The Big Brown Lie...

Life and labor relation's policy as a United Parcel Service Teamster Union Steward, and as a union reformer during the battle for Local 402.

By
James R. Earls
Former Chief Steward - Teamsters Local 402

Copyright © 2002

RLM Publishing Co.
P.O.Box 265
Hazel Green, AL 35750-0265
ISBN: 0-9718697-0-7
Printed In The United States Of America

This Book Is Available At Quantity Discounts For Bulk Orders
Write to above mailing Address for information

I dedicate this book to the two most important people in my life after God. My loving wife Lesley, and my daughter Mattie. I love you both very much.

James Earls / March 2002

Introduction

The American worker probably rarely gives much thought about the intricate anatomy of their workplace and of their working conditions, and often at times dismisses their working environment as just being typical corporate functioning...but typical it isn't.

In the United States alone, over $236 million was spent in the year 2000 on implementing, maintaining, and enforcing industrial labor relations policies by employing thousands of 'specialized' consultants, both 'in-house' and outside, to handle the burdonsome task of this field. This expertise was once considered as becoming extinct with the 'perceived' demise of organized labor by corporate America in the 1970's and 80's, but the reality is that there is now a resurgence, and once again corporate America has found a need for these 'professionals' and their services.

What exactly are industrial labor relations, and just how big of a role does it play in your everyday life? I think the findings will surprise you. Industrial labor relations is the field of business management, which deals with the 'relationship' between the employer and the employee. It is often times associated with organized labor which conjures up the stereotypical visions of combat booted security forces who are hired by companies who are attempting to bust a union drive at their plant through the use of violence, but every company both large and small employs some sort of policy that encompasses the principles of labor management whether it be establishing a vacations policy, sick day policy, work schedules, policy compatibility within the constraints of the various labor laws, and balances and applications with the interaction of the employee. There is a need for this 'tool' of management in order to allow a business to operate as efficiently as possible, while attempting to maintain a sort of harmony between the management and the workers. But often times many employers choose to pervert that relationship by employing immoral tactics, and enforcing ritualistic policies all in the name of the god that most of corporate America worships...which is greed.

Often times a demoralized, weakened, and destroyed worker, both mentally and physically is all that is left in the wake that is generated by the speed up engineers, and the malevolence of management who are hell bent on squeezing out every dollar, and ounce of production from their workers no matter what the cost. Many times it is the worker who pays the price for the companies profits by giving not only their sweat, and in some cases their blood as well from the dangerous conditions of work that is often times created from this practice.

UPS workers suffer more than a staggering 60,000 injuries a year with more OSHA complaints being filed against it than almost any other company in the United States. From the result of the doubling of the package weight to 150 pounds then coupled with the killer work pace that management has always employed only results in the lives of the workers being slowly destroyed, but to management this is just another business expense that must be factored in, and what a business expense it is with UPS's management paying almost $1,000,000 a day in just workman comps claims on less than 350,000 employees. These injuries are readily observable on the surface and they are thought to be minor, but in reality below the surface...the damage is often more devastating than one may perceive. The long term effects of a highly stressful working environment have a defined impact not only on the employee in question, but on society as a whole with resulting cost that run into the millions of dollars a year, in which most cases...society pays the price for providing the security and avenue for the increase in corporate profits which come at any cost.

The elements of stress is a clear and forceful state which consist of several idiosyncratic sets of poignant, rational and physiological responses depending on the motivation. The motivation can be a restriction, a requirement, or even an opportunity to perform, which the employee believes that the outcome from their action is important although it   remains uncertain. According to McLean in 1980:

"Occupational stress is the sum of all the factors in the workplace, which elicit a response in an individual." It has been further defined as a perceived disparity between occupational stress and the individual ability to adequately perform when the consequences of failure are thought to be important by the employee."

In this specialized research field it has been longed believed that employees who experience very high levels of stress develop an assortment of varying mental and physical disorders. Just to name a few of the 'disorders' which include; depression, anxiety, mood disorders, altered behavioral and home lifestyle patterns, sleep disorders, drug abuse and alcohol abuse as well as several physical ailments which include; hyperacidity, peptic ulcer formation and various other gastro intestinal conditions and ailments. Also included is various respiratory disorders, with asthma being the most predominate illness, which has long been suspected as being associated with stress. With high, and unattainable workloads, the worker experiences an increase in their psychological perceived demands coupled with little work environment control have dramatic effects on the smoking habits of these sort of individuals, which with the increase in smoking comes the end results which often include heart and lung disease, and various types of cancers that are associated with smoking such as mouth, esophageal, and lung cancer.

The mere health cost alone, which is a derivative from highly stressful working conditions, and are result of a ruthless labor relations policy are astronomical not only in monetary value, but come at a cost to the workers who pay with a diminished quality of life. In reality the price for increased production, at no matter what the cost, offsets the profits of society by a long shot, but it has very little negative effect on the profits of the indiscrimanately perpetrators, whom passes the cost onto insurance companies and ultimately...upon society.

In recent years the International Brotherhood of Teamsters, who represent the workers at United Parcel Service, commissioned and contracted a study that was conducted by the Illinois Health Hazard Evaluation Program (HHE), at the University of Illinois, to investigate the occupational stress among package car drivers who are employed at United Parcel Service. The participants in the study were from various administrative centers, which were situated within hubs located in Saddlebrook, New Jersey; Oshkosh, Wisconsin; Houston, Texas; and Concord, California. Of the 317 drivers who participated in the study 95% were male, 5% were female with an average age of 35 years. The length of their service ranged from one year to 31 years, with an average of 9.6 years in service to the employer. The levels of education that were exhibited by the participants were that 35% completed high school, 47% completed some college and 17% were college graduates. The marital status of the participants ranged from 72% being married, 18.5% being single and 10% being divorced or widowed.

It was reported that 85% of the drivers tested experienced physical pain which they attributed directly to the job with the back being the common site with 221 of them reporting that they had experienced some sort of back pain, followed by pain in the leg or foot (46%), and the 28% of them reporting pain in the hands and arm. Twenty-eight percent of the participant reported having had a back injury while working at UPS. The initial evaluation of UPS' workers compensation experience indicates that the rates for its ENTIRE workforce are increasing yearly. The rates of injuries for UPS are three times the national average.

The professional study found that the package car drivers at UPS were well above the norm for psychological distress, which readily placed them in the 91st percentile, or within the top 9% of the general working population nationwide for this psychological suffering! The most staggering and consistent factor that is associated with the above defined symptoms of psychological anguish and strain on regression was "ROLE OVERLOAD". It was reported that the drivers were suffering from a variety of symptoms and diseases, which are quite possibly related to work stress, as well as experiencing a "burn out" phenomena after a short period of years on the job. When it came time to measure the participants ability to relax and find satisfying activities outside the work environment during their free time...they scored below the national average in that category as well.

All of these drivers who participated in the study reported that at each of their respected locations there existed a punitive rather than collaborative approach when they had dealings with members of UPS'smanagement. They all experienced daily a high level of supervisory pressure for 'increased production' through the implementation of longer work days, working through lunch, extremely stressful and combative supervisory personnel presences on the trucks with them during the day while they were on their routes, and pressure from replacement drivers to "OUT PERFORM" those drivers who were out from either vacations or illnesses. Every participant complained about conflicting expectations, which emanated from differing members of management, and a ruthless disciplinary system at which, even for minor infractions of the established labor relations policy, they all were "JUDGED GUILTY", and sentenced before the "Trial" and well before arbitration of their grievance. Finally, they all reported a stressful social environment at work which borderlines on being hostile, which is fostered in part by a lack of social support from supervisory personnel.

At the conclusion of the study the findings ranked the UPS drivers in the 91st percentile, which placed them at the top of the scale amongst the most stressed adults in the United States. These job characteristics are greater for the UPS drivers than for the general working population with only 8% of the population scoring higher than the drivers who work at United Parcel Service.

The non-monetary cost associated with this particular job class at UPS is a decrease in the quality of life for the employees and their families, as well as a likely increase in workers compensation claims along with a monetary increase in health/disability cost to the employer and to society.

So it can be without argument that a ' abusive labor relations policy' can be extremely costly to administer, and that such a policy should be readily open for review to allow for a much needed restructure once failure has been recognized, but remember that by doing so...it would then begin to cut into their profits, and often times it is deliberately overlooked and it's considered as just being another expense at doing business. The top level corporate managers often have a clever way of masking and diverting attention from this problem by employing carefully scripted 'spin and damage control' after something that they'd wished would've remained in the closet has been exposed, and quite often they attack the 'complainant' unmercifully by unleashing their million dollar attorneys onto their prey in a desperate, last ditch attempt to quash and suppress whatever thing it was that they have perceived to be a threat to their reputation, and how it may adversely affect the public's perception of the policy which has been brought into question. But this is one unique, and different case study in which that tactic will be unsuccessful in hiding and perverting the truth from the world. The argument will likely be made that what I have written about is nothing more than a disgruntled fabrication, which lacks in truth...but in the end the labor contract that we work under does not lie.

Organized labor plays an important role in the implementation and enforcement of these policies. They are the ones who had been designated to protect and prevent such abuses from happening, and I'm happy to say that not all labor organizations are blind to the plight of their rank and file members, but some 'factions' of the AFL/CIO affiliated International Brotherhood of the Teamsters are allowing the travesties to continue all in the name of the same motivation which drives the corporations...greed. Often times this selfish act incorporates the principles, and/or becomes cleverly transformed and disguised as corrupted power and unethical union politics, but the end results from this tragedy are even worse than the 'crimes that are committed against the American worker by Corporate America'. The ultimate crime which is committed against organized labor by the leaders in the organized labor movement is their betrayal to the membership they represent, but the end revelation as to the ones who may ultimately be responsible for this tragedy may surprise you.

From the ashes of empty representation, individuals are born who decide without caution to make a stand for what they believe is right and prepare themselves to do battle with the rampant union corruption, and the ruthless styles of management all in the name of reforming their work place, and their unions. These brave individuals actively engage the brutally abusive labor relation policies that they work under in a heroic attempt to protect the rights of their oppressed and abused fellow workers. Often times they are the ones who pay the ultimate price while doing battle with corporate America and often they have to wage a personal war on two fronts. One of the fronts being the corporate battlefield, and the other...within their very own union. This is just one of those such stories about a thirty-two year old Teamster reformer named James Earls, and his fight against management and the old guard Teamsters all in the name of defending workers rights. This is his story...

Chapter 1

"I don't know how much more of this I can take? I'm working over 70 hours a week and not making a bit of money at all and they're constantly looking for new ways to screw us over. I just need to move on and start a new life...a real life, instead of like this one here at this dead end job. I don't know if I can last long enough until I can find another job. Is there even another job out there, better than this one, with what little I know?"

I was still working part time in the summer of 1987, while still a senior in high school, for a local grocery store. I was doing the usual "high school" part time job routine working for a local grocery store in Huntsville. I was the typical American teen being lazy and loathsome from having to work, but I was quite content with what little responsibilities I had that entailed being a bag boy. It was getting closer to the time for me to graduate from Buckhorn High School, located in New Market Alabama, and I really didn't have any idea of what path or career that I wanted to embark on in the real world after graduating. To say the least, I probably represented the epitome of teenagers, and was like most teens at the time, I was only concerned with taking a short time off before starting college in the fall and "rest". I wasn't too interested in seeking a real job, and only wanted to party because my father was subsidizing my expenses and me. I had no bills at the time, and with that came a feeling of complacency and no desire to improve my 'wealth' at the time.

This was one of my first real mistakes that I would make, which would eventually have a broad, defined impact on my perception of being a worker, an average worker if you will, on down the road called life.

This job at the grocery store had no benefits whatsoever other than it afforded me the opportunity to make minimum wage without insurance. I qualified as one of the many million's of people who didn't have any luck in working for a company that had a union and honestly...at the time I had never even thought much about a union. I had failed to realize that with my dad working for Chrysler in Huntsville, and he being a member of the U.A.W union, what real impact that a union had on my life. I mean we weren't rich by any means, but we did manage to live a fairly comfortable life, hardly ever wanting for anything.

I was making a little over three dollars an hour and part time wasn't cutting it anymore. I needed more hours than just the measly twelve and thirteen a week that I was getting, so I had decided to go ahead and register for college to try and pursue a degree in Engineering. I thought that I had matured a little in those few months since after graduating, or so I thought, and found it necessary to increase my 'wealth' because I was growing tired of going to daddy and asking for more money. I managed to get the chance to go full time with the grocery store, which meant that I'd get more hours to work, plus a whopping twenty-five cents an hour raise to boot.

Several months at working full time for this grocery store proved to be a better move financially for me, but I would have one pivotal incident that would eventually change the way I viewed most management personnel. We had received word that our new area supervisor for our district, named Raymond, was expected in the next couple of days to visit our store. Raymond had got to where he was the old fashioned way...he had family in high places.

This had always been a sore spot, and a very touchy subject for most of the managers of the grocery store where I worked. They had been stuck in the same position for many years with no prospect for moving up the ladder, and they too felt exploited and victimized by their upper management of this grocery chain, which only damaged the morale of all the managers who worked under them.

This particular manager was in his mid thirties and very young to be in the position that he was in. We received a confirmation that Raymond was indeed coming and then the store went into full alert as if an air raid siren went off. Raymond had held various titles and positions throughout his career, and he had even obtained a reputation to suit his management style and personality as well. Everyone called him 'Rectal Boy". Raymond, in essence, was unable to work for himself, and he whined about every little thing that everyone else did in relation to their work and nothing anyone ever did was ever good enough for this man...even if it was right. Nothing that any store manager would do would be done right. They couldn't ever please him. The day before Raymond was due to arrive, all the managers of our store were running around panicking while trying to figure out what else needed to be done to a store that was already perfect. They were barking out orders at us like they were army drill sergeants.

We wound up staying at the store well into the early morning hours just hours before his visit, cleaning, mopping, hiding merchandise, scraping the floor, and scrubbing toilets, and about everything else under the sun that one could imagine.

When Raymond finally arrived early that morning, you'd think the king of grocery glory had arrived. We were immediately instructed by our store managers to lay low, look busy and most of all...stay out of his way. We were even told not to communicate with him at all unless he spoke to us, and I found this to be rather strange and this did not sit too well with most everyone who had already been there. After a minute or two, the managers came back and said that Raymond was making his way back over towards us and for us to get lost quick, but it was too late, because Raymond saw us before we could escape, and hollered at us to wait where we were. While standing there several employees began to tuck in their shirts and try to improve their appearance the best they could. Raymond came walking up to us and then walked down in front of us as if he was inspecting the troops. He never stopped to introduce himself to any of us and he actually thumbed his nose up to several of the dirtier employees. I found this to be rather sickening. I mean the arrogance of this pathetic man who actually thought we were beneath him, and every since this one little incident...I had taken on a different view of management.

After about eleven months of declining working conditions I decided it was now time to move on. I was in desperate need of a career change. Towards the end of my career with the grocery store, I was working in excess of sixty hours, six days a week and I was still without any health insurance, although I was still covered by my dad's plan through the U.A.W union. I was trying to go to school full time and with working like a slave for the store, I was becoming mentally exhausted. I had a girlfriend at the time, and between work and school, I never had any time to spend with her, which was beginning to strain our relationship at the time. I felt that I didn't have a life outside of the store.

After deciding to search for a new career, I phoned my employer and informed him that I needed to take a sick day, which I received a lot of grief from the manager over this request, but I let in go into one ear and out the other. Actually I really didn't lie to him because I was sick. I was sick and tired of all the crap I had to put up with while working at the store. I went ahead and drove on down to the employment office that morning to stand in line, and wait to fill out the various applications and screening forms for local companies. As I waited for my turn, I began looking around at the different people who were in there searching for a job as well. I decided to perform a mental catalog of my talents and I began to wonder how I compared to the other people that were there waiting along with me. I didn't have any experience at anything other than the grocery business.

Finally I spotted an empty seat, and hurried over to it before anyone else saw it, and boy was I glad to sit down and finally rest my feet. The floor of the building was made of concrete and very, very dirty. I remembered thinking to myself at how filthy this place was. It was almost degrading to just be here, and I began to question my worth, and I wondered if what I was asking for would be considered a handout or something. Heck it was that depressing to me to even be in here. I wanted a change in life, and I dismissed my feelings as just being apprehensive and stupid. "This place needs some light," I thought, as I looked at the ceiling which had several of its lights missing their bulbs, and I let out a long sigh, and rested my head in my hand with my elbow on my knee.

Finally after about twenty minutes of analyzing the place, and counting the missing ceiling tiles my number was finally called over the P.A system. I had been there for almost two hours. I stood up and peered over the half partition separating the waiting area from the receptionist desk, and I saw that a lady was waving her hand and pointing at me to come to her. I began making the snaking maneuvers around the other desk, which all had applicants sitting at them, and noticed that most of the applicants looked really enthused to be there. I managed to make it back to her desk and took a seat. She immediately began to drill me with questions and began asking me what I was looking for without any formal introduction to whom she was. I wasn't really sure as to what it was I was looking other than something besides the grocery business. I explained to her that I didn't have any skills other that the grocery business and I knew that my choices were going to be very limited. The lady was rather nice to me, but sort of impersonal as well. I could tell that it was sort of a scripted verse that she was going through, and I could tell that she evidently wasn't very happy doing what she did either. She typed into a computer as we talked and she would look at her watch about a half a dozen times as she typed and she'd let out a sigh. This bothered me a little, and it made me feel as if I was burdening her by asking her to help me. This made me sort of uncomfortable and I began to become restless and started fidgeting side to side in my seat. The longer it went on, the worse it got. My tax dollars was paying her salary, but yet I was being subjected to this sort of treatment. After a few more minutes of typing she called out several companies to me with UPS being one of them, and ironically so was a company named PPG. I went ahead and filled out the screening forms for them both and handed them back to her as she began to tell me what little she knew about both companies in regard to wages, working conditions and so on, and I perked up little.

I was really drawn towards UPS, because of the hours of work, the wages and the fact that they were interested in hiring college kids. I was in college at the time and this sounded really good to me. I mean...I could work far fewer hours than I was working now, and make more money, have insurance and other benefits that were superior to what I had at the grocery store. I was very excited at the prospect.

I returned to the grocery store the next day and I was called into the office and told that Raymond had ordered a crackdown with all absentees. I was written up for taking a day off sick after hardly ever missing a day at all while being with the store. This new series of events only added fuel to the fire that was raging. After this little stunt I was well on my way to being an unhappy grocery employee. Several of us found different means to vent our frustrations towards the management of the store. All were by non-violent and non-destructive means of course. We usually hid spoiled fruit and meat around the store until it stunk so bad that the customers would complain of the smell and various other childish things.

After waiting in agony for about two weeks, I finally received a letter from the employment service stating that I was scheduled for an interview from a representative of UPS and that I was required to report back in two days. I was very happy to say the least, and I could hardly contain myself. I went back to work that night with a different attitude, and I decided that I was going to be a good boy for the next couple of days.

I didn't manage to sleep a bit the night before the interview. I was experiencing several different emotions all at the same time, which was very confusing to me. I was happy though that I had decided to make a change, and felt that it was for the better. I wrestled with this until finally drifting off to a light sleep.

I awoke and drove on down to the employment office that morning and signed in with the front desk. Nervously I sat in the section that was marked for interviews with several other people who were all smoking and drinking coffee. My knee was going ninety to nothing, and I must admit that it didn't relieve any of the stress that I was experiencing. After having been there for about ten minutes an older lady in a dress came walking up to the roped off section and called my name. I stood up, as if snapping to attention, and briskly walked over to greet her.

"Hi, my name is Dana and I'm the human resources manager for Alabama," she replied, while smiling rather big.

"I'm James Earls and it's a pleasure to meet you," I replied, and followed her on back to her room.

I decided early on to apply all of the 'job interviewing training' that I had received while in high school, to help me any way it could.

I was courteous, clean-shaven and well dressed, and I was there to sell myself to her company. I wanted her to see me as the southern gentleman that I was.

She opened the interview with a standard question, "tell me about yourself," as she began to lay out a tablet on the top of the table and prepared to write down what I was about to tell her. I drew a blank. I was caught off guard and I panicked. This wasn't what I expected as one of the first questions to be. I had been going over all this in my head of the order of things that would transpire during the interview, but now...I couldn't remember anything. I nervously began to selectively tell her about my work history, hobbies, interest and education. Dana smiled a lot and this made me feel a little at ease.

Dana went through her spiel about UPS and their history as a company. I really didn't tune into her until she reached the part about $8.00 an hour with insurance and paid vacation. If I got the job I'd be working part time in the morning for about four hours with every weekend off. I hadn't had a weekend off in months. I thought I was in hog heaven. This is what I was looking for, and I knew she could tell that I was over eager and really wanted this job. I thought it sounded more like a cakewalk compared to what I was doing now and I tried to contain my outward expressions of wanting this job, but my enthusiasm was expressed with every answer I gave her. At the end of the interview that she told that she would review my interview and if the company were interested she would give me call in a few days. I was sure to thank her for interviewing me, and brother did I lay it on thick.

I returned home and I could not take my mind off of that job. I wanted it more than anything in the world. I prayed a lot to God that if he wanted me to have it then it would be his will. Several days went by and I hadn't received a call from UPS, and I had begun to lose hope. After giving up, after a week and a half had passed, later that afternoon the phone rang and I answered it. It was Dana and she told me that I had the job and she told to report back to the employment office the next morning. I decided play it safe and arrived about an hour early. Dana was already there and she noticed me sitting out in the waiting area, and reminded me that I wasn't scheduled for another hour. I told her that I knew that, but I wasn't going to take a chance on being late. She laughed from my 'concerned' punctuality and brought me on back to fill out the application, insurance forms, finger print forms and so on. The last document I was asked to sign if I wanted to, was to join the Teamsters Union. I really didn't know anything about the union other than what my grandpa and father had told me and decided it couldn't be a bad thing if they were in the union so I signed the card to join the Teamsters.

Little did I know that I had embarked on a journey that would forever change, and have a detrimental lasting impact on my life? I was on top of the world when I left there that morning, but if I had known of the hell that was in store for me over the next thirteen years, I would have done things differently. A lot differently...

Chapter 2

"How much longer until break? I've been steady at it now for two hours and it's not even beginning to look like it's going to slack up. I can't keep the sweat out of my eyes. My back and feet are killing me. Everybody is pissed and throwing the packages that I've missed back up toward me. I know they hate me. I feel like I'm going to throw up. It's not so much from being nervous but is from the stale, hot air from inside this building. The managers are running around screaming at me "to get it in the car." What in the world do they mean? I'm lost in here amongst the packages in this man made hell. Is that another truck I hear pulling in? Please God, not more boxes? I'm beginning to think that I've made a serious mistake by coming here. I can hardly breathe from all the diesel fumes. I'm really beginning to get seriously nauseous from the fumes. I don't know if I'll be back tomorrow for more of this.

I barely slept that night before my first day at UPS, anticipating the start of this new job and what was got to be involved. I had no idea of what to expect and I tried to imagine what I would be doing. I even role played in my head someone asking me where I worked with me replying, "I work at UPS." I didn't have a clue about UPS other than they delivered boxes, yet I was ready for a change. I decided to go ahead and get up, well before the time I set on my alarm clock. Why not? I couldn't sleep anyway. I had a stomach full of butterflies and I was even shaking a little from the sudden rush of adrenalin. "Was I getting up too early?" I thought, as I stood and stared at the clock, with each passing second it felt like I was a dead man walking. It was around 3:00 a.m or so, and I went ahead and got dressed and fixed my water jug for the day and plopped down in front of the T.V to watch cartoons for a while. I wasn't required to report to work until 4:00 a.m and it was only a fifteen-minute drive from my house to the plant. I watched TV for while longer and decided to go ahead and go into work and just wait there until time to report.

When I pulled onto the property, I noticed a door at one of the corners of the building. I climbed out of my car and walked up to the door. I reached toward the door and turned the doorknob and found that the door was locked. I attempted to open it again and it still wouldn't open. I shook the door several times, but it wouldn't open. "Maybe they won't let us in until it's time to start," I thought, as I turned to walk back to my car, not really knowing for sure. Employees began to come into the parking lot and park their cars on the other side of me. I stopped walking as employees began to walk towards me and then file by me to go in the other door. I was trying to look cool and play off the fact that I couldn't open the door so I wouldn't look like an idiot or something. I was sweating like I had run two miles in a fur coat. It was a little too hot to be so early in the morning, even for August. There wasn't even a breeze stirring. Nothing. It was just hot and humid as hell. Everyone began going inside the building as I stood there holding the door smiling at them. I really felt stupid now and waited a couple of minutes before I went inside.

I went on inside and the first thing I noticed was how stale and heavy the air was inside the building. It was hotter in here than outside. "This place must have air conditioners?" I thought, as I began to hear a series of loud buzzers sounding off that lasted only a few seconds, and then the sound of machinery starting up.

The inside of the building left a lot to be desired. The steel beams, which supported the building, were exposed along the ceiling and down along the sides, stopping at the cement foundation, with insulation exposed on the ceiling. There were three small cement block buildings inside the main building, which contained the offices, and another small cement block building, the customer counter, located in the front of the building. I noticed above the brown trucks parked inside on one side of the building that there were several large conveyor belts that ran the length of the building climbing to a height that was almost as tall of the building itself. I walked a little farther into the building towards the offices just looking around a bit not knowing what to do or how to even find the person I was looking for.

I was amazed at how they got all those trucks into the building all parked so close together, side by side, and all backed up to a concrete dock that was about knee high. I stood around outside one of the offices waiting until I could see someone who looked like they were in charge. People walked by me as I stood in front of the office never speaking to me just smiling. I didn't feel any more nervous than before, and I was starting to relax a little and began to ease out of being anxious.

I stood there admiring their operation and I watched the birds fly around inside, which were fighting with one another when a young lady approached me.

"James Earls?" she asked.

"Yes I'm James and I'm here to see a Mrs. Townsend" I replied nervously.

"I'm Ms. Townsend and not misses okay," she snapped back as if she had been insulted. "Everyone calls me Alli," she replied.

Alli instructed me to wait for her in the middle office until she came for me.

I went on inside the office and noticed that it was actually a break room, as I sat down at a small table after buying a soft drink. I didn't mind waiting in here because this room was air-conditioned. I heard the buzzers go off again except this time they seemed to last a little longer than before and ended with three small chirps. I peered out of the window in the door and noticed that people were really starting to move, and were running around like they were sort of lost.

After about ten minutes of trying to stay awake, Alli poked her head into the office and told me to follow her. We then walked around the corner of the offices toward one of the two docks that were on the inside of the building and she stepped up on it. The dock itself was about ten feet wide, and about 100 feet, or so, long. The dock had a conveyor belt running down the center of it, which was about thigh high and three to four feet wide. There were brown trucks parked on both sides of the dock from one end to the other. The belt started on one end, and was connected to a huge metal slide, which was angled, and was about 40 feet wide. Everyone on the belt, about eight people on this side, were digging through a pile of charts that were thrown on top of the belt in one huge clump. They were looking for the ones that belonged to them.

Alli looked for the ones that belonged to the trucks that I was going to be trained on that morning and she couldn't find them. She asked everyone standing there if they'd seen them and everyone replied no. Alli went into a fit of rage.

"That son of a bitch carried them home with him and kept them," she replied, while slamming a box of crayons on the belt with several rolling off of the belt and onto the floor.

I looked at her with surprise. I wasn't used to women talking like that. She meant that the person who she was training before me kept the charts she gave him and didn't return them when he quit. The more she dug through the charts the more she cussed. I was shocked to say the least, and just kind of stepped back watching her display of anger, as everyone became somewhat uncomfortable, as I could tell by the looks on their faces. She instructed one of the loaders named Gary that I would be loading by him, and for him to help me get my truck set up while she went to print me some more charts.

"Fantastic," Gary replied, sarcastically as he turned to walk to his loading area.

The charts she was going to print out for me are used in loading the brown trucks. Each street in a particular area is assigned what is called a sequence number. The sequence numbers are arranged in such a way, which depends on how the route is set up and how the driver is to deliver it. This sequence number is what determines where the package is loaded in the truck in accordance to the way the driver runs the route.

Gary walked in front of me, down to the other end of the belt, shuffling his feet, with his charts tucked under his arm and carrying a cup of coffee. He raised the back door to his truck and placed his coffee in the rear of one of the shelves. Gary helped me set my trucks up because I hadn't any idea what I was doing.

I tried to help him the best I could but decided to just stay out of his way until Alli returned. Alli had been gone now for about ten minutes and another blast of the buzzer came, as I looked up toward the beginning of the belt and noticed a guy standing at a control panel that was bolted to the edge of the slide pressing what appeared to be a button. The belts began to run and I looked up toward the head of the belt and noticed about five people beginning to pull packages off of the slide and placing them on one of the three belts.

They were sorting the packages and placing the on one of the three belts depending on which part of Huntsville they went to. Finally, before the first of the packages made their way to me, Alli came running up to the belt and jumped on the belt and slid across to our side. She handed me a tape gun and told me to tape the charts to the rear of the trucks while she got the stop count papers set. I nervously took the tape gun from her and taped the charts to the back of the trucks after looking at how the other people had their charts hung. Before I could get the charts taped to the trucks, she had already begun to pull packages off of the belt and began to sit them behind our trucks. She began to explain to me the concept and fundamentals of loading "package cars". That is what UPS prefers to call the brown trucks.

She was explaining all of this while walking in and out of the rear of the trucks that were assigned to us.

I tried to strain and hear what she was saying and telling me to do. I would catch part of what she was saying and acted like I heard it all.

Alli would stop and take a sip from her coffee and look down the belt and then turn and shake her head in disgust. I was standing there looking around trying to see what it was that disgusted her so much. I only saw a lot of boxes coming down the belt rather quickly. Alli came back out and screamed, "Somebody crank the damn belt down!"

I watched another loader as he walked up to the front of the belt a kneeled down and slid open a little steel grate. He began to crank a lever and the belt became slower and slower until Alli finally yelled, "Fine." He slid the grate back and walked back behind his truck.

Alli didn't do too much talking to me except to tell what packages were mine. I didn't have a clue what was going on now anymore than before I started. She worked with me for about twenty minutes when someone came from around the end of the truck, across the belt from us, and told her that she had a phone call. While she was gone she instructed Gary to help me pull my packages and just sit them behind my last package car.

Gary just rolled his eyes and nodded his head yes. When Alli walked off I heard him say, "damn it," in a disgusted tone, and I knew it had to have been because of him having to help me.

Everything was so fast paced that I couldn't begin to keep up with the flow of packages. Gary now had to pull for seven package cars instead of just his four. I could tell that he was starting to get upset, because he started to throw the packages behind and into his package cars. I tried to do better and increased my pace.

"Man it's hot in here," I thought, as I looked up and noticing that we had fans but they weren't cut on. We needed some air moving. The building was still hot as hell and with the fact that there wasn't any air moving only made it that much more miserable.

I tried to hold the crayon in one had, that was used to write the sequence numbers on the boxes, while carrying the packages. It didn't work. I dropped the crayon time and time again while carrying the packages and attempting to mark a stop on the stop count sheet of paper. I thought I was doing a fairly good job. I mean I was finding the streets on my charts and placing them in the appropriate section of the package car. I was just slow in doing so.

After about ten minutes Alli came back from her call to help me. She walked into my truck and came back out and asked me, "What in the hell have you been doing?"

Now imagine my position. I have been on the job for less than an hour, without any understanding of what was required of me or how to do anything in relation to loading these trucks, and now I had to deal with this supervisor who was acting as if the world was coming to an end. Maybe if she didn't stay on the phone for half the morning things would've been better. I was doing the best I could. I didn't say anything to her and I just stood by and watched her rant and rave, and kick and throw packages across the belt and up into the truck with many of the packages bursting open and spilling their contents onto the floor. I felt as if I had killed Mickey Mouse or something as I tried vainly to pick up their broken   contents as she unremorsefully trampled the customers merchandise.

Over the course of the next hour I tried to appease her the best I could. It only seemed though that the more I tried the worst I did. I tried anyway and I paid really close attention to everything she said and I asked questions, but when I did this she only got angrier. I felt as if I asked her any questions, concerning what I was supposed to do, she stood there and would look at me like I was an idiot or something. I really began to con-sider the thought that maybe I had indeed made a serious mistake in tak-ing this job. At least at the grocery store I wasn't exposed to this type of supervisory training. The packages that were coming down the belt never seemed to end.

The belt was unrelenting and it didn't matter if you had packages piled behind your trucks or not. They just kept coming. Finally, after about two and a half hours of getting slammed by boxes they called a break. The belt stopped after a supervisor rang the buzzer with three short blasts, and everyone stopped loading their trucks, and placed their cray-ons on the lipped edge of the belt, and left to go to the break room to smoke or buy a soft drink. I stopped for just a minute to go to the restroom. I went on up stairs to the bathroom after asking someone the location of it and entered the men's locker room. It was cool in there. I had soaked my clothes from sweating and I was dripping sweat from my nose as if a faucet was running. I stayed up there long enough to cool off some and I dreaded going back down there and finishing the job. I finally mustered up enough will power to make the ever so long trek back down the steps and back onto the belt. I was going to have to leave the air-conditioned confines of the bathroom.

When I arrived back onto the belt Alli was still loading the truck. She looked at me with a look that could kill and asked where I had gone. I informed her that I had gone to the restroom and to get some water. She shook her head and continued to write numbers on the packages for me to load while throwing them behind my different trucks. The buzzer sounded again a few short burst and the belt started back up and we were thrown again...back into the thick of things. My main objective that morning was just to survive, and try not pass out from the heat and lack of air stirring in the building. I had forgotten about the fans that were mounted up above the belts, which had still not been cut on. I asked Gary why they weren't using them and he stated that they hadn't worked in a while. The only thing that kept the air from getting any staler was the fact that the huge garage like doors on the side of the building had been raised at some point during the morning. The hourly people who were loading the trucks, in an attempt to keep cool normally raised them before the start of the shift.

The only problem with this is when the tractor-trailer truck drivers, called feeder drivers, pulled onto the yard they left their trucks running and then the diesel fumes would creep into the building which usually caused several of the workers to become ill.

Finally as the sun came out, my body could feel it. It was getting around 7:30 or 8:00 a.m and finally the packages on the belt began to thin out, which was a signal that they had began to unload the last trailer from the hub for that day.

This is the part of the morning when the supervisors would come around and ask each loader how many stops they had on their package cars. This is how they leveled out the work to determine what the average paid day for each driver was going to be.

I was primarily working on one car by myself, and had been all morning, and Alli loaded the other two. A man in a UPS drivers uniform, called a set of 'browns', came up to me and asked me what my count was.

"250 stops," I replied, waiting for praise to spew from his mouth.

He started to write this number down and stopped and slowly raised his head and looked me and asked me, "What did you say?"

"250 stops sir." I replied nervously as I began to get a bad feeling about this.

The man called out to Alli who then came running up to him, and he asked her at how I arrived at this number when the driver had on average about seventy-five stops daily. I stood there not knowing what the problem was, or if this was just something routine or what? The man's name was Dick, and he was the center manager for the Huntsville east side. Dick told Alli that he'd be back in a few minutes and that she'd better have a 'good' count for him and know exactly what was on that car.

As soon as Dick walked on down, and out of sight, she threw her clipboard onto the ground, and asked me just what in the hell I'd been doing all morning and whether or not I'd been listening to her.

I was completely floored by this. I stood there tired, hungry, sore and mad as hell about the whole situation. I was filthy from the sweat and dirt on the boxes and from all of the soot flying around in the building. I wasn't in the mood at all for this kind of crap from her. I was awful close to telling her where to stick this job. I didn't know what I had done that was so wrong.

The problem I had caused was in fact her fault. She had failed to instruct me that I had to mark a new stop for each new address. If the same address received more packages it wouldn't count as a new stop. What I was doing was counting boxes. Each time I carried a box onto the truck I marked on my paper a count for the box. There weren't 250 stops on there but somewhere close to 250 packages. I wasn't told any different, and thought I was doing a good job at the time.

Alli told me that I could go ahead and go home and for me to carry the chart I was using that day home with me and for me to learn all the information on it. I was told to learn all the sequence numbers and streets along with the number ranges and breaks. I had to know if the street was east or west, a road, avenue, or street which all would determine what sequence number would be assigned to the package. It had to be right. Alli told me that I would be tested on my knowledge of the chart at the end of the week, and Alli added one little bit of encouragement. "You'd better know it if you want this job," she replied, as I walked off.

I walked down the length of the belt and climbed over it and stepped off of the dock. My back was sore and I stretched a little in an attempt to try and make it feel a little better, as I walked on over to the counter to place my jug on it. The jug had been empty since right after break, and my mouth was dry and it hurt my throat to talk. I went on over to the water fountain and I must have drunk twenty gallons of water. I stood there thinking about the whole morning, and began entertaining the thought of keeping my charts like the boy before me had done and not come back. I knew what must have made him not want to come back, and I wasn't sure that I'd be back the next day or not. I walked on out to my car and climbed inside and immediately cut the air conditioner wide open. I sat out there enjoying the sunlight and fresh air. I blew my nose and must have blown out a pound of black-sooted dirt. I just sat there with my head on the headrest for a few minutes trying to gather enough strength to drive the fifteen minutes back home. I was worn out.

I had just finished a job that was, at that time of my life, one of the most stressful both mentally and physically that I had ever experienced. The job was tough enough with all the physical factors, but when you threw Alli into the equation, and how she showed her butt all morning only made it worse. I hoped it would get better than it was this morning and drove straight home and went to bed.

I managed to stick it out for a few days and I slowly began getting better at loading the one car when they decided that they needed me to work in the unload for a couple of days. The unload area is the area which entails unloading all of the trailers that arrive from the various hubs that had the packages to be delivered that day. I was sort of relieved when I heard the news that I would be doing this now for at least a week.

I walked on under the slide that morning, where the un-loaders were assembled prior to the start of their shift, and I quickly analyzed the situation and realized that this was a job that involved more brawn than brain. This is what I was looking for. I could do this job with no problem. I unloaded grocery trucks at the grocery store while I was still employed there, and I could unload one of those in about three hours by myself. I would later come to find out that this was one of the biggest jokes I have ever told myself.

I was now working for another supervisor named Johnson who was at one time in the Navy. He was a nicer person than Alli and had a totally different attitude than her. I thought to myself, "I could work for this guy." Johnson gave me a very brief introduction of the fundamentals of the un-loading of UPS trailers. Johnson trained me in about a minute. It was that straight forward. All I had to do was keep the address labels turned up so the sorter could read them without having to look for them as they came down the slide. I had to keep the rollers full with packages and unload about 900 packages an hour, which didn't seem like too much to do with these short twenty-eight foot trailers.

Johnson instructed me to unload one of the first trailers that had already come in and was already backed on the door. Johnson walked over to the ladder with me in tow and picked up a set of bolt cutters. I thought to myself, "What in the world is he going to do with those?" Johnson climbed up the ladder and onto the catwalk and kneeled down, and he placed the bolt cutters on a little steel wire and cut it. The little steel wire is called a seal. Whenever a trailer leaves the hub and is 'sealed', a super-visor then places this little wire through the lock on the trailer, and twists it, which prevents the trailer from being broke into while in the possession of the driver.

Johnson cut the seal off from the handle of the trailer, and placed it into his pocket so he could later verify the numbers that were on it to whether they matched the numbers on the seal control record. Johnson threw the bolt cutters onto the metal dock and raised the door. Packages began to fall out of the back of the trailer with several of them striking Johnson in the head.

"You've got to watch out for that kind of crap there James," Johnson replied, while shaking his head hard.

I was ready to get started and when he finally raised the door all the way where I could see into it, I noticed that it was full, or at one hundred percent as UPS likes to call it. Johnson removed a retaining net that was supposed to keep the load from falling out onto you whenever the rear door was raised on the trailer. I stood the waiting to start and I began hearing a noise that sounded like "ker-chook", "ker-chook". I stuck my head out around the side of the trailer and noticed that a feeder driver was jacking the nose of the trailer up and this was the noise I was hearing. This is what UPS calls a 'gravity feed system" thus deriving the name "feeder" because, it "feed's" packages into the system.

Johnson pulled out a small conveyor belt that slid in and out and placed it against the set of rollers that were built into the center of the trailer. The trailer I was unloading had compartments under the floor flaps, which contained additional space to put more packages in. These kinds of trailers are called drop frame and they utilize all available space.

When I stepped into the rear of the trailer it was like stepping into an oven. Heck... I thought working on the belt was hot. The temperature inside the trailer was considerably higher than inside the building.

There was dust and tiny pieces of paper flying around in mini torna-dos caused from the vacuum effect that was from the bad seal from the building against the trailer.

I stepped onto the edge of the trailer, just inside the rear of it, trying not to fall into the crack that was in between the trailer and the dock, and I began to put packages on the belt at a rather fast pace and it didn't seem bad at all. I managed to work a steady pace for about six or seven minutes and began to get stiff from bending over and pushing the packages that were on the rollers, out. I was really starting to sweat now. Sweat was running down the small of my back and soaking my pants and underwear. The fumes from the tractor exhaust had begun to seep into the trailer where I was working. I lasted for about fifteen minutes until I began to vomit and get dizzy with a tremendous headache. The more I bent over and stood up to push the packages out the worse I got. The bending and standing up, then leaning down, then back up again was beginning to take its toll on me. Every time I bent down to get a package and stand up to place it on the rollers the sicker I got. I was working under the flaps, and with having gotten sick I puked my guts out onto the floor of the trailer. With the heat and the smells, and from having to stand in my own vomit and work only made me even that much sicker. I desperately needed to go outside and get some fresh air.

Johnson came up to check on me and told me to come out of the trailer and get some fresh air. I climbed on out and all I wanted was to just go somewhere and lie down and die. I had become that sick from the heat and fumes in the trailer. I didn't see how people managed to do this on a daily basis.

I managed to have drunk all my water and I had drunk way too much. On top of everything that was wrong with me from the fumes and heat, I now had to contend with the diarrhea from all of the water I drank. As I walked around I noticed that my butt had become raw and it hurt when I walked. I had sweated so much that I was chafed in between my legs and crotch. I had managed to rub myself raw. I was miserable. I didn't think I would be able to endure the same kind of conditions again.

I finally managed to get half way straightened out and Johnson put me back into the trailer and placed another part timer in there to help me the rest of the day. I couldn't muster much effort, and I must say that the other worker did most of the unloading the rest of the morning. They all could tell that I was sick and Johnson never said anything to me other than, "Just hang in there."

There was no way I could've kept up that pace. The 900 pieces an hour, which was the mar, or the required amount of pieces per hour, was almost a whole trailer itself. We had just roughly one hour to unload a whole trailer by ourselves. This wasn't worth $8.00 an hour to me.

As the week progressed I became accustomed to the heat and the working conditions, and was able to keep up with the demands and meet the mar. I was still very sore from the continuous and repetitive motions of bending and twisting for four hours at a stretch.

The following week I had to leave "the unload" area and return back onto the belt and work for Alli, and when I returned to the belt she started me out on two cars this time. Alli was still working with me, and she was trying to help me get the whole concept down, and Alli continued to act as if I should have been born with the knowledge of loading trucks and acted accordingly. I had only loaded for a week before they stuck me back in the unload. I didn't even have a real chance to apply my memory of the streets or learn my charts that well yet. She showed no relief in her criticism and disgust in the many mistakes I had made that day.

When the supervisors called for a break and shut the belt off, I was still loading packages and trying to get the area behind my truck cleaned up, because I had a lot of packages just piled in three-foot high piles. I wanted to straighten the trucks up and make sure everything was just perfect. This is a common practice even today of new hires who don't know any better. They want to make a good impression and want to portray an image of being concerned and wanting to do a good job, so they work during their break. They fail to realize that this practice only takes money out of their pocket every day. I was busy trying to get as much as I could into the package car before the end of the break and the belts started back up. I noticed an employee standing behind me, across the belt, who asked me what I was doing. Her name was Dee.

I had noticed that Dee worked at the head of the belt, but it was still only my third week there, and I was more concerned with surviving than making friends...at least for now. I knew that she was loading several package cars in the number one position, which was all the way at the head of the belt. She was a few years older than me, and seven months pregnant. She was pregnant and doing this job. What kind of woman was this? She stood there decked out in a pair of overalls, and a pair of black combat boots that were only laced halfway up and wearing a red bandanna wrapped around her head. She qualified as a redneck if there if was one but I didn't care and I immediately knew that I liked her.

Dee struck up the conversation with me and I decided to stop and take a breather. Dee told me that I should stop and take a break because we had a ten-minute break in the contract and that we were paid for it anyway. I explained to Dee that I just wanted to get everything I could into the package car so Alli wouldn't jump on me. She said that she understood my line of thinking and told me to do the best I could until I qualified.

"Qualified. What's that?" I asked.

Dee began to explain to me that I only had thirty days as a trial period to see if I could do the job. UPS would then make a decision based on my performance and then they'd decide if they would keep me or let me go. This put an added strain on me since I was not told about this up front before I quit my job at the grocery store. I had no other choice now but to work 110 percent harder than I was or I'd stand to lose my job.

I chose to carry everyone of my charts home everyday after work and I spent all of my available time studying and taking self made test. I worked harder and harder, and I improved everyday over the course of the next week.

This is when I first started experiencing health related problems from the stress of being employed at UPS. I was required to start off on an anti-anxiety prescription to help try and curb and control the frequent panic attacks that I was having. I feel strongly that this could be attributed to my newfound career at UPS.

I had made a mistake that almost cost me my job shortly after I returned back to the belt. I had missed the stop counts on one of my package cars by almost 55 stops short, and this was a serious problem, at least to management. With me missing the stop count by that much had caused the driver to work an extremely long day. Not only was management upset, but also the driver was really pissed off at me at the time.

The next morning after that little mistake, I received a top grade butt chewing from Alli during our daily PCM. A PCM is just a pre-communication meeting that management holds to tell everyone how well they did the day before and to set goals for that day as well. The same man I had seen before, Dick, came up to me during the course of the day and asked Alli to be present when he spoke to me.

Dick was rather a short man, with a deep voice and sort of intimidating to a little pee-on like me. He was again dressed in a set of 'browns' and stood across the belt with his arms folded.

"James, what's your problem?" He asked without expression.

"I don't know what you mean." I replied nervously and slightly offended from his tone.

"Do you realize how much money you cost me yesterday? Do you?" He asked in an upset tone while staring at me.

"No I don't," I replied.

I didn't have any idea what he was talking about 'costing him money'. Dick then asked Alli what did my stop counts looked like that morning. She told him that she hadn't checked them yet. Dick pulled her off to the side and told me to get back to work, and I tried to get caught back up from having to stand there and answer his questions. The belt had been running the whole time and packages were filing by me unchecked. Gary had to pull my packages and sit them at the edge of my work area and pull his packages as well.

I looked over to where Alli and Dick were standing down from us and I noticed that Alli kept looking at me and I could tell she was really pissed off about something. I acted like I didn't notice her and when she returned all she had to say was, "If you don't do better by Friday you're gone."

It took everything I had to keep from telling them both to stick that job right then and there. I decided after thinking about it that I wasn't going to let them get the best of me. During any free time I had, and during the breaks, I studied and the other loaders helped me out by showing some short cuts and tricks of the trade. Everyone worked with me for the next four days and by Friday I had qualified.

Several months would pass and I didn't have too many problems other than having to deal with my three drivers everyday and anytime I made a mistake that they didn't like they all chewed me out. Each of my drivers wanted their package cars loaded different despite the way management wanted me to do it. I ignored them and loaded them the way management wanted me to.

I had one driver in particular that reminded me a lot of Barney Rubble from the Flintstones. His name was Tommy. It seemed that I hadn't been loading his truck just right and he was a rather loud crybaby about the whole thing. Finally one day he started in on me about something petty and began cussing me, and I then returned the favor back to him and we got into a pretty heated exchange. Tommy cussed me out again the next day and I once again returned the favor. Before he left that day he told me that he would make my life miserable.

The next day Tommy had turned in a card that said I made a lot of mistakes the day before, called a 'misload card', which only got me reamed by Alli that morning. Tommy had turned a card in on me, which read like a short story or something. Alli told me that the next time this happened I would get a warning letter, which was the next step of discipline after getting a write up in our file. Tommy continued to nitpick me for the rest of the week and he even went as far as making up a couple of things that were not true.

I thought all morning about he intentionally lied on me just to get me in trouble and I decided on a course of action. The next day when it was time for the drivers to start work I told Alli that I had became sick and that I needed to leave. The preload was at the end of running the sort and she told me to go ahead and go on home. I walked on over towards the time clock, and punched my time card on it, and I then began walking on up towards the front of the building and noticed that the drivers were just coming out of their PCM. I saw Tommy walk out and he looked at me and shot me a bird and several of the other drivers laughed at him. "We'll see who has the last laugh," I thought to myself and waited for him to walk to his package car. I hid around the corner and after a second or two I heard the drivers erupt into laughter. Tommy came out of his car cussing and screaming for Alli to come over to his truck to see what I had done to him. They couldn't see me standing there, but I could see Tommy talking to Alli while pointing towards the inside of his truck. Alli stepped into his package car and she went out of my sight for a couple of seconds then she came back out laughing her head off. Tommy was pissed. I hollered at Tommy, and he looked around for me and finally saw me hiding behind two package cars. I shot him a bird and then took off running to my car and left.

Tommy worked well past 9:30 p.m that night and the following Monday, and I believe that's when I received one of my first warning letters for my actions from that previous Friday. All I had done was to load his entire truck backwards, and after I did this I never had any more problems out of Tommy or any other of my drivers.

I had begun to come around and everyone began to accept me. That helped me a lot with adjusting to the newfound stress at UPS. Most of everyone I worked with was going to college except for Dee who was studying to be a mortician.

One of the first retaliatory incidents perpetrated by management that I could remember involved a loader who worked in front of me named Scott. Scott was getting ready to graduate from college and later in the week he was going to just up and quit without even working out a notice with UPS. He simply wasn't going to show up. Sure enough when Friday rolled around Scott didn't show up.

The pre-load had begun that morning and boxes were coming down the belt. Scott's truck weren't set up yet and the packages that were undelivered from the previous day were still strewn across the floor of his package cars. Alli went around asking everyone if we knew anything about Scott, and we all denied any knowledge of him quitting. She knew that he was planning to graduate that week but wasn't for sure as to what day it was. With Scott not reporting for work meant that Alli was going to have to load his cars. She wasn't familiar with his trucks and what stops belonged to him, and she was missing packages left and right. Alli began throwing things up into the truck and kicking packages. She was really, really, really pissed off at us, but she was finally getting a taste of her own medicine.

"Pull your stuff," Gary would yell out at Alli who then would just turn and stare a hole through him. We'd step into the back of our package cars out of view and laugh. I sort of got the impression that Alli didn't like getting what she'd been dishing out to us for so long. She wasn't any more proficient than the rest of us as she made out to be, because she had one of the biggest messes out behind her trucks that I had ever seen in my life. There were packages piled about chest high behind her package cars...no lie.

Finally, Dick had to call in the drivers of those cars to help her clean up the mess that she had made. At break time Alli was wringing with sweat, her hair was a mess and her clothes were filthy. She had black dirt all over her face. As she walked by us she just stared everyone down. She knew that we knew that Scott was going to screw her over and we kept silent about it.

That following Monday after Scott had quit, during our PCM, Alli decided that our work would take on a new twist. She told us that if this was how we wanted things to be then we would just have the relationship of employer and employee. Heck that's the way I thought it was supposed to be, and besides the only time she ever treated us with any kind of dignity is when she needed something from us like swapping trucks or something.

We almost immediately began to get hammered by management and were written up for every little infraction we committed whether by accident or not. If we missed our stop counts by more than plus or minus five stops we were written up for it. Even if we just missed the count by just six, that one extra stop would cost us a warning letter.

If we had any misloads whatsoever for any reason, on area, or off, we were disciplined. The management in Huntsville even went as far as to ban any talking on the belts while we were on the clock. This only backfired on them because when they came up to ask us something we'd pretend to lock our mouths and throw away the key.

One of my friends, Kenny, who loaded right down from me had missed one of his drivers by more that fifty stops. He was indoctrinated as an honorary member of the infamous 'fifty club'. That unwanted membership wound up costing him a two-day suspension.

Management was determined to make our lives as miserable as they could from day to day. Time would march on and we managed to dodge the bullet and keep our jobs and Alli finally graduated college and moved on up in UPS somewhere out west in human resources. We went without a supervisor for a couple of days until they could find another sucker to take her place.

I had been relocated to the front of the belt and was given only two cars to load, just after I managed to learn the three I had since I started at UPS. I had been at UPS now for over a year and tried to do my job everyday the best that I could and just lay low. I really didn't care about what was going on at UPS and who was who.

One morning Dee and I were joking around when we noticed a stranger standing in the sort aisle barking out orders. Neither one of us had ever seen this man before, and he was standing up there snapping his finger yelling, "more flow". The sorters had to sort a certain amount of packages an hour as their mar. They were supposed to maintain a steady rate of flow, which allowed us to do our jobs and keep our trucks clean. It made it easy on us and reduced misloads and so on.

Well, with this idiot yelling orders, the sorters started increasing their rate and boxes were coming down the belt piled on one another and falling off onto the floor. He had managed to mess everything up in a matter of minutes. Packages began to pile up behind everyone's trucks and it was getting out of hand. We couldn't sort the sudden surge of packages and put them on the right side of the belt. Labels were turned upside down and we began tripping over the packages that had begun falling on the floor. I managed to miss most of my packages and had stumbled over packages on the floor as I followed the piles of packages on the belt trying to split and sort them out. Out of anger I finally had enough of what he was doing and yelled up toward the sort aisle, "Ease up, you're killing us."

The stranger immediately came running up to me and got right in my face, nose to nose. He stood there for a few seconds and told me that his name was Jed and that he was the new preload manager in Huntsville. He continued on with what I needed to do and that I had better get used to the way he did things if I wanted to work for him. I stepped back and he finished by telling me to mind my own business and do my job. Dee looked at me and asked me "What his problem was?" I told her that I didn't know, but I didn't appreciate him getting into my face like that.

Before the day was over Jed had managed somehow to climb onto the top of the package cars that were parked on the inside of the building, and had somehow got his hands on a bullhorn. He walked up and down the roofs of the package cars yelling and screaming at us to "get the packages in the car." Here this idiot was in a suit and tie waiving his arms around and pointing at us while screaming at us with a bullhorn. He was about thirteen feet off the ground. He had everyone shook up and scared to death. He was turning out to be a real slave driver if there ever was one.

I had never seen anyone like him, at least not as of yet, and he would become notorious for doing similar display's of idiocy on more than one occasion and management didn't seem to mind his tactics as long as he continued to get the preload down on time.

I remember one incident that still bothers me to this day and I was quite scared that the same thing might happen to me while I was employed as a loader.

What had happened was that UPS delivers to different labs to have customers specimens to be analyzed. This one day in particular involved a loader named Hanson who was a rather short guy around five feet two or so. Hanson had difficulty in putting the packages in the top shelf of the package car when he had a stop that went on the top shelf.

It seems that a small Styrofoam cooler made it's way through the UPS system, and had become damaged somewhere along the way. The package made it all the way down the belt 'leaking' its contents. This was years before UPS had began enforcing its policies regarding 'leaking packages'. Hanson picked the package up and carried it into his package car to be loaded in the top shelf, and as he stood on his tiptoes to sit it in the shelf it slipped and fell into his face. Some of the contents, probably dry ice or something in liquid form, spilled into his eyes and mouth. Hanson ran out of the package car and he told a supervisor that something had spilled into his eyes and mouth and asked to go wash them out. The supervisor was rather uncaring about his situation and gave him a lot of grief when he walked off the belt to wash out his eyes and mouth. The supervisor had the package and the top of it read "viral specimen". The fact that this supervisor gave this man any problem at all should be a testament to the mentality of management at the time.

One of the first major run in's I had with Jed, which would wind up requiring the representation of the union, occurred when I had 'allegedly' caused several misloads for my drivers. Someone had called in sick that morning and I agreed to help out Jed by picking up an extra truck to load. I had earlier in the year received a warning letter for the same offense and had managed to go four months without receiving another one. Management keeps the discipline on the record for a period of nine months and if no other similar infractions happen then it is wiped clean. If something does happen then the company proceeds to the next step of discipline, which would be a suspension.

Upon learning of this, I became somewhat nervous, considering the next step for me would've been a suspension and then a discharge. I now had a reason to be worried. Everyone slipped up pretty often and nine months was a rather long time to go without making a mistake. I mean we'd handle (700 - 1000) packages apiece each day and were responsible for everything being just perfect when in fact it was nearly impossible to do. It was a tedious and exhausting attempt just to keep from getting fired for making a mistake.

Jed came up to where I was working and stepped into the rear of the truck while I was inside placing something in a shelf.

"James you need to get a steward at break and I want to see you in the office." Jed replied.

I nodded my head as I marked my paper for a new stop. As break time neared I began to get a serious case of the butterflies. I told Marsha, our part time union steward, that Jed needed to see us in the office at break after I told Marsha what was going on and she said she'd come get me as soon as the buzzer sounded. I was getting quite nervous now and I wasn't too sure as to what was about to happen to me whether I'd get suspended or fired.

The buzzer sounded as the belt shut off and Marsha walked down to my truck to get me. We walked around to where the offices were and walked into the front one that Jed was using as his own. We both walked in and sat down waiting for Jed to show up. Marsha rehearsed with me what might be said and what for me to say and not say. I was rather nervous and everything she was telling me just went in one ear and out the other. She finally just told me, to reduce any chances of me cutting my own throat, to let her do most of the talking. This was the first time that I was going to see the union in action. Up to that point, I had no knowledge of what actually went on in these offices concerning a possible discharge, and other serious offenses. Was it going to be any different than when I had received my warning letters? I didn't know.

Jed came busting through the door like his butt was on fire. He came in and sat down on the corner of his desk and stared at me for a few seconds and then went through his spiel about how he couldn't allow this sort of behavior to continue and asked me what my problem was. I was lost. What in the world is this moron talking about?

"I didn't know I had a problem." I replied, growing tired of them assuming that I had a problem.

Jed went through his routine describing what had happened and I still didn't know what he was talking about. What he was claiming I had done was something that I actually hadn't done.

The problem was that the acting supervisor over the east belt didn't tell me, at the time, that I was to pull off a section of packages off of one driver to be placed on another.

Jed sat back up straight and thought for a minute and asked me to step outside while he talked to Marsha about what was going on. I stood up and walked on outside as he shut the door behind me.

I stood outside the office door for a minute or two, and I was finally called back into the office and asked to sit down. Jed told me that there wouldn't be any discipline since it wasn't my fault and for me to just go back to work. I had wasted my whole break period in the office fooling with him that morning and now I wasn't going to get to eat the sandwich that I had brought from home.

One of the most horrible experiences any new worker at UPS has is their first 'peak season'. Peak season is the time after Thanksgiving up to Christmas Eve. Peak season is really strange. Everything is going along pretty normal and then all of a sudden the bottom falls out. Packages start coming in by the hundreds. Volume spikes and talk about a mess. There are usually packages piled out about chest high behind all of the cars from one end of the belt to the other. It's almost as if management holds these packages in a warehouse somewhere and then all of a sudden, bam, here they are.

I never new what a hectic schedule was until peak season arrived. Every driver we had suffered from our poor loads. There was, in fact, very little we could do during this time other than to just survive. With all the packages piled up as high as they could on the belts it was impossible for everyone to do their jobs. I mean, even with management hiring seasonal help it was still not enough. We just couldn't do it. No one could. Not even Superman Jed.

About one hour into the sort during peak season you couldn't walk down either side of the belt. You'd either have to walk, crawl, or slide over the boxes to get anywhere. I mean a person could honestly wade through mounds of cardboard.

Then all of the supervisors would be screaming at us to "get it in the car" and we'd be screaming at everybody we could to slow down and help us. The drivers normally would have to be called in to clean up the mess every morning. The drivers would spend, at times, in excess of an hour just trying to figure out what went where. It just didn't make sense. Why didn't management just start us an hour earlier and pay us that extra hour to do the job right? Instead they'd rather pay a driver time and a half to do a job that would cost them $20 less an hour to let us do it...go figure. The supervisors would be screaming and yelling and kicking boxes in an attempt to intimidate the drivers so they'd get on the road quicker. It was just a vicious cycle.

I would stay on the preload for a few more months and would finally have the chance to go full time. I signed the bid sheet, which had been posted on the wall announcing the new openings into the package car ranks. I went ahead and quit college because now I wasn't going to have time to go. I was about to start making the big bucks.

Chapter 3

"11:22 a.m: So far this morning I've been cussed out by two customers for delivering their packages two hours late and I can't even begin to get caught up. I don't know which is worse the heat or the irate customers. Surely it's got to get better than this."

I was sent to the UPS center, in Birmingham Alabama, to attend a three-day driver orientation class that was required by the company to be trained in the fundamentals of driving professionally. I left Huntsville the Sunday evening before having to report and made the eighty-five mile drive to Birmingham. I checked into my hotel room, that UPS was paying for, and found out I was having a room mate. The other guy I was rooming with was a part timer out of the Gadsden Alabama building. His name was Terrell.

I introduced myself to him we were both fairly excited and apprehensive about going full time. Our conversation shifted from what we were expecting from our trainers the next day to what we could get into that night in downtown Birmingham. We were both twenty one years old and decided that it would be best if we just hang around and visit Sammy's. We weren't going to get too wild because we did have to get up early the next morning.

We put our things away and walked down the hallway of the hotel to the lounge that was located next to the reception area. We walked in an ordered a couple of drinks and made our way back to a table to see who would come in. We received our drinks and were joined by several more UPS employees who were there for the same thing. There were two part timers from the Montgomery hub and one from the Winfield Alabama center. After several drinks we all had loosened up a bit and we all just sat around spilling our guts about what went on back at our home centers. We compared war stories of who had the worst managers to work for. It was sad though. No story was really any different than the other. It was as if they were all cut from the same cloth. Everything sounded pretty much textbook UPS management style.

We stayed in the lounge until I had grown pretty tired, and I excused myself from their company and walked on back to the room to go to bed. We were going to be in class for a long three days and I needed some rest to be sharp for the 'quality' training I was about to receive.

I awoke to a courtesy call from the front desk, still feeling the after effects of the previous night's social gathering. I rolled out of bed and slowly rounded up my gear and drove over to the Birmingham center to start my class.

When I arrived at the center, there were only a few other people there besides me. I found my way to the classroom after asking several people for directions and walked in and took a seat in the rear of the room. The classroom was actually a small conference room with a whiteboard up front and several D.O.T, Department of Transportation, posters on the wall. There was a TV and VCR on a cart at the front of the room. I was rather early with the exception of a few supervisors roaming the halls and had decided to just lay my head on the desk and catch a few winks before the long day started.

I must have dozed off and I did not notice the instructor had walked in. It was Dena, the lady who had hired me. I stood up and she smiled at me while sticking out her hand.

"How are you doing today James?" She replied, while shaking my hand.

"Fine Dena and yourself?" I asked.

"Just fine." She replied as she began sitting out books and forms at the various seats in the room. Shortly after doing this she stepped out for a few minutes and then she came back with several boxes of pastries and soft drinks in a cooler. I was standing around flipping through the books trying to see what we were going to be doing for the day.

Other people started to come in by now and everything started to liven up a bit. Some managers had come into the room, while we were all busy discussing our previous night's adventures and they walked around introducing themselves to us. The appointed hour had arrived and passed and class had still not began. I thought to myself, "Looks like we'll be here all day." Finally Dena walked back into the room and asked us to settle down and for us to take our seats. She introduced herself to everyone, but we all knew who she was, and introduced the UPS driving program.

During the course of the next few days Dena covered everything from driving habits to safety regulations. She especially discussed the 'fundamentals of driving' according to UPS's standards. Dena told us to forget everything we thought we knew about driving because it was probably all wrong. We were bombarded for hours on end with everything you could think of that related to UPS driving and D.O.T laws. At the end of each ten-hour day, we were given a written test to evaluate what we had learned from that day.

The odd thing about management is that when they give you a test they review the answers with you. I always thought it defeated the purpose of testing an individual when you'd give them answers. Maybe that's how they account for the perfect scores on most of their training packs. They still practice that to this very day.

At the conclusion of the last day of class Dena had to take us all out for a road test in Birmingham. We all stood up and followed Dena outside to where management had parked a gutted out package car which had been fitted it with seats, like a van, and windows all around. It was absolutely the ugliest thing I had ever seen and it was painted that Pullman Railroad color brown. We all piled into the 'ugly wagon' and took time about driving. We all managed to pass the driving class and now we were sent back to our respected centers to be trained by the on-car supervisors back home.

I reported to work the following Monday morning, arriving well before the assigned start times for the drivers. I didn't want to be late and I found the supervisor that was going to train me for that week. His name was Harry. Harry was running around the center before time to start the meeting walking and trying to talk to me at the same time. He was telling me about the route and what to expect and so on, while he was trying to finish his duties, and answering the phones, and trying to answer my questions all at the same time. You see... management has certain routes that are used only as training routes and nothing more, and usually the new drivers stay on these routes until they have sufficiently picked up on the "fundamentals' and then they are moved to cover other routes.

The training route that I would be assigned to was called "The Park". This route made deliveries in an industrial park, which was located just down from the building. It consisted mostly of business stops and about thirty residential deliveries with about thirty pickups in the afternoon. It was tagged by all the other driver's as being a 'gravy' little route, meaning it was easy.

Harry walked into the east center office to get his training packet while I waited outside the office for him to return. We then headed up to the customer counter room to attend the morning PCM. We walked into the meeting which had already begun, and we kind of blended in with the thirty some odd other drivers already in there. Dick was the one conducting the meeting and he continued to talk to the drivers while looking at Harry in a very strong way. I knew that Dick didn't like us interrupting his meeting.

Dick finished going through his spiel and then introduced me to the rest of the drivers. I remember that there were a few snide remarks made that I was the 'new meat' and for me to go out and have a good time with Harry. This was all common and I guess a rite of passage as well. I just laughed along with them. I was nervous enough as it was. I really tried not to think about it, because I had enough to think about as it was with Harry being with me. At the end of the meeting Dick excused us all with the usual, "Lets go to work."

Everyone filed out through the three doors leading back into the building and Harry and I were two of the last ones to leave. I followed Harry to our truck that was parked just right outside the customer counter door. We made our way around the stacks of packages that were leaning against the truck and were blocking our way, and I managed to avoid the mess and stepped up on the dock and he began to look at the packages that were piled out behind my truck. I knelt down to hand him the ones that were hard to reach and had fallen in between the dock and the truck onto the floor. Some lay under the bumper of the truck and we'd have to wait until we pulled out away from the dock to get those.

"When you pull out I'll get them okay?" Harry replied.

I said okay and we continued looking at the address labels that were stacked out behind my truck. Harry explained to me the importance of making service on every package and the severity of the punishment if for some reason I was unable to deliver any of them.

"You do know that you are to deliver everything you have on this truck...period. Do not ever bring back anything unless it can't be found and then you'll need to call us and we'll tell you where to take it ...understand?"

Harry replied, while making sure I understood.

"Deliver everything regardless, right?" I asked.

"Right." Harry replied while checking a package against the chart on the back of the truck.

I had butterflies and I was a nervous wreck. I had a thousand things running through my mind at the time and couldn't think of a single thing to ask him. My mind was shot.

Harry fired up a cigarette and instructed me how the packages were lined up in the shelf in relation to the way we would run the route. All the overnight packages, called Next Day Airs, were in tote boxes behind the truck for us to sort through. These packages were extremely important and had to be segregated from the rest of the ground delivery packages. As Harry and I went through these packages it reminded me of my first experience of seeing the local union in action.

Shortly before I went full time and while I was still pre-loader, I had allegedly loaded several overnight packages in the shelf with the regular ground packages, which this was a big no-no. The driver had missed the committed time of delivery, which in turn had caused what is called a 'service failure'. UPS had to refund the cost of shipping the packages because they were guaranteed by a certain time. So in that case UPS delivered the packages for free.

I met with the Huntsville east center manager, Dick, and with my union steward Marsha. The company had decided that due to the seriousness of the offense that it warranted a one-day suspension. I was shocked and I was immediately told by Marsha to file a grievance to protest the suspension. This was typically done anytime a Teamster received discipline. I filed the grievance just like Marsha had told me to do and later in the week I learned that a local level hearing, called a 'local', was set up to hear my grievance concerning my suspension.

What did all of this mean to me? It meant that I probably had screwed up really bad, but the more and more I thought about this whole case the more it didn't make sense. Something wasn't right with this, but I couldn't quite place my finger on it.

The local level hearing, being the second step in the grievance machinery process, is when UPS's labor manager and the local union representative meet to try and resolve the grievance.

When the day finally came for my hearing I waited down stairs by the water fountain waiting for the man that was going to represent me. In through the back door walks a man in a suit that I had never seen before carrying a briefcase. He walks almost up to me, and then turns to go up stairs to offices up there. I didn't know what to do at all, so I decided to go ahead and just stand there until someone came for me.

After a few minutes had passed, in walks another man that I had never seen before either and he walks up to me and asks me, "Are you James?"

"Yes sir." I replied.

"Follow me and don't worry about anything okay?" He replied, as we jogged up the steps to the office. We walked on into the office and inside was the man that I had seen earlier, and sitting beside him was Dick.

"How are you doing? My name is Chet." The older man replied, while shaking my hand. Chet was a district labor manager for UPS.

I told him that I was glad to meet him and sat down beside Huey, the local union representative at that time, before Matt, and Chet began.

I could tell immediately from his arrogance and grim look on his face that he was a hard ass if there ever was one, and I figured on just taking my day off and serving my suspension.

"James do you understand that we lost money because of your error?" Chet replied, while looking over his glasses as he replied in a cold, hard tone while rocking his chair back and forth.

Chet really laid it on thick to me and I felt like a real piece of crap. I had given up on even trying to work it out. Huey asked Chet about my previous work record, and Chet turned to Dick and made a facial expression that made Dick speak up. Chet didn't know anything about me nor did he really care. He was there to enforce the labor agreement between UPS and the Teamsters and could care less what kind of employee I was.

Dick spoke up to Huey and told him that I was a fairly good worker. Huey then turned to me and asked me what had happened on the morning in question to which I explained to him everything that had happened.

I explained to Huey that I didn't remember loading the airs onto the truck. In fact, I remembered that I had left early that morning to get my class schedule straightened out.

"Huey, Jed told me that I could leave early that morning." I replied in an excited tone.

"Dick I want to see a copy of this man's time card for that day." Huey replied smartly.

"I don't have it with me." Dick replied.

"Well hell, go get it, I'll wait." Huey popped off in a smart tone while Chet sat there turning redder by the minute.

After a couple of minutes of waiting, Dick came back into the room and sat down beside Chet. He handed my timecard to Chet first and then Chet handed them to Huey. It was some sort of little game they liked to play, and I figured they did it to try and piss Huey off. Chet sat up in his seat and pushed his glasses up on his face.

"Dick what time did the airs run the morning in question?" Huey asked, while examining my time card.

"I don't remember?" Dick replied, while looking at Chet.

"You mean to tell me you don't even know what time you run your airs? That's a bunch of bull '@#%*', and you know it!" Huey replied, while becoming pissed.

"What time on average do you run them?" Huey asked again.

Dick looked at Chet, and answered, "About 8:15 a.m."

"8:15 a.m right?" Huey asked.

"Yeah." Dick replied.

"Explain to me then how this man could load the airs if they were ran at 8:15 a.m that morning when his time card shows him punching out at 7:15 a.m?" Huey asked while tossing the time card on the desk.

Dick never said a thing. He just sat there. I could tell though that Chet was rather upset from the whole thing and was fuming, because Dick had just made Chet look like an idiot in front of the union.

Dick had failed to check that aspect out before hand and just assumed that it was me who made the mistake.

The thing with that is that when ever there is a service failure the management in the center had to explain to their bosses why they had the service failures, and they had better have a good reason for it or it could cost them their job. They decided to make me the scapegoat for these service failures. Only this time it didn't work.

"James step out a minute while I discuss this with them." Huey asked. I stood up and walked on out to the bathroom, which was just right across the hall. When I came out I could hear Huey cussing and raising hell with Chet and Dick. After a minute or so Huey came out of the office and got me, and we walked back into the office and sat down. Dick apologized to me and told me that I could leave that the suspension was dropped and that was that.

Well anyway, Harry began loading the overnights, sometimes called "red's", into the top shelf in the first section, and he said that we would deliver them as we went along that morning, breaking off only as we had to, in order to meet the commitment time on the packages. We finished loading the truck and he pulled down the back door using the strap hanging from the door slamming it shut. He then walked around and climbed in the drivers side and I slid over and pulled the little 'jump seat' on the passenger's side of the truck down and fastened my seat belt.

All the drivers began pulling out of the building and Harry told me that he would drive for the first day and for me to just observe and help him carry packages. We both waited until it was clear and then he pulled the car outside and stopped it in the parking lot. He climbed out and instructed me how to properly pre-trip a vehicle.

We checked all of the safety equipment, tires, horn, and lights and so on as required by D.O.T regulations on a daily basis. After checking everything, which took less than three minutes, Harry signed of on a little book called a D.V.I.R book. The Daily Vehicle Inspection Report listed any mechanical problems of the vehicle which when the driver would request to be repaired. After this we headed out for our first stop of the day.

It was pretty exciting, at least to me, to be out riding around in this vehicle. With the large glass in front and the height of the seats, I could see everything that was going on ahead of us that was normally limited to view from within a car. The ride and quality of equipment, due to age of the vehicle, left a lot to be desired though.

We delivered the first part of our day and we stopped at around 11:30, after finishing all of the business stops, and pulled into the parking lot of a store to buy some lunch. Harry parked out front, away from everybody, and locked the vehicle down. "This how you secure your vehicle when you're going to be away from it and out of sight." Harry replied, as he slid all the doors closed and we both began walking towards the store.

It was real nice outside. It was early March and it was sort of cool that day. We stopped at a local store, which was on my area, and I bought several things to help me make it through the day such as cokes and chips. We didn't stay in the air-conditioned section of the store very long. Harry paid for everything and we headed back out to the truck.

We walked around to the rear of the truck and Harry sat his drink and hot dogs down on the bumper and dug through his pocket for his key.

"I thought we had to keep the key ring on our finger," I replied jokingly.

He never answered. He just looked at me and smiled. I wanted to poke fun at him a little and try to relax us both.

Harry opened the back door and it flew up and rocked back and forth until stopping. He then stepped up into the truck while taking a bite from his hot dog. He placed his food in the empty part of a shelf and I climbed in behind him and sat on the wheel well on one side of the truck. Harry proceeded to tell me that we were on a tight schedule and that we couldn't stop to take all of our lunch. Although according to our labor agreement, the 'contract', I had a one-hour time allotment for lunch to take at my choosing. He failed to tell me this. We spent a small part of the break setting up the rest of our deliveries that we still had to make before begin-ning our pickups. There was a rather strong breeze blowing and it blew into the back of the truck where we were sorting the load causing dust and Styrofoam peanuts to blow all over the place. It reminded me of something like a sandstorm except there wasn't any sand, just trash.

I had begun eating the hot dogs that I had bought while standing up beside him eating with one hand. Harry was moving packages around and I was trying to follow his logic of placing the packages just right. We sat there for about ten minutes, until we had finished lining up everything that was left, and arranging what we couldn't deliver that morning in a corner of the truck just behind the drivers seat. Harry opened the front doors and we fired the truck up and headed for our first set of residential stops.

The neighborhood we delivered in was in north Huntsville, and for the most part all were nice houses. We had to drive about fifteen minutes one-way to get 'on area' and begin delivering.

The way the stops were arranged in the shelf was amazing to me. I didn't have any knowledge of my delivery area and was totally lost at how the driver knew where to turn and so on. I sat over in the jump seat and looked over a map of my area that Harry had highlighted earlier. All of the street's and cross street's and the number breaks just confused me tre-mendously. I couldn't figure it out and it was clearly a display of science.

The "production" standards management uses to calculate the 'ex-pected' level of performance for each individual drivers route is another type of science as well, or at least they like to think so.

We, according to Harry, were required to run seventeen stops an hour regardless of the many different variables that are injected into the equa-tion on a daily basis. Many variables such as traffic, construction projects, wrecks and so forth did in fact interfere and hamper us and it prevented some drivers from achieving the desired production standard. The other variables would also include the number of packages, how many steps to the door, if it was a C.O.D package and so on. Management didn't really care what problems you ran into, as a driver, as long as you met their 'production standards', that were established for your route. They seemed to treat you more like a machine rather than as a human being.

We managed to achieve this quota, and at some times exceed it due to the fact that there was two of us working. I, unknowingly at the time, would run the packages up to the door and jump in the truck which was unsafe, and we'd take off to the next one. I thought it was the norm but in reality I was slowly cutting my own throat.

Harry instructed me in the 'world famous' delivery methods designed and taught like a religion by management. The methods were supposed to be the most efficient way a driver could go out and deliver the packages. Management had spent thousands of dollars on perfecting this production tool, and this was the company's most cost effective tool to ensure maximum performance at minimal cost. It was a number thing. There's more than just the perception of us "riding around all day" to deliver packages. This is where the time allowances and other factors come into play.

The average driver should be able to do the following as according to management.

As the driver is preparing to deliver his next stop he is aware of the next five stops in the shelf as well. Once the driver begins his approach to the stop, say a house for example, he scans the area and the house to make sure it is the correct number. As the driver begins to signal their intention of stopping they put on their blinker and then their four way signals, or emergency flashers. The driver then prepares to stop completely and sounds the horn to alert the homeowner of them stopping. In one fluid motion the driver stops the package car, shifts into first gear, pulls the hand brake while starting to stand and simultaneously releasing the lap belt with their right hand. When the driver stands they turn to insert the key that has already been removed from the ignition and inserts it into the door that separates the cab from the package storage area, called a bulkhead door. This fluid motion should have taken no more that seven seconds.

The driver then turns the key and enters just inside the area behind the bulkhead door. The driver selects the package from the shelf and checks the next five stops, or thirty-inch selection, while sliding up his whole shelf. Depending on the size of the package he places it either on the steps inside the cab or holds it under his arm. The driver does this since larger packages run the risk of causing an injury while exiting the vehicle. Lets say that the driver has a small package. He then steps out from behind the bulkhead door, and back into the cab, and closes and locks the door. This should have taken no more than fifteen seconds.

The driver then grabs his clipboard, and while using the handrail, the driver exits the vehicle. The driver walks up to the house and writes the shipper number down all the while keeping his eyes moving and looking for obstacles that could cause him to trip. As the driver walks up to the door he looks for a safe place to leave the package that will prevent it from being seen and getting damaged from the elements. When the driver does this they ring the doorbell and call out "UPS", they then turn and hide the package out of view from passing people and then while on his way back to the truck the driver sheets up the next stop. This should take, depending on an average house, no more than two minutes. The driver prepares to enter the vehicle and in one fluid motion, steps into the truck, inserts the clipboard into the holder, inserts the ignition key, cranks the truck, fastens his seat belt, releases his hand brake and check over his shoulder before pulling out into traffic. This should take no more than seven seconds. We're looking at a total of about three minutes for this one stop. And this was a perfect scenario without any C.O.D's, or having to use your hand trucks for multiple packages, and no dogs and so on.

Harry and I finished all of the residential deliveries we had, and headed back to the "Park" to start our commercial pick up stops. We couldn't start these any earlier than 2:30 p.m., and we ran through these in record time since there were two of us working. We returned back to the building at around 5:15 p.m that afternoon. Harry made the 'suggestion' that we could go home early if we didn't take the rest of our lunch and work what is called a "code five". Harry left the decision up to me, and I chose the latter and took the code five and went on home to visit my girl friend, Kelley. I chose, like most people would do, and went on home early. It was rare for any driver to get off that early and Harry decided that he would review my ride the following day.

The following day Harry let me do all of the driving and I was not accustomed to this size of vehicle and I was extremely intimidated by it. I was being trained in what UPS calls a 'P-1000', which means package-1000 cubic feet of space. This was one of the larger package cars in UPS's fleet. It was harder to drive than it looked. I was very uncomfortable with its size and cut corners too short and came close to clipping several mailboxes on more than one occasion, while Harry sat over in the jump seat smoking his cigarettes like a freight train. As the week progressed I became more confident and increased my skills somewhat overall. Harry must have smoked a carton of cigarettes a day that first week with me.

Finally Harry turned me loose the next week to do it on my own. Harry told me that he would come out and check on me during the day to see how I was doing, and if I wasn't doing well he'd get 'on-car' with me and get me caught back up.

I left that morning a nervous wreck, and I couldn't remember where a thing was, and I drew a total blank and felt lost as hell. As I began to pull out onto the main road I forgot about the dip in the road just in front of the UPS building, and instead of taking it easy and ease on out into the street...I gunned it. The angle at which I left, coupled with the dip in the road had caused the package car to rock back and forth violently. I gripped the steering wheel as I heard packages falling out of the shelf and into the floor. There were some that even struck the bulkhead door. I'm glad I had it closed because if I didn't I'd probably had packages all over me, in the cab, and then out into the street.

I drove onto my first stop, which was PPG, hoping that the mess wasn't as bad as it sounded. I arrived to the plant and parked out front to check out the damage. I stood up and tried to open the bulkhead door and it wouldn't open. It was jammed shut. This was not a very good sign. I walked on around to the rear of the truck and opened the door, and as I raised the door, packages tumbled out into the parking lot.

"Crap" I yelled out as my stress level shot to the moon. The clock was ticking and I was running out of time. I had only an hour and a half to deliver all of my overnights and be at a predetermined stop to be 'on time'.

I began to sweat profusely and climbed over the packages to begin moving the ones that were blocking the bulkhead door. I had a terrible mess. I couldn't remember where anything went. I didn't know what to do and I began to panic. I thought I was going to have a stroke right there on the spot. I just began to throwing things back in to the truck and shut the door. I had lost about twenty minutes already from having to screw around with this mess. It was starting to get hot and I was sweating like a dog. I tried to catch up, but the harder I worked the more mistakes I made. As I went along that morning customers had begun to complain to me that I was running behind and they needed this stuff earlier that morning. I thought about quitting. It had become that bad.

I was late getting to the store and Harry was sitting out in his truck waiting for me. I pulled in and jumped out and ran inside to buy me something to drink. I was thirsty as hell and hungry too.

Harry walked over to the truck and opened the door and looked inside. I had packages in the shelf that I had already been to earlier that morning. The whole truck was one huge cluster. Harry fired up another cigarette and took several draws while standing there surveying the damage. He could tell that I had a terrible day and only smiled at me. He climbed on board and rode with me to finish the day on time. I felt relieved. Harry told me not to worry about it and just learn from the mistakes I had made.

During the next couple of weeks, I managed to get better and finally I had arrived at the point that I was required to be at by management's standards. I had qualified for the job and I was now a driver.

Chapter 4

"2:30 p.m: I met with Mr. Stacy in the receiving area of PPG and we had a huge fight. He wanted me to stay and wait on him to finish processing an important shipment to one of their facilities out west. I told him I don't have time that he should have had it ready for me before I got there. I told him if he wanted it shipped he'd have to wait until tomorrow. He's threatened to call in on me. So what? Let him. I'm just doing what Stan told me to do."

I had been a full time driver now for several months and our center manager at the time, Dick, we had heard through the grapevine, was being sent away on a special assignment somewhere out west. This was news to our ears and we all danced a jig of joy. Everyone was in a pretty upbeat spirit after the news had spread. Later in the week, while we all were standing around discussing who may be in line to replace Dick, it was pretty much a toss up between several people. The next day we received word that an on car supervisor from the Huntsville west center, named Stan, was going to be the new Huntsville east center manager. We all found this to be no surprise because Stan had the right mentality for the job. I mean...he was a rump kisser if there ever was one and it was rather sickening to see him in action around all the big boys. He received his promotion via the "brown nose" method, which was the order for the day.

Stan was the type of 'political' person upper management needed to carry out its daily directives in their labor policy and he was rather young to have had become a center manager. Stan was well liked by most of the drivers in both centers. We all had believed that there wouldn't be that much of a change in Stan once he assumed full control of the center, but needless to say we were all wrong. It was almost an overnight transformation from an easy to get along with kind of person to a ruthless diehard.

Management was very heavy into trying to keep a tight reign on us through the close monitoring, and relentless scrutiny of our production numbers, and Stan would prove to be no different than his predecessor. Stan immediately turned the heat up on us all in a flagrant display of trying to show us 'who's in control'. Stan was dead set on establishing who was the boss and the 'buddy-buddy' from days of old was no longer the order of business.

I remember two weeks after his promotion and having returned to the center from one of "Uncle Busters brain washing schools", Stan singled out the four least best drivers and began to systematically harass and nitpick everything they did. This was done in an attempt to intimidate everyone else into falling in line.

Stan wanted to make those drivers 'successful' at their jobs. This is what management always liked to say when they're preparing to begin hammering someone for production.

"Let us help you into becoming a better driver," they rattle off with no conscience or thought about what they are saying. It sounds innocent enough, but little do those people outside the world of UPS know what that this actually means. This is one of the 'carefully' chosen words management uses to justify the unbearable grip on each driver that has been selected for their 'campaign' of production hell.

In the real world there are really no bad drivers, because not everyone is the same. I mean, if we were the machines that management believes and considers us, then it wouldn't be a problem to achieve their 'desired' elevated level of production. But everyone is not the same. Not everyone is as athletic, or in the best shape as the younger drivers and there are many factors that should into play when management makes this determination. There are many health variables, that are in most cases discarded such as age and physical condition. Then management would tell the Teamsters Union, once the production 'harassment' started and after the grievance procedure had been invoked by the employee that 'it's not economically feasible' to allow the driver to continue on the path of 'poor', and I use that loosely, poor performance. The fact of the matter is that under our current collective bargaining agreement there is such language that applies to this very issue which clearly states that "age and physical condition will be considered when determining a 'fair day's work'. The language was created to protect employees from this kind of harassment, but the problem with the issue is that the language itself is too broad. Management does consider it, and they even take into consideration, and then they throw the consideration out the window because "THEY HAVE CONSIDERED" and thus have fulfilled their contractual obligation. The solution to this problem is that we need a stronger and a more defined language clause, which outlines a clearer and defined penalty for managements blatant displays of abuse and have stiff and immediate penalties, which would be pursued vigorously by the union.

There is a clear and defined difference between an employee being used and exploited versus doing an "honest day's work for an honest days pay". No one would disagree that we all work very hard and rightfully should. In the fiercely competitive market that UPS shares with other companies like Federal Express, RPS and the U.S Postal Service an employee has the obligation and duty to ensure that the best interest of the employer is kept in mind at all times, but not at sacrificing their rights. We must make this company, our company, successful but in the same breath the management of the company has the moral and contractual obligation's not to exploit and underhandedly abuse the employees in the process. The perceived result from the employee perspective toward the management does in fact have an impact on production. This cannot be denied. There is far more involved in the world of labor relations than just a simple union contract as most perceive exist, which has a dramatic ripple effect on production, health and so on. There are, in fact, real and even imaginary rules and morals to be considered in the act of human resources and employee relations within all corporations worldwide.

I was still a new driver and had not yet figured out that management was using me. I was still running my route wide open, hurrying, and short cutting customers and the whole bit. I was only concerned in wanting to do a good job, and as well, I was being intimidated by the management of UPS to do more and more everyday. I was running more stops per hour, and was being dispatched with the most stops on this route than any one driver before me had ever been done. Were the other drivers capable of achieving and exceeding the same production standards that I was achieving...yes, and every bit more. But they've been down this road with management earlier in their careers and they knew what was going on, but yet I was blind to it. I was in fact being manipulated and used.

I had become labeled as a 'butt kisser' by my fellow workers. I thought they were just 'jealous', and I had failed to realize that I was hurting them as well. I received ridicule on a daily basis from them, but truthfully at the time I really wasn't too concerned with how they thought about me and I concentrated on just trying to best my previous days record. But sadly I should have been concerned, and I should have seen the tell-tale warning signs that were being thrown up by the actions of management.

It had gotten to the point that management was egging it on with the other drivers. The supervisors would make comments during the PCM about how well I was doing and why couldn't they go out and be a good driver like me. Management went as far as to say that the other drivers, some of them were twenty-five plus year drivers, could take lessons from me in a sickening attempt to boost production numbers by inflaming the employees against one another in a disgusting pit of competition. I was flattered for the comments by management, but I could tell that the sentiment towards me was not very favorable and it was in drastic decline.

This practice was of no one's benefit, but that of the local management in Huntsville. Simply put, the center was only allowed a certain amount of 'over-allowed' hours per day for all the drivers combined. The average can be taken by totaling the combined number of over allowed hours worked for that day by all the drivers, and then dividing the answer by the number of drivers. Keep in mind that the over allowed hours for a driver may range from one minute of 'over allowed hours' to a driver running two hours over allowed. For example if the Huntsville building was allocated only five hours of over allowed hours for a given day, and then exceeded the allowance, then the upper management comes down on the local management, and then they came down on us.

Then the vicious cycle begins with the systematically singling out of the 'problem', meaning worst production, drivers and then the harassment and intimidation begins in a to attempt to 'bring the driver in line'. Some say it's good business sense and should be expected, and I agree if the driver is out there screwing around, but if the driver is out there doing the best they can do, then it can only be interpreted as harassment and intimidation which there exist only a fine line separating the two.

Then enter into the equation that a center has five drivers, like me at the time, who go out and 'burn' these routes up. They run sometimes up to two hours under allowed. With those five driver's each running two hours under allowed for the day gives the center a much needed cushion of ten hours of under allowed time to counter act all of the over allowed that came on a daily basis from the remaining drivers. Keep in mind that not all drivers run over and the majority run under allowed. This ten hours of under allowed carries the weight of the building in terms of the under/ over allowed time allowance, which makes the managers jobs in Huntsville that much easier while hurting the other drivers who then become expected to follow our suit. We 'new' drivers, the runners, were working unsafe. We were out on our routes, running from the truck, and up to the house, and then back to the truck. We were wide open all day long, which only increased the likelihood of injuries and accidents due to 'aggressive' driving habits as a result. In fact, one side of the coin was that in the process of this practice we were neglecting the customers when in fact our business was to "service" the customers.

In the early 1990's, in my opinion, management had not yet become totally concerned with 'servicing' the customer and/or had fallen away from that founding principle in order to generate a higher profit. I don't disagree that generating higher profits for the shareholders should be a goal of any company, but not at sacrificing the integrity and commitment of our service in the process.

We were instructed by our Huntsville management team, from my beginning as a driver, that we were only allowed a certain amount of time for each stop. We were further instructed that mainly during our pick up portion of our paid day NOT to wait around at the customers place of business for any late shipments that were not processed and ready. When I would arrive to a customer's place of business in the afternoon to make a pickup and they weren't ready that was their problem and not mine. They had from the time I arrived and began to start loading what they had ready until I finished. If it wasn't written in the book, and ready, then I instructed them that it would have to wait until tomorrow. I left many a package sitting on the customers floor simply because the pick up book was not filled out correctly and the package had not been entered into the record. Even worse, on days that I was running behind, I had told customers that their urgent packages would have to wait until the next day and for them to call management if they had a problem. I told them I could not wait. This was all while 'Uncle Buster' was still the only big dog on the block. The practice of 'Service' was not to service the customer but to service the O.R, Operations Report, for management, no matter what the cost. Did they do this to all the customers? No not all of them, but it was prevalent in the "mom and pop" businesses, at least in our building.

I continued to burn my route up that I was still on at the time, "The Park". My record of the total of stops ran on that route before 5:00 p.m to this date has not been broken. It's something I'm not proud of because of my actions at the time, I hurt my fellow drivers and that performance record from that earlier time reflects on the drivers now who currently run it, now some ten years later.

I had been a package car driver for little over a year now and managed to avoid having any accidents, scratching the paint on the package car and breaking any mirrors which I could have been charged with an 'accident'. I received my "Safe Driving Award" from UPS marking my achievement for being a safe driver. I received my award during the morning PCM,in front of the other drivers and although it was supposed to be an achievement I considered it a symbol of surviving not being fired for having an 'accident'.

I was making a pick up one afternoon at a local computer distributor just outside Huntsville. It was, at the time, one of Huntsville's biggest accounts. I met up with another driver named Murphy who was covering for the driver on vacation. We talked to each other as we loaded the packages onto our trucks.

"How many stops are you going out with now James?" Murphy asked, as he placed several rather large packages into the shelf of his truck.

"Around 125 I guess." I replied, boasting of my efforts.

Murphy looked at me and grinned as he continued to load his truck.

"What time do you normally get off everyday with 125 stops?" He asked again.

"Uh, around 5:30 I guess," I replied.

Murphy didn't say anything else for a while as we continued to load our trucks. When we had finished loading what packages were on the pallets he stood there grinning at me like he had something to tell me.

"Why are you grinning for?" I asked, while wrestling around with him. Murphy was the type of person that liked to aggravate you and he was constantly wrestling around with everyone, just harmless horseplay.

"Ask me how many stops I used to run on the Park when I ran it?" He asked, trying to draw my curiosity.

"Okay, how many stops did you run?" I replied, while trying to keep him from putting me in a headlock.

"75 at the most." Murphy replied.

I immediately pulled away from and asked him what did he mean. I wanted to know what he was talking about.

"Yeah, and do you know what time I got off everyday?" He asked, while wiping off his forehead.

"5:45 at the latest." He replied, as I stood there shocked in disbelief.

"They're using you and you're too dumb to realize it Earls." Murphy replied.

It had felt as if I had been hit with a ton of bricks. I felt stupid, and yes, even used. Here I was running 50 more stops an hour than he had and I was still getting off at the same time.

"If you're doing such a good job for them and they appreciated you for helping them then why don't they let you go out with the same amount as I used too and get off around 4:30 everyday?" Murphy replied, as the sound of the tow motor began to get closer. These were excellent eye opening revelations. I began to think back to when I had started out on the route the first time Harry had trained me. We had roughly 55 stops. Then over the course of the year management gradually, and unsuspecting to me, began to increase the number of stops up until it was maxed out at the 125 that it was at now. I had been buffaloed and I felt very angry towards them for using me.

I asked Murphy what I needed to do. Murphy told me to slow down and work safe. Emphasis on the word 'safe. I needed to take all of my one lunch, whereas now, I was unable to do and I had to eat on the road most of the time due to the number of stops, and if I did sit down for that hour I wouldn't have been able to get finished for the day. My eyes had been opened and I realized that I had been slowly manipulated into this position and predicament that I was now facing.

I decided to take Murphy's advice and slow down and work safer. I went back to the fundamentals of how I was trained and began to apply the 'UPS methods' and I worked more efficiently. I was concerned about the response that I would surely get from management as soon as they realized what was going on with me, their two hour under allowed cushion provider.

Little had I realized that it was costing me more money to skip my lunch, and getting out there and running like a scalded dog than I was thinking.

If you figure that I was being dispatched with a ten hour day and 'running' it in eight hours I was cheating myself out of two hours of overtime a day, ten hours a week. Then add into the equation the one hour lunch I was giving back to the company, because it comes out of my check REGARDLESS if I take it, and losing that one hours pay was costing me dearly financially, but saving the company tons of money nationwide with this standard deceiving practice. The fifteen hours a week at the overtime rate that I could have worked, but 'gave' back to the company was costing me almost $3400 a year in forgone wages. It was hurting me economically.

From the managers perspective...say that across the country there were 10,000 drivers doing the same thing that I was. At $3400 a year for each driver multiplied by 10,000 drivers comes to $34,000,000 a year the company 'saves' from just this practice alone. From a business policy standpoint WHY should or would they attempt to cease this practice?

Well, anyway, I had begun coming in a little later and later each day from taking all of my lunch and for taking longer to finish my route. The Huntsville east center manager, Stan, asked me one morning after the PCM what was going on out there on my route and was everything all right. I had become somewhat harboring hard feelings from my perception of having been used and misled.

"Everything's all right Stan." I replied nervously, as he stood there looking at me with concern in his eyes.

"I'm just tired of being used by y'all." I replied. Stan stood there shocked and not knowing what to say. Evidently it wasn't the response he had been expecting from me. I was beginning to cut into his over allowed cushion and with me being one of the primary drivers carrying the bulk of the centers 'under allowed' time and this undoubtedly began to concern him due to the sure to come impact from this sudden decline in under allowed.

I just told Stan that I needed to start working safer because I had begun to have adverse reactions due to the stress load. I wasn't lying at all when I told him that. My knees, feet and back had begun to ache more and more each night. I simply told Stan that I wanted to do my job like I was supposed to do.

Stan stood there looking at me with his arms crossed and his finger resting against his mouth. Stan just turned and walked off. My heart was pounding and I felt like crap. "What have I got myself into?" I thought to myself.

A couple of days would pass and finally Stan called me into the office during the PCM. Stan told me that I would need Joseph, our job steward, to accompany me. As Joseph and I walked to the office he took out a cigarette and lit it. He didn't have anymore of an idea as to why I was being called into the office than I did.

We walked to the office door and knocked, and Stan hollered for us to come in. Joseph walked in first and I followed behind him and shut the door. There weren't any chairs to sit down in so we both stood up, leaning against the wall.

"James I've called you in here to discuss with you why all of a sudden your numbers have dropped off." Stan replied, while looking over several printouts.

I explained to him about my health problems and how I had decided on trying to work safer and the whole bit. Stan didn't seem to care about that at all. I knew this wasn't going to be looking good.

I sat there expecting something to happen, but nothing came. Stan just sat there looking at me, then at Joseph. After about a minute or so of this, Joseph spoke up and asked Stan if this was all. Stan said that it was and for us to go to work. What was the reason for that pointless meeting anyway? The answer is simple... intimidation.

Joseph and I walked out of the office and I immediately began to ask him questions about what had just transpired. Joseph just took a draw off of his cigarette and exhaled. Joseph said to just simply walk lightly for a while and that I had possible became a 'targeted' man.

Over the course of the following week I had began to try and get some of that work taken off of me to bring me more in line with the other drivers and the way they had run it in the past. This was proving to be a problem. After the second week of working safer Stan called me back into the office, and this is when the harassment would start.

I walked back into the office and Stan sat in his chair rocking back and forth with his arms crossed staring at me as I walked in. Stan had a rather smug look on his face and he never said anything as I turned to close the door. Just as I closed the door I heard a knock on the door and Joseph walked in. I knew then what was about to happen.

Stan opened the meeting with a presentation of my previous performance numbers obtained from the previous O.R's. He asked me why I had gone from running two hour under allowed to just 30 minutes under allowed, a loss of one and a half hours.

"I'm just trying to work safer." I replied.

Joseph recognized what this was leading into and he stepped a little closer beside me. Stan was attempting to lead me into to admitting that I was slowing down with the purpose of 'stealing time', which simply was not the case. I had simply started taking my one-hour lunch and I was driving and working much safer than I had been doing before. My reasons were innocent in nature in my eyes, but were a possible avenue for him to exploit.

I was still running under allowed everyday anyway. Joseph stepped in immediately after this and he asked Stan, "What's the problem?"

Stan spoke up, interrupting Joseph, which I could tell made Joseph mad. Stan told him that it wasn't the fact that I was still running under allowed, but it was the "sudden" decrease of the one and a half hours that concerned him. Stan once again implied, in a round about way, that it could easily be mistaken for stealing time.

Joseph sort of blew up and instructed Stan not to even say that word, "stealing", unless they had some damn good proof. Here I was caught in between these two guys going back and forth like I was at a tennis match or something. I didn't have a clue as to what was going on. I was lost.

Stan finally said, "Well, I think I'll schedule Mr. Earls a ride for next week to see what the problem is."

"Do what you have to do Stan, and if it turns into anything else I'll get the union involved in this." Joseph replied.

Stan looked away from Joseph, breaking eye contact and began looking down at the papers that were on his desk and began to ignore Joseph.

"Do what you have to, now go to work." Stan replied coldly, and we turned to leave.

I was still lost as ever. I knew enough though that Stan didn't like it one bit when Joseph mentioned 'bringing' the union into play. We both walked by several supervisors sitting at their desk who had been listening to everything that went on in the office.

We both walked on out into the building, away from everyone, and we both stood outside the office for a minute or so. All that Joseph told me was that I needed to make sure I did everything by the book the day that they rode with me.

"Just do your job James." Joseph replied.

I wasn't sure as to why I was getting a ride. Joseph told me that I wasn't a team player with them anymore and that they were going to 'tighten me up'. It had been almost two years since I was trained, and I hadn't had anyone on car with me since being trained. I thought I was doing a good job for them while I was running like an idiot and skipping my lunch. I had gone from being one of their best drivers, receiving daily praises, to one of their worst one's that ever wore a brown uniform. All this transpired in the span of about two weeks. I knew then that everyone was right.

Chapter 5

"9:25 a.m.: While at my first stop Harry is making a big deal about what side of the truck I was getting out on. Finally he's going to see why it takes me so long at this first stop and maybe Stan will finally get off my back and let me do my job."

I arrived to work a little earlier than usual on the morning that my ride was scheduled, and as I walked on into the center I immediately began looking for Joseph. I noticed that packages were still steadily coming down the belts and the hustle and bustle from the loaders stepping into their trucks made an ominous sound. I walked through the whole center peering down the belts and checking the offices for Joseph. I knew he was there because I saw his truck, "Old Blue", parked outside. A driver who was standing at the bottom of the stairs asked me if I was looking for Joseph, to which I replied yes, and was told that he was upstairs changing into his uniform.

I ran up the stairs and walked into the locker room where Joseph was finishing putting on his uniform. He could tell from my impatience that I was extremely nervous about the ride. Joseph talked to me as he tucked his shirt in about what to do and not to do. He said that he had already talked to Harry and Stan about the conduct of the ride, and Joseph told me not to worry that Harry was a good supervisor, and that he'd be fair in assessing my strong and weak points.

He then proceeded to tell me what to do and not to do in regard to taking advantage of the extra time one would gain by following UPS' delivery methods. I needed to be sure to think about what I did before I did it so I wouldn't cut my own throat by losing time somewhere from short cutting the system. It was going to be hard to change almost two years of running wide ass open in just five minutes. Harry would also know if I was out there jerking him around and that wouldn't look good at all.

I walked out of the dressing room that morning a nervous wreck. I felt as if I was going to be fired. I began to think about losing my car and all the other things a person in my situation would think about. I managed to collect myself and I walked on down the stairs and into the break room and bought myself a coke to try and settle my stomach. I was almost to the point of throwing up from being nervous.

After punching in, I walked over to a group of drivers that I usually hung around with before I started work and they all knew about my ride. I was bombarded with questions and advice from all of them. I tried to soak up everything that they were telling that I could, but it was way too much to try and remember in a two-minute span.

It was about time for the PCM to begin and we all began to make our way up to the customer counter where it was being held. When I walked into the room Stan immediately singled me out in front of the other drivers, and in a very degrading tone, he instructed me not to run off after the meeting that I had a rider for the next three days. I looked around the room and noticed Harry standing over to one side of the room intermingled amongst some of the other drivers and he was wearing a set of 'browns' instead of his usual suit. I had managed to let Stan work me into such a panic that I thought I was going to wig out right there on the spot and have a spell or something.

I managed to hold it in and when the meeting was finally over, Harry walked on outside and waited for me. I walked out being one of the last drivers to exit, and Harry told me not to worry about today and for me to just 'concentrate' on doing my job and that everything would be okay. But this would prove to be easier said than done.

I climbed over the packages that were piled up in the middle of my truck to put my supplies and personal affects into the cab of the truck, as Harry had sat his cup of coffee down on the rear of the shelf inside my truck. He immediately began to write down something on his clipboard. I thought to myself," What a way to start out a day with a mess like this." There were packages everywhere. Drivers were calling out loud to each other asking if so and so street belonged to them, and they were trying to work the packages around to the drivers that they belonged to. It was a usual morning. I began to check the packages that were lying behind my truck to see if they belonged to either my neighbor or to me. Those that belonged to me I loaded in the appropriate shelf and marked a count onto the paper with my pen. Not that it really mattered anyway.

After about fifteen minutes of loading all the 'stacked' out packages, I finally came across my overnight packages and I began loading them in the top, first section of the shelves. We really weren't bound to a early commitment time like we are today, but none the less they had to be delivered by noon. I loaded an extra twelve stops or so, mostly bulk stops that were placed under the belt that was saved to be loaded last after the sort went down. This is done so the loader doesn't have them in his way all morning, which would impede his ability to maximize   production.

The whole truck looked odd for some reason inside. It wasn't as full as it normally was and the packages were loaded better in the shelves than I had been experiencing. I looked for the stop count paper and noticed that it had 115 stops marked on it, but the truck was way too empty to have had that many stops. I picked up the sheet and walked down the belt looking for a supervisor to ask him how many stops were on the truck. I finally found a part time supervisor and asked him how many stops were on the truck, and to my amazement I had roughly forty-five fewer stops than I was normally dispatched with, excluding the six that I had just loaded myself. I was finally going to have a good day for a change. My days were just long rather than 'bad', because I had a lot of work that was just taking me longer to deliver since I decided to start working 'safer'. I began to feel at ease and had become rather eager and ready to go out and a good job by the numbers.

While driving, Harry began to question me about the five seeing habits and various other UPS safety training phrases that all drivers should know. I hadn't thought about them twice since I was first trained and drilled on them years ago. I hadn't heard the phrases since, and I couldn't remember what exactly it all stood for. I went out and just concentrated on delivering the packages and at the moment nothing else mattered. Harry went through his spiel, and questioned me several times about various topics as I headed for my first stop. Upon arriving, Harry asked me what my first five-floor section stops were. I didn't remember and drew a blank. I couldn't remember a single one of them. I couldn't remember if I had even looked at them before leaving the center. I told Harry that I didn't know and he wrote something down on his little note pad and told me that I needed to work on that the entire day. I agreed and immediately felt a sudden and drastic decline in confidence, but I tried to bury it and do the job at hand.

Our first stop was at PPG in Huntsville and as I pulled onto their property you have to go to their guard shack and sign in before they would open the gate. I stopped the truck beside the long concrete ramp that led into the plant and climbed on down exiting the vehicle on my side, because Harry was too slow in getting out of his seat. I didn't want to wait on him to unbuckle his seatbelt and step down so I went out on the driver's side and walked around the front of the truck and began the walk up the ramp that led into the building. Harry hollers at me to stop and then he comes walking up to me, and he asked me why I had done what I did?

"What in the world is he talking about?" I thought to myself as Harry tells me not to stop walking and I then asked him, as I turned to start walking again, what he was talking about. Harry told me that it cost me too much time to exit the car on the driver's side and walk around to the right side. By me doing this cost me roughly six steps. Six whole steps and here he was making a big deal out of it. I became somewhat perturbed towards him about this, but tried to overlook it as merely nitpicking. I told him that I would work on it.

After I signed in and was walking back to the truck Harry asked me where my keys were. I kept walking and just held my hand up over my head and jingled them. They were around my finger on my right hand just as he had trained me to do. I stepped into the cab, cranked the truck and off we went.

My "start car routine" was a little slow and he was sure to point that out. I just ignored him as I made the circle in front of the dock and sounded my horn and then backed up to the dock, being mindful to follow every 'backing rule' UPS had. I secured the vehicle and exited out of the passengers side door just like I had been instructed to do just three minutes earlier.

"What are you doing James?" Harry asked me while stopping in his tracks.

"What are you talking about now?" I asked getting upset.

"Why did you come out this side for?" He asked smartly.

"I thought that's what you wanted me to do?" I replied sarcastically to him.

"Which side is closest to the door you're going in at?" Harry asked, while placing his hands on his hips.

"The drivers side." I replied.

"Why did you waste all those steps by walking around the truck again?" He asked.

I didn't want to argue with him about his trivial subject. I simply told him that I'd use a little more common sense instead of working as instructed. I knew then what kind of ride this was going to be.

The step issue that was going on here involves wasting six steps. If you have 75 stops and you exit the 'wrong' side of the vehicle each time, then those six steps cost you roughly three seconds per stop of wasted step time. If you multiply those 75 stops times three seconds that will cost you almost three minutes in lost time. Lost time means 'unproductive' time and unproductive time meant cutting into shareholders profits. It was all about production and meeting that production number.

We walked into the receiving office and in there sat a man in a small office, which was about the size of a bathroom in a house. Behind the desk sat the man who ran the receiving part of PPG. His name was Barry. One thing about Barry is he doesn't get in a hurry for anybody. It was just the way Barry was. Harry had begun to become impatient. After all we'd been standing there for almost four minutes. Those were four minutes of 'unproductive' time. I was losing valuable time in Harry's eyes, but to me, I could care less. This is what I went through on a daily basis. This stop, in all fairness, should have taken me no more than fifteen minutes total, round trip, to complete. The fact of the matter is that it sometimes cost me in excess of thirty minutes to complete. Thirty minutes of dead time and sometimes longer if I had to wait for another carrier who was on the dock at the time I arrived.

Finally, Barry got off the phone and he said he'd be with us in a minute. Harry then looked at his watch and the shook his head in disgust. Barry saw him do this and I knew right then we'd be here all day now. After about seven minutes or so Barry came to the back door and unlocked it and I then jumped down onto the bumper and raised my rear door to the truck. I began to unload the truck lining the packages up in rows and pushing them out across the floor. I did this because it was easier to write down the shipper numbers from them. PPG was my heaviest customer and received at least eighty packages a day. It took me a few minutes to unload them all and write down all the shipper numbers, ID numbers and tear off the tracking labels and place them in my pocket to send to Birmingham, Alabama to be recorded.

The whole stop took about twenty-five minutes. Harry was extremely upset. He enlightened Barry that "his" driver could not and "would not" wait like that anymore. Barry handed me my clipboard back, looked at Harry and said, "You will wait and if you don't like it call my plant manager about it." Harry took out his pen and began writing down his name and asked for the phone number to the plant manager.

Nothing ever came of this, but that was the 'big dog' attitude that UPS management had at the time towards the customers. The rest of the morning went pretty well and we stopped for lunch around 11:45. I wanted to stop and take the whole hour, but Harry told me that if we did it would mess the pick up stops that we were going to start later in the day and he felt that it would be better to just hold off until later in the day. At the time I knew no better and agreed to do that and off we went.

The rest of the day went fine and we returned to the building in record time, just with barely eight hours of work.

Harry called me into the office the following morning to review the previous days ride. He told me that I needed to work on several 'trivial' things, but said I was doing very well and that I would only get better as time went.

"What about the rides today and tomorrow?" I asked curiously.

"There's no need for them James." Harry replied, while looking for a pen.

Harry scooted a piece of paper across the desk towards me and asked me to sign it. I picked it up and read over it and noticed that there wasn't anything really negative on it and out of stupidity I signed it.

What I had unknowingly done was to break the Teamster rule of self-incrimination, which was to "NEVER TO SIGN ANYTHING BUT MY PAY-CHECK!" What I had done was to unknowingly commit myself to running their 'required' number of stops an hour, and I had in essence cut my own throat. Management could now hold this over my head in the future.

Unfortunately, I didn't find this out until the following Monday, when after starting work, I looked into the rear of my truck, while it was still parked on the dock at the center, and wondered if I had the right truck. This truck that I was staring into was packed solid. The stop counts were back to normal with the usual 120-125 stops that I had been running during my 'stupid' days, and the truck was in the usual mess as it was before the ride. I was floored. I yelled out, "What the &$*!! Is going on here?"

Stan was walking along the belt and made a beeline straight towards me. He came up to me and asked me what my problem was. I asked him why I didn't have the same kind of load and dispatch as when Harry had rode with me. His only answer was that the volume had dropped off those days, and before I could say anything else he said, "18 stops an hour," and walked off. I was screwed. For going out and doing my job like I was trained to do, management had rewarded me with this.

Needless to say, I worked my butt of to try and run those numbers and after awhile I did manage to meet the production standards that were set for me, but while doing so I wore myself down and worked very unsafe. I went back to short cutting the customers and really did a poor job in my eyes. The managers didn't care how you did it as long as you didn't make them look bad. I learned a valuable lesson from that experience.

Chapter 6

"I worked for free this week after I had my first encounter with a dishonest customer who lied to both UPS and me. The customer said I collected cash for a C.O.D. I'm so disappointed that they believed him over me. I have no other choice but to pay for it."

Over the course of the next few months I practiced 'UPS' delivery methods everyday and at times even went as far as pretending that a member of management was on car with me. I got the routine down with each passing day. I had decided that if I could hone these methods to a fine edge I could even the playing field and possibly beat them at their own game. I was still delivering the same route, "The Park", and unfortunately ran across a very dishonest customer. I was about to learn a valuable lesson in the school of hard knocks.

I delivered to a company that was laying on the edge of the Chase Industrial Park that received something pretty much everyday. I back up to the dock and sounded my horn waiting for Tim to open the dock door like he did everyday. I stood in the rear of the truck with my back door open and I was looking to make sure I didn't miss any of their packages that had been on the floor. When I finished doing this, Tim still hadn't opened the door. "Maybe he doesn't hear me," I thought to myself.

I walked on around and went inside the receiving area and unlocked and raised the door myself, and I jumped down into the truck and began to unload all of their packages. Tim still hadn't walked up to me so I called out "UPS" and waited for someone to arrive. I finally gave up on them and pulled the C.O.D tag off of the package and walked up front to the office to let them sign for the packages and to collect my check. I only had one C.O.D for that day and it was a personal package from a sporting goods store. The package contained a fishing reel from what I could tell, and from the tag I noticed that it was a rather expensive one at that.

I walked on in and the lady working there told me that the boss was on his way to the back. I thanked her and turned to walk back into the receiving area to meet him. Finally I met a man that was dressed in a dress shirt and slacks and not the usual attire associated with the employees.

"Good morning, I have a C.O.D for you sir." I replied cheerfully.

He stood there not saying a word at all. He just held out his hand and I handed him the C.O.D tag. I thought to myself, "What a real jerk."

He turned and walked back to the office, and after a couple of minutes he emerged with a check in his hand. I took the check and looked it over to make sure it was filled out for the right amount and noticed it was a personal check, and I then checked for any restrictions on the funds that may have been stated on the package. It was safe for me to accept personal checks, and I handed him my clipboard and he scribbled something undecipherable on it and handed it back to me. He started to reach for the package and I told him that I need the C.O.D tag back that he carried with him up front.

"It's in the office." He snapped off smartly.

"Sir I need it to turn back in so the shipper will get the check." I replied cautiously. I knew this had the potential to turn ugly rather quickly, and I chose my words and actions carefully trying to diffuse the situation.

The customer turned and stormed off back up front. "What a jerk," I said again under my breath. Finally after a minute or two he came walking back up to me with the tag and threw it on the floor in front of me. I stood there looking at him like he was an idiot. There were a lot of things I tolerated while delivering, but actions like this was not one of them. I was still holding the package he wanted and just stood there defiantly. I wasn't about to pick the tag up. Finally he got the message and picked it up and handed it to me and boy was he fuming. I decided to stall a little bit longer and began to check the tag to the check. This wasn't really the procedure but he didn't know it. Finally I handed him the package and he popped off, "What about my receipt?"

"It's on the box sir." I replied coldly, and stepped into the truck and closed my door. I heard him slam his door down hard. "I'd hate to work for that moron." I said to myself and stored the check and drove away.

Several weeks later, after reporting to work, Harry hands me a letter from the UPS Collections Department. It was a formal collection form from UPS concerning a shortage in my C.O.D turn in. I had to go back out and do what was called a "driver follow-up" with the customer. In other words I had to try and find out what happened to the money and if a check was written, I had to collect another check, and man...I hated doing this. I asked Harry what was going on. He looked over the form and stated that the C.O.D was turned in, but there wasn't a check with it. Harry had crossed checked my money drop to see if I had turned cash in for the C.O.D. I told him that I was given a check for it by the customer and relived the confrontation from that day with the customer. I thought to myself that maybe I was making a bigger deal out of it than it really was. I thought there wouldn't be a problem with collecting another check. Boy was I wrong.

I arrived back that stop as usual that morning. Tim, the normal receiving guy, was there. I felt relieved to see him and figured I'd just hand him the driver follow up form and tell what I needed and I'd let him take it up front. Tim took off up to the office and after a minute or so he came back with the owner. I started to become uneasy and began to anticipate a confrontation. I explained to the owner what happened and asked him if I could collect another check, minus any stop payment fees he might have to pay from his bank, and I'd be on my way.

The owner stood there for a minute thinking, when out of the blue he says, "I didn't write you a check, I gave you cash that day." I reminded him that he didn't give me cash but he had indeed written a personal check for it. He continued to have no memory of it and threatened to call UPS on me if I didn't leave. Basically the dialog went back and forth a few more times and I left. He was lying through his teeth. I was pissed the rest of the day and when I arrived back to the center that evening I went straight to the office looking for Harry. I found him working on some paperwork and told him what had happened.

Harry told me that I was still responsible for the money if I couldn't get it worked out. I was stunned. I flat out told Harry that I wasn't going to pay for anything before thinking about what I had just said. Harry proceeded to tell me that if I failed to pay for the package that it would look as if I may have stolen the money and they'd fire me for dishonesty. I knew of several drivers' in the past that had been caught stealing C.O.D money and they'd all been fired. I sure didn't want UPS' loss prevention department to get wind of it. That's all I needed was to get UPS' version of the Keystone Cops mixed up in this with their ' Gestapo' style tactics.

The following morning Stan called me into the office after the PCM and I found that Joseph was waiting in there for me. I walked on in and Stan told me to shut the door. The mood of them both was unsettling. I could tell that something bad was about to happen.

I sat down beside Joseph, and Stan asked me about the package in question. I explained in detail as to what happened and how the customer had treated me. I told him that the customer was a liar, and that he gave me a personal check for it and not cash like he was claiming.

Joseph asked Stan how much the package was for. Stan said it was for several hundred dollars, and Joseph shook his head and asked me, "Are you sure he gave you a personal check for it?"

"I'm positive Joseph. It was drawn on a local bank here in Huntsville." I replied nervously.

Joseph sided with me and told Stan he needed to get loss prevention involved. "Maybe if they pay him a visit he'll cough up the check." Joseph told Stan. My stomach just sank. I didn't want to get loss prevention, often called LP, involved because there's no telling what that nut might tell them. Stan reluctantly agreed to do this, and in the meantime, Joseph told me to go ahead and get the grievance ready to file in case management was going to make me pay for the package. In reality it was looking like there was little the union could do to keep me from paying for the package.

Within a few days I received a certified letter from management stating that I would have to pay for the package. It seemed that the liar had stuck to his guns. The next day I was brought back into the office by Stan to let me know that I was going to have to pay for the package, and Joseph handed him the grievance outlining my protest concerning this C.O.D incident. I would later lose the grievance in the local level hearing.

I met back with Stan and Joseph to discuss the detail's of paying for the C.O.D. I told Stan that I couldn't pay for the whole package up front although I could've if I had wanted to.

"No problem James we can take a little out of your check each week until you pay for it." Stan replied.

I agreed and signed the form authorizing UPS to deduct eight installments from my check over the course of eight weeks. In a moment of anger as I walking out of the office I told him that I'd get my money back from UPS for this. Stan jumped up out of his seat like a mad man screaming at me in front of Joseph, "Are you threatening to steal time from me because if you are I'll fire your ass on the spot! Do you understand me?"

What could I say? I had said a bad choice of words. I was shocked and caught totally off guard and before I could reply Joseph stepped in.

"You've misunderstood James. He didn't mean it the way it came out Stan." Joseph replied.

Stan leaned across his desk and said, "Just let me catch you doing it James." We got out of there very quickly after that.

I walked on out and Joseph got on me pretty hard about my comments. "If you run over allowed now they could say that you're doing it in an attempt to recoup some of your money back." Joseph replied shaking his head.

I hadn't even thought of that. I had to pay for that dishonest customer's several hundred-dollar fishing reel. I hoped and prayed he'd lose it in the river somewhere. I had learned a valuable lesson from the experience. UPS has one of the best insurers in the world... It's drivers.

Chapter 7

"This is one company party that I'll never forget. Between the center manager kicking drivers in the groin, to drivers copping feels off the center manager, to cussing and fighting... I don't know which is worse."

I was trying every way I could to be a good driver and keep my nose clean. I was still on the same route, "The Park", and everything was going pretty well. I managed, as I gained more and more experience, to work just hard enough to keep management off of my back. I was running under allowed and I was getting off around 6:30 p.m everyday. This was pretty well the norm except for an occasional day of having to work past 7:00 p.m

The district report came out showing how all the centers in the Alabama District ranked in regard to over allowed hours, missed pieces and various other 'management performance' measuring tools. We found out in a rather unceremoniously display of unhappiness, that we were the worst in the District. The Huntsville east center was ranked at the bottom of the list out of about thirty or so centers District wide. This ranking, in regards to the 'overall' performance, reflected in the eye's of UPS' top brass that the management in Huntsville east were not cutting it and desperate measures needed to be taken. It was always our fault, as Stan quickly pointed out, no matter what. They never addressed the possibility that it could have been due in part to a 'poor labor relations' problem between them and us. It was definitely in the 'quality' of management for the way they were running the show.

Slowly over the course of the next few weeks we began to notice that there was an increasingly steady 'crackdown' on all drivers again. It was as if it came in cycles. With our ranking being so low meant that were about to be 'occupied' by outside management who were being sent to Huntsville to find out what the problem was. Management had mounted another one of their infamous 'production kicks' in a vain attempt to increase production straight across the board. The threats of discharge were relayed frequently between managers if something didn't change. And change it did.

The harassment escalated everyday to include the least little petty infraction. Management had decided again to start following the company policy word for word and the contract as well. Everyone was in turmoil. The threats of being fired for running over allowed concerned me, not that I was running over allowed or anything, but I was still very concerned for my fellow workers.

Although management couldn't contractually discharge anyone for failing to run production, although it has happened in rare cases, they went about it under different pretenses.

Say for example the driver they singled out, for what ever reason, was running over allowed. They'd then initiate the discipline process by meeting with the driver and his job steward. The company would then do a three-day lock in ride and try to force the driver to sign a form committing him to run the numbers they wanted. If he did sign this and he continued to run over allowed, after 'displaying' that he could do the job, he then would be suspended and subsequently discharged for "failing to work as instructed" if his production didn't change. Accompanied with this directive would probably be comments from management to intimidate him along the lines of "you must not need your job" or "You must not want to work here anymore" to help coerce him into speeding up.

Odds are too, that when the driver works a few days later, after his ride, his loads will be back the same, and the same number of stops will be back on there as well. Management wouldn't leave the stops down and improve the loads as were done on the day's they rode with the driver while conducting a production ride. If the driver had signed anything in the office committing to running the pieces per hour they wanted him to...then he was truly screwed. My advice to everyone is not to sign anything. Tell them that you will do the best job that you can and leave it at that. But remember...do your job!

Most drivers would be intimidated into giving in. The systematic breakdown of them just from the psychological tactics alone would prove to be enough to fulfill the desires of management. This driver would've become so concerned about not being able to provide for his family, feed them and provide a place for them to live. Think of the tremendous amount of stress placed on this driver from this ruthless display of "psychological corporate terrorism" and having to deal with that on an everyday basis. Does this employee carry this fear home with him at night? Does it diminish their quality of life at home? How about their family's happiness and quality of life? Do they lash out at their loved ones? The mere social aspects of this sort of 'abuse' have detrimental affects not only on the driver but on their spouse and children as well.

Top management fails to see this or do they? I feel that they know, without a doubt, that this tactic will spark the 'production' concerns of the individual and force him out of fear alone to speed up. They may be holding this over the heads of the drivers in an attempt to strong-arm them into increasing their production. The social ramifications alone from this practice is overwhelming and sickening. But management doesn't care... remember? Increased production equals increased profits. They want that extra ounce of production out of that driver, no matter what the cost.

This is when the union should've stepped in and stopped this   practice immediately. The steward should be the one in the office to stop this practice from progressing. In most cases though it wouldn't end, even after numerous attempts by the stewards to stop it. Some drivers would, at some point of this process, practically beg not to be fired. The management would make the driver grovel for his job while most of them sat back enjoying the power trip. They did seem to enjoy it, knowing they had this man in their clutches, I've seen it in their eye's. I've seen it a few times after becoming a steward and I had fought with management over it numerous times.

Most drivers would not choose to fight management and would sim-ply give in. They would opt to give management their lunch and thus would gain the extra time from their lunch hour to be used to bring their over allowed times down. This is what management wanted in the first place anyway. It was a win-win situation for management regardless of the means they used to achieve it.

First, management would increase production by intimidating this driver and thus make money by him reducing his hours spent on road out of his fear of being disciplined for running over allowed everyday.

Second, they would save the money that they were going to have to pay him, if he had taken his lunch, if he stayed out longer. Management didn't care about this driver taking his lunch, because they were still nickel and diming everyone to death, which, across the nation, made them a profit.

The whole production ride ploy used by management is a cleverly orchestrated labor management tool. Management knows that a lot of the times it is impossible to achieve these goals by only using conventional tactics. The day's that rides are picked is an art all of itself.

Local managers pick the day's to perform the production rides de-pending on the volume projection forecast for that day which is taken from averaging the amount of package volume from the previous few years for a particular week, and then they check the 'feeder forecast sheets" transmit-ted from the hubs. The forecast sheets from the hubs contain the expected volume capacity of the loads that are inbound to the centers on a daily basis.

How can they determine this you ask? It's really simple. Manage-ment checks the data concerning the volume from previous years. Say for example the average daily volume over the past three years for the last week of May shows, for example, roughly 15,000 packages in bound, figu-ratively speaking of course. Then local managers know a rough average of 'projected' volume inbound for Huntsville and plan to run the minimum amount of drivers for that day to deliver the 'projected' 15,000 pieces. Nothing is for certain and volume fluctuates. Management schedules driv-ers for vacation using the figures and some times they are surprised by 'volume spikes' and are at times understaffed. The 'feeder forecast' are transmitted from the hubs once the Feeder Drivers depart showing, what time they left and the percentages of the trailers. The percentages of the trailers are a key tool. A standard H-Type and W-type twenty-eight foot trailer can hold roughly one thousand packages and would be at 100%. If a trailer was forecast at being 50% then there would roughly be 500 or so packages on it and so on. Now if you have fifteen inbound trailers at 100 % each then you could expect roughly 15,000 packages for that day to process.

How is this adverse to the driver you ask? Take for example a driver is scheduled for a ride on a day that the 'volume manipulation theory' is in effect. That day the center is forecast for 3000 fewer packages for that given day. That means that all the drivers in the center are going to have fewer packages to deliver, thus lowering the overall paid day. That lower paid day translates for that particular driver a drop in his total package volume for his route and in turn...fewer stops. This means that he would have to handle fewer packages per stop, and fewer over all stops. If he lost twenty-five stops, due to a drop in volume, and if he is required to run eighteen stops an hour he roughly gains to his advantage 'a loss' of roughly about an hour on his paid day. Bear in mind that the conditions of his load have also improved as a result from the loaders having more time to put quality loads on the trucks, which comes from having to handle FEWER packages.

The driver's psychological perception and mental performance have been changed as well. His overall measure of performance, including all of the 'non-average' attributes, will reflect on the O.R a 'better', and thus, a more productive day on paper. In reality it's not a fair evaluation, but it works to managements benefit.

How does this benefit management? It benefits them for this simple reason. Whenever a driver rebuts their claims citing insinuating circumstances it gives them a little leverage to counter his claims by manipulating the system. Thus giving them a defense in justifying bringing the driver in line. Management would, and has made claims during grievance hearings statements like, "Look we rode with him on these days and he did the job and ran the numbers we wanted, why can't he do it now?" Chances are that too, management has given this man great reviews and has arbitrarily pointed out a few things he needs to work to legitimize their scheme.

But management fails to interject "ALL" of the story. Those days they rode with that driver were probably not typical days and chances are his volume was light and the conditions, including weather, were more "ideal" to benefit them than him. It's intriguing the amount of effort management puts into this labor relations practice.

Management knows that this isn't a perfect world and volume spikes and drops off un-expectantly due to trends in the market and with customers shipping needs. If a ride has been scheduled for a week when the volume is projected to be low and then the volume spikes, management has been known to have sudden 'emergencies' arise and then become unable to ride which is usually accompanied by a sudden 'surge' in package volume for that given day.

Now on the other hand management have been known to take off stops to lighten a driver up which is a little harder to explain if the grievance process is invoked by the driver concerning the question of management harassing them. It's all about 'time'.

I happened to be in the office one morning with Harry discussing a new pick up account that was on my route. We began to hear a lot of yelling and cussing coming from Stan's office. We both stopped what we were doing and strained to hear what was being said. I knew that Dick, having just completed his special assignment, was promoted to division manager for North Alabama drivers. I knew as well that he was in Huntsville this morning. We listened to Dick raise hell with Stan and we heard Dick tell Stan that if he couldn't run Huntsville better that he needed to find another job. " Whoa," I thought, man this heavy.

After a few more minutes of screaming Dick came out of Stan's office and looked at Harry and me as he walked out in the center. We both acted like we didn't hear him blazing Stan in the office and ignored him. Then a few seconds later Stan came out of his office visibly shaken from the ream-ing he had just received from his boss.

"I need to see all of the supervisors in my office Harry." Stan replied nervously with his voice cracking.

Harry walked on out and Stan turned back into his office and shut the door. I stood there thinking, "Better you than me for a change you loser."

Come to find out later that Stan wasn't running the numbers Dick wanted him too and he gave Stan an ultimatum to either shape us up, or he'd be shipped out. This wouldn't come to pass because it was impossible for Stan to run the numbers he needed us to so he could keep his job. Although the suspensions and warning letters increased daily towards us but in the end it proved to be a useless effort.

We never really found out why, but Stan quit, and we were shocked to learn that it was so sudden. We knew it was coming but didn't figure it would be this soon. His job could've been saved by us, but once again when you live by the sword you may die by the sword.

We would go about two weeks with Harry acting as temporary man-ager until Birmingham could find us another center manager.

That second Monday after Stan quit we were all standing around the check in counter just before time to start work when several 'suits' came strolling in. We all noticed that there was an unfamiliar woman with them. We all debated who she was and what she did at UPS. We couldn't figure out who she was. She was a fairly nice looking woman, kind of "Amazon'ish." She was about six feet tall and 175-200 pounds. She was a good size gal to say the least. We all walked towards the middle of the building so we could see what was going on as they all filed by us and walked upstairs to Dick's office and shut the door.

By this time Harry had come down from using the bathroom to where we all were standing around talking.

"How do you like your new center manager?" He replied, while ad-justing his pants.

"What? Her?" William asked.

"Yeah her." Harry replied, while still straitening his pants.

William being a comedian said, "Well hell, if we run over allowed she wouldn't give us a warning letter. She'll just stomp the crap out of us!" We all erupted into laughter and Harry walked away shaking his head.

She was the buzz for the time before the PCM started. We all began to walk up to the customer counter for the meeting and stood around inside it until they showed up.

Finally after a minute or two passed in walked the suits like a parade of monkeys. She followed in last and Harry closed the door behind her. Dick announced to us that they wanted to introduce our new center man-ger. Her name was Eliza. Eliza stepped forward and said she was glad to be here and looked forward to 'working with us'. Actually she should have said 'for her'. The suits went through their spiels describing Eliza's accom-plishments and career highlights. They were trying to sell her to us. Eliza said she wanted to meet us all and that she'd wait and talk to all of her drivers tonight after work.

We left the PCM talking amongst ourselves and walked to our

package cars to leave. It was in usual fashion that the preload was wrapped up and all of the trucks were loaded and ready to hit the streets. This wasn't normal for us but very normal whenever we had 'visitors' in Huntsville. We left the building on time for a change and all had pretty good days. The dispatch was light, which meant we'd get in early enough to meet Eliza. I returned to the building that evening and walked up to Eliza after completing my turn in and she held out her hand to shake mine. I grabbed her hand and it was almost twice as big as mine. This old gal had hands like a boxer. They were huge. She was a well-groomed lady and was decked out in gold chains, rings and other jewelry. She was a stout looking woman who looked like she'd be a handful for any man down there.

The next couple of day's Eliza just met with the supervisors and hung around us more than most of the last managers would. She claimed she wanted to get an idea of Huntsville and what it was like. This was her first time at being a center manager and she seemed to be all right, or at least we thought. I try to give all of them, when I first meet them, the benefit of doubt.

During the course of the next week she conducted all of the PCM's and one morning she dropped the bomb on us. She described a plan she had concocted to decrease our paid day to get us home with our families earlier than we were accustomed to. We were shocked. What were we hearing? This was the first time I had heard a center manager state that they were interested in getting our paid day down. We all stood around with our mouths open waiting for the punch line to come. We thought she was joking. Eliza asked us to work with her and if we took care of her she'd take care of us. She wanted us to help her run the numbers that Stan had been unable to do. We actually, as a group, had a feeling of hope that the harassment was finally going to come to an end. Most important we thought that finally we were going to get off at a decent time for a change.

Over the next couple of weeks things improved at the center. Everyone's attitude started to get better and Huntsville was coming around. The harassment began to disappear and along with that, the number of grievances we were filing had diminished as well. It looked like we were going to work together for a change and things were looking good.

There was one incident though, that stands out in my mind that involved a package car driver and a pre-loader in the Huntsville center. What had happened was the driver had accidentally left a plastic soft drink bottle on the top shelf of the package car filled with urine and the cap was not screwed on tight.

Many of the residential drivers aren't around places that have restrooms and are forced to relieve themselves using whatever they can. Only thing is that when we do this we're supposed to throw the container away when we are done.

The loader was working one morning when he accidentally tipped the bottle of urine over and it spilled onto his head and face. It was a very nasty mess and was in a close second to the 'virus specimen' incident back when I was on the preload.

We were all standing around in the PCM that morning that it happened, when Eliza came busting through the door she was decked out like a space man or something. I mean she had on goggles, an apron and a mask. She was carrying this bottle that had some urine left in it with a pair of salad tongs. We all immediately erupted into a roaring laughter from just the mere sight of her in that get up. Heck...she looked like Ralph Cramden off of the honeymooners or something.

Eliza went bonkers. She began to scream at us to "shut your damn mouths!"

We all tried to silence our laughter the best we could. We all had become shocked from her mouthy outburst. Heck, even Harry was laughing and he tried to hide it by turning his back to her to keep her from seeing him laugh. Needless to say that we were all shocked by the language she continued to use in her flagrant display similar to that of a lunatic. We all tried to quit laughing, but there would be an occasional snicker and someone would try to conceal it and then here we'd go again.

Eliza started into her presentation about the events that had happened that morning on the preload. She explained that the end result was that the part timer had to go home because he had become ill from the "spill". Eliza then singled out the driver and proceeded to humiliate him in front of us. This didn't sit too well with us at all. She had made a mistake that would begin turning us against her. She had attacked one of our own. I understood that she needed to prove a point but the manner at which she went about it was totally uncalled for. We could tell that this upset the driver tremendously.

Finally she ended her raging hostilities and swearing with a nice little statement.

"The next time this happens I will fire the hell out of the one who does it." She replied smartly to us. We began to the have our doubts about her but later she came to us and apologized to us evidently after someone went to Dick and told him about what had happened.

Other than this one incident, everything was going smoothly on the surface. The center was running better numbers over all than when Stan was here. Yet the center was still ranked towards the bottom of the list. This was unacceptable to Dick and he immediately ordered a crackdown on us wanting her to use the usual brutal tactics to 'tighten us up". To our amazement Eliza refused to comply with Dick's demands, and in a bold and unprecedented statement during the PCM, she told us that it was the supervisor's fault. This was an about face from the standard procedure of blaming us for everything. It was in fact their lack of managing the building that had caused the center to be ranked so low. She cracked down all right...only this time on them. In the meantime though, it was rumored that in an attempt to cover her own butt, she had made a call to the district manager and made allies with him and attempted to cut Dick off at the pass. This move infuriated Dick to no end. He would bird dog her and he would inspect every little thing she did. He was looking for a reason to nail her butt. Eliza was the only manager at the time to have stood up to Dick like that and she was running Huntsville like it was her center.

The peak season we had with her went as smooth as silk. We didn't have to work late during that time of madness and it was one of the smoothest ones I could remember.

Eliza was wanting to schedule a little Christmas get together, the first of its kind, for the drivers and her at a local restaurant named Lord Nelsons. We all agreed to it and looked very forward to it. Eliza had redeemed herself with us and we all liked her once again.

It was no secret that Eliza had her eye on a couple of drivers and she made no bones about what she wanted to do with them. It was common knowledge amongst us all. This was of course inappropriate, and in total violation of UPS' Company Policy. In other words a big no-no.

The get together was planned for a Friday night after work. Eliza had dispatched us with a very light day and we all had time to go home and clean up after work. I left work and drove out to pick up Kelley, my girl friend at the time, to go to the party. Well anyway, Kelley and I arrived at the party and walked inside and found us a table. Everyone was there from work and was evidently having a good time, and most of everyone who were already there was busy getting plastered. I ordered us both a drink and we sat around at a table with some other drivers and discussed UPS of all things. Eliza came walking over to my table and asked me to introduce Kelley to her. I obliged and introduced them, and Kelley became 'extremely' uncomfortable.

We ordered our food and everyone was having a good time. Eliza had come with a rather nice looking friend and they were sitting around at a huge table just across from where we were sitting. I noticed that Eliza was drunker than Cooter Brown and she began cussing and raising hell and the drivers who sitting with her were egging her on. It was beginning to get out of hand fast. The manager of the restaurant walked over to her and told her she needed to settle down that several customers had begun to complain to him about her. I got up and went to the bathroom and as I walked by Eliza's table I noticed that some inappropriate contact was going on underneath it. I didn't know what to think. I met another driver in the restroom and asked him if he had seen what I had just saw, and he explained to me that it had been going on all night. We both started laughing about it and went back outside. It seemed that some drivers were copping feels on Eliza and in turn Eliza was returning the gesture. Eliza even went as far as to try and kiss an unwilling employee.

Our meal finally arrived and we ate it quickly because Kelley told me she wanted to go on home. The party was out of hand by the time we finished eating, and we left without telling Eliza good-bye.

The following Monday Eliza couldn't be found. The mood of the center was as if someone had died and I asked a driver what was going on? The driver started into the story of how she tried to kiss an employee and was grabbing other employees on the genitals in front of other drivers, but the kicker came when, shortly after Kelley and I had left, Eliza really got out of hand. The driver proceed to tell me that she hauled off and kicked Joseph in the groin for no reason. I asked the driver where Eliza was and she said they hadn't seen her all morning.

By this time Joseph came strolling in and I asked him how the ol' family jewels were.

"She's lucky I didn't punch her lights out." Joseph replied, while squinting and holding himself.

I started laughing and continued to aggravate Joseph about the incident as Harry came walking up to us and said that we were going to be starting early today.

We all met at the customer counter again and we asked where Eliza was. Harry replied that she hadn't made it in yet. That's when Joseph yelled out, "She's probably in the hoosegow!" Everyone started laughing.

William asked Harry where she was which his reply was, "I don't know and I don't want to know."

Come to find out she was so ashamed to come in face us that she waited until we left the building that morning before coming in. She managed to sneak into the center and she hid out in her office all day. Within a few days it was all over the District. Eliza stayed in her office for almost two weeks. We never saw her but we knew she was there because we saw her car everyday.

It wasn't long after this incident that we received word she was being busted down and transferred out of Huntsville. She had screwed up so bad that she was lucky not to have been fired for her actions at the party. She knew better, but she was just too wild for UPS to control.

Chapter 8

"Early July, 1999: Management is accomplishing what they've set out to do. I've been called into the office a total of three times this week. I've fought with Davey over him keeping people in the building and violating the contract. It's time the union does something other than to talk and put a stop to management before we do."

This is the time frame at which I had really begun to stop and take notice to the surrounding feelings of everyone working in the Huntsville center. I had been married now for over two years, and my wife and I was expecting our first child. I was out delivering my route one morning and met my wife at her Obstetricians office, which just happened to be on my route, and she informed me that they were going to have to induce labor and that she was on the way to the hospital.

I was in the middle of making my deliveries that morning and walked over to the phone and called the center to let them know that someone had to come get the truck that my wife was about to have our baby. After a few minutes I finally got through to my supervisor and I told him what was going on, and his reply was for me to keep on delivering and they'd try to get someone out there in an hour or so. Wrong answer Jack. Here my wife was about to deliver our child and management wanted me to keep on delivering and take a chance on missing the birth of my child. Yeah right. They may put the packages first in their lives, but not in mine.

I told them where the truck would be parked at and the keys would be hid in the cab, and I followed my wife over to the hospital. I parked the package car across the street in the parking lot of one of my customers' store.

I still remain bitter about that selfish episode still to this day.

I no longer looked at the 'world' at UPS through rose-colored glasses. I no longer had a selfish, self-centered viewpoint, and I was concerned for everyone at the center and was looking at things through a collective point of view. I had seen the constant shifts in management's 'labor policy' between each new faction that arose in Huntsville, which only resulted in everyone's morale, and solidarity being put through a test on a daily basis.

Harry didn't want the responsibility of the center, although he had no choice in the matter, and just did enough to keep Dick off of his back so we all tried to help Harry out the best we could. The management of UPS had always been rough to work for but we dealt with it the best we could, but it was nothing in comparison to what we were about to experience.

In the early spring of 1995, Joseph was having some health problems and was becoming unable to perform his duties as a steward in the way he felt we needed. Joseph decided to step down, and not wanting to take away from representing us. We all hated to see Joseph step down, but we all understood.

Management was giving Joseph a hard time about accommodating him with creating a job for him as our labor agreement provided for. The D.O.T had pulled his physical card and the company was then forced, I say that jokingly of course, to create him a job. Joseph was having terrible and sickening inner ear problems, and had problems keeping his equilibrium without medication. In fact he had a hard time walking and standing most of the time, but like any loving father he had a wife and children to provide for and needed to work. Joseph's condition could be controlled with medication and he looked forward to starting work again. The job management created for him was working in the unload area, including unloading trailers, of all places.

Unloading the trailers was a hard strenuous job for anyone who was young and in good health, much less a mid-thirty year old broken down package car driver with inner ear problems. Joseph tried to do the job, but with the constant, repetitive bending over, then standing up, and then over again he just couldn't do it, not in his current condition.

Eventually Joseph would have to go out on temporary disability because of his medical problem and was unable to do the job that management had so graciously created for him. I had often asked management why couldn't they just let him push a broom so he could get his eight hours in? Like any other thing of this nature they had the usual response of, "No comment."

Joseph left the center for a couple of months, and the local union who was now being ran by a man named Matt, asked if anyone was interested in becoming the steward for the Huntsville east center. This time they were going to appoint an assistant steward as well to help with some of the workload if that was any indication to the steady increase in labor relation issues. This move of appointing a chief steward and also an assistant union steward revealed to me that the union knew that there was in fact a unique problem between management and employees in the Huntsville center and the chief steward needed extra help.

Well I discussed it over with Lesley, my wife, and I decided that it was something that I would like to do, something I felt I needed to do, and I decided then to throw my hat in the ring. I felt strongly, and often voiced my opinion, that we needed to head in a new direction, one that was a lot tougher with the management and a position to flex the union muscle when times so warranted the need.

Another driver, Wally, threw his hat in the ring also.

Well, I campaigned for a couple of days with the people in the center and tried my best to sell them on what I had to offer them. After a week or so, the Local 402 business representative, Matt, brought over a ballot box and conducted the election before were scheduled to start work one morning. After everyone cast a ballot, the box was carried into the west center office and the votes were tallied. Abel, Wally, and Alvin, who was the Huntsville West job steward, witnessed the tallying of the ballots. I managed to have won by a few votes and it was now official. I was now the chief job steward for the Huntsville east center and the local union representative handed management a letter confirming my appointment and recognition as being a steward for Teamsters Local 402.

I had decided early on that I was going to take a much more aggressive position with the management on several key issues. One being the constant harassment of the drivers concerning the way management dealt with the over allowed issues. Second, was the daily 'illegal', meaning uncontractual, use of cover drivers to circumvent the hiring of full time drivers. The management in Huntsville was abusing this language in our labor agreement to keep from promoting part timers to full time.

In a previous labor contract that was voted on and passed by the Teamster members of UPS, called for the company to create a new position of driver called cover drivers. It sounded good at first but the way that the cover drivers were supposed to be used was to only cover vacations of regular full time drivers and in cases of illness or something else along that line. What management was doing was using them like regular full time drivers, which they were not. They were using them to run half day routes, run over flow, and run bits and pieces pulled from other routes to form a 'cut in' route. All of this work should have been offered to a full time driver first, and then management should have forced the less senior full timer to run this stuff, but this was not the case. The company had, in their eyes, a full time driver who was being paid part time wage and benefits. They were saving money by replacing the retiring full time drivers with these new disposable throwaway part time jobs.

How is this possible you may ask? If you figure that in wages alone, there was a difference in pay of about $5.00 (for example) an hour. If they worked that cover driver full time for 40 hours that week at a saving's of $5.00 an hour then management saved $200 for that week in wages, but got the same amount of work at a cheaper cost, and a more productive cost. Then if you figure the benefits side of not having to pay into the pension fund at a "full timer's" contribution rate, and then the case of insurance, look at the money they were saving then. Keep in mind as well that when a cover driver, who worked at time's in excess of 50 hours a week, weren't on vacation they did not get paid for that 40 hour week like the full timers? Remember now...that they had been working "full time" for many months. NO! No they weren't. Management was only paying these people their part time vacation rate and they didn't receive 40 hours vacation pay. They received only 20 hours, which was their daily guarantee as a part timer. Management only wanted them to be on board as a "full timer" only when they weren't on vacation, and in regard as well to when it came to paying them the substandard wages and benefits. This proved to be extremely unfair to the part timers who were working as full time drivers with only the protection of being a part timer. This was great for management in term's of labor policy. They had disposable full time jobs at their fingertips and could lay off the cover driver's anytime they so desired as volume dictated. There wasn't anything the union could do because of the language in the contract. What were the cover drivers supposed to do? They wanted to achieve the American dream of buying a house and wanting some of the finer things in life for their loved ones, but were unable to do so because of the insecurity and fear of being laid off back into the part time ranks. It was a sad catch twenty-two. What were they to do? Maybe complain so that upper management could get upset and tell a center,where the controversy had arisen, to cut out the cover drivers altogether?

They weren't 'committed' full time jobs like our full time jobs were. They had no security and in reality no guarantee of working full time everyday other than the way the language was written and intended for. It had provided a lot of false hope in regards to a higher, secured wage. Management knew this and used it as another means to turn a profit.

Harry was once again forced to act as our center manger until Birmingham could find someone to come into Huntsville and turn us around. We had been through three center managers within the last three years and everything was stroking along rather smoothly and we all liked working for Harry. We often asked him why didn't he want to be a center manager. His reply was, "Are you crazy," and he walked off laughing and shaking his head no.

We had obtained a new CEO in the meantime and began to notice a lot of changes beginning to take place. There was almost a new air of attitude amongst the management in Huntsville and as if there was a new vibe being given off. It was sort of like a newfound discontent for us, the lowly Teamster employees. Harassment once again started back up, but in different, subtler ways than what we were used to. It was almost like instead of the old full, in your face kind of action it was now like we were being prodded a little at a time to see how far they could push us before we 'snapped'. Management would often push some people to the edge, but not over it. Maybe they were testing the waters for something new? I was a little uneasy about the new shift in labor policy and tried to interpret what was going on with the managers and what they were up to, but later just gave it up to being untrusting and just plain old paranoid.

As a union steward I now had the duty of going into the office quite often to represent employees for various infractions of the contract for reasons both real and perceived. I was new as a steward, and very inexperienced, and the company exploited that fact every chance they could without any help or concern from the "old guard" local union officer, Matt. I had began to purchase books on my own and read everything I could get my hands on about work place rights and so on. I simply took the initiative to educate my self in the ways and workings of organized labor.

I had arrived to work earlier than usual that next Monday morning, to get an 'intelligence' report on what was going on in the building that might need our intervention. As I walked toward the offices I noticed that several tables had been set up with food on them that looked like something out of a buffet in a restaurant.

Management had set up three tables covered with biscuits, doughnuts, cakes, and cokes and about anything else you could think of under the sun. I figured they must have really liked this person that they were doing this for or were planning to buffalo us some way. The rest of the drivers began to trickle in and everyone was standing around eating and joking. They were all having a good time. Frank, who had replaced Dick on the District staff level, had walked into the building through the back door undetected and like usual, had his entourage in tow. We all began to settle down a bit and everyone turned to see what was going on and who all was with him.

The meeting started a little after 8:00 that morning and Frank intro duced our new center manager after giving us a detailed account of his career while at UPS over the years and all of his accomplishments. "Big whoop," I thought, as I took another bite out of the free biscuit while listening to them ramble on.

Then a man walked up to the microphone and tapped on it to check and see if it was on and said, "Good morning Huntsville my name is Davey."

I looked over at Alvin, and he glanced at me and shrugged his shoulders in answering the question I didn't ask, "What do you think?"

Davey went through his spiel and I had the gut feeling that something wasn't quite right with him from his speech. There was something elusive and I wasn't too sure of him. I smelled a rat. During his speech he revealed what corporate management wanted to do, in regard to labor relations, and was to take a new approach and policy on the way it did its 'business'. Davey went on to say how outdated the O.R was and blah, blah, blah. I thought I was dreaming. "Has this man lost his mind?" I thought. The one new shift in the labor policy was when he told us that management wanted to start over and that everyone's discipline records, known as the 'Pittsburgh file", would be thrown away. Everyone would start with a clean slate. I thought I was going to choke on my biscuit. "Was I hearing him right?" I asked another driver. Everyone began to look around and a small muffle of noise from everyone discussing what he had just said. Had management finally saw the error in their ways? Unknowingly to us, the management's scheme to bust the Teamsters union had just been set in motion after they had appeared to have just won our hearts and minds.

Davey went on and said he was brought up to Huntsville to implement a new style of management-employee relations program. It was called the "Team Concept". No one knew what in the world he was talking about and he immediately began to explain it citing several other corporations, Unionized corporations like Saturn and Goodyear, that had similar programs and everything was working just fine for them. He was a good salesman and he didn't appear to be like all the replacement center managers that came before him and we bought it. Davey continued to outline just the 'basics', only enough to wet our appetites, and then he said that he'd get into the specifics later on down the road. He was there, as a salesman to the Team Concept program that management wanted so desperately to implement nationwide.

We, as a group and even I, had taken their bait with the exception of Wally and Josey, the feeder driver and mechanic steward. They both smelled a rat from the very beginning. Wally was pretty well up on what was going on in the labor movement in regards to labor trends and policies and he immediately began to discredit the company's intentions and motives and became an instant thorn in their side in his own personal attempt to derail this program. Josey just didn't trust them. He'd been around for almost 28 years and he knew that they wouldn't do something unless there was something substantial in it for them. I didn't really see a problem in it at the time, because I didn't hear any opposition from the Teamsters Union about it. I figured if it was all right with the IBT, International Brotherhood of Teamsters, then it was okay with me.

What management was wanting to do was create several, independent work groups that would address some of the business aspects of running the company, and handle the day to day operation of the center. This would be accomplished by using the hourly employees within a particular job classification, and then they would be broken down again into work groups known as "teams". Then there would be an 'appointed' "team leader", whose position would rotate amongst everyone after a few weeks and who's job was to solely focus on the individual teams objective for the week. Included into this were some of the daily supervisory duties, such as dispatching for example, and the responsibilities associated with it. Who else knew better at how to do our jobs besides us, and what it would take to achieve optimum production. We were 'empowered" by the management to make decisions and the majority of the drivers were just ecstatic about the whole deal.

In a series of carefully orchestrated PCM's over the next few weeks Davey was slowly accomplishing what he had set out to do. The team concept was in full bloom in Huntsville in a matter of a few short weeks and management had practically done away with the O.R and had all but eliminated any perceived 'production related harassment' like they said they would do in all shapes and forms. That was the one and only time in my career that I didn't mind going to work. After six years while being employed at UPS and dreading everyday of having to come to work, I no longer had that gut wrenching, nauseas apprehensive anxiety in my stomach as the closer I came to the building while driving. It was quite pleasant to work there. It was a welcome change, and this change also reflected at home. I was much more pleasant to live with and everything was much, much better. I was able to spend quality time with both Lesley and my new daughter named Mattie. The company had reduced our paid day and we were given more time to go out and actually spend time with our customers, quality business building time, and service the customers like we were supposed to do, and like they so much deserved.

This program was going quite well into the fall of 1995 and continued through the start of peak season, and that's when problems first began to surface.

I was half-heartedly participating in the program just like Alvin was. The action of us even participating at all in the team concept was drawing flak from Wally and Josey. They were sort of upset about us participating, and after pressure from them, I agreed to step down and not participate at all. I didn't condemn it, nor did I endorse it either. There had slowly been a growing discontent within the ranks of the package car drivers about how the management was choosing who would stay in the building to work on what for that day. The problem was that there was no real observation of seniority between the drivers who were having to stay in the building and do what was once a supervisor's job.

The management in Huntsville still wasn't following the contract in regard to observing seniority and the use of cover drivers. The problem once again was when the management pulled a full timer off of his route to work in the building and replaced him with a cover driver, which they couldn't 'legally' do although they could use a full time unassigned driver to replace the full time driver who stayed in the building, but not a part time cover driver.

The common and monotonous excuse management would use after a grievance had been filed to protest this contract violation was, "We don't have anybody trained to cover the route." Contractually this was a loophole to some degree. They were citing that in order 'to make service' they invoked the language in the contract that gave them the authority to use whomever they could to make sure the route would be delivered. This is a poor argument from their position. If that was the case and management was concerned with the 'making service' question then why did they not just keep the full time driver on the route, and keep the part time driver in the building to work on the team projects. The reason was that they couldn't do this without running into a major contract problem, because there wasn't a defined position in the contract for a part time Teamster to stay in the building and do a 'new job'. This would raise a whole new question regarding legitimacy to their plans which would have resulted possibly in the contract being opened again and these new jobs to created 'permanently', which wasn't in managements plan.

Once again it was all about money. By using that full time driver in the building management could control cost for that day in regard to over time pay and the driver's full time pay scale as a whole, because he would work only eight hours straight time and then go home. He was going to have to work eight hours anyway because contractually he was guaranteed that. Management was having to try and get this "team scheme" into place and were going to have to use someone to cover a route and stay in the building anyway. By replacing that full time driver with a cover driver who was making $3.00 less an hour than the full timer, and who may have had worked an hour of overtime for that day, would have saved UPS $127.50 a week (with one hour of overtime per day). Multiply this times 10,000 drivers nationwide for fifty-two weeks...that comes to $6.6 million dollars.

Does it make sense now? By management following the contract it was, in one sense, actually costing them money, which would've been paid in the form of higher wages and overtime.

Whenever the 'heat' got to be too much for the management they'd start 'offering' days off to the drivers. This was rare, up to the team concept, and any time you wanted or needed a day off prior to the team scheme it was like pulling teeth.

Prior to the team concept anytime you'd call in sick or was needing off you'd be given the third degree by management and made to feel like you were abandoning your job, and even at times you were threatened that if you didn't show up you'd have hell to pay when you did. Most of time the norm was for a driver to call in and just tell their supervisor they were sick and to hang up the phone before the supervisor could say anything. Then chances were they'd try to call you right back and leave you a nasty message on your answering machine. I had even known of some supervisors coming out to driver's houses to see if they were in fact sick.

Management was 'bribing' people to keep controversy down from the problems that the team concept was causing.

Management had also managed to implement a training program almost in sync with the implementation of the team concept, in which drivers were cross training other drivers on new routes. That in itself relinquished just about all responsibility, and need for a supervisor. We had taken on almost all of their job responsibilities now and they felt concerned for their jobs. In a bold move the Huntsville management reduced an on-car supervisor position and the ones that were left felt threatened, and I was even approached one morning by a very disgruntled supervisor with what was happening in management from the team concept.

UPS was offering a buyout of managers and supervisors with a certain amount of time in service of the company. A substantial amount of the management took the buyout which left UPS, unexpectedly short staffed at some facilities. Management was figuring on the employees who were actively engaged in the team scheme to fill their places, which once again would save the company millions of dollars. Say for example that if 5000 supervisors had taken the buyout and UPS was no longer having to pay them a salary and stock options that totaled for example $55,000 a year, then multiply that times 5000 managers...it comes to $275 million a year just being saved from not having to pay in management salaries. Bear in mind that these are conservative numbers, and figures, so the amount would've been much, much higher. These 5000 jobs would just be passed onto the hourly people to do. Heck they were killing two birds with one stone.

Management called the class's fancy names and really hammered it up to us. But in essence they were nothing more than 'brain washing' classes. These drivers, after attending these classes, would come back to the center with a different outlook. They were concerned with management's perception rather than the with union's perception. It was as if you were talking to a die-hard UPS manager when in reality they were nothing more than just a flunky. These drivers were acting different and a little more 'professional' which stood apart from the rest of us, only not in the way they thought.

Slowly through the next peak season of 1996, the Birmingham, Alabama feeder department tried to implement that same program within the Huntsville feeder drivers. Josey flatly and firmly told the company during one of their 'forced' meetings that it wasn't going to happen with Huntsville's feeder drivers. Sadly though it did happen, but in the case that there were only a limited number of feeder drivers who participated in the program. Birmingham feeders even went as far as to try and get some of the feeder drivers in Huntsville to train any new feeder drivers. This is the manager's duty and responsibility to train new drivers, and with the type of equipment we use, in excess of thirty tons, and the safety concern that was involved, it should be the management's responsibility. There is one word that pops into mind and that is 'liability' of these hourly people training new drivers. I never could get a straight answer on the question of who's liable for the quality' of training that is involved in driving heavy commercial motor vehicles in excess of thirty tons down the highway at 70 miles an hour.

Josey and the other feeder drivers unanimously refused that mandate and told management that there was no way they'd do that. It was way too much responsibility.

Everyone was beginning to grow weary of the deliberate and obvious highly visual displays of favoritism that was going on in the Huntsville center, and crap started to hit the fan slowly by the end of the Christmas rush. Management was using the same drivers every time to stay in the building and had modified the 'rotation' that had been in practice. Management decided not let the strong and influential union members lead the groups, because they thought that it was in the best interest of the survival of the team scheme to maintain the integrity of the group with not having to inject a 'radical' into the equation. I thought to myself, "what's going on here?"

With the 'authority" and "responsibility" of being a team leader came some newfound perks such as dispatching your own paid day, and staying in the building to perform 'critical' duties and jobs that was levied on you by the local management, which usually happened on very rainy and stormy days.

What happened after management realized that their team scheme was unraveling, and causing problems amongst the rank and file members was that they started identifying some of the weaker members of the union and began courting them. This was not actually courting, but cleverly disguised manipulation and deceit into supporting and continuing their agenda. This was one of the biggest mistakes that management could have done. They actually thought that we were too stupid to not see what was going on. It might have taken us a while to come around, but the writing was clearly on the wall now for everyone to see.

Problems associated with the team scheme began to mount, snow-balling everyday. The team leaders were continuing to dispatch their routes with a lot less stops than their neighbor's routes, which butted up to theirs. The majority of the 'leaders' were coming into work about an hour or two earlier than everyone and then working the rest of their six hours on the road delivering. This meant that they got to go home around 4:00 p.m everyday while the rest of us worked till 6:30 or later each night. When the team leaders pulled work off of their truck to dispatch to other drivers it was usually in the form of apartments, hilly houses and the very worst stops they had. When they pulled the packages off of their truck to go on another, called pulling a 'split', they'd normally pull the heaviest packages they had. I've even caught them sorting through their loads and picking out the worst houses and all the Nordic Track boxes they could to pawn off on other drivers.

Local management turned a blind eye to this practice and encouraged us to work it out amongst ourselves. We handled it usually with a cuss out fight on the belt and even some went as far as to call them out into the parking lot after work.

Management was proving to be successful in their endeavor to divide us, and in turning us against one another. On or about February 16, 1996 the I.B.T directed all local unions representing any UPS members not to participate in the team concept program. The I.B.T demanded that UPS provide the Teamsters with a complete program of details and objectives to which management's reply was that all they wanted was to create the 'spirit of one big company family". Behind the curtain management was secretly refusing to negotiate a final agreement on key safety issues and was feverishly engaged in fighting to get Congress to gut labor and safety laws.

Upon hearing of the news, from a T.D.U, Teamsters for a Democratic

Union representative, Josey put a call into the local union representative, Matt, and asked him why it was still going on in Huntsville if the International had ordered it stopped. Matt's reply to Josey was that he didn't see a problem with it.

What kind of bull crap was this? Here the IBT has issued a directive for us not to participate in the team concept but our local union officers were supporting the program. Were they supporting management or us?

Josey called a meeting with all the stewards in the Huntsville building and discussed how we were going to combat it. The only thing we could decide on, as a way to defeat it, was to hold management accountable for every little contract infraction and unleash an avalanche of grievances. This would prove to be easier said than done. We were in for a battle, because we had to stand-alone. Our own local union and its 'old guard" leaders was in support of it and turned a blind eye. How did we expect to get a fair shake at the grievance hearings at trying to bust this program in Huntsville from the local union? Josey and Abel thought that it would be a good idea to have a meeting with the drivers and discuss the problem to finally expose it for what it was and what damage it had done to us as a group.

I called the meeting for the following Tuesday and pretty much everyone from both centers attended, except for those drivers who was still supporting the team scheme. Alvin started the meeting off telling the drivers about the position of the IBT and the opposite position of Matt and the local union. We immediately discredited Matt and the position of the other Local 402 officers and we all agreed to side with and follow the instructions given to us by the IBT and then Teamsters General President, Ron Carey. Everyone was given a chance to voice their opinion and concerns and we then formulated a game plan to bust this team scheme up, and to get rid of this plague once and for all. We, the stewards, instructed the drivers that if they had any question in regard to the legality of something management was wanting them to do, to simply come to us AFTER they did it, and for them not to depend on the management to truthfully tell them the legality of anything. We all agreed that the stewards was the final authority in deciding if something in question was "legal" or not in regard to the team concept. We did not say refuse to work as instructed but to do so, then contact us and we'd all file a grievance to protest it. To defeat this was in reality very simple. Just don't participate or volunteer for anything.

After our meeting, as we dismissed everyone, Wally and I noticed that there were several members of management standing just inside the building, smoking cigarettes and watching us. I walked on around to the rear entrance and walked on in with Josey and Abel and noticed that Davey and Randy, an account executive, were pulling drivers over to the side asking them what went on out in the parking lot as they came in. Most of them told Davey to ask a steward if he wanted to know. Davey had tried to interrogate them trying to find out what the meeting was about outside and what was discussed, and to the best of my knowledge no one divulged any information to a member of management about the meeting. A few days later we surprised management with an onslaught of grievances both collectively as a group and individually. We filed so many grievances in those three days that we had literally ran out of grievance forms and had to use notebook paper. We were relentless in our endeavor to bust this program up.

Davey did not know what to do about this new situation in Huntsville. He pulled me into the office one morning, after the PCM, and closed the door behind us. I was standing there with my heart racing from the rush of adrenalin. Davey walked around me and took a seat on the edge of his desk and just looked at me, and I started looking around the room trying to ignore him. His intimidation wasn't going to work on me. Davey crossed his arms and took a deep breath and said, "Is there something I need to know about James?"

"Like what?" I asked, while playing dumb.

"All of these grievances. What's the problem that warrants all of this paper work James?" He replied, while holding up about a four-inch tall stack of grievances.

"Well Davey we're having a problem with the way ya'll are violating the contract every time we turn around with this team crap. How many times have I came to you about working these drivers in the building three days out of the week while loading the rest of us up? Davey you don't seem to care about it at all. " I replied, while being a little cocky with my response.

"A few times James." He replied cautiously.

"Why haven't you done something to fix the problem?" I asked.

"James I don't see a problem with it. Do you think that you may be making more out of this than it really is?" He replied sounding like a father figure. I could tell then that he was attempting to manipulate me into thinking that maybe I was blowing this out of proportion. It wasn't going to work and I stuck to my guns.

UPS management is experts at both conventional and unconventional coercion and manipulation. I wasn't going to buy into what he was attempting to sell me any longer. I decided to put an end to our meeting and told him that the grievances would continue to come in swarms until we eradicated the last remnants of the team concept in Huntsville. I made sure he understood that we had been directed by the members in Huntsville to do whatever we had to in order to end it. Davey became extremely agitated from my response and I waited for him to blow up. I was nervous and judging by the bright shade of red on his face, I expected us to tie up at any moment. He made the wiser decision and chose to contain himself and looked at the floor and said," If that's the way you want it," and told me I could leave.

I walked out of the office and let out a long sigh of relief. I didn't have the experience at the time, to feel comfortable in handling them in an explosive incident and dealing with those kinds of confrontations by myself, but after that meeting with Davey I did feel more confident, and competent, and more like a steward than before I had entered the office that morning.

After about two more weeks of grievances and with people constantly questioning management on a daily basis on whether or not they had to attend these meetings before their start times, Davey had enough of the questions and opposition from everyone. During a PCM one morning he made it mandatory that if your name appeared on a list that you had to attend the meeting. Everyone came to us after the PCM and asked what they needed to do. We told them to go ahead and attend the meetings and just look at it as easy money. The management was bringing everyone in thirty minutes before their start times and it was in one sense overtime. We instructed everyone who went in there to just sit in their seats, and not say a word, and not participate in any part of the meeting.

Whenever a manager called a meeting that was 'mandatory' and started a less senior driver than me, I would simply file a grievance protesting the violation of my seniority rights in regard to extra work. Management would pay a lot of money out to us all due to these grievances. We were winning the majority of the grievances that were being filed in regard to the team scheme.

Management had become very upset that they were paying us just to come in a sit at these meetings. They decided that they'd still make us come regardless if we participated or not, and it was something to see. The managers were acting like a bunch of babies about the whole deal and pretended like they were getting responses from us whenever they asked a question when in fact we weren't saying anything at all.

After a few more weeks of these tactics, UPS, in a company decision, disbanded the whole team concept after the Teamsters filed an Unfair Labor Practice charge, or ULP charge, with the National Labor Relations Board, or NLRB, in Washington D.C. We had beaten them as a "team", but it was a small victory before the upcoming war. We were going to have hell to pay.

Just exactly what was the "Team Concept," and why did management cleverly try to infiltrate this cancer into the body of the union. The answer to that question isn't as surprising as one might expect. The answer being ... to undermine and destroy the union from within. The cost associated with implementing this ploy was miniscule in the sense of dollars, and it was probably considered just merely a small investment and a gamble, which could have resulted in one of the largest payoffs known to Corporate America ... the demise of the Teamsters Union.

Programs like the 'Team Concept' and various other work groups, and yes even the pride and joy of UPS' management now, the CHSP or the safety committee as it is commonly known as, have been around for many decades and they all serve the same purpose no matter what fancy, deceiving name that management affixes to them. They all have the same goal and purpose in mind upon their birth..., which is to prevent unions from coming into the work place, and/or to get rid of established unions, or as this practice is commonly known as, "To bust a union."

It has always been a fundamental tool that is often used by professional labor consultants, both 'in-house' and outside, that is used to win the trust of the employees and offer alternatives to union representation. One of these such programs is the universal "round table," or "rotating" committee's. Management creates a committee, which the participants are taken from the particular audience of employees and they then offer them a 'formal' way of bring their complaints, their concerns, a avenue to influence company policy and yes to even air their ... grievances. According to Martin Levitt's book, "Confessions of a Union Buster", he writes:

"These groups become management's tap into the worker grapevine and it's repressive thumb on the informal worker power structure. The regular group

meetings provided management with a system for planting information, and as well for identifying and controlling the leaders amongst the employees, and by continually changing the makeup of the employee committee, management could keep abreast ofcomplaints and rumors circulating without creating a bond amongst the participants or inadvertently creating leaders."

As it was demonstrated during management's failed attempt to implement this debauchery, it is evident from their actions that this was one of those programs, which was designed to cripple the Teamsters union, because remembering that there are roughly 222,000 UPS Teamster members, and just try and imagine the devastation that could have come if this program was allowed to continue. Management's program, which entailed rotating the leadership positions, was just like using this before mentioned blueprint. They deceived the members into believing that out of fairness to everyone that the leadership positions should be rotated bi-weekly ... or so, but in reality it was being done to prevent any strong leadership from being born. Management tried to replace the established procedure for resolving grievances and issues, which is through the grievance machinery language, with their own, and in the process tried to manipulate the thoughts and feelings of the rank and file members to begin questioning themselves whether or not they actually needed the union at all.

The old guard, deadbeat, do nothing controlled local unions actually helped foster and promote this program in two ways. One of the ways they achieved this short-lived hold that is probably being overlooked, and it was quite clever on managements part was the members discontent. It's evident, and without question that management hears and knows the discontent that the majority of the members hold for their old guard controlled local union officers and how they routinely 'sell out' the employees during the grievance procedure, if and when the grievances we file are even heard, and what better way to offer the employees with a system of resolving their concerns and disputes other than to offer it directly with the company by 'en-powering' the employee, and by bypassing the union's grievance procedure altogether, because the members often say, "What difference does it make anyway? Because, the company is going to, more than likely, get what they want and bamboozle the union into throwing up the white flag during the grievance procedure." This is in reference to Local 402. Management capitalized on this sentiment, and guess what ... people bought it. And all of this was simply from the old guards lack of enforcing the contract and truly doing their jobs. Management simply offered an 'alternative' ... one, in their own words and actions ... that worked, which in reality it was, and is, nothing but a manipulative deception born to garner sympathy and support for their cause.

These programs still exist at UPS and they maintain many of the core fiindamentals of this union busting tactic all the while the old guard controlled local unions ust sit back and out of ignorance, they allow them to continue, even after warning has been given from the rank and file members. One such example of this new found 'scheme' is UPS's CHSP program, in which you will read more about it in later chapters, but the end result is the same. I look at these programs and it reminds me of an old saying I heard, which I feel these programs deserve to be made in reference to. It goes like this:

"You can dress a turd up, and call it fancy names, but no matter what you do to dress it up and no matter what you call it... it's still a turd."

These programs are without a doubt a serious danger to the survival of the union in every facet of the imagination of what one may believe the union is, but it is imperative that the participants realize that by participating in these programs that they are allowing their union to be undermined and destroyed, and it is being done by their own deception. One underlying question I have is why the old guard officials allow it to continue to happen? Read on and find out why.

Chapter 9

"4:38 p.m: I just got off the phone with Davey and we had another fight. That makes for the second one today. There's no way I can get done and be back at the time he wants me to. After him telling Tommy to tell his wife to quit work and stay home and raise their kids, when they were sick, to him trying to fire me for leaving my pager on. I'm about to the point of telling him and UPS to stick it."

The level of retaliation levied on us by management for defeating the team concept in early 1997 was swift and immediate. Davey called us, the stewards, into the office right before the morning PCM was to begin. We were being forced to attend a meeting to discuss some new changes in managements 'labor policy'.

"I'm not here to debate or to answer any questions or discuss any issues at this time with you about what is fixing to come down from above. I just need y'all to stand here and listen." Davey replied very coldly.

He was about to reveal to us what new shifts in policy that was coming down from corporate. We all stood in front of his desk, all very attentive, and listened to him read from a prepared statement concerning how the company was losing money from doing away with the O.R, and how the company had rethought its position and decided that once again they had to control cost. The way that this would be accomplished was to bring us back under the dark days of the O.R.

We all knew what this meant, as I looked at Alvin who just nodded at me and winked. This meant that management was going back to the production standards of old, and we all knew, too that the harassment and production rides associated with it would be following it as well. We wouldn't have time to let the other employees in on the fact that this meeting had taken place, because management caught us before we could notify the members. But we found out they were being presented with the same prepared statement during their PCM while we were in the office listening to ours.

We were all dismissed and told to go to work right after Davey wanted us to tell the drivers what to expect in the next couple of days. Davey had a real smart-ass attitude and almost a smirk on his face while he fed us this line of bull crap. We all left the office and walked towards where Alvin's truck was parked.

"Tell your drivers on your side that we're going to have a parking lot meeting this Friday before work." Alvin replied excited from what just transpired in the office. I told him that I would and walked over to my side of the building and stepped up on the dock and walked on down to where my truck was parked.

This meeting with management concerning this new position happened on a Monday and by that Friday the supervisors were unleashed on us and they had begun to single out the 'problem' drivers, those running over allowed, and began the discipline procedure the following week.

By that Friday morning management in Huntsville had stirred up a hornet's nest. Almost every driver, with the exception of a few who were afraid to be seen exercising their rights as a union member out of fear of being retaliated against, had shown up in the parking lot of UPS. We tried to get the meeting underway several times and were running out of time before we had to start work, and finally, after about five minutes we managed to get everyone calmed down long enough to begin the meeting. It was evident that everyone was fired up about the "sudden" about face of the company. Everyone felt betrayed and felt used by management and everyone was very anxious to stick together as one and to support us, the stewards, on whatever course of action we decided to take to try and combat it. We instructed the drivers to go out and do their jobs by the book. No more, and definitely, no less. No longer were we going to do 'favors' to help management out and the buddy-buddy days were gone as well. If they wanted a 'business' relationship then that's what they'd get, and brother this was a two way street.

I feel very strongly that this was the final act of betrayal by the management of UPS towards, not only against myself, but also against us as a group that finally turned my heart hard towards them and started me on the path to making me the way that I am today towards them.

During our parking lot meeting we covered the UPS methods the best we could in the time we had, and we told everyone what to possibly expect and how to counter it. We directed that no one went in the office without one of us. No matter the reason. Everyone was real receptive to the things we were telling them to do and not to do and what their rights were not only under the Labor Agreement, but Federal Labor laws as well. After completing the meeting we dispersed everyone so they would not be late and be subject to discipline for that.

When we returned back to the building to start work, after having established a game plan, we noticed a collection of management personnel at all the entrances writing down the names of those who attended the meeting as they filed past them.

First let me say that this is against National Labor Relations Act, which is against Federal Labor Law. This was an act of illegal 'spying' on a group of union members that were engaging in protected concerted union activity and is an Unfair Labor Practice in the eyes of the Federal government. It was clear that the battle lines had been drawn. It was us against them. So much for the "one big happy family" management tried to portray to us just a few weeks ago. That's the way these managers are...just a bunch of two-faced sore losers.

I was immediately singled out by Davey, and by the other members of management in Huntsville, as a "trouble maker" and chief instigator in arousing the employees to side with the union, and I was beginning to become a threat to them. I had filed several grievances concerning the still rampant use of cover drivers illegally by management, and also that Davey still had a few drivers handling the dispatch, which was still causing a serious problem amongst the other members. Davey had met with me on several occasions to try and work this problem out, and we mutually agreed that this practice would be phased out totally within the next two weeks, at least until he could get some help in there with additional staffing of management personnel.

The few weeks we had agreed upon had turned into a month and I immediately began to file a grievance everyday that they illegally used a cover driver. Davey had managed to crawfish on me and I then had evidently become a major thorn in his side. Everyday I handed him at least two grievances for something...anything, and this was not counting what everyone else gave him on top of mine.

The labor manager for UPS' Alabama District, named Hembry, had scheduled a local level hearing with the Teamsters Local 402 representative, Matt, to discuss the dozens of grievances we had filed over the past few weeks. The local level hearing was the second phase, or second step, of the grievance procedure. This is invoked only after the steward and local management cannot settle the grievance and an impasse is reached on that level. This is step is normally scheduled within a couple of weeks following the conclusion of the first step.

I was told by Davey to report to work a little earlier that morning of the local hearing so I could sit in on the meeting. This would be the beginning of many 'locals' I would sit in on and it gave me a totally different perspective into the world of labor relations between UPS management and the Teamsters Union.

I arrived to work early that morning and walked on inside the building and stood around at the bottom of the stairs waiting for Matt to show up. The preload was just finishing up with their shift, and I watched as workers struggled to pull around the heavy carts loaded that were loaded with rolls of fabric and other "e-reg packages" as I waited anxiously for my side, the union, to arrive and the hearing was scheduled to begin in ten minutes.

After a few minutes Hembry walked in through the back door carrying a briefcase and dressed in a suit. He walked up to me and introduced himself. Nothing fancy was said between us, and the introduction reminded me of a politician and the way they would shake their hand. He asked me if Matt was here yet and I replied, "No. I haven't seen him."

"Tell him, if you will, that I'm up the stairs in the office waiting on him okay?" Hembry replied waiting for my answer.

"Okay." I replied, and Hembry proceeded on up the stairs to the office and I watched as the door shut.

I was still waiting for Matt to show up and he still hadn't arrived. The meeting was supposed to start at 7:30 a.m and here it was almost 7:45. I walked on into the west center office and called over to the union hall and Jamie, the secretary to the local hadn't arrived yet either. "Where was he?" I thought to myself. I hate waiting on someone especially when something of this nature was involved. It doesn't look good for the union in my opinion. It's as if it portrays a perception to the member of not caring enough about our business and our needs to be prompt.

Before I could hang the phone up, I caught a glimpse of Matt walking by the window in the door, and I hung the phone up to catch him before he went upstairs. I didn't know what he wanted me to do, so I hollered at him as he climbed the steps and he turned to me and motioned for me to come on up. I walked on up the steps to the office upstairs and followed Matt inside.

As we walked into the office, Hembry was on the phone and held his finger up to let us know that it would be a minute. We went ahead and sat down in front of the desk and Hembry hung the phone up and looked at his watch. He was thinking the same thing I was. Hembry stood up and shook both our hands and then sat back down and began to pull copies of our grievances out of his briefcase. Matt was carrying his copies in manila folders. We were ready to start the local hearing and were just sitting there waiting for Hembry to get done with what he was doing.

I had begun to grow somewhat impatient with Hembry's lack of urgency and importance. I was almost ready to say something to him when finally after a few minutes of stalling I began to sense a loss of momentum, and a resulting loss of confidence for our side before the meeting had even begun. His stalling and subsequent control of the tempo of the meeting had served its purpose of being the psychological tool that it was. After a few minutes of paper shuffling Hembry began the meeting by selecting the countless number grievances I had filed against Davey as well as some others that pertained to other members.

Matt, was concerned with some issues involving the complaints of harassment that were made by several drivers, after the defeat of the team concept, and he wanted to discuss those first.

It had seemed that supervisors had been directed by company 'henchmen' to begin riding with the problem drivers and the out spoken critics of the team concept and had begun the discipline procedure.

I had been called into the office, prior to this local hearing, to represent these drivers who all had received discipline for running over allowed and various other minor infractions of the labor agreement. Management tried to put the fear of corporate back into us all in an attempt to restore the power and control that they once had on us prior to the failed team concept attempt.

We had heard several of the grievances and after Hembry and Matt failed to resolve the issues of harassment, they then agreed that the grievances would be heard by the next step of the grievance procedure, the National Grievance Committee, or the "Panel" as it is often called. That took several minutes of back and forth debate, and dialog, and finally it was my turn for my grievances to be heard.

My grievances were concerning the use of cover drivers, the team concept and a couple of other infractions. I sought on several of my grievances as remedies to include charges filed against management with the NLRB. I was sitting there waiting for someone to say something when Hembry asked me to walk down and get Davey for him. I looked at Matt and stood up and exited the office and noticed that Hembry was watching me leave not saying a word as I turned to close the door behind me.

I walked on down the steps and went into Davey's office and told him that Hembry wanted to see him upstairs. He dropped what he was doing and told the supervisors in the west office that he'd be back shortly and to take any down any messages that came in for him. I followed Davey back up the stairs and he knocked on the office door as Hembry told us to come in and take a seat. I sat back down beside Matt and Davey sat over by Hembry.

"What do you know about this?" Hembry asked Davey as he handed him the grievance to read.

Davey sat there looking over the grievance while looking dumbfounded as if he didn't know what Hembry was talking about. Davey proceeded to tell Hembry "his" side of the story, after he suddenly and miraculously remembered what had happened, and how he and I had discussed the problem extensively. Davey managed to leave out how long ago we had spoken, and how I allowed him enough time to re-staff both centers and phase out the use of drivers doing managements work. In Davey's testimony regarding his use of cover drivers, he told Hembry that he didn't know that it was still going on, and that he'd talk to Harry and the other supervisors and put a stop to it.

That's how long it takes to lose a grievance due to a lying center manager telling their "version" of the truth. As far as the use of the cover drivers, he knew all about it. I, along with Alvin, had gone to him several times demanding that he stop this practice and both had filed the grievances to protest it. Davey's favorite defense was, " I've got a business to run."

The sad thing about the whole deal was that Matt had bought Davey's story and it was mutually agreed upon that this practice would stop and as for the drivers doing management work, that too would be phased out over the course of several weeks. The management in Huntsville had bought themselves another block of time and had paid for it with a lie.

After the meeting was declared closed, I walked into the restroom and Matt followed me in there. He began to talk to me about what I had written on the grievances as remedies, that I wanted the local union to seek, against the management. I told Matt that Davey was nothing but a liar and Matt even agreed with me that he knew that Davey was lying.

"Why in the hell didn't you do something then Matt if you knew he was lying?" I asked Matt in a rather upset tone.

I'm trying to work out several grievances on some other issues with them and I don't need anything like this to screw it up." Matt replied.

That said it all for me. Evidently Matt was more worried about trading some grievances off rather than enforcing the contract and protecting our rights and jobs. Matt was nothing but an "old guard Teamster official" and boy was it starting to show. I became furious on the inside but just held it in and blew it off.

Before Matt walked out he said, "Oh yeah, one more thing. The panel doesn't know what you mean by filing charges with the Labor Board as a remedy to your grievance, so don't use that anymore okay."

"What the hell do you mean they don't know? Who are these morons anyway? Don't they know that's my right to do that?" I replied almost exploding from the anger.

"They do, but...they don't want to get mixed up with stuff like that. Just let me work it out okay?" Matt asked looking for my reassurance.

"Trust me." He added while patting me on the back as we exited the restroom.

Trusting him would later prove to be my biggest mistake in my career in the Union and at UPS. That is...for me to trust him.

I headed on back down stairs to the office to get my D.I.A.D, a computer clipboard, and punched in on it and walked over to where my truck was parked. I began to go through the packages that were piled out behind the truck. I looked up, while reading the address labels and noticed that Hembry and Davey were standing off to the side and both of them were watching me. When I looked back at them, they noticed that I had caught them looking at me and they turned their backs to me. I paid no mind to them and went about my business.

Otis, the driver next to me, was in his truck and he came out and looked around asked me what was going on in the office upstairs. I told what Matt had said and the outcome of our grievances and his only reply was, "So what's new?"

I thought to myself, "Yeah, what's new?"

I finished up with what I was doing and loaded all of my overnights and the remainder of my bulk stops that were still under the belt. I crammed the last of those in, and slammed the rear down closed and walked around to the cab of the truck. I was sitting in the seat of the truck waiting to leave and here comes Chad, who was an east center on-car supervisor, hollering like an idiot for everyone to leave. He looked at me and screamed out, "I need you to leave James! Now!"

"How do you expect me to leave when I can't even move Chad?" I popped back off to him. The position and location of my truck on the inside of the building prevented me from simply pulling out. I was stuck beside two trucks with one in front of me. I wasn't going anywhere until they pulled out first.

Chad wasn't interested in us leaving per say. He just wanted us to pull far enough out of the building to be considered off of his time. You see, while we are still in the building we have not 'left' yet, thus the time we spend on the dock doesn't count against our 'on road time'. That time is then charged back to the building, which they are only allowed to have a certain amount of "sort and load" time in the building for each morning. Leaving the building, in the eyes of management, would be to simply pull out of the building, then that time goes on our 'on road time' and thus becomes our problem and not theirs. Drivers are simply instructed to pull up as little a fifteen feet away from the dock, and this places the package cars just outside the building and this then constitutes "having left" the center.

In my case, I couldn't move so I charged all of the eighteen minutes that had I lost while sitting there back to the center. I didn't care though because it wasn't my problem it was the preload management's.

I finished my day of delivering with nothing out of the ordinary happening. I had once again changed routes with another driver a few weeks earlier, and I liked my new route very much. I was now in downtown Huntsville and it wasn't bad at all. I was being dispatched with around 80 stops over all, mostly business stops, and I enjoyed the scenery. I hadn't had any real problems from Davey for a while until after that local level hearing.

I was called into the office to sit in on a meeting with all the stewards in regard to the new division manager's decision that the number of stops we were being dispatched with everyday day needed to be changed, and some of the routes realigned with new delivery sections. Our route was to incorporate our adjacent driver's delivery area into ours in a sort of an overlapping system. We never received any information as to why this was being done other than the statement from Davey, "This is still our company and we'll run it the way we want."

"No problem," I thought to myself, as he continued to reveal what was about to happen that would be phased in over the course of the following week.

"How convenient." I thought. Here they can screw up a driver's route within a week or less, but it took them several months to phase out their use of what was their last vestige of their destroyed team concept.

Well, anyway, after all the mumbo jumbo from Davey, we were all excused and began preparing ourselves for the upcoming question session, or better yet, a gripe session, from the other drivers that would be affected as a result from the changes in their routes.

The stop counts were raised to reflect a more 'proportionate' day that had been determined by upper management as to what constitutes an eight-hour paid day in relation to the dispatch. Management was now including on the load diagrams of the trucks a low, medium, and a high paid day dispatch. No longer were they just dispatching us with eight hours of work, they were now going to implement this new system, and their goal was to keep the driver in a medium dispatch level, which itself was actual an eight and a half hour paid day on paper. The increased dispatch along with this new system, it didn't fairly represent the dynamics involved in determining a paid day by the subsequent increase in the number of stops to justify their actions. This could only been done through a time study of all the routes. There was a time study conducted in the next couple weeks and as a result most routes lost time and very few gained any. It didn't make sense, because Huntsville had seen a boost in new house construction and new businesses and with this prosperity came the added congestion and even more construction.

How was it possible that we could lose time on these 'congested" and condensed routes, in the time study, with all the positive variables that were sure to be a determining factor in the equation? The answer is a combination of two things actually.

First, as a result of the cover drivers, now being a major contributing factor, in the everyday use as 'on road' drivers, we had a lot of new, inexperienced drivers that weren't totally knowledgeable to the ways of management and their underhanded means of obtaining high production from the use of fear and intimidation. Simply put, they weren't trained in using the methods like they should've been due in part to the use of hourly people training other hourly people. The cover drivers went out on the routes those days they had the time study personnel on the trucks with them and wanted to do a good job for whatever reason, by either out of ignorance and out of vanity, they cut corners and ultimately cut their own throats while on the routes. This was all too familiar to me, because I had done the same thing when I had started out as a new driver.

Second, was the use of lazy, in-experienced, and incompetent time study supervisors. On my particular route, for example, it had many steep, long driveways, which required a lot of walking by the driver because of the grade, and angle of the driveway the package car would drag the bumper and I would be unable to climb the driveway in the package car. The time study supervisor would just wait at the truck, out of laziness, instead of walking with the driver and recording everything that would influence the amount of time that would be allotted for his route.

For whatever reason my route had picked up a portion of the medical district, which butted up to my route, from the 'adjacent' driver to me, and this translated into roughly another thirty stops, and seven new pick up stops, one of which was a heavy and time consuming stop. This increase of thirty stops translated into roughly a two-hour increase in my overall paid day, which I was still expected to run in a little over an hour's time.

My daily dispatch was increased as well, from the original 80 stops to 110, which managed to put me into my residential deliveries later in the afternoon, which that would have an impact on my over allowed time as well. Anytime I delivered my residential stops before 3:00 p.m., I didn't have a problem, but anytime after that, and now it was 5:30 p.m, you could hang it up it was near impossible to remain on schedule. Traffic was bumper to bumper and I delivered on a dangerous portion of the highway that had claimed several lives already from accidents. I wish I had a dollar for every time I was shot the finger from passing motorist for parking on the side of the road like I had been trained to do. I could probably retire from UPS today. My safety had become such a concern to me that I had decided to start parking in the turning lane and take my chances there after I had several close calls while making deliveries. I asked Davey about parking here, in the turning lane, and he told me that if I was hit by another car, while parked there, it would be my fault no matter what. Now what was I to do? Was I to worry about being fired for parking in the turning lane or was I to worry about parking on the side of the road, like he wanted me to do, and run the risk of causing an accident and possibly getting run over myself? What would you have done?

My original stops per hour went from nineteen stops an hour down to about eleven stops an hour due to me running my residential stops two hours later, after the afternoon rush hour started, and along the extra business stops as well. I had begun to run over allowed pretty much everyday since they implemented this new system. I began to be called into the office by Davey everyday to discuss my sudden decrease in production and my evident "lack of interest in remaining employed with UPS". After numerous complaints and fights with Davey I was scheduled for a new time a study as well were several other drivers whom all had similar complaints as I. Management had bussed in several veteran managers from our sister centers in North Alabama to help 'evaluate' our claims of unfairness.

Everyone was pretty upset from the fact of what was going on in Huntsville so I made a call over to Matt, at the local union, and asked him what was going on with this new change in Huntsville. As usual, I didn't get anywhere with him and he proved to be nothing more than a waste of time and that they could do whatever they wanted to until they violated the contract some way.

"No duh?" I thought as I hung up the phone. I was scheduled for the ride with none other than Chad, my supervisor, and I knew what kind of ride it was going to be. From the very beginning he was very, very nit picky and criticized every little thing that I was doing.

Nothing I would do could pacify him. I had made the mistake of letting him get under my skin and this had done nothing more than to cause me to make more mistakes.

Finally at the end of the day I went ahead and filed a grievance against him for harassment, and for the way that he had talked to me in front of several of my customers. I was demanding that he never ride with me again. Davey looked over the grievance and agreed to take him off the car with me and put Harry in his place instead. This was a welcomed solution. At least now I would get a fair shake during my day, and I did manage to have a good ride the following two days with Harry.

The summary of the three days ride reflected that I was doing a good job with my methods and that the route needed some work taken off of it, that it was too heavy. That's what I'd been trying to tell them all along. It was dangerous for me to run those residential's during that time of day after Harry found out the hard way and was almost was run over by on-coming traffic. Harry agreed that the route could be changed around in a way to not only make it safer, but also more productive as well to meet the new requirements as directed by Davey.

A couple of days passed after the ride and Davey called me into the office. He wanted me to bring my steward in with me, Alvin, to discuss my production ride.

We walked into the office and Davey had Chad in there with him as a witness for management. We all sat down and Davey began to review with me my past three days ride evaluation. I was not questioned as to why this or that had happened, and all that really took place during this meeting, was that I was ultimately expected to run eighteen stops an hour on a route that had, only days before, been determined to only being able to put off twelve stops an hour.

"Where's Harry?" I asked Alvin.

"You don't worry about where Harry is James, we're talking about you right now." Davey popped off in a smart tone.

This smart answer had only upset me. Here I was being subjected to this sort of inquisition without being afforded to bring the one man in the office that could clear this whole thing up.

"What about what Harry had written about the route needing to be changed?" I asked becoming agitated.

"I don't see anything like that in here." Davey replied, as he thumbed through the pages acting as if he was searching for what I had asked him about.

"Well someone's lying like Hell then." I snapped back.

Needless to say that was when the crap hit the fan. Chad jumped to his feet like he was going to do something and that's when Alvin put his hand on my shoulder and stepped in.

Alvin blazed up one side of them and down the other. He told Davey that this was nothing more than harassment and demanded to see the records from my ride.

"Since you like to file grievances James, you can file one if you want to see the records." Davey replied, while looking at Alvin. He proceed to tell me that I would run the numbers he was showing and pushed a sheet of paper across his desk for me to sign.

Davey had now opened the door for the next step of the discipline process that if I failed to 'work as he was instructing me" and failed to comply with his demands then management could carry it to the next step which would've meant a suspension and then a discharge for me.

I looked at the paper and slowly began to laugh as I read it.

"You've got to be out of your mind if you think I'm going to sign this Davey." I replied, tossing the paper back onto his desk.

"You'll sign it or I'll fire you." Davey replied, while pushing it back to me.

"I'm not signing jack. Do you understand me Davey?" I replied angrily.

"Alvin, you'd better tell Mr. Earls to change his tone or I'll give him a few days off to think about it." Davey replied, trying to intimidate me. Chad stood behind Davey with his arms crossed trying to look menacing and by this time my blood pressure had blown through the roof. Here they were sitting here lying and trying to get me to sign a form to commit to running a production number that was impossible to do.

"Well if he won't sign it," Davey replied, as he turned to Alvin.

"You sign it as witness Alvin." Davey replied, while pushing it towards Alvin.

Alvin picked it up and read it and then signed it and threw it back on his desk. It took everything I had to keep from cussing him out right then and there. I started to say something, but I was interrupted by Davey and told to go to work.

I stood up and walked out followed by Alvin to outside the offices and back into inside the center.

"What was that all about?" I asked, while trying to calm down.

"Looks like they got a problem with something you've done, probably those grievances you filed a few weeks ago. Just watch your back and do everything by the book." Alvin replied, while putting his glasses back into his shirt pocket.

I walked on up to the customer counter for the PCM and Harry told us some more good news. Management had decided that we were getting in too late with our pick up volume and they were having a problem on the local sort, or the reload shift, in processing it all, so they sat a curfew for us to be back to the building with our packages by no later than 6:30 p.m., and if we saw that we weren't going to make it for whatever reason they wanted us to call them so they could make the call for us to come back in or to stay out and finish.

I raised my hand to ask Harry a question.

"Harry since we now have a curfew are y'all going to take some work off of us to compensate for our loss of delivery time?" I asked, while drawing looks from everyone who then turned to Harry and waited for a response.

"You'll have to take that up with Davey, James. I don't know?" Harry replied. By this time Davey walked in to the room and I asked him the same question that I had Harry.

"You're expected to do your job like you were trained and if you do that then there shouldn't be a problem with getting back before 6:30." Davey replied. Everyone began to talk amongst each other. That question I asked Davey had disrupted the meeting and all of a sudden he yelled out, "Shut up! This is my meeting and you will not talk in it do y'all understand me?" Everyone just stood there looking at him like he was an idiot or something.

"I want to see Wally, Joseph, Dee and Willy after the meeting. The rest of you can go." Davey said to everyone.

All of the drivers were subjected to the same kind of treatment that I had experienced in the office just before the PCM and it all involved these drivers running over allowed on their routes. Davey wasn't interested in hearing their side of what happened to have caused them to run over allowed, and tried to get them to sign the same form that he tried to get me to sign earlier, stating that that they would commit to running the numbers he wanted, which was like in my case, impossible for the to do without working 'unsafe'. He managed to have upset all of the drivers too, and like me they refused to sign the form and when he turned to me and asked me to sign it as a witness, I told him I wasn't going to. He was stunned and at a loss for words.

"But...but you have to sign it." Davey managed to stutter out.

"I don't have to sign anything but my paycheck. I decide, as these peoples representative, what's legit and what's a crock, and Davey...this is nothing but a crock and you know it. I'm not going to sign anything and neither are they." I replied drawing the attention of everyone in the customer counter.

"Go get Alvin, Willy," he said, and Willy walked out to find Alvin, and after a minute of two, he came in behind Alvin and he began putting on his glasses

"What's going on here Davey?" Alvin asked.

"James won't sign these 'write-ups' as a witness and I want you to Alvin," Davey said.

"Whoa, whoa, whoa, just a minute. Now hold on." I said stepping over in front of Davey and Alvin. Davey just did the wrong thing by trying to go around me. This was not about to happen. There was not any 'going around, over, or under me when it came to my drivers and me.

"I run the east center Davey, not Alvin, and he has no say when it comes to me representing my members." I replied in a stern tone.

Davey looked like he was going to cry. He didn't know what to do.

"He's right Davey. He's the one you need to deal with and not me." Alvin replied and walked out.

Davey looked like he was about to have a stroke right there on the spot. What was he going to do now that I challenged his authority to choose who these people wanted to represent them? I knew enough about the labor laws to know that the members had the right chose whom they wanted to represent them in the office and not the management. I stood there and explained to the drivers what their Weingarten Rights were right in front of Davey who was clueless about what I was rambling on about and just stood their with a stupid look on his face.

"Do you all want me to represent you?" I asked the group as a whole. They all said yes that they wanted me to represent them.

Davey rolled up the forms and walked out without saying a word and slammed the door shut, shaking the counters on the wall from the force of the door.

"I guess that means to go to work?" I replied as everyone started laughing out loud. It felt good to use the law in our favor for a change.

I had demonstrated in front of the drivers that I was willing and wanting to stand up and fight for them. Over the next couple of weeks, I had gained ever more knowledge and wasn't afraid to use it when the actions by management warranted it.

It became increasingly difficult to make it in before the curfew and I was forced to file a grievance on February 5, 1997.

DATE GRIEVANCE FILED: February 5, 1997

EXPLAIN GRIEVANCE: *I had talked with Davey before leaving the center this morning and told him that I had too heavy of a paid day to be through in time to make it back before the 6:30 p.m. curfew. He showed no signs of interest and went even as far as to turn his back to me while I was talking to him. I have been working over 9.5 hours a day, in violation of the contract, and I'm doing the best I can do.*

REMEDY SOUGHT: *Compliance with the contract and a lighter paid day.*

The grievance was heard and settled on the local level and both management and the local union agreed that they would take a look into my allegations of not being able to get done with my route on time. This proved to be a waste of time. Neither the company nor the union looked into what they said they would. The only thing that was happening was that the company was gathering evidence in building their case against me.

Needless to say, over the course of the next few months I was constantly being threatened of being fired for not 'working as instructed' and life at UPS everyday had become a living hell. Everyone was miserable, and even though we filed grievances to protest this rampant display of 'labor abuse', it didn't do any good, because management did what they wanted to do the majority of the time anyway and the local union just turned a blind eye and let it happen.

I, along with several other drivers, worked many eleven and twelve hour days. There was no way I could get done in the allotted time and now I had 45 fewer minutes to do it in.

I was beginning to get home later and later each night as the weeks progressed, and with a newborn baby I hadn't any time to spend with her during the week. When I arrived home at night I ate a 'cold' dinner, and by the time I took a shower, and got everything ready for the next workday it was time to go to bed. My wife was becoming exhausted from the UPS lifestyle and this was the beginning of our marriage problems. It began simply as making little smart comments to one another and then into full-blown verbal fights. I was feeling guilty for not spending any time with her and Mattie and tried numerous times to make it up to them both by buying them things. One thing I would later learn is that there is no substitute for quality time. I hadn't eaten supper with them since the fall of the team concept and Lesley couldn't understand what was going on. She kept bringing up to me how months earlier I had been home before 6:00 p.m.

and how we'd sit down and have a nice dinner, and how we got to spend a lot of time together, but now I was coming home late every night upset, tired and mentally exhausted from fighting with management. I had unknowingly begun on a voyage of withdrawal from the ones that I loved which was accompanied with sporadic mood swings.

Many mornings I would wake up and I would have to literally make myself get out of bed and go to work. The closer I came to the center, as I drove, the worse I became. I was even contemplating on quitting and finding something else, but heck... I couldn't do that, though, and quickly dismissed the thoughts as just being foolish. Where was I going to go, making what I made here with just a high school education? I wasn't.

I felt as if I was though I was trapped, and I was. I was living in a new $100,000 house, had two new cars, credit cards, the whole bit. I was just like most drivers out there with debt up to my armpits. I just became that much more depressed from being trapped.

There were a lot of nights after coming back the building and unloading to go back out to finish my route, I would make a delivery to a house and the front door would be open and I could see the family all sitting around the table eating supper, fathers playing with his kids, or getting ready to go to a ball game or some other family function, and here I was out working till 8:30 p.m delivering boxes.

I had been complaining of arthritis and joint stiffness in my hands and knees. I had to have Lesley massage my hands and feet every night just so I could get a little relief from the deep pain in the joints so I could sleep. There were times at night that I stayed awake for hours at a time lying in bed with my knees hurting so bad I would almost cry from the pain. Lesley told me to go to the doctor and find out what was going on with me both physically and mentally.

I went to see my family doctor and after he examined me we sat and talked for a while. He said he wanted to start me on an anti-depressant and he wanted me to work on changing my lifestyle.

"Depressed? He's got to be crazy to think that that's what was wrong with me," I thought as I drove home. I started not to accept his diagnosis and get a second opinion and after I arrived home and told Lesley, she went right then to the drug store and had my prescription filled.

Lesley and I sat down when she got back and she asked me to tell her about everything the doctor had said. I told he that he thought I had a little arthritis in my knees from the strenuous activity from climbing in and out of the package car some 200 times a day. I was told to do a little warm up exercise to help with the symptoms but basically there wasn't anything he could do other than prescribe and anti-inflammatory medicine and muscle relaxers. As far as my fingers and hands, the problem with them was the same as with my knees and feet. There was no way to fix the problem other than to begin taking a prescription to help with the symptoms of it.

I began to take the prescription and it began to work, and over the next few months, I worked at trying to straighten out my marriage problems. I thought they were getting better, but in reality, I had become so consumed with hatred towards management that I had began to neglect my family once again and I failed to even notice my digress. Lesley just accepted it and me as the norm and tried to make the best of it. I still really hadn't bonded with my daughter anymore than when Lesley had first brought it to my attention before. Management's tactics were unknowingly beginning to affect and have an impact on innocent people…my family.

I was worried about losing my job and everything else just didn't seem to matter much to me at the time. We were at war with management. I was in a constant, daily battle with management about everything. I was still being harassed by Davey in regard to running over allowed and I began to grow weary of it all. I had had enough of it and I decided to just give up and cave in to their demands. I began to work a lot harder than was required contractually and in the process I once again began to neglect my customer's needs in order to serve management's needs, the OR.

After about three weeks of neglecting my heaviest shipping customer they called in a complaint on me. Or so I was told. She allegedly said that I was unwilling to work at meeting her needs and they were considering using another carrier if the problem wasn't fixed. I was called into the office, which had become pretty much a daily thing, and sat down expecting the usual bit about running over allowed and that I was going to get another warning letter or a suspension.

Alvin came in as usual and Davey started off by saying that a customer had called in a complaint on me. I sat up in my chair shocked, as I tried to think of who it could've been and when he finally told me I couldn't believe it.

"What did I do Davey?" I asked curious and hurt.

"They say that you will not stay long enough for them to finish their shipping and you refused to come back later and pick it up." Davey replied.

"What do you expect?" I snapped back.

"Hell I can't even deliver what I have much less go back by there after I've already been there and then be back to the building by 6:30." I said upset.

"You will go back by there if they want you to and you will be back here by no later than 6:30 p.m. Do you understand me?" Davey snarled.

"How can I do this Davey? It's impossible to do." I asked.

"Hell I can't even get done with what I have now." I replied.

"I'm instructing you to quit using that language in front of me." Davey snapped back

"Just make it happen. Now go to work." He replied, and shut his door behind us.

I felt like I was beating my head against a brick wall, because it was going to be impossible to meet that demand, and I felt like quitting right then. It had ruined my whole day. "If they want to they can just fire me because I don't care anymore." I thought to myself.

My whole day was shot to hell and when I arrived at the customer who'd called in the complaint I greeted the ladies in the back who were acting as if nothing was going on. Cathy, one of the ladies in the shipping and receiving department, asked me if UPS had talked to me about the problem they were having.

"Yeah, they talked to me all right." I replied sarcastically.

"What do you mean James?" She asked, as she walked over to where I was standing.

" I got in big trouble this morning." I replied, and began to tell her the whole story of what Davey had said to me, and how he had threatened to discipline me for this incident involving them.

Cathy didn't say a word. She turned and stormed off up front to get Angie, the manager, and she told her what I had said,

"That's a lie." I heard her shout out. Angie came walking back to where I was and asked me to tell her what happened. After I told her she turned and went to her office and slammed the door shut.

The truth was that Angie had called to see if they could schedule a later pick up and Davey said it depended on the driver. She had not called in a complaint as management had claimed. They didn't have the backbone to tell her about the curfew and tried to place the blame on me. While I was loading their packages into the truck she came out on the back dock and said she had corrected the problem and she said she had blazed Davey for lying to her.

I left out of there and continued to make my pick ups while finishing delivering my business stops as well. It was an extremely hot day and I was sweating like a dog, and while I was in the back of the truck sorting the packages I heard a car pull up and a door slam shut. It was Davey. Davey stormed over to where I was and climbed up into the truck and jerked his glasses off. He was fuming and quite visibly upset.

"What in the hell gives you the right to tell customers on me?" He screamed at me.

"I'm instructing you to stop using that language in my presence. Do you understand me? I find it disrespectful, and furthermore..." I said while rambling off parts of the contract. After about five minutes of a heated exchange he jumped in his truck and sped off like an idiot almost causing a wreck as he pulled out into traffic with wheels spinning.

I proceeded to finish my route although physically shaken from that confrontation and decided I wasn't going to let him get away with that and filed a grievance for harassment on March 27, 1997.

DATE GRIEVANCE FILED: March 27, 1997

EXPLAIN GRIEVANCE: *I was approached by a manager, Davey, and was forced into a verbal confrontation while on my route. I was cussed at by him and treated very disrespectful. He lied to a customer on me and I was unduly disciplined for this action.*

REMEDY SOUGHT: *I request an apology from him and the warning letter removed from my record.*

Needless to say, I didn't receive an apology and as a result of this confrontation what I did receive unknowingly was an audit that night after I left work. I had come into the center early the next morning after the fight with Davey and was called into the office. I was expecting an apology from Davey about how sorry he was for acting like he did and for lying and so on. Boy, was I wrong.

Alvin and I walked into the office and sat down after shutting the door.

"James, last night, I was going over your records and noticed a couple of things wrong." Davey replied, never looking at me.

"Are these your packages?" Davey asked while sitting the packages on his desk.

I looked at them and replied, "Yes."

"You failed to complete a service cross on these packages." Davey said. I looked at them along with Alvin, and sure enough I had failed to complete the crosses on them.

"Is this your pager James?" Davey asked very cold and methodical.

"Yes it is Davey." I replied, while the anger slowly began to swell inside.

"I found it in your truck with it cut on. We can't afford to buy you batteries because you're too lazy to cut it off," he said, while taking a cheap shot at me.

"First of all Davey those aren't your batteries they're mine. I had to buy them myself because you're too cheap to do it." I snapped back.

"Besides, I left it in there so I wouldn't lose it." I replied, with Davey never looking at me.

Management had assigned us the pagers to contact us, since the DIAD wasn't using its cellular capabilities to communicate with us yet, which were in the clipboard. Management had begun to discipline drivers several weeks ago that had lost or forgot to bring their pagers to work with them. I figured it was their property so I'd leave it at their building, because I couldn't afford any problem's that could stem from this trivial situation so I just simply left it at work.

I reached over and picked up the pager and took the battery out of it and tossed the pager back onto his desk and said, "You owe me for a battery Davey." He sat there unamused from my actions.

"One other thing James, you failed to sign off your DVIR book last night. With all of the grave violations I'm going to have to suspend you for 'failing to work as instructed." He replied.

"What do you mean suspend me? You can't do that for this. I haven't even been given a warning letter for this yet." I replied standing up now. I was trembling from the adrenalin running through me after Davey's actions. I knew my blood pressure was up, I could feel it pounding in my head.

"I can, and I have. You'll work until the outcome of your hearing," he replied.

I was really pissed off and was about ready to just knock his block off, when I had a little light bulb go off in my head. I leaned over to Alvin and whispered a question I wanted him to ask Davey.

"Davey, how many drivers did you audit last night besides James?" Alvin asked.

"That hasn't anything to do with this." Davey replied nervously.

"Oh yes it does. Answer the question. How many drivers did you audit last night besides James?" He asked again.

"None, I just happened to catch James' records while going over several..." he replied realizing he had just contradicted himself.

"Something isn't right here. I seem to be missing something Davey. You just said that James was the only driver you audited and now you just said that you audited several so which is it?" Alvin asked.

Davey knowing he had been caught in a lie tried to change the subject and quickly end this meeting as soon as possible.

"Alvin I need you to sign this stating what I had discussed with James." Davey said.

"No Davey, I can't do that. You've singled this man out because of him filing a grievance. I'm not signing anything. In fact I'm going to call the union as soon as I get out of here and on the road and tell Matt the crap you just tried to pull." Alvin replied, sounding upset.

Davey was shocked and to say the least he didn't know what to do. He was like a fish out of water. We stood up and just walked out.

After going in the office against Davey and the way he constantly lied about things I decided I needed to leave a paper trail. I went ahead and filed the grievance anyway that night.

DATE GRIEVANCE FILED: March 28, 1997

EXPLAIN GRIEVANCE: *The center manager called me into the office on 3-28-97. I had failed to complete a service cross on several packages, sign off my DVIR book, and I left my pager on in my package car. I was written up and suspended. I feel I was singled out and disciplined due to the fact I am a union steward and also that I had filed a grievance on 3-27.*

REMEDY SOUGHT: *I want the union to carry this as far as possible.*

The grievance was never heard and in fact it was settled before the local level hearing, and I didn't receive any discipline at all for this. What Davey had done was that he had retaliated against me for exercising not only my contractual rights, but also my rights that are guaranteed to me under the protection of the National Labor Relations Act. I was in fact SINGLED out and held to a higher standard than the other employees and I had received discipline due in part for being a job steward.

Davey screwed up when he only audited me. If he'd audited several other drivers as well at the time, then I wouldn't have had a leg to stand on. Everything was settled, or at least I thought, but more of the same harassment continued to happen over the next couple of weeks.

There was one other incident that involved a driver who rarely ever got into trouble. The incident really bothered me a lot and still does to this day. A driver named Tommy came up to Davey and asked to take off for two days to care for his sick children who had the chicken pox. Davey turned him down on the spot. There shouldn't' have been a problem with this since Tommy had the sick days to spare, his personal option days. But it wasn't the fact that Davey turned him down that bothered me, but it was what he told him in the process.

I saw Tommy leaving after this had happened, and Tommy was visibly upset. I stopped him and asked him what was going on. Tommy told me that Davey asked him if he was married, to which he answered yes. Davey then asked Tommy if his wife worked, at which Tommy answered yes. Davey's reply was, "Sounds like she needs to quit work and stay home with your kids. The answer is no." For management who 'prides' itself in portraying an image of being a 'family oriented' company to say something like this to this man is nothing, but a lie of deceit...but typical of them.

Tommy called in for those two days anyway and received a warning letter for failing to show up to work, but it was later thrown out after the local level hearing and it was determined that he did have personal days to use.

Chapter 10

"Friday morning: Management is cutting the routes back to reflect that there will be a large number of scabs if there is a strike called. What are they thinking of? This may very well be the end of the UPS that we know."

It's been rather routine for management to begin a pre-contract campaign to slack off of the 'production standards' and the daily harassment associated with it. Their propaganda machine usually started in the months prior to the labor contract, between the Teamsters Union and UPS, expiring, but this time it was kind of different, a lot different. Nothing was being said about what management was going to offer us or what they thought the outcome from negotiations would be. It was almost as if they had a secret about something highly sensitive and they were almost taunting us as a child might do with, "I know something you don't know." They were indeed playing mind games with us. The truth is that it was totally the opposite of management's past negotiating tricks and tactics to 'wine and dine' us in an attempt to woo us over to their side and run the contract on through. They immediately, in the last days before the contract was due to expire, began to escalate the tensions by stepping up the levels and frequency of harassment. This action came close to having several flash points within our center.

The IBT had previously organized an informational picket that was carried out a short time before the contract was due to expire. I remember that most participated and had a good time out there and the news crews and newspaper reporters were taking pictures of the whole ordeal and they were eating it up. There were a lot of good signs we carried in protest, but my favorite and the most ironic one read, "Just Practicing."

All the managers in the center came out to the edge of the building and watched us picket during this sanctioned demonstration. It was supposed to had been a nationwide coordinated event that took place at all package centers and it was primarily orchestrated to turn the heat up and display a show of union muscle and member solidarity directed towards management who were at the time, dragging their feet through the negotiations.

After the picket that morning, we all returned to the center and were 'greeted' by the management who all said that we probably had cost them some business, and sure enough their phones began to ring off the hook that day once the reports of the picket got out with people wanting to know if we were on strike.

Every time a contract nears expiring the competition, Federal Express and RPS, begins their scare tactics on our customers. They would tell them that they needed to go ahead and start diverting their volume to them and if they waited to see whether or not we would go on strike that it may be too late to help them. Federal Express and RPS began, with their campaigns, to steal our volume and with this informational picket starting early, which didn't help matters much for UPS's management.

The harassment continued to escalate in nature and frequency. Management began to use new tactics, up to the last week of July 1997. Davey was still on me and several other drivers about running over allowed, but we dealt with it in our own way. We had other things of importance other than Davey being a bully.

The contract was due to expire on July 31, 1997 at midnight, and as of yet the IBT and UPS management had not reached a tentative agreement for us to vote on. With all the other past contracts, they had reached an agreement for us to vote on well before the contract was due to expire.

That's when rumors had begun to surface that management might actually try to force us out on strike in an attempt to bust the Teamsters Union once and for all at UPS. Tension was at an all time high in Huntsville, and I was being bombarded throughout the days leading up to the expiration with questions from everyone on whether or not I had heard anything new on the contract. I hadn't heard anything not even from the union, and that in itself was strange.

The mood of the managers in Huntsville was that of arrogance. They weren't saying anything about the contract and they were all being tight lipped and told us they had no information. What a bunch of lies, because we knew they all had attended a meeting in Birmingham Alabama a couple of days earlier and the main topic was about what to do in the event that a strike was called.

The network news stations had been reporting on the 'impending labor crisis,' as they called it, for several days now and I managed to find out more from them than I did my own local union. That was where I first heard that the Teamsters had agreed to a contract extension with UPS management in a last ditch effort to try and come to a tentative agreement. That was what management was claiming, but with all indications they were still cleaning the system out and trying to make arrangement's to transport the volume once a strike was called. They were just buying time.

With this news I began to get an uneasy feeling about the whole thing, I thought that the management at UPS might be crazy enough to force us out, but what would it accomplish? They were actually contemplating taking this course of action knowing that in the end it could ruin them, and I became somewhat distressed after learning of this latest round of news.

That Friday, while at the center, before the contract deadline, the center management team had begun to cut routes out and some routes back in anticipation of a strike. We had already suspended making pickups in an attempt to 'clean out' the system which meant that whatever packages where in UPS's delivery system was going to be delivered and that no new packages would be picked up that could become 'stranded' in UPS's delivery system in the event of a strike.

I became somewhat concerned and finally they began to talk. They were indeed planning for a strike, and to top it off they were figuring on at least 80% of the Teamsters at UPS to scab and cross the lines within the first couple of days.

"Most of you will be here at work on Monday morning." A supervisor replied, as he continued to cut out routes.

What was going on in their minds? They were actually going to force us to go out and they thought the majority of us were going to scab. This was not just Huntsville's management way of thinking, but the general mentality of the company nationwide. Management actually thought the majority of the members wouldn't support a strike and would scab by no later than the third day into the strike.

Just a few weeks prior to this bold move by the management, the stage had been set for a showdown after we had received ballots in the mail from the IBT to vote on whether or not to authorize them to call a strike if negotiations failed. With an overwhelming majority, the UPS Teamsters voted to authorize the IBT to call a strike and I have to admit that I thought that this alone would be enough to give the union a little more leverage in reaching an agreement and to show management that we weren't playing games with them. I would have never guessed that it would've come to this.

I left for home that Friday evening after delivering my route and I was scheduled to attend my ten-year class reunion that very weekend. I couldn't think of anything other than what could be possibly going on in the management's minds at UPS. UPS' CEO was sticking to his "last and final offer" to the very end and it began to look very bleak. I continued to watch the news networks only to find out that UPS had taken out a full-page ad in the Washington Post late edition that Friday evening, July 31, telling our customers to expect a disruption in service. I knew then that it was on.

Finally, on Sunday morning I received a call from Matt that the Teamsters IBT General President Carey was still meeting trying to reach a tentative agreement before the midnight deadline, after granting management an extension at the request of John Wells, Director of the Federal Mediation and Conciliation Service, but it didn't look too promising though. Matt would go ahead and send the picket signs over to Huntsville via another member, and he told me to hang around by the phone that day until he called me to let me know about what to do, and he wanted me to call Alvin and Josey, and the other stewards to let them know what was going on.

I stayed at home that whole day Sunday, glued to the TV, watching everything I could just trying to find out something about the marathon talks that were still underway. Finally about 10:00 p.m., I was watching CNN when the Chief Negotiator for UPS emerged from the meetings to state that no agreement had been reached and that all talks had been called off.

Shortly after a few questions were posed by the reporters, IBT President, Ron Carey, walked out and immediately called a press conference. Ron Carey stated, "A strike was imminent" and he went on to declare that management had not wanted to negotiate, and in fact wanted a strike. He then stated to the public that he was on his way to his office to get word out to the 206 different Teamster Locals that represented the members who worked at UPS. It was on.

At 12:01 a.m., we would strike a company that in its 97-year history never had a nationwide strike called against it. I finally received word from Matt who told me the decision from IBT was to strike and for me to be at UPS picketing at 12:01 a.m. I needed to leave as soon as possible so I could meet everyone down there to help get everything set up.

Lesley was up watching the news and after I hung the phone up she asked me what were we going to do? I kissed her on the forehead and told her not to worry about it that it probably wouldn't last a day or two and that everything would be all right. I gathered up my things and headed to the center.

As I pulled out of my driveway, I called Alvin on my cell phone and his wife answered the phone and said that he had already left on his way to the center. I remember while driving to the building that I was feeling a bit of relief that we were finally going to show them something. UPS's management had brought this on themselves and it was way past time for them to get a taste of what they had been dishing out to us for so many years.

The closer to the center I came I actually began to get excited about it, and the uncertainty of what was actually going to happen and I began to look forward to it. Little did I know what was in store for us in the coming days.

As I turned the corner onto Winchester road off of Highway 231, I immediately began to see some people already there and they were busy setting things up in front of the building on the street. I looked at the clock on my radio as I began to slow down and it was now about 11:45 p.m.

I slowed down to pull into the parking lot of a business situated across from the UPS building and Josey came walking over to where I was parking. I got out of my truck and stretched a little to try and ease the tension and anxiety that I was feeling. I looked over to where the other three people were busily working laying things out and I noticed that it was Petey, a feeder driver and a mechanic named Gary, and 'Burr. They were setting up some lawn chairs and laying out picket signs.

"Well, I never thought they would ever go through with it Josey", I said.

"Well this thing may be over by Monday morning when they realize they really goofed up and the customers start calling them complaining, but who knows for sure?" Josey replied. Josey asked me to help him unload some things that were in the back of his truck and asked me if I had called Alvin. I told him yes that his wife said he was on his way. "Good" he replied, "Help me carry this stuff back over to the sidewalk in front of the building," Josey asked. I leaned over and looked into the bed of his pickup truck and Josey had about two dozen signs, hammers and various other things that would at least get us through the night until we figured out from Matt what the outlook was on the strike and see what we had to work with.

I gathered up an armful of things and walked on across the road to where Gary and Petey were and laid everything that I was carrying out onto the sidewalk. They both stopped what they were doing and came up to me and I greeted them both and shook their hands.

Besides Josey, Petey was probably one of the most experienced members we had involving something like this, with them both experiencing the nationwide truckers strike in the 70's. Petey came from Local 299 out of Detroit. He was a member of that local when Jimmy Hoffa Sr. was the Business Agent and often told me what the Teamsters were like then, compared to now. Petey was a "real" truck driver. He stood about 6'1 and about 240 pounds and was strong as a bull. He was one rough looking character if you didn't know him, but if he liked you...he was very friendly to get along with, and if he didn't like you, he just wouldn't have anything to do with you.

I helped them finish setting everything up that we had at the moment and we all stood around discussing the events from the last couple of days that led up to this moment. It was a clear, humid summer night with a slight breeze blowing. Alvin came pulling up to where we were standing and we stopped talking and Josey leaned over to see who it was, he didn't know what Alvin drove and Alvin leaned over the seat and rolled his window down and asked us where we had parked at. Gary pointed toward across the street, and Alvin pulled in over there to park and got out. Alvin was combing his hair as he walked across the street asking us what we knew and if we had heard anything else. We all shook our heads and told him we hadn't heard a thing yet.

By this time a couple of other employees were starting to show up and it wasn't quite 12:00 a.m. yet. Josey held a sort of informal meeting with those who were already there, to let us know what we could and couldn't do on a picket line. We didn't want anything that would warrant management going to the courts for an injunction to limit the number of picketers allowed on the line at one time. That action itself would have a very detrimental effect on the expression to the public that we so desired to obtain. Abel came walking from across the street, as Josey was wrapping up his speech, and by now there were about two-dozen or so people there, with a continuous trickle of others as the deadline of midnight approached.

There wasn't anyone of importance at the building that night representing management in Huntsville. There were only two part-time supervisors inside. I would have figured that UPS would have had at least a full time manager there when all this had started.

Josey and I were talking when someone hollered out that there was someone standing in the door of the customer counter with a flashlight. Josey walked over to his truck and came back with a huge flashlight, and as he cut it on, it looked as if it was a searchlight or something. Josey shown the light over to where they were and there were two figures standing in the door, and when the light hit them, they both jumped back out of the door like two roaches would do after someone cut the lights on.

We all began to laugh and Abel said that it's almost time. It was almost to the point of being ceremonious. Everyone looked at their watches to count down as the midnight deadline approached. Ten, nine, eight, seven, six, five, four, three, two, and then one. We were officially now on strike.

Everyone who had a sign began walking up and down the sidewalk in front of UPS. We didn't really know what to do, but at the time it seemed appropriate to start picketing, after all we were now on strike. I grabbed a sign and began pacing back and forth, trying to get a feel for it. It seemed odd and strange, but it didn't have the monstrous feeling of power that I had envisioned it would feel like. At this time of morning there wasn't any traffic moving. I couldn't help but think how stupid management was for forcing us out on strike. I really, at the time, didn't fully understand the "big picture" of everything encompassing the reasons why we were out here in the first place. I thought it was for something trivial but it didn't matter much to me at the time, because I had put my trust in the Union and IBT President Ron Carey, and without fail I was going to support them both for as long as it took. I understood the principles and issues that were involved, but I had my doubts to why really it had happened. Was it the fact that management was truly the 'evil giant' that was hell bent on crushing the working man or was it for other reasons?

Very few people came by that early in the morning, even though it was a main road for several small towns on the outskirts of Huntsville, and those people who did drive by slowed down to take us all in. Some of those who drove by honked their horns in support and some told us to get our butt's back to work and gave us the "finger".

Abel was standing next to me when one person came by cussing us and revving his engine as he passed. We just looked at each other and laughed. "What a dumb ass," Abel said.

Josey came up to us and asked us if one of us wanted to go with him to pick up a Huntsville feeder driver who was stuck in Atlanta. I looked at Abel to see if he wanted to, and he said that it didn't matter to him, so I told Josey that I would ride over there with him.

Atlanta was nearly four hours from Huntsville, and before we left, Alvin and Abel said they'd keep everything straight and all the steward's exchanged cell phone numbers just in case something came up.

Josey went to get his truck while I called my wife to let her know I was going to ride with Josey to Atlanta and that I would be back soon. Josey pulled up to where I was standing and picked me up and we were on our way.

The driver we were going to pick up, Mack, was covering a run for the driver who started on Sunday nights and ran to the Pleasantdale hub over in Atlanta. He got caught at the hub after midnight, and once the picket lines were set up he refused to pull his loads across them. Mack stated that the management at the hub was threatening some of the drivers that were caught there and were stating that if they refused to pull the loads that they had ready for them when the strike was called that they would face abandonment of their jobs and would face being discharged. They didn't have his trailers loaded when the deadline came and passed and everyone in the hub walked off the job including Mack who made arrangements to try and catch a ride to get back to Huntsville.

That left a lot of the hubs supervisors trying to finish the work, but their attempt was in vain because who was going to pull the loads? Josey said that Mack had caught a ride with an employee of the hub that lived over in Rome, Georgia and then caught a ride from there to the UPS center in Fort Payne Alabama. We were to pick Mack up at a truck stop right down from the center that he stopped at regularly when he was on the P'dale run.

We arrived at the truck stop and I climbed into the rear seat of Josey's truck and Mack came strolling out to the truck still wearing his browns. Mack climbed in and buckled up and began to tell us what was going on over at the P'Dale Hub in Atlanta. Mack said that management had begun to encircle the hub with all the trailers they had on the yard in an attempt to close the Hub off from view of everyone including the media. "The lines are up over there with probably a couple of hundred people or so on them. It sounded like a party over there or something," he said.

We arrived back to Huntsville and Mack asked Josey what he was going to do about getting his personal truck back, which was still parked on the company property and that he had some reservations about crossing the picket line. I think back to that moment and I knew what was he was thinking. He was wondering if he crossed the line to get his truck would that make him a scab? Josey quickly dispelled any concerns Mack had to this thought and we both decided to accompany Mack to get his belongings.

His truck was still on UPS's property and he also had some personal effects in his locker that he wanted to get as well. Josey said that he and I would walk over there with him and go inside to give them back his key to the building. So we all three began walking towards the building and walked around to the back door of the center. Josey pounded on the door with his fist and replied, "That'll wake them up." We all laughed about it.

"Or...get us put in jail for scaring them to death," I replied.

Finally after about a minute or so of standing there beating on the door we heard a voice on the other side ask us, "Who's there?"

Mack looked at Josey and me and then Josey said, "The big bad wolf, let me in or I'll blow the door down." I couldn't help but to laugh. The voice asked nervously, "What do you want?" "We want to give you your building keys back and Mack needs to get some things out of his locker," Josey told them.

"Hold on a minute," he said. After about two or three minutes we heard the door unlock and a supervisor stuck his head out and looked around. He was acting like he was expecting an ambush or something, and finally after checking everything out he opened the door all the way to let us in.

"I had to call Davey to find out what he wanted me to do." He said it would be alright, but he wanted me to ask Mack where his loads were and the tractor he had left from Huntsville in were at?" said the other supervisor named Casey.

"They are sitting in Atlanta at the hub," Mack replied. Davey wanted me to tell you that if that's where they were that you've abandoned your equipment," Chuck said.

Josey stepped forward and pointed his finger at Casey, "Now listen here bubba, those are struck goods and the contract states that he doesn't have to cross a picket line." I thought for sure Josey was going to do something crazy. He was a Christian man, with a rough past, and I knew that he was unpredictable in his actions, and so did management, especially when it came to organized labor. "If Davey has a problem with that then he needs to come on down here and we'll talk about it out front," said Josey.

Needless to say, nothing else was said about it at that time, but Davey would try to make it become an issue later on.

Josey and I stood there waiting for Mack to come down from his locker upstairs and after he came down, we left, not saying anything else to either one of the part-time supervisors. We were no longer on the same team, not that we were to begin with, but now it was different, and they both must have felt like they were now truly the 'real enemy'. Mack drove his truck back across the line and parked it across the street with all of ours.

By now the pre-loaders who had been scheduled to start late this morning, in anticipation of the strike, began to show up and park across the street with everyone else. The sun was beginning to poke over the mountains that surrounded Huntsville and traffic was beginning to pick up. Josey gave the order for everyone who had been assigned to picket on the Parkway to take positions up on both sides of Highway 231/431, which is one of the main arteries that lead into Huntsville from the outlying county.

Several members picked up signs that were in a pile beside some lounge chairs that were arranged on the sidewalk in front of the center. As they walked up the sidewalk to take their positions to picket, Davey came driving down in front of us and proceeded to turn into the parking lot of the center. Several people shot him the 'finger' as he drove by and many more yelled and thrust their signs in the air as a sort of defiance against him and what he represented I guess, as he passed them. Davey and I made eye contact and I grinned as he passed me, and he became somewhat disturbed and gunned his truck into the parking lot.

Now the local news stations had arrived and began sitting up their cameras and linking up with the station via satellite to broadcast a live report from the picket line. They were attempting to be 'the first on the scene' and were hurriedly getting the cameras out as other news trucks began to arrive and pull up on the curb just in front of the building. Alvin was standing there with Josey and myself and he asked the two of us who wanted to talk to them. Josey said immediately he didn't want to and Alvin said to me that it really didn't matter to him so I decided for us.

We had decided early on, and presented our decision to the members at our site that no one other than a steward was to give interviews to the media while on the picket line. That way no one could run the risk of giving false or misleading information that could jeopardize the chance of losing any public support that we may have had at the moment, or as far as that goes, any future support.

I met with the reporter across the street and she asked several routine questions in regard to why we were striking, if we supported the leaders on this and what our plans were. "We didn't have any plans," I thought to myself but did not let on to her any different. I didn't have time to rehearse for the questions that were presented to me and I answered the best that I could. I simply told her that we would be out here until we won, no matter how long it would take.

The time was now around 7:30 a.m., and the morning rush hour traffic was at its peak. A lot of the people that drove by blew their horns and gave us the thumb up while a few just drove by and gave us the 'finger'. "What a bunch of morons," I thought to myself as a driver shot me a bird and yelled at me, "get back to work". I kind of laughed it off, although I wouldn't have minded so much to put a brick through his windshield.

Everything calmed down after the rush hour and the majority of the drivers had reported to us to find out what was next. Alvin called for a meeting.

Everyone came walking back up to our temporary base camp and laid their signs down on the side walk, with the exception of a dozen or so who remained walking the line, and the steward's explained to everyone how they were to conduct themselves while out on the line. We explained to them that right at the moment, we didn't know anything more than they did and that Matt was scheduled to come by sometime later that day, after he visited the three other centers that were in our local besides us.

What we didn't know though, was that the Independent Pilots Association, UPS's pilots, who had been without a contract since June of 1997, had honored their threat to walk off the job when we did. They were the pilots of the UPS fleet of aircraft that transported the largest majority of the Next Day Air packages

At the headquarters of the IPA in Louisville, Kentucky they had a recording on their phone, which stated that there would be no company duty of any kind. This included no flying, training or company directed deadheading after the initiation of the strike.

A UPS spokesman said in a statement to the Washington Post, "That if the 2000 IPA pilots did not show up for work, the company would try to maintain some level of air traffic by calling 138 management level pilots." This would prove to be more fiction than fact since over the course of the next couple of days the managers would run out of hours and be grounded.

UPS would now be unable to limp along without the help from their bread and butter, the Next Day Air volume. We all found this welcome news and rejoiced and we tried to remain focused on our particular objective here in Huntsville, which was to just hold the picket line.

Meanwhile, we explained to the members how we wanted the lines set up and how we were going to rotate the picketers. Everyone was real receptive to our orders and rules. They knew that this was business and that we weren't trying to boss anyone around. We were charged with the responsibility to maintain order and enforce directives handed down to us by the union. By now the morning sun had begun to poke out from behind the haze and it started to get hot, real hot, and as anyone who has ever visited or lived in Alabama knows how the summer days can be hot and humid.

Josey walked to his truck and retrieved a clipboard and paper and he began to write down what supplies we had and what we needed to sustain us until we could get supplies to us. First and foremost we needed shelter from the elements and I, along with two others, said that we has some tarps that we used while camping.

I left immediately to go home, and then drive over to my father in-laws house to get the tarps and everything else that I thought we could use. Others went home and got their ice chest and chairs, lanterns, and just about anything else you could imagine.

By that afternoon when Matt arrived we had set up a real, more permanent base camp. It might have looked like a hobo village or shantytown, but hey...it worked. We had tied several of the tarps together and placed all of our belongings together under them, and during the course of the day other unions began to come by with money and supplies, food, ice, drinks, snacks and support.

UAW workers Local 1413 had taken up a collection for us the night before and had pledged to do so every week until we had won.

The United Rubber and Steel Workers had done the same thing and even offered us manpower if we needed anything done that we didn't want to dirty ourselves with. I declined any enforcement at the time, because there was no need for it, but I was sure to write down the names of several 'black shirt' contacts just in case we would have any problems out of scabs. The 'black shirts' were experts at dealing with the problems of scabs and had become well know for their 'strong stands' when it came to protecting their jobs. I appreciated the fact that they were willing to stand and fight with us if things came to that. They too offered, and delivered money as well as supplies.

During the course of the life of the strike, we would receive monetary donations, food, supplies even the use of a gas station on the corner, which allowed us the use, their restrooms any time we needed to.

We were doing a lot of business with one store, at the start of the strike, that was across the street until one of the clerks, whose wife was a supervisor in Huntsville, had popped off to one of the part-timers who was in there using the restroom and buying a cold drink. He had made a smart comment that warranted a little visit from some of the hard line, old timers. Needless to say when they showed up to discuss with him what was said, he changed his story real quick and apologized to them. After that incident a lot of us, including myself, will not do business with that store still to this day.

Matt finally showed up late that evening and we all gathered around to find out what was going on. Everything was going fine and in our local we had only one driver, at the time, to scab and she was from the UPS facility in Florence, Alabama, who mysteriously received a dump truck full of gravel in her driveway one evening courtesy of the Teamsters.

Management was still being defiant and they thought that we'd give in after a day or two, and start crossing the lines in masses. UPS's CEO was still sticking to his "last and final offer". We'd stick this out and show them and we became even more so determined to do that very thing. After the years of the daily abuse and mistreatment by the management of this company it was a welcomed and warm thought that we could now engage in an act of revenge. If they just knew how much fun we were having on the picket line in Huntsville they would have settled right then.

The members would continue to take turns at working shifts and I along with Josey, Gary, Alvin, and Abel, along with several others, all spent 15-20 hours a day during the beginning of the strike at the picket line. We'd sleep in our cars and trucks, and would eat most of our meals down there trying to keep an eye on everything. Not for one moment did that line go without a watchful eye of one of us being present, not that it was necessary, because we had very strong brothers and sisters down there fighting management every step of the way. We really didn't have anything to worry about except for the possibility of someone showing up drunk, drinking on the line, or fighting with passing motorist, which would have had you sent home if we caught you doing it.

The first confrontation with management happened within the first three days of the strike. Davey had walked out there to where we were standing being followed closely by a Huntsville City police officer who had been hired by management to remain on the property 24 hours a day for protection. Davey came up to just the edge of what he perceived was the property line of UPS. Management had planted a row of pine trees at what they thought was the property line and he stood there with the police officer. Davey approached us and Josey stepped forward to kind of meet him half way. "Y'all are going to have to move this tent off of our property now!" Davey said.

"We're not moving anything," Josey replied. "For your information 'Jack' we have 50 feet from the center of the highway and our tent is on our side," Josey said.

The police officer was kind of nervous thinking how this could have very easily escalated into a confrontation, like in the past with the 'black shirts', and stepped a little closer toward in between Josey and Davey.

By now several people standing around watching this had picked up a couple of signs that had some heavy sticks on them and Davey stepped back not knowing for sure if he was off of UPS property or not, and out of protection.

The police officer radioed in to his dispatch to find out about the property line disagreement and after about three or four minutes later the answer came over the radio. The officer told Davey that he was standing on the state right of way. Davey stormed off mad as hell with his tail between his legs as several picketers whooped and hollered, and taunted him.

Josey told several of us that we were going to be moving the tent as Davey headed back towards the building. I thought to myself, "What are you talking about, heck we just won a small victory and here you want us to move this tent?" We wound up moving the tent, only closer to the UPS building under the pine trees that they had planted. Seems that they had mistakenly planted those trees on public property and we were now hanging support ropes and signs from the trees. The move under the pine trees provided a little more shelter form the sun. It was a good slap in the face for them and another small victory for us.

The negotiations between the Teamsters and UPS yielded very little progress, even though the use of a Federal Mediator. UPS' Chief Negotiator was sticking with the 'last and final' offer presented on behalf of UPS to the Teamsters. IBT President Ron Carey refused to even entertain the thought of presenting that dime store offer for us to vote on.

August 5, 1997, the Teamsters Union asked the U.S Labor Secretary, Alexis Herman, to try and help restart the stagnated talks with UPS. President Clinton had stated in a later interview about the UPS strike and what impact it has had so far on the country, "I'm worried by the spreading impact of the UPS strike but I am not willing to intervene yet."

So far, as of August 5, only eight people had been arrested for picket line altercations and with a total of sixteen nationwide.

Tuesday morning we had begun a tactic called a "rolling picket which is where we, about four Teamsters with picket signs, would load up in a vehicle and follow the supervisors as they left the center to make business deliveries. While they were inside the business making a delivery we'd get out and picket the business. This proved to be very effective and we had a lot of businesses refuse to accept deliveries after we began doing this. Everyone who was scheduled to report for the evening shift had reported and Alvin relieved me that afternoon after giving another interview with Chan nel 19 news. I then drove home to be with Lesley and Mattie.

I pulled into the driveway of my home after the twenty-minute drive and they walked out into the driveway to meet me. Mattie had just turned nine months old and was very eager to see me. I took her from Lesley and she immediately took my hat off of my head and placed it onto hers half cocked. I hugged and kissed Lesley and asked how their day had been. She replied that everything was fine and asked me if I had heard any news on progress in talks. I said no that they had scheduled talks for Thursday and maybe they'd get this thing settled so we can go back to work.

I went inside my house and started to sit Mattie down on the floor. She began to cry and clung to me not wanting me to let go of her. I sat her down anyway for just a second and she immediately stretched her arms out and worked her fingers calling me and crying like the world was ending. I bent over and picked her back up. I was tired and didn't feel like fooling with anybody. Lesley looked at me, and I could tell that my reaction to Mattie had really upset her, and she just turned and walked back into the kitchen. She was fixing dinner and this would be the first time I would have been home to eat with them in three days.

I sat down in a chair in the living room with Mattie in my lap playing with a book while I flipped on the news and kicked my shoes off. Lesley was slamming cabinets and shuffling pots and this was wearing on my nerves. I got up and cut the TV off and walked into the kitchen where she was, and I was going to be a stupid man and ask her what was wrong? Her reply was a simple one; "You just worry about what's going on down there and not worry about us at home."

I just walked out and went back into the living room and sat back down and hunted for the remote to the TV and turned it on to CNN. It was getting close to 6:00 p.m and the national report had come on. The UPS strike was the main story as with all the stations and it was reported that no progress had been made that day. I thought to myself, "I thought the talks were to resume Thursday." What was happening was that management had asked President Clinton that evening to enact the Taft-Hartley Act.

"Oh crap," I yelled out and Lesley came into the living room peeling a tomato and asked me what was going on. I told that management was trying to get the President to step in and enact the Taft-Hartley Act.

"What's that?" She asked curiously. The President can step in if a strike poses an imminent threat to National health and safety. That would force us to possibly vote on UPS' proposal, which we didn't want to do. If the President does that then we've lost the strike. We would've been beaten and most of all our spirit would have been broken.

I stayed at home until around 10:00 p.m., and tucked them both into bed and headed back down to the picket line. I turned the corner to where the picket lines were set up and as I looked them over while parking I thought of the conversation between Lesley and me earlier. "They could make it without me after all," I thought to myself, and climbed out of my truck and walked across the street to where everyone was congregated.

I got the lowdown from Alvin who was still there and fixing to go home. Everything had gone as planned for the evening with the exception of an interview he had given earlier and the news station had distorted the facts. I told Alvin that I would take care of that problem myself when they showed back up for another interview.

I walked Alvin back across the street to his car was parked and we discussed a 'possible' problem that we might have. We possibly could have a scab right here in Huntsville. We went through a mental check list of the names of the people we knew weren't out here and crossed checked them against each other's memory. We narrowed it down to about six people, but we were still unsure of whom it could be.

"We'll find out who they are." I replied confidently to Alvin and patted him on the back.

Management wasn't moving any volume, to our knowledge and what little they did move didn't amount to much to even be concerned about. I told Alvin about how UPS was trying to get the President to step in and he felt the same way as I did about it. If he did we'd be finished and they'd bust this strike. Alvin left and wished us luck and headed home.

I walked back across the street where Abel and several others were clustered together talking and telling jokes. It was a cool, clear night and the humidity had tapered off. They were calling for rain to move in towards the end of the week. It felt good outside and was a welcomed relief from the heat we had to deal with during the day. Abel was having a little fun with a stick he had and would jab people in the butt with it and then wave it around pretending to be a lunatic. It was real funny and he helped relieve some of the tension and stress everyone was feeling.

I asked everyone if they had heard the news about what management was asking Clinton to do? Everybody said no and asked me what it could mean for us. I explained to them what the consequences could be if President Clinton invoked the Taft-Hartley Act and everybody was concerned about it.

"He's not going to do that." Josey replied, while whittling on a stick.

"What makes you think that?" Ronnie asked curiously.

"Because the Teamsters gave him a lot of money for his election." Josey replied, drawing the interest of everyone around.

Josey was right. The Teamsters Union had endorsed him in both elections and had contributed millions of dollars to his campaign and there was no way he would crap on the Teamsters like that. It would damage his political career.

"Just be glad we don't have a Republican in office like ol' Reagan." Someone interjected into the conversation.

Everything was calm that night and on in to the early morning hours we heard the sound of a big truck gearing down fixing to make the turn around corner heading towards us. Sure enough it was an 18-wheeler that had just turned off the highway running wide open.

"It's a shiny wheels," Petey yelled out, meaning that is was an independent driver using his personal truck to pull struck goods, which made him a scab.

We all jumped up and grabbed our signs. The driver was running wide open by us and turned into the entrance to UPS's property barely slowing down enough to safely make the turn into the entrance which caused both trailers to rock back and forth violently and almost causing the rear trailer to turn over. We were running along beside him yelling and calling him a "scab". He must have been terrified from the sight of twenty-five men with sticks screaming at him.

"I'm going to follow him and see where he goes when he leaves," Josey replied, as he ran across the street to wait in the shadows inside his truck. We all stood on the sidewalk screaming and hollering profanities at him.

The driver pulled around to the side of the building and blew his horn for what seemed like minutes trying to get a manager to come out and help him. Chuck, a part time supervisor, ran out from around the back of the building to meet the scab driver. We could see the scab driver jump out once he saw Chuck, and run around his tractor trying to unhook from the loads as fast as he could. We then saw the scab hand Chuck something, and it looked like Chuck signed it and the scab driver took off headed back towards us wide open.

We were all at the entrance and it took everything I had to keep from throwing something through his windshield. We were powerless other than to hurl words and insults unless we dared to cross that point of no return. The only thing I could think of was violent thoughts. I wished for about two-dozen 'black shirts' then but I thought if that's what this is to come to then we'd need to do it ourselves. It was our strike and our jobs that this vermin scab was taking away from our families and us. I then understood at how picket line violence erupts. The scab didn't even have the backbone to look at us in the face as he tried to avoid eye contact like the coward he was and he sure wasn't about to say anything or gesture to us out of fear of being pulled out of his truck and us stomping his ass right then.

The scab pulled on out and headed toward the light at the intersection of highway 231/431 to make the left back towards the Interstate. The light turned red and the scab ran on through it afraid of being caught there with us in pursuit. Josey pulled on out and gave chase. Josey had a CB radio in his personal truck and was talking to the scab while following him. Josey told us that he followed the scab about twenty miles outside of Huntsville while the scab slammed on his brakes trying to get Josey to run into him. Josey said that he told the scab that by the time he bought a new set of tires from rubbing flat spots on his tires from skidding he'd probably lose money that night. Josey said that the scab was begging for help on the CB and Josey was telling everybody that was listening that he was a scab and not to help him.

The truth is the scab was all alone. He was not only a scab in just our eyes, but everyone's else's as well who just happened to be listening to the CB that night at his pleas for help. Josey said he had the scab so upset that the scab got off on the wrong exit, heading into oncoming traffic. After about 45 minutes of chasing the scab, Josey returned and tried to calm everyone down.

A few minutes later Chuck, a part time supervisor, came walking up to where we were and asked if one of us would walk down and break the trailers down, or separate them, for him that the scab had brought in. We laughed him all the way back down to the building.

That was all the excitement we had that night and we had our first taste of scabs. We were all left thinking about how we would deal with scabs in the future. Would we be willing to cross that line and act out in violence if need be to protect our jobs? We debated the issue and decided we'd take that up the next time it happened…if it happened.

The morning crew arrived just before the morning rush hour was to start with news that Clinton had declined to step in and ruled out any intervention at this point and stated that he thought that management's top brass should consider negotiating with the Teamsters and settle this dispute at the bargaining table. This was indeed sweet music to our ears and we had won another major battle against management that would ensure us the right to continue with the strike.

We had received word from other members in the local that the IBT was only going to be able to pay us $55.00 a week in strike benefits, which was a far cry from the money we were used to making while on the job. Mr. Sweeney, President of the AFL-CIO, put an end to any rumors that the Teamsters weren't going to be able to pay the strike benefits for long, because the IBT was hurting for cash and low on funds from an earlier strike which had depleted a lot of the funds that the IBT had on hand. Out of this check that we were going to get, we were going to have to pay union dues, which were $42.00, so in reality we were only going to draw $13.00 in strike benefits. Mr. Sweeney pledged to loan the IBT as much money as it took to ensure our victory. So now the IBT had the funding to sustain the strike for as long as it took. I'm sure that management had known the financial condition of the IBT and used that in determining the decision to force us out on strike thinking that there'd be a mutiny once the IBT declared they couldn't pay us anything for being out here, but management failed to consider the resolve of the AFL-CIO. They were probably thinking that this strike would bust the Teamsters Union financially, which would have destroyed the union, as we knew it. But management failed to 'get the big picture' that this was not just the Teamsters fight but organized labors as an institution as well. It was costing them dearly.

In a bold, rare, and one of the only 'good' things the old guard regime, in Local 402, did in the thirteen years of being a Teamster was to call a special meeting and vote unanimously to match the IBT's benefit check to all of Local 402's UPS members. They did this by cashing in a $25,000 CD that was being held by the bank they used. This would help and I give them credit for that move.

I talked to my Father in-law who was a USPS Letter Carrier and a member of the National Association of Letter Carriers Branch 462, which had their local here in Huntsville. He told me that he had talked to their President that evening and told me to give him a call. I called Lew that night at home and discussed in great detail, what was going on in our struggle and what we needed in regards to support. I was invited to attend their union meeting that Thursday night and to go before their members with what I was asking.

That Thursday evening I rode down with Jim, my father in law, and was introduced to everyone who was present for the meeting. I was then asked to join the local's officers at their table that was situated in front of the members until they were ready for my presentation, which would come at the end of their meeting.

I knew a lot of their officers real well, because they were carriers downtown with me, and I spoke to the daily and had even eaten lunch with them numerous times not knowing of their positions in their union.

My time had come and I didn't have a prepared speech to read from. I spoke from the heart telling them that if UPS were successful at winning this strike then what union would be next? I went as far as to say as well, that if the Teamsters lost this strike, then this could very well set the stage for their contract which was coming up soon. They were really receptive and sat there with looks of encouragement on their faces. I explained to them everything I knew, and how this was not just about the Teamsters who work at UPS, but it was also about the very future of organized labor in America. I explained to them that although we may be competitors and when this is over that'll we'd go back to trying to put the other out of business, but this wasn't about that. We were "ALL" brothers and sisters in organized labor, and we needed to support one another. This was not only our fight but theirs as well. If UPS's management were successful at busting this union then who would be next?

I spoke for about fifteen minutes straight and the end of my speech the room erupted in applause. I was beginning to see how big this had become. I was asked to step out of the room while they discussed it amongst themselves and took a vote on what to do.

About five minutes had passed until I was called back into their meeting room before the members, and their President told me what they had decided to do. They were immediately writing a check to us, to the members of local 402, for the amount of $500.00 and pledged to do the very same thing again the following week if the strike was still going on. Lew had also pledge the use of their facilities, equipment and the most valuable asset they possessed...their members to come down and walk hand in hand with us. I was deeply moved and had never been so proud of my union family that I was there that night. It made me feel proud to be a union member and this is what solidarity was all about.

I was handed the check and thanked Lew, Glenn, Charlie and Max and everyone else I could, and was very anxious to get back to the picket line to tell the others what I had received for us. I walked up to Matt and told him where I had been and handed him the check. He looked it over and then looked at me in astonishment. I told him that Huntsville would get $200.00 of it since we had two centers in one and the other three centers would get $100 each. $100 would help buy ice, soft drinks, sign materials and other supplies that we needed. Everyone was really grateful for Branch 462's generosity in helping us financially and with manpower. Word had soon gotten out to the other unions in the area about what the Letter Carriers Union had done for us, and then the money started pouring in. We were getting money everyday and could now equip our lines with much needed supplies. Customers, and other union members were still coming by and dropping off food, money, drinks, ice and most of all prayers. We ate real well after that while on the line. Whenever we grilled out something, which was pretty much everyday, we'd fix an extra plate and carry it over to the police officers that were guarding the center. We never had one problem out of the police the whole time while we were out on strike, and management would have died if they knew we were smoozing up to their hired guards, and that we were feeding them every time we would eat. We were told by more than one of them that they were there just to do a job and hoped we won the strike. We understood their position and thanked them for being understanding with us, because there were a few times that probably warranted a little negative intervention by the police for some of the things we had done. It was rumored that the police were even stopping some of the management personnel nationwide, who were out in the package cars delivering to see if they had their physical cards and checked for faulty equipment on the vehicles, and were writing them a lot of tickets...it was great.

One thing that happened during one morning that had the potential for violence involved a package car driver named Murphy and a passing motorist. Every morning this motorist, the same guy everyday, just like clock work, would drive by the picket line and roll down his window cussing everyone out and shooting us the finger. After three or four days of this Murphy had enough. This guy drove by yelling obscenities at us and made the mistake of shooting Murphy a bird. One mistake the motorist didn't figure on...was being caught by the traffic light. Murphy saw that the light had caught him and he took off running out into the street and up to the intersection where the motorist had stopped before we could stop him.

Murphy stopped running when he got up to the car and walked over to the window and pecked on it. The motorist was shocked and became fearful of getting his butt kicked as Murphy told the guy to roll his window down, which the motorist refused to do it. Murphy then asked if he wanted to shoot him a bird now to pull over in the gas station parking lot and get out that he'd love to 'discuss' it with him like a man instead of like a coward. The guy begged Murphy not to hurt him and must have apologized a hundred times. Murphy told him that if he ever drove back by there and did anything like that again that he'd take care of the problem. Murphy walked off as the light turned green and everyone was watching him from their cars. Little did that driver know how close he had become to being a statistic.

We had noticed that management was now staffing the package cars with drivers from all over the southeast. This concerned us because we didn't know if any scab drivers were being used from another District. We didn't know if they were supervisors or actual drivers. Some of the people acted like they had never driven a package car in their life much less rode in one. They would stall the trucks as they pulled out from the center and were grinding gears. Every time something like that would happen we'd all start yelling at them laughing and pointing our fingers mocking them. This really unnerved them, and finally when they left the building or were coming back in from delivering the struck goods, they'd close the doors on the truck until they were safely back onto UPS property.

Another thing we were beginning to notice was that management had been towing in a lot of package cars since the first couple days of the strike. It seemed that the people they were staffing these trucks with knew very little about the equipment they were operating and were putting gasoline into trucks that used diesel fuel. We got a real kick out of that. Management was now sending out every truck they had with at least two people on them now. Supervisors driving the feeder equipment were bringing in what volume they had still in the system. It was reported that there was very little volume on the trailers, at times...less than ten percent, which contradicted management's claims of 80-90% full trailers. Lots of the trailers that were on the road were in fact empty, and were only out there for the public to see in an attempt to deceive the public into thinking that they were doing just fine without us, but this was hardly the case. They were struggling.

The strike was going well and there was no new information on any end in sight to the strike. The Letter Carriers Union, U.A.W workers, Steel Workers, Grocery Workers, I.B.E.W and many other different unions were there with us everyday now along with a UPS pilot from the IPA. He was out there with us three days out of that week dressed in his pilots uniform. It felt good to have the solidarity and support we were getting from everyone.

Many customers were beginning to instruct the supervisors not to come back onto their property citing, "Until our drivers are back we won't accept anything from UPS." They were going to do the best they could until we were back.

August 10, 1997, UPS's top brass were beginning to feel the pinch from the strike and coupled with the constant losses to the Union in regard to public support and a lack of Governmental intervention were running out of options. Despite the breakdown of negotiations, the Teamsters weeklong strike still posed no threat to the nations welfare that might prompt President Clinton's intervention. Labor Secretary, Alexis Herman had said Sunday, "The President recognizes that these are serious issues: The nature of part-time work, pension protection for American Workers. These are all issues that we care about," Herman said on NBC's Meet The Press. "But we don't believe that this situation has reached the state of what we define as a national emergency." The work stoppages damage to small businesses throughout the country has Governor's and business leaders clamoring for White house intervention. Herman said that the White House was sensitive to the plight of small businesses and is closely monitoring the strikes impact on the economy.

"The question of Taft-Hartley...is one that seems to me lies in the future, but not now." Treasury Secretary Robert Rubin said in analyzing the strike's economic implications. Counseling caution, Rubin said on ABC's This Week that, "The Act has very stringent requirements. It hasn't been invoked in over twenty years. In fact the last time a President tried to use it, he was rebuffed by the courts."

UPS's CEO questioned on CBS's "Face the Nation," urged the President to step in and stop serious damage to the economy. Without such intervention he doubted an agreement could be negotiated soon. A UPS spokesperson said today that more than 15,000 Teamster jobs were being eliminated. UPS top brass were once again trying to get the public involved by claiming economic concerns. The top brass were on the run and were grasping for straws.

We continued to hold the lines and had received the second installment of the money pledged to us by Branch 462 of the NALC. I had planned on holding onto it and only cashing it of we needed it and then once again dividing it among the five centers in North Alabama. It was time for us to get paid our last check from UPS, who still owed us one more payday. Matt had wanted management to meet us on neutral ground but they refused and we were forced to walk onto their property. They sat up a table in the parking lot and walked up to the picket line to let us know what was going on. I strongly disagreed with this because I knew management wanted to instill in everyone that they were still "in control". We instructed everyone to simply get their checks and come straight back and not talk to a single manager while down there. Josey walked on down with everyone and stood by as an observer to make sure management didn't say anything out of the ordinary to any Teamster that was down there getting their checks. We were sure that they'd be on the phones to their bosses to let them know the morale of the strikers. At the end of this 'show of power' the managers packed up and waived to everyone as they walked back into the building.

CNN had now begun to report that strike support was waning among some UPS workers nationwide. They began each interview with several "suspicious" employees on the news. The only question I had was why didn't they ever show anything that would indicate that they were even on the picket lines? They appeared to be acting in an event that was being staged to try and hurt the morale of those of us that were still out here. I strongly felt that this was just a strike-busting tactic instigated by management to try and press the issue of putting their "last and final" offer to a vote.

UPS's top brass mailed us a copy of their contract proposal with a 'heart felt' letter from the CEO portraying the IBT as a greedy monster who wanted to exploit the workers and deny us our rights to vote on this offer and that they were the lone and righteous savior. If the hell they put us through everyday, prior to the strike, was any indication of their interpretation as being a savior then I'd hate to see what a devil was like. The truth is we did vote Mr. CEO. We voted to strike and support our union and we weren't about to accept their offer.

There's no denying that the strike was beginning to hurt some drivers financially. That's when customers and local farmers came by offering anyone who needed it temporary work until we won the strike. We told anyone to come to one of the stewards and we'd get them what they needed before they even considered crossing the picket lines. We decided, as a group, to offer the work to the people who needed it the most and several drivers started work that day and I'm proud to say that they still came by and pulled their shift. It was fantastic.

We decided to make this strike as personal as we could when word began to get out in the news that certain companies were trying to turn the public against us. Naturally they sided with management and in turn were feeling the pinch in their profits and decided to do a little negative campaigning on UPS's behalf.

They tried to display that we were hurting their employees who had families and were being laid off as a result of our strike. We countered this by bringing our wives and children down to the picket line to walk with us (see photo insert). We wanted these turn coat-union hating companies and the general public to see that we too, had young children and families to provide for. This tactic made it very real as to the reason we were out here. We were out here not only for our children but theirs as well. Was America to turn into a part time employed country? Were their children to grow up and look forward to only part time jobs and never have a chance to achieve the American dream? We were fighting their battle as well, and they knew it.

Our plan was working. On August 14, it seemed that UPS's top brass was beginning to crack. Labor Secretary Alexis Herman described the talks that were going on between both parties as "substantive and detailed." Although the talks themselves were billed more as discussions rather than negotiations. After twelve hours of back and forth exchanges, the company suggested that there was room for compromise. Even UPS' CEO said that the company was willing to consider a deal that could be substantially different from what UPS had insisted was it's "last, best and final offer." UPS management was still insisting that the employees be afforded the opportunity to vote on its offer that they have mailed to our homes. The Teamsters weren't going to budge on this one bit.

By now the Independent Pilots Association began to warn UPS customers that even if the Teamsters strike was settled, service could soon be interrupted again. They had been operating without a contract since December of 1995. IPA President Bob Miller said," The day may soon come where we go out on strike and they honor ours." This turned the heat up on management and with increased pressure from customers for them to get this dispute resolved. We now had a commitment from three other airlines, Evergreen International, Southern Air Transport and Trans Continental not to transport struck goods for UPS. They were becoming unable to limp along now since they were running out of ways to move their struck goods.

One of the most low down and disgusting things UPS management had done during the strike involved an incident that happened on August 13, 1997. According to Lyn Gerry, "At 3:00 p.m., homeless residents at the Ridge Shelter, in Philadelphia Pennsylvania, had come forward stating that a brown UPS van regularly visits the Ridge Shelter to pick up homeless residents, which sneaks them back into the UPS facility, and pays them $5.00 and hour to cross picket lines set up at UPS.

The Teamsters Union and the KWRU, Kensington Welfare Rights Union, demanded an investigation by the mayor as to why city subsidized shelters are being used to recruit homeless individuals to break a strike and eventually throw striking workers into the ranks of the homeless." This was a new low even for UPS management. They didn't even have the decency to pay these poor people the $8.00 an hour they normally paid a part timer and here they are concerned for our health and rights. This clearly demonstrated managements lack of humanity and decency but at least they managed to save $3.00 an hour by screwing these poor homeless people.

On August 18, 1997 we received word that the Teamsters and UPS management had reached a tentative agreement that night to possibly end the fifteen-day strike. Secretary of Labor Alexis Herman announced the deal at 12:30 a.m., with Teamsters President Ron Carey and UPS's Chief Negotiator by her side. A UPS spokesperson later made the comment while being interviewed after the announcement of the agreement," to our Employees: We hope to welcome you back very soon." Little did we know the amount of hell that was in store for us in the upcoming weeks.

We had received the word that evening that the strike was over and we all decided to stand out on the roadsides thanking the public for their support. We received hundreds of thumbs up from people that passed by.

Everybody by that afternoon had begun to help at the dismantling of our camp and clean up the area. It was hard to believe that we had just beaten the management of UPS. The IPA pilot was there and we thanked him and took several pictures with him and pledged to go back out with them if the need arose. We received word to report to work the next day to 'begin the healing process' as management called it. I was relieved to have won the strike and that it was finally over but in the same sense I was worried like never before as to what was in store for myself and the rest of us once we returned. A supervisor, who had quit during the strike, in Huntsville, told us all about a 'hit list' management had comprised that detailed everything we said and had done during the strike. I was one of the ones at the top of the list. We all knew that they were going to be gunning for the leaders of the strike. Hell was coming.

We received word that there were only four scabs in the whole state of Alabama, that we knew of, with one being a driver in Florence, a mechanic at the hub in Montgomery and the one in Huntsville.

The only major thing that happened during the strike in Huntsville involved a supervisor named Woodson and a feeder driver named Petey. Before the start of the afternoon shift we decided to implement a new tactic that would hamper the driver leaving the building to deliver struck goods.

What we had decided to do was to walk at a normal pace while on the sidewalks and then slow down once we came to the entrance of the center, but not stopping. The police told us that as long as we kept moving and didn't stop that everything was okay and legal.

There were about thirty of us picketing at that moment when someone yelled out here comes another one. We noticed that a driver pulling out of the building and was leaving to possibly make pickups. It was Woodson, a supervisor from the pre-load. He was driving one of the new trucks, of course he wouldn't drive one of the crappy trucks we had everyday to deliver in, and he was by himself. Everyone took their positions and we began to slow down our pace in front of the entrance.

Woodson came driving up rather fast, to be in a parking lot, and stopped about fifteen feet from where we were picketing and began to race the motor in an attempt to intimidate us. I was watching the whole thing and he was looking us over real well. Woodson had now moved up to about three feet or so from where we were walking.

First of all he was a member of management who had been trained by UPS to drive safely and why he pulled up to us that close defies all logic. It was very dangerous to us and he knew better than to do it.

I had stopped just left of the truck and by now a police officer had stepped out of his patrol car and begun walking up to where we were telling us to stop and make him a hole so he could leave. Woodson was fuming and his whole head was red and it looked like he was going to burst a blood vessel in his neck. Several of us had begun screaming for everyone to get out of the way but it was drowned out due to Woodson racing the engine.

"Get out of my damn way," Woodson screamed while laying down on the horn and continuing to race the engine. There were several pickets who could not see the policeman walking towards us or hear us screaming for them to get out of the way because of this idiot blowing his horn. Finally everyone was trying feverishly to make a hole so Woodson could pull out. He then let out on the clutch and the package car lunged forward hitting several picketers. Petey was hit and fell to the ground screaming in pain. This UPS supervisor had just injured this man from this 'accidental' act. Woodson didn't show any emotion and he sure in hell didn't get out of his truck.

By now the police officers had called for an ambulance and for additional back up fearing a riot was about to break out.

Davey came walking out of the center and walked over to where Petey lay on the ground writhing in pain.

I dropped my sign on the ground and ran to a phone to call the local union and Jamie answered the phone. I asked for Matt, who was not there and was out visiting other lines. I proceeded to tell her about what just happened and she couldn't believe. She told me to hang up that she was going to call Matt immediately. I hung the phone up and ran back down to where an ambulance had already arrived and had begun treating Petey who was still on the ground.

Petey complained of neck and hip pain and the EMT's placed a brace around his neck and loaded him up to take him to the emergency room. Everyone on the line was outraged and was ready to drag Woodson out of the truck.

UPS took Woodson out of service for a day and then paired him up with another driver for safety reasons later that afternoon.

What Woodson didn't know was that the new truck he was driving had what was called a 'button clutch' which was different that a conventional clutch in terms of when it engaged. A conventional clutch engages gradually as you let out on the pedal whereas a button clutch engages fully with minimal pedal travel.

If this would have been one of us, which it wouldn't have been because we are more professional than him, we'd been fired on the spot and would've NEVER got our jobs back. Go figure.

When Woodson left that evening to go home he was escorted by Huntsville city police, because people had begun calling the center making threats against his safety. Several drivers had erected signs, and lay on the ground and made chalk out lines and various other tactics were used to let him and management know that we would not forget about this.

In the September 1997 issue of TDU's publication *Convoy Dispatch* they reported on the position of IBT General Presidential candidate Hoffa Jr. concerning the strike at UPS in which his supporters denounced our strike with "encouraging" phone calls being made to UPS criticizing Carey for even calling a strike. With many of Hoffa's big backers, such as UPS and Yellow Freight, pulling his chain he readily panhandles to their side while abandoning ours. This is from a man who has NEVER, EVER worked a day in his life as a Teamster and was only "allowed" to join a Local union just to satisfy the election nomination requirements! Corruption prior to his election runs deep with one such example being when a freight employer in Canada was found in violation of the election rules by placing pro Hoffa literature in their employees pay envelopes. Hoffa's own personal legal counsel during the 1996 campaign is on many Teamster employers' payrolls as well.

In an interview on Larry King Live on August 22, Hoffa said, 'I am calling for a trusteeship of the Teamsters Union" in a display of concern to the members regarding our rights while he has secretly joined sides with the anti-union members of Congress in an attempt to get the Government out of the Union and to gut our rights."

According to TDU in their September 1997 issue of *Convoy Dispatch*:

"In Chicago-based Teamsters Local 710 which covers some 6000 UPS Teamsters in downstate Illinois, and parts of Indiana and Iowa. They have a separate contract from the national one. Hoffa's key ally Frank Wsol and Hoffa running mate Patrick Flynn are the secretary treasurer and president of this local.

It seemed that the leaders of this local would not join the contract campaign to inform members. The IBT made resources available to Local 710, but they refused although the members of Local 710 wanted so desperately to join in the picket.

UPS management repeatedly asked IBT General President Ron Carey to give a contract extension but he refused. Local 710 broke ranks to do it. And, even worse, they gave UPS a signed deal that requires the union to give management five days notice before ever calling a strike. Once the strike was called, Local 710's officials stood on the sidelines as 'neutral' bystanders. When members from other locals traveled into 710 territory to picket, the Hoffanite leaders dutifully passed along managements threats that members had to stay away from picket lines."

This is the type of traitorous leadership we had to look forward to when Hoffa would later be elected as IBT General President.

Chapter 11

"Thursday, 7:23 p.m., Smitty and I get into the biggest fight yet. He is just looking to push me over the edge, but I will not allow him that pleasure. He drags me into the office and proceeds to discipline me for no reason. I have no respect for this 'rat'."

The IBT had filed numerous unfair labor charges against management during the course of the strike, and as part of the terms of management dropping their complaints against us, was for the Teamsters to drop theirs. Both sides were given amnesty for whatever actions were conducted legally within the realm of the law, but were questionable to the company and to the union. When the contract was voted on, and ratified by the members, only then did the IBT withdraw the charges.

We were all scheduled to return to work the following day, at the conclusion of the strike, and I have to admit that I was a little nervous about what to expect. I pulled into the parking lot and immediately noticed that several drivers were standing by their cars and talking amongst themselves.

I parked my truck and walked over to where they were. "What's going on guy's?" I asked.

"We're just waiting for one of y'all to show up," replied a driver.

"You don't need one of us to walk you in do you?" I answered jokingly.

"No, but we'd feel better in case they start in on us." He replied.

We finished our little conversation as we walked through the big open door in the front of the building and I looked around as we walked in and noticed that the belts were still running packages down them. "The preloads not finished yet," I thought to myself as I looked at my watch. I was surprised at this because there shouldn't have been but only a very little bit of volume that was still left in the system to be processed that had become stranded before the strike. Several supervisors passed us by as we walked further into the building without anyone of them speaking a single word to any of us. Not even a good morning. Nothing. This didn't bother me a bit. I just figured they were just being sore losers like they have always been. We walked on over and pulled our clipboards, called DIAD's, out of their holder and punched in. Most of the drivers that were already there were standing around in front of the offices talking amongst themselves quietly and every once in a while turning to see who might be standing near them that could be listening.

Everything seemed back to normal for the most part, but there was a gigantic presence of tension in the air. You could honestly almost reach out and grab it. The presence was overwhelming, to us, it was like a huge cloud engulfing and smothering everything in sight. Everyone was on edge from not knowing what was going to happen or what would be said at the first PCM since the strike had begun.

Davey came by and asked to see me in the office while he never stopped walking. I walked on over to his office and opened the door and noticed that all of the stewards had already been called and were waiting in the office for us. I walked on in and stood over beside Alvin and Davey shut the door.

"We need to put this behind us and concentrate on getting our business back." Davey replied getting right to the point with no formal greetings.

"I agree," Alvin said, "Provided the company can put this behind them," he finished.

"Well, we're going to move forward and try to forget the strike the best we can and like I said, concentrate on getting the business back." Davey replied, while reaching for several papers stacked on the edge of his desk. Everyone was in agreement about what needed to be done, but I knew that they had something in store for us in the near future or at least for those of us who were on their hit list.

"What about the so called hit list the company has on us?" I asked anxiously. Davey gave a poor performance in trying to look puzzled and acted like he didn't know what I was talking about.

"There's no list," he replied in a cracked smirking tone while continuing to stack forms on his desk making sure that they were all nice and neat, and then he folded his hands on top of his desk and just sat there staring at me. We all knew then that he was a liar. The list did exist because we had two UPS supervisors tell us about it, and that we were all on it. Management had documented what we, the stewards, were doing everyday on the lines, if we were the one's conducting the meetings, and what we were saying while on camera and so on. The list indeed existed.

"I'll cover the specifics in the PCM, but I'll need your help as stewards to help everyone get over this," Davey finished saying, standing up gesturing for us to leave.

We all left the office and Alvin turned to me and said, "Watch your back," as he walked off. Davey stepped out behind us and stood in front of his office smoking a cigarette looking at people as they passed by.

I went to the PCM that morning, and as I would have expected, the supervisors was reading from a prepared statement sent out by corporate management from over in Atlanta. No blame had yet to be placed as they read it aloud to everyone and it mainly talked about what we needed to do in regard to getting the business built back up to pre-strike levels. We were instructed at telling the customers what the management wanted them to know, kind of like a little spin control, and what to say if we were posed any questions. I stepped in after the PCM was read and told all the drivers just to tell the truth and not lie about anything. This infuriated Davey but he chose to keep his mouth shut for now. The meeting was over in about five minutes and we all were excused to go to work.

We left to go out on our routes for the first time since the strike and during the course of my day all of my customers was glad to see me back. I was welcomed back with open arms. Not everyone agreed with what we did but they respected our stance and that was good enough for me. The day went well for all of the driver's with no real reported problems.

Within a few weeks we noticed one morning that we had what appeared to be a new on-car supervisor who had been sent from another center. He was sent over to help Harry out since he was short handed from managements 'bungled' buyout program several months ago. The supervisors name was Smitty.

Right off I could tell he was a hard-core company man and would have the potential to cause a lot of problems if judging from his attitude was an indication to what type of manager he was. Smitty was introduced to us in the usual way with a detailed account of his work history, accomplishments and achievements. At the end of the meeting he stood in the doorway and shook everyone's hand as they left. Several others and I went out another door to keep from having to shake his hand. We've heard and seen this all before, how did they expect us to think that he was any different? That day of delivering was not much different than the one before. My volume seemed to be at the same pre-strike level that it was at before the strike and seemed to contradict what management was claiming, at least on my route.

Finally toward the end of the week management would bring in their account executives, or company salesmen, to give a presentation to us to show how much volume had been lost and the financial status of UPS as a result of the strike, and what we needed to do and so on. After the presentation, which was nothing more than a load of propaganda crap, management proceeded to go around the room handing out 'sale lead's' cards that they wanted us to fill out for new accounts and those accounts of previous customers who had diverted their volume to one of UPS's competitors during the strike.

I declined their offer and handed the cards back to them and told them, "Y'all wanted the strike and y'all lost the volume, then you go out and get it back." After I did that, the majority of the drivers followed suit and began tossing the cards back onto the counter that had all of their propaganda spread out on it. The account executives didn't know what to say, but all eyes were focused on me. Nothing else was said as they told us all to go to work.

As I walked to my truck, which was parked just outside the customer counter door, Smitty was waiting for me on the belt standing behind a pile packages.

"James I see that you were late getting back last night. What happened to you?" He asked while thumbing through several pages of a report.

"Yeah, that's what happens when you get us out on the road late Smitty." I replied in a disgusted tone and bent down to look through my overnight packages that was scattered behind my truck on the floor trying to make it obvious that I was trying to ignore him.

"Well, I need your help okay. Have it here by 6:30 and no later," Smitty replied, while clearing his throat several times and walked off. I just turned and started loading my airs into the rear of my truck so I could leave. I just wanted to leave and get away from all of the lying that had gone on that morning.

I left the building that morning around 9:15 a.m. and had barely delivered all of my overnight packages by the 10:30 a.m. commitment time.

That had given me roughly an hour to deliver an hour and a half's worth of work but I did make it on time. I delivered my business stops until around noon and stopped for lunch. I would only take about 45 minutes of my lunch break and decide to save the other fifteen minutes for later in the day. I started back delivering the remainder of my business stops and I was getting close to the 110 stops I was supposed to have been dispatched for that day.

After making the next stop, I walked into the back of the truck and began sorting through the three dozen or more packages that were still in the shelf that remained to be sorted through and lined up for delivery. I knew then that the loader had probably missed my stop count for the day. I had about 55 more stops than Smitty had told me before leaving the building this morning.

I came back to the building by the 6:30 p.m. curfew, with about twenty stops left that I couldn't deliver in time. I backed the truck onto the dock so the local sorters could unload the outbound volume I had picked up that day from my customers.

I found him in the office working on a computer and told him how many stops I had left and that it would take me at least two hours round trip to deliver them. His reply to my concern was "Don't go over twelve", meaning not to work more than twelve hours that day. No problem I thought as I walked off. I know how to play this game with him.

I walked back over to the dock and looked inside my truck noticing that it hadn't been unloaded yet. I yelled at a supervisor that I needed it unloaded and sat in my truck waiting for the unloaders to finish what they were doing. I then left the building once they slammed my rear door down and set out to finish making my deliveries.

It was around 7:20 p.m., when I pulled out of the parking lot. It would take me another twenty minutes to drive back to the spot where I had made I my last stop, to make the drive back to the building in time to meet the curfew. That would then leave me with roughly and hour and fifteen minutes to deliver roughly thirty-five stops and then make the drive back the center and check out before my twelve hours would be up, which would've been at 9:30 p.m. This was going to be impossible to do since the area I was delivering, the last 35 stops I had left, only allowed me to run just roughly fifteen stops an hour. And that was during the day not at night when the house numbers jumped wildly to one another and was difficult and near impossible to see. This wasn't counting the extra time it would take me to walk up to the house avoiding objects that could cause me to trip and avoid the dogs that I couldn't now see.

I went ahead and delivered the best I could, running the packages up to the door and then running back to the truck, which is something that I normally didn't do but with everything that was going on at the time in Huntsville, since the strike, I wanted to avoid trouble. Seeing that I wasn't going to be able to deliver everything, I stopped a little earlier to punch in on my DIAD all of the packages I couldn't deliver as 'missed', meaning that I was unable to deliver them.

I returned back to the center and punched out just before my twelve hours were up, and drove home tired as heck and my legs were killing me from the pain of jumping in and out of the truck, and from running up to the house and then back to the truck, while just trying to save some time.

The following morning Smitty called me into the office while I was still on the belt loading my truck to leave that morning, and as I walked in to the office I noticed that Alvin was in there with Davey. I knew right then I was fixing to get reamed for something as the door slammed closed. I walked over and pulled the seat away from beside Davey and positioned it in front of his desk beside Alvin.

"James explain to me why you had thirteen missed packages last night?" Davey asked smartly.

"I had to come in and go back out Davey." I replied.

"Why didn't you tell someone you wouldn't be able to get done?' Davey asked.

"I did Davey. I told Smitty that I had over thirty-five stops left that I had to go back out and finish delivering everything and all he told me was not to go over twelve hours." I snapped back.

"I didn't tell him to miss packages, Davey. Smitty nervously replied, while looking at me then Davey.

"You knew what I had left and you told me to go and deliver it," I replied as I began to get upset.

"Don't ever let this happen again or I will discipline you." Davey replied, while cutting a small grin.

I didn't say a word and just left the office. I couldn't believe that little 'rat'. Smitty was standing in there lying like a dog in an attempt to cover his own butt. I decided that it would probably be in my best interest to file a grievance to protest this whole incident. I'd been in the office with other drivers in the past and I knew right then from that little meeting what management was going to have in their plans for me and I tried to head them off before it started.

I didn't get credit for the time it had taken me to drive back to the building, although I did get an allowance for the miles I had traveled in the drive back and forth which failed to compare. I had lost roughly 55 minutes of 'on road' time to which I probably only received about a twelve minute mileage allowance, which still left me with roughly 40 minutes or so of dead time. Dead time that attributed to my over allowed time for this day and time that I can hardly make up.

I saw Davey standing over by the time clock and I walked up to discuss with him several problems that we were beginning to have again, such as using cover drivers and everyone working over 9½ hours a day, which both were in violation of our labor agreement. Finally as he walked off from me, he popped off, "If you're tired of working that much then do your job," while increasing his pace and acting as if he was reading something. I followed him on around the corner just outside his office and told him that if they were like a real management person they'd fix our problems. This got his attention. He turned around and walked back over to where I had stopped.

"James, if you don't like the way we treat you here, then I suggest you need to find another job." Davey said and then stormed off. I couldn't believe it.

I went ahead and filed several grievances to protest his 'lack' of action and for his comment he had made to me about quitting. I wasn't about to let this go.

DATE GRIEVANCE FILED: 8-22-97
EXPLAIN GRIEVANCE: *I'm having to leave the building from 9:15-9:30 with too much work to have the pick up volume in by 6:30 p.m. My new loader is missing my stop count causing me to two-trip every night. I'm working over 9 1/2 hours a day, for more than three days in a row. Management is not concerned or the problem would've been fixed.*
REMEDY SOUGHT: *a lighter paid day.*

DATE GRIEVANCE FILED: 8-23-97
EXPLAIN GRIEVANCE: *Management is using cover drivers to run bid routes while driver are continuing to stay in the building to work on team concept items. I met with Davey and didn't receive an explanation for why this was going on.*
REMEDY SOUGHT: *To use cover drivers according to the contract.*

DATE GRIEVANCE FILED: 8-23-97
EXPLAIN GRIEVANCE: *I was told that I was going to have a heavy day and they said I could work a code 5 to help them out. Later before leaving the building, another driver with a similar heavy day was given a rider to help him get in early. The management also ran two cover drivers for a few hours to help even the paid day out. I was told that I would be paged and given help but never received the call from management.*
REMEDY SOUGHT: *Compliance with the contract.*

DATE GRIEVANCE FILED: 8-23-97
EXPLAIN GRIEVANCE: *I was asked by management why I was about 1-1/2 hours over allowed and when I tried to explain the center manager he wouldn't listen. I feel that day, in question, was out of my control. The truck was packed front to back and I had to work around bulk all day and with a poorly pulled split cost me an extra 22 minutes for just two stops. I feel that I am being harassed and I also feel that I have not been given a fair days work for a fair days pay.*
REMEDY SOUGHT: *Stop the harassment and fix my load.*

DATE OF GRIEVANCE: 8-23-97
EXPLAIN GRIEVANCE: *I was told that if I didn't like my job that I could find another one. I feel this is unacceptable behavior coming from a manager. I was off of the clock and feel that I am being singled out because of me being a steward. This was witnessed by Abel.*
REMEDY SOUGHT: *The harassment to stop and an apology.*

The management and the union had held a local level hearing to discuss these grievances and it was once again agreed that this abuse would stop for about the fifth time now. Truth was it would only escalate.

Tensions had begun to mount higher and higher each day during the week between the management and the drivers.

During this week I had my normal loader, a veteran of two years, replaced by another loader who was new. This new guy was killing me everyday. He was putting the worst load on me possible and was missing my stop count by at least 40 everyday. It was not his fault though because the management would not train him right and had just threw him in there to basically figure it out on his own. I tried to help him the best I could, coming in a little early and helping him with whatever problem he was having for that particular day. I knew how he felt because the same thing had happened to me with Alli. The supervisors who were training this young man couldn't do the jobs themselves much less train anyone else how to do it.

I was called into the office everyday that week. I tried to explain to Davey that some of the splits Smitty and the other supervisors were pulling to me were stupid and costing me more time. I was delivering just three stops some days that were costing me over twenty-five minutes for just those, whereas I could have delivered at least ten stops in the same time period if not for this poorly pulled split. We were constantly being blamed for the shortcomings and poor decisions of the management in Huntsville.

I was not only paying the price at work but at home as well. I had now been getting home at around 9:45 every night. I missed dinner with my family daily and every night they would both have gone to bed, and Mattie would be asleep before I got home. I hated management for this. This was beginning to cause some major problems to say the least. I was beginning to become extremely stressed out and remained on edge, and the amount it took to instigate a confrontation at work was severely dwindling.

Management began handing out warning letters and suspensions like candy, and every driver who was affected by this harassment became very militant and lashed out at management every chance they had.

Management had laid off about seven drivers in both Huntsville centers and divided those routes up amongst the other drivers. I was far enough up the totem pole in seniority that it didn't affect me other than the fact I was now being dispatched everyday with an eleven hour paid day instead of the eight and a half hour paid day management had committed to doing prior to the strike. We all worked many long hours and missed a lot of packages. Management had laid off several part timers as well and during one morning that I came in early to check on things, I found two supervisors loading the trucks for the people they had laid off.

I immediately asked them, "What in the world are you doing?"

"Just mind your own business," was their reply.

I filed the grievances to protest this action and the continuing action of management to use part timers in violation of our labor agreement. This matter had already been ruled on, the prior week, after the conclusion of the local hearing and the management agreed to end it. Needless to say it didn't end, but in fact it escalated.

Management was now using the part time air drivers in the afternoon to pick up ground volume when they were solely restricted to only picking up overnight packages that were called in after the driver made a pick up, which was in violation of the contract once again. When I brought this to the attention of Davey, he shrugged it off and told me to file a grievance. So I obliged him and did so.

One, major problem that was happening in the west center, more than in the east, was full-time drivers being forced to vacate their 'bid' routes. I wasn't about to sit back and allow cover drivers to run these bid routes, simply because the cover drivers didn't know any other routes from a lack of being trained. These senior drivers had picked the routes they wanted and now they were being forced to vacate them because the cover drivers didn't know where they were going. This upset a lot of the old timers and caused an even greater divide between management and us. The management clearly had no respect or integrity to honor the contract.

DATE GRIEVANCE FILED: 8-25-97
EXPLAIN GRIEVANCE: *Supervisors working while Teamsters are laid off.*
REMEDY SOUGHT: *Bring back part timers with back pay.*

DATE GRIEVANCE FILED: 8-26-97
EXPLAIN GRIEVANCE: *Management using air drivers to pick up ground volume.*
REMEDY SOUGHT: *Comply with contract.*

DATE GRIEVANCE FILED: 8-26-97
EXPLAIN GRIEVANCE: *Management is still using cover drivers to help 'heavy' drivers in the Huntsville East Center.*
REMEDY SOUGHT: *Bring laid off drivers back to work with back pay and a lighter paid day.*

DATE GRIEVANCE FILED: 8-26-97
EXPLAIN GRIEVANCE: *Management is continuing to abuse the use of cover drivers and is forcing full time bid drivers to vacate their routes in the Huntsville West Center.*
REMEDY SOUGHT: *Comply with agreement and cross train cover drivers.*

Everyone disliked Smitty from the very beginning, I mean the very day he arrived in Huntsville. Smitty thought that the world revolved around UPS, and he in fact thought that UPS was the world. At times, he was so hard-core that it seemed that if he were to be cut, that he would bleed brown. He was that pathetically gung ho and one side towards UPS. He was strictly by the book, as long as it benefited him, and if not, he would 'put the interest of the company' before what was actually the right thing to do regardless of what the labor agreement called for.

During the two weeks after our return, management had begun a crackdown on us, and they orchestrated and carried it out against us with a vengeance unlike anything we had known. I personally had managed to file a record total of grievances for various infractions and harassment by management since the strike. I was not the only one, though, being harassed, in fact the majority of all the drivers, in both centers, were being treated the same way as I, but it seemed that they enjoyed making an example out of me.

During the last week of August 1997, while I was delivering my residential deliveries in the late afternoon, I had a 'sudden' urge to go to the restroom for a bowel movement. I was about four miles, up the mountain, and from the nearest restroom and there wasn't anywhere closer for me to go, so I had to stop delivering and "immediately" drive down the mountain to a gas station that was at the foot of the mountain. The total round trip time I lost was about thirteen minutes. I went ahead, as a precaution, and punched over on my DIAD board to show what time I had' broken trace', or left my delivery area, and in fact I had a total of about nine minutes left on meal. I thought I could make it back in time, within the nine minutes, if I hurried but failed to do so. I ran four minutes over my allotted time of one hour that I received for my meal period, but keep in mind that I did show this extra time, and returned back on trace to complete my route. I finished the day with no real problems other than having to work late again that night.

The following morning during the PCM my name was called out loud along with about five others to be seen in the office. This had become so routine that I was no longer surprised by it and in fact, expected it. After the meeting Smitty followed all of us into the office and I went in and represented the other five drivers for various trivial things ranging from running over allowed, missed packages and so on. They all received warning letters and one had even received a suspension. Alvin came in after all his drivers received their discipline, with a record number drivers that morning having received discipline for about the same infractions as my drivers. Davey shut the door behind me as I walked in and took a seat beside Alvin, and he started the meeting beginning to talk to me as he walked around where I was seated and sat behind his desk.

"James, I'm going to have to give you a warning letter for going over your one hour for your lunch." He replied.

"Davey I had to take a dump." I replied. "What do you want me to do crap in my pants? I said in a loud tone.

"James we give you an hour for lunch to take care of that business." He replied. "I'm also going to have to give you a warning letter for failing to record your time properly." He finished saying.

I was shocked but Davey wasn't finished yet.

"James you will also receive another suspension for the attitude you had with Smitty the other day while discussing your route." Davey rattled off.

My blood began to boil. I thought I was going to have a stroke while he was naming off the various for of discipline that I was about to receive.

"Oh, and also, you will receive a warning letter for failing to record your time properly for yesterday." Davey said. "I need you to sign these papers showing I discussed this with you," he asked as he slid the paper over to me to sign.

"You know what you can do with that paper don't you Davey? And I do mean that in the utmost matter of respect...sir!" I replied angrily.

Davey then pushed the paper over Alvin who simply said, "James, call Matt as soon as you can and get him over here." Alvin refused to sign the paper, which infuriated Davey, and then he had Smitty to sign it saying that we both refused to sign it.

So after that meeting I was in no real condition to go out and deliver. My head was pounding from my blood pressure and I was feeling lightheaded. My stomach was killing me and I felt like I was going to throw up all over the place from this latest ordeal. I had no business going out on the road while in this shape. It wasn't safe for the public or me to be out driving that day.

That event really shook me up and all that night, after I got home I could not relax or even begin to unwind. That was all I could think about and I just couldn't get it off of my mind. Another two or three days shot to hell after that meeting. I received three warning letters and a suspension all-stemming from just having to use the bathroom. I couldn't believe it. What did management expect me to do? There wasn't a bathroom in the truck. Did they just want me to hold it or go in my pants? I just couldn't understand it.

Matt's and the local's 'old guards' position was a very relaxed one to say the least. "Don't worry about it James," Matt would say not only for this incident, but every other time I would call him. I did worry about it. It was my job and my health. Every night I would come home drained from being so sick and tired of what happened that morning and from all of managements bull crap attempts at disciplining me, that I would be thinking again of quitting. It was making my life miserable wondering if I would even have a job the next morning when I reported to work. I had a family to provide for, a house and car payment. I spent a lot of sleepless nights lying in bed playing out the past days events in my mind, and what I needed to do the next day to prevent the management from getting an upper hand on me. I, in fact, had a right to be scared of getting fired because I was dealing with a labor relations policy that was notorious for firing people for just cracking a fifty cent mirror on their truck or scratching the paint on it and then charging the person with an accident, and never...ever thinking twice about doing it.

Several weeks would pass and eventually a local hearing would be held to discuss my discipline that I had received for my last incidents, and once again, Davey denied everything, even after bringing Alvin in to the meeting as a witness for me. Nothing would come of the suspensions and warning letters, which all were reduced to just write-ups on my Pittsburgh file. There should have been more of a fight or at least some sort of effort from Matt and the local union other than just sitting around joking with Hembry about it after it was settled. Shortly after this happened, the rides and 'REAL" harassment began.

Davey and I tied up several more times while being in the office with drivers and the way he would talk to them like they were a bunch of dogs. It came close several times of one of us crossing that 'line'. It was pathetic about some of the crap he was bringing these drivers in the office and disciplining them for. It was on the borderline of being just plain stupid. The reasons for discipline ranged from where they parked their trucks at night to leaving coke bottles in their trucks, and even one driver... a banana peel being left in the shelf of his truck.

One thing from that morning that stands out and still does to this very day was when Joseph was disciplined for 'failing to work safe'. Joseph had lifted a heavy package and strained his neck while out delivering on his route one day. He had to miss a day or two of work because he couldn't turn his head at all due to the severe pain. They honestly disciplined this man for this and Matt and the local union just sat back on their dead butts and let it happen. This was nothing but an outrage and this would prove to be one of the main catalyst that would begin building discontent from the UPS members toward Matt the other 'old guard" officers that were in the local.

After the meeting ended and after Davey handed out the last of the warning letters that morning and he stood up as I was walking out behind Joseph and Davey said, "James."

I turned to him and looked at him waiting for a reason why he was calling me.

Davey paused a few seconds...and said, "You're excused to leave now..."

He was trying to have the last word I guess, but as I started back out the door I bent over and curtsied and said, "Yes sir, master," and quickly shut the door behind me, and not giving him a chance to reply.

I walked on out and rounded the corner to pick up my DIAD and the other things that I had left on the counter and "Smiling Eddie" was standing there waiting on me grunting. It was Smitty. He looked down at his watch and asked me what I've been doing.

"It's 9:10 and we're late." Smitty replied.

"I'm not late for anything you are." I replied. "If you've got a problem with me being late then you need to take that up with Davey." I said loudly.

"Oh, I didn't know you were in the office with him." He replied, while trying to look surprised.

"What a liar," I thought to myself. He knew I was in there because he was the one that called out my name during the PCM this morning to report to the office. I don't know why he would play dumb like this unless he just wanted to get me rattled, or something.

I gathered up my stuff and I bent over and opened one of the cabinets to get out some supplies for one of my customers. "What are you doing?" Smitty asked smartly.

"What does it look like? I'm getting some supplies," I answered.

"No-no-no-no. You need to do that before you start work and not now, we don't have time." Smitty said.

"First of all let me tell you a little secret Smitty. I don't work off of the clock, and I'm not going to do anything for any of you before I start work. If it's that big of a problem then just forget it," I said, and put the supplies back and walked over to the dock and stepped up on it.

I was parked all the way on the other end and began walking down behind the trucks stepping over packages that were still piled out behind most of the trucks. The drivers were steadily digging through the piles of cardboard. I remember glancing down at my watch. It was now about 9:25. I stopped to turn around and tell Smitty that we were going to need some help with delivering my overnight packages and he ran into me as I stopped to turn around. It seems that he was right on my heels.

"Why are you following me so close for. Back up and get away from me before you cause me to fall and get hurt or something." I screamed out so everyone could hear me. Everyone stopped what they were doing and began laughing at him. Smitty was pissed now more than ever.

"Hm, hm, hm, hm...everyone get back to work," Smitty yelled, while grunting and clearing his throat.

I turned around and finished the walk back to my truck and the door was pulled down most of the way but was not locked. I stopped and looked around at everyone else's truck that still had packages piled out behind it and how everyone else was still loading their trucks and I wasn't going to have to. "This is a first," I thought as I raised the door. The door opened all the way and behold. Everything was in the shelf and there were very few packages on the floor. I knew right then that something was wrong...very wrong. I asked Otis, who was parked beside me and out behind his truck digging through his pile of packages, "Who loaded our trucks."

"Chester loaded yours and Scott loaded ours." Otis replied, as he carried an armful of packages into his truck. Chester was a part time supervisor who was one of the best loaders Huntsville ever had.

"What's going on here Smitty?" I asked.

"We want to make sure you have a good load on here so we can see what the problem is." Smitty replied.

"Smitty, the load 'IS' one of the problems." I replied, while growing frustrated. "Why didn't you use Scott so you could see how sorry of a load I was going out with everyday?" I asked.

"You need to take that up with Davey, James." Smitty replied in a smart tone.

I was floored. I was so upset from this screwing that I could have blown up just from my blood pressure.

"What good are you Smitty?" I asked.

Smitty never answered and stepped off of the dock grunting and sat everything he had up in to my seat in the cab.

"James, we don't have time for this. You need to get this stuff in the car." Smitty replied, while looking at his watch.

"All I have out is overnights, Smitty." I replied, as I scooped them up and carried them around to the driver's seat of my truck. I managed to pawn off on Otis and Denny, the other downtown driver, some of my overnights that lightened me up a bit and help relieve some of the stress of meeting the 10:30 a.m. commitment time.

I pulled the truck out and made sure I did everything by the numbers. I checked every single safety item on the truck that was mandatory to inspect by the D.O.T. We left the building after this, and I went about my day with Smitty in the passenger seat. I made sure to stay within the speed limit and he then made the smart-alec remark, "You must not drive the speed limit everyday if you have to keep looking down at it?" I didn't say a thing. I wouldn't even look at him.

As we drove to our first stop I noticed that Smitty was looking for something. He would stand up in the cab looking around in various places for something but I couldn't just figure out what it was that he was looking for. Finally after about a minute or so it became obvious from the brown stream running out from the corner of his mouth. He needed to spit.

"Don't you even think about spitting in the floor of this truck Smitty," I said while staring a hole through him. He sat there for a few seconds more and slid the side door back and spit about a gallon of tobacco juice down the side of my truck and shut the door back.

"I'll have to get the car washers to wash that off tonight." He replied, while wiping off his chin. I was sickened from this lack of respect for company property that he had just displayed. Although appalling, it was quite typical.

We arrived to a delivery stop and I walked inside with an armload of packages followed closely by Smitty who was writing something on his pad. It was the sewing store, and one of my favorite stops and I liked all of the ladies who worked there a lot.

"Good afternoon James, who's your friend?" A lady asked.

"He's not my friend Katy, he's one of those managers I've told you about." I replied.

Smitty stopped writing and immediately looked up at me and then to Katy. "How are you doing m'am?" Smitty asked. No reply.

I knew Smitty was uncomfortable because he began clearing his throat in that annoying way that he does when he gets stressed out. I finished punching the packages into my DIAD and walked over to where Katy was sitting. There were several other ladies in there working with her and several more had walked back to where I was to get a glimpse of this 'person' that I had described to them as if he was part of a freak show or something.

"Where are those supplies I asked for yesterday, James?" Katy asked.

I realized I had the opportunity here to teach Smitty a lesson in customer commitment and service. "I started to get what you requested this morning before leaving Katy, but Smitty here told me we didn't have time for them so I had to put them back." I said looking at Smitty who now had turned a bright shade of read and his lips were moving, but nothing was coming out of them. If he wasn't clearing his throat and grunting before coming in here he was sure enough doing it now.

Katy flew into Smitty like a wild woman. Smitty didn't know what to say or do. I finally had to walk outside because it had embarrassed me so bad for him. Smitty got right on the phone and called the center right then for an air driver to run some supplies out to her within the next thirty minutes. Chalk another one up for the good guys. I walked on out to the truck and sat in the seat waiting for Smitty to emerge from the reaming he had just received from a customer. Finally he walked out and I could tell he was visibly shaken and quite upset.

"Why did you do that to me?" He asked upset.

"I told the truth," I replied, as I started the truck and pulled away from the curb as he sulked up. We we're about to start delivering my residential's at an unheard time of 2:45.

I brought this up to Smitty who replied, "I'm not wanting to stay out here all night with you, I've got church tonight." Big deal. How about the nights I missed church? Did that matter?

There was hardly any traffic that mattered. I didn't have the stops on me that caused me all of my problems and delays. After sorting through the packages in the shelf I noticed I was missing some key neighborhoods.

"Where's Covemont?" I asked Smitty.

"We had to pull that section off because we had some light drivers," he said, while writing on his little clipboard.

"How convenient," I said as I finished sitting up stops to begin delivering.

The Covemont section, which was the name of a street in the influential part of Huntsville, which on a daily basis cost me about 45 minutes of my total over allowed time everyday, because of all of the traffic on the highway during rush hour, I couldn't make any time delivering that section, but without this section on me today the whole day was wasted. It wasn't anything like what I had to contend with on a daily basis. This whole day was nothing but a set-up for Davey to try and hold me to running a certain amount of time under allowed.

We arrived back to the building at around 5:50 p.m with roughly twenty-five fewer stops than I was normally sent out with. I was finished and off the clock by 6:15 and on my way home.

It was rare to have gotten off this early, for the fast few weeks, and it was like a treat to my family when I pulled into the driveway. I tried to explain to Lesley what was going on today with me getting home early and she asked a simple question, "Why can't they do this everyday?" Sadly the answer isn't as complex as one might think. Simply management wanted to do this to us. I enjoyed that evening with my family, because inside I knew it was going to be short lived.

During the course of the next couple of days I had more of the same kind of "ideal" loads and perfect conditions while Smitty was riding with me. I never worked any later than 6:15 and I was really enjoying getting off early even if I had to put up with Smitty, but I tried not to fool myself. I knew that chances were, after a few days of this, things would be back to normal and the 9:00 nights would be back.

I was called into the office after the conclusion of the third days ride, that evening, and sat down with Davey, Alvin and Smitty who were in the office as well. Davey went over the past three days ride, which were pretty much textbook rides and had noted that I had improved in the "so-called" areas that Smitty, had pointed out to me during the last three days. I never had a chance to see the OR during the mornings when Smitty was on car with me. Every time I asked, I was told that the report just failed to be printed and would be available that evening for me to see. That never came to pass so I just gave up on ever seeing it.

"James, you have demonstrated that you can run eighteen stops an hour in this area and fifteen in this area and so on." Davey said while looking over the OR from the last day. When it came down to the number of stops I had run in my residential's, I noticed that the number of stops an hour was inflated quite a bit. I had come close to running almost double what I normally had run in that area.

"Davey," I said interrupting him. "That number isn't right."

"What's wrong with it?" He asked while looking at it and flipping the pages back and forth.

"I didn't have Covemont any of these days. I had only the lower end stops, Davey." I replied.

"What difference does it make, James, they're all in the same area?" He snapped back.

"It makes a lot of difference Davey. The houses in Covemont are way off the road up steep hills and driveways. You cannot drive the speed limit without packages falling out of the shelves, because of the steep hills and sharp curves, whereas on the lower end all the houses are about ten yards off of the road and all of them are on flat ground." I said turning to Alvin who was looking over the OR that showed a breakdown of each of my delivery areas. "Alvin, there's a huge difference." I replied, waiting for Alvin to say something. Anything.

And there was a huge difference indeed. Everything in the Covemont section, I could only run about eleven stops an hour, but everything in the lower part I could run at least twenty-five stops an hour and have ran thirty plus during peak season...by myself!

Davey wasn't going to budge on this, but I had caught him in the middle of his little scheme. "James, you've demonstrated that you can do the job with Smitty riding with you and you will do it from here on out or I'll fire you." He replied, while pointing his finger in my face.

"Get your finger away from me," I said while starting to stand up. Alvin could tell right away where this was heading and tried to diffuse the situation by putting his hand on my shoulder and began pushing me back down in my seat.

"Well do what you have to Davey, I need to get on the road," I replied.

"James sign this saying that I covered this with you and that you'll run the stops an hour we requested." Davey replied, as he was pushing the form over towards me. I looked it over real well and noticed that it only said that he had covered this meeting and nothing more. This was odd. I didn't see anything on there about running the stops an hour that he was requesting me to run.

"I'll sign it," I replied to Davey and Smitty's amazement, "On one condition."

"What would that be?" Davey asked.

"You put in here that Chester will load me everyday and that I will go out with the same number of stops everyday and without Covemont." I said.

"We can't do that," Davey replied.

"Then I can't sign it Davey. What would be the problem with guaranteeing me the 'ideal' conditions that you provided for me the past three days, every day Davey?" I asked.

"Well volume fluctuates and we never know what each day holds," he said.

"That's the biggest crock I ever heard." I replied.

"Alvin sign..." he started to say, but Alvin interrupted him.

"Don't ask me to sign any thing. You're not doing anything but railroading this man here. Nobody's signing it." Alvin replied while sounding upset.

"Get out of here and go to work!" Davey said hatefully to us as we stood to leave.

Alvin and I stood up and thanked them for their time and walked out of the office and walked over to our trucks. I arrived to find the rear door to my truck closed. I walked on around and stepped off of the dock and climbed up into the cab of my truck to find that it too had been closed. I pulled the key out of the ignition switch and opened the bulkhead door. The truck was packed with things falling out into the cab of the truck as I slid the door back. I couldn't believe what I was seeing. I jumped out and walked to the back of my truck and raised the door up. It was my usual mess. I climbed over the pile of packages that were in the middle of the truck and looked in the shelf where my residential stops were loaded. I had the Covemont section...about 35 stops for that section total, back on me. I sorted through all of the packages in the shelf and noticed that they had pulled all of my lower end stops that were my time saving stops, and put them on another driver. I liked to have gone off of the deep end as I climbed out from inside the truck and set off to find Alvin.

Alvin was in his truck going through all of his stops, and getting ready to leave when I climbed up into his truck, "Come and take a look at this crap over here Alvin." I said. Alvin took off his glasses and followed me back over to my truck.

"Look at this, can you believe it? They wanted me to sign that form committing me to run those numbers with this kind of load," I said. Alvin didn't say a word for a few seconds and I could tell he was getting madder by the second.

Finally he said, "Lets go." I followed him to the end of the belt and started to step off when Davey stepped up onto the dock.

"What's the problem? Why are you over here?" Davey asked Alvin.

"Come down here and look at this," Alvin said. We all walked down there and peered into back of my truck, which had packages falling out of it.

"Is this how the truck was loaded like those days that Smitty rode with him?" Alvin asked.

"No," Davey replied.

"Then why is it like this today then?" Alvin answered and began drawing a crowd of drivers.

"Well, we had a couple of loaders call in this..." Davey started to say and was cut off by Alvin.

"You need to put Smitty with him today, Davey." Alvin demanded.

"We can't do that today." Davey replied nervously as the drivers began to talk amongst themselves about what was going on.

"I want a rider today and I mean right now!" I said while beginning to shake from the anger that was swelling inside of me.

"If it was no problem to ride with him the past three days then what's the difference if you ride one more day?" Alvin asked Davey, who had now turned a bright shade of red.

"Either it's time to put up or shut up." I replied, as the other drivers began hollering at Davey to ride with me and see what life was really like. Every driver in the Huntsville east center knew what management was doing to several others, and to me as well. They too, had been growing tired of the rides. Davey was beginning to have a serious problem on his hands and finally he agreed to make Smitty ride with me. Smitty stormed off and got his clipboard, and told me to pull out of the building and wait for him in the parking lot.

I walked back to my truck trying to regain my composure and I pulled the door down and locked it. I pulled on out and waited for Smitty to come out from inside the center after completing my morning routine.

Smitty came out followed by Davey who had stopped at the large door that led into the building. He just stood there smoking a cigarette, watching us as I pulled off of the property.

The morning was typical and by the time 11:30 came around I was right on schedule...about an hour behind where I had been the previous three days with Smitty's "ideal" load. At around 12:30 that time had grown to about one and a half hours behind. I thought to myself that I was finally going to be given the credit I deserved, and then the harassment would stop.

Around 12:45 Davey came pulling up in his personal truck. "James, Smitty's going to have to come back with me. I need him at the center." Davey said.

"Who's going to finish the ride?" I asked.

"You can do the job. Just finish it and don't run over allowed today." He said as Smitty stepped down from the package car and opened the door to Davey's green truck, and climbed in and drove off.

"Don't run over my butt," I said. Here I was almost two hours behind after fooling with Davey all morning and he knew...he knew that I was behind and never said a word about it. "Forget them," I thought and decided to stop and take my lunch break. I shut it down for 50 minutes and after eating lunch I was really behind now. I wasn't going to be able to finish my commercial deliveries, and I had to call the center to tell a member of management that I was going to need some help with my business stops or I'd wind up missing a whole lot of packages. I never got a reply from anyone who had authority to make a decision. Where was Smitty? I thought he was needed at the center to do something urgent? He wasn't anywhere to be found.

I delivered what business stops I could until about 4:30, and then finished what pick up stops I had left. That day I wound up missing around thirty some odd packages, and even had to come in and go back out which that resulted in me missing about ten of those, as well for a total of about forty missed packages for the day. I had managed to go over my twelve-hour limit, which was a big no-no with management. Crap was sure enough going to hit the fan the next day.

I came into work the next morning and naturally I was called into the office by Davey and received a two-day suspension and three warning letters for failing to work as instructed (one for going over twelve hours, one for missing business stops and one for missing residential stops because I was instructed "NOT TO" miss anything,). I tried to plead my case with Davey, but he was not interested in hearing anything I had to say. I just filed the grievances.

DATE GRIEVANCE FILED: 9-10-97

EXPLAIN GRIEVANCE: *A member of management rode a half-day with me to evaluate my performance. I feel this is excessive (4 rides) in a two-week period and is unfair to me. I feel that I am being harassed for my actions during the strike.*

REMEDY SOUGHT: *No more rides until a Local hearing.*

DATE GRIEVANCE FILED: 9-10-97

EXPLAIN GRIEVANCE: *I am continuing to work over 9 ½ hours a day.*

REMEDY SOUGHT: *Lighter paid day.*

DATE GRIEVANCE FILED: 9-10-97
EXPLAIN GRIEVANCE: *I was called into the office on 9-9 by the center manager, Davey, to receive discipline for several offenses. I was not allowed to present my side of the story as to why I was 'over allowed' for 9-8 and was given the excuse of "A lack of time." I feel that this is a total lack of respect on his part for me. I feel that I am being harassed.*

DATE GRIEVANCE FILED: 9-11-97
EXPLAIN GRIEVANCE: *Whenever a member of management rides with me (production ride) they pull my regular loader off and put a good one to load me for those days they ride.*
REMEDY SOUGHT: *Train my loader and straighten out the load.*

DATE GRIEVANCE FILED: 9-12-97
EXPLAIN GRIEVANCE: *I protest the three warning letters and the two-day suspension.*
REMEDY SOUGHT: *Remove warning letters and suspension from my record.*

The next major thing that happened was when Davey decided that the extra time we were taking over our one-hour lunch was going to stop. I was called into the office and Davey explained to us that this practice was now going to stop and he had planned to hold a PCM that morning announcing his intentions. "No problem," I thought, and I headed off to the PCM. Everything seemed to go as planned.

Several days later I had heard on the radio that according to a report in *Traffic World* magazine found that UPS might owe in excess of a billion dollars in back taxes. I found this very interesting and I became curious as to the reason why they owed that much money. I'd find out later, because at the present time I had more important things to worry about as I stopped for an emergency visit to my dentist to have a tooth fixed. My dentist wasn't too far from where I was delivering, so I called Harry to see if I could drive over to my dentist and have my crown put back onto my tooth. He agreed but told me to try and not go over my one-hour lunch or to call him if it looked like I was going to exceed my hour. I left the dentist with ten minutes to spare and headed back to my area. It seemed that an accident had just happened as I sat at a light a couple of streets before the intersection I needed to cross to get back on area and be able to punch off of lunch and back to on road time (UPS' time).

You see, the minute you break off of your route you begin coding out onto your time, and until you return, and pick back up where you broke off at, you are still on your personal time, which was on your one-hour break period. I saw that this was going to put me over my mealtime of one hour as I sat there waiting for traffic to clear a path for me to get around, and it was looking like I was going to have to detour. It just so happened that I went over my one-hour break by about three minute's due to the wreck.

I was called into the office by Davey the next day, and he notified me that I would be suspended for two days and I would receive another warning letter for failing to properly record my meal. I tried to explain to him what had happened and what Harry had told me and he said," you work for me, not Harry. What did I tell you about your hour lunch, James?" He asked.

"Do what you have to Davey and I'll file the grievances." I replied.

The "three minute " issue was a little more complex in nature that it first appears to be. I am required to 'properly' record my meal period and if fail to do so then I can be disciplined, like I was in this case. For example lets say that I have one whole hour to take a meal with. If I break trace at 11:00 and drive to Taco Bell and eat and when I leave to drive back to my route I arrive at 12:05, thus going over by five minute's. This is the core of the issue. Lets say that on this particular day I was being followed by management and was being videotaped from the time I had broken trace, while I ate and as I drove back to where I had broken off to go eat. Lets say even further... that instead of entering into the DIAD, the times of 11:00-12:05, that I should have in the first place, I enter instead the times of 11:00-12:00, thus shorting the company five minutes. What management would do now is sometime after I arrive back to the center and check out, they'd then pull my records to see what time, and how much time, I had coded out for lunch. If I had recorded 11:00-12:05, then they have nothing other than my case, but if I record 11:00-12:00 then that's a different story. What I have done now is 'falsified my time card' and have stolen time. This is an act of dishonesty to which they would have had the videotape evidence of to prove their case and then I'd be discharged with no chance ever of getting my job back.

I've seen it before and have sat in on discharges for this very thing. So I elected to show whatever time I used and never...ever...hid anything from management.

DATE GRIEVANCE FILED: 9-23-97

EXPLAIN GRIEVANCE: *I was called into the office by Davey and was notified I would be suspended for two days, and given a warning letter for taking a one hour and three minute lunch. I tried to explain to him in front of Alvin, that I had got caught in traffic.*

REMEDY SOUGHT: *Remove discipline from my records.*

The management and local union held a local level hearing to discuss this and everything was reduced to a warning letter or thrown out. It was evident by the actions of Davey that he was indeed harassing me and setting me up for a constructive discharge, which is illegal.

The stress from this period had resulted in having to change level of dosage on my medication. These two months, since the strike, was a pure living hell.

I carried this home with me every night and it drove a wedge deeper between my family and me. I might have been winning the battles at work, but I was losing the war at home.

I had grown tired from the daily antics of management and finally after the local union wouldn't do anything to make management stop I decided it was time to get a lawyer involved. I had to literally obtain the service's of an attorney to send Davey and UPS a letter stating that if they didn't stop the harassment that we'd take it up in the legal system. It had gotten that bad.

Chapter 12

"Monday morning- we managed to show another sign of solidarity. Management spent close to a hundred dollars on biscuits this morning and we threw it in the garbage and told them what to do with their food. It was great."

I managed to remember about the report on the radio about the back tax issue and I asked Harry about it. He simply said he didn't know anything about it and kind of blew it off. I figured there was something to it if he was brushing me off about it so I'd just wait and see what I could find out from watching the news during the next couple of days. Nothing ever came on the news about the tax thing, at least that I saw during my time off at night. During the course of the next few weeks everything seemed to taper off in regard to the harassment and the frequency of rides after the local union no choice but to force management to back off of me.

We had been through about three different District Managers in the past two years for the Alabama District and we received word that we were going to be getting another new one.

This man was coming from up north, and was supposed to be a real, no nonsense kind of tough guy. We received word that he was going to visit the Huntsville center and the "big-wig reception" plan was put into motion and for anybody who doesn't know what this is...it's simple.

The center that was going to receive the visit, cleans the building beyond belief, washes, waxes and paints the wheels and armor all's the tires. Everyone is required to wear perfect uniforms, shoes polished the whole bit. The management even gives you instructions on how to act and what to say. The preload goes down in record time and everything is loaded in the package cars with the doors "down and brown". It was a sickening affair, and it brought back memory's from my days at the grocery store.

Well, the morning before the scheduled day of "his highness'" arriving, we were told in the morning PCM for us to come in early the next morning and they'd have biscuits there for us to eat along with soft drinks and various other things. I decided to go ahead and arrive to work early enough to eat and when I walked in the building pretty much everyone was already there. I walked on over to the check in counter, and sat my radio on the counter and walked back over to where the east drivers had congregated.

"Why isn't anyone eating?" I asked.

"Dick told us we couldn't till Lenny gets here," a driver replied.

"Who?" I asked.

"Lenny, the new man." She replied.

We stood around for about twenty-five minutes and finally Lenny walked in the back door with about fifteen different managers in tow like a bunch of stooges or something.

"Maybe we should have carried him from his car so his feet couldn't get dirty," Joseph said getting a laugh from everybody.

Lenny began making his customary rounds introducing himself and shaking everyone's hands in the process. Dick still wasn't allowing us to eat and everyone was hungry. After about five minutes or so, Lenny made it to where I was and held his hand out to me. I reluctantly shook it and introduced myself to him. "Pleasure to meet you," he said, and moved on to the next person. He went on down the row of people like a politician. Several high ranking, but below Lenny, managers were bringing up the rear behind him and doing the same thing that Lenny was doing. This was the first time that any of them were going to 'greet' me although I'd seen them some two dozen times in the past. There was one manager that was almost to me, who I didn't like, and I decided to walk off before he made it to me, because I didn't want to shake his hand...much less talk to him.

I walked on across to the other side of the bay inside the building where some other drivers had congregated around the food table awaiting the order to eat. I stood there with them for a couple of minutes or so, and Lenny had made his way back around to me, and went through his whole routine again with me. "I just met you and shook your hand five minutes ago and you don't even remember me you cracker head," I thought. I just laughed inside while shaking my head.

Finally after all that Dick, started the show and Lenny went through his speech about his accomplishments and what he hoped to do with the Alabama District at which, by now his speech had carried over into our time to get on the road. When it was finally over everyone was waiting for the order to eat. It came all right.

"Everyone get you a biscuit and carry it with you and go to work," Dick said. You talk about pissing everyone off. Here we had all come in thirty minutes or more before our scheduled start time...on our own time, and with having the opportunity to eat all morning they made us wait and now we couldn't even eat. Most people got a biscuit and walked to their trucks talking amongst themselves about how sorry this was from the treatment by the management.

This flew all over me. I went right over to Lenny and asked him if I could talk to him alone for a minute. I went through my whole bit about how Dick told us we couldn't even eat after being there up to an hour early. I told him that I thought that was pretty sorry. He agreed and, and offered to make amends by making it up to us the next day. After Davey found out I had complained to Lenny about being screwed out of the biscuits he was pissed off to no end. Davey called me into the office that night and proceeded to tell me that he got chewed out about it and blah, blah, blah, wah, wah, wah.

I went on home after that meeting with Davey and thought about a solution for the "crisis." That following morning I went in early and got with several other key drivers and told them about the way Davey acted and how he talked to me the night before and let them in on my idea. We all agreed on my solution to the problem.

When the morning PCM began, Davey apologized about what had

happened from the previous day, and about the whole biscuit ordeal and that everyone would be able to eat a biscuit on ten minutes of 'their' time immediately after the PCM. Smitty began bringing in several bags of hot, fresh biscuits and sat them on the counter.

We all knew what we were going to do. William slipped out right after the PCM had ended and dragged a huge garbage can over by the front door that led into the customer counter. We all filed by and got our biscuits and immediately walked out the door with over 90% of us throwing them right into the trash as we walked by.

"We don't want your biscuits," a driver replied, as they threw theirs into the trash. This pissed Davey off to no end and I thought he was going to have a stroke right on the spot. We never would receive any food from management for a long, long time, while Davey was there, because of the "World famous Biscuit Revolt of 1997." We managed to get our point across though, and believe it or not it was a strong act of solidarity.

Huntsville was beginning to become to be known as a "problem center" in the Alabama District when it came to the labor relation policy and the employees. We were slowly beginning to become notorious for our strong stance of supporting each other and management hated it.

The spirit of the union was strong in our center, including the support of the stewards. Within two and a half months after the strike I had filed roughly twenty three grievances and had received discipline in the form of roughly seven warning letters and five two day suspensions. Some employees manage to go the span of their whole career (30 years), and never even receive a suspension, much less five in less than three months with several of them coming in one day.

Management had agreed to create jobs as part of the agreement that was reached during the strike when we voted on and ratified the agreement, but they weren't living up to their end of the bargain.

Management was still handing out revenge without an ounce of conscience in the form of intolerable harassment, warning letters, and suspensions. Management was continuing the practice of using part time cover drivers to keep from hiring them full time. Why would they want to give up a source of revenue and this gravy train, when newly elected Hoffa wasn't going to complain about it?

The argument that management would use was that the reduction in volume had warranted them not to hire drivers. This could be proven to possibly be false and here's why. First there's the question of volume. Management never would say if it was it a decline in actual volume or projected volume. What I mean is, If UPS was projecting to deliver say...a ten percent increase over last years volume, but only achieved a marginal two percent increase in total volume then on paper they could say that there had been an eight percent "DECLINE" in volume, only it would have been in projected volume instead of actual volume. I understand that due to the strike we did lose some volume, but I can only speak for what I saw in my center in regards to using this excuse to keep from promoting drivers to full time status. It would stand to reason that if the decline in volume existed, as they were portraying, then it would be logical to cut out the cover drivers and roll them back into their 'original' part time jobs they had worked before going to cover driving. But, this wasn't the case. Management was still running these guys everyday on routes that weren't 'vacated' as the contract had called for. Management continued to run them everyday for months to come, while crying about not having enough volume to justify hiring them full time.

Some cover drivers would go for two or three years before finally being promoted, and this was with them driving everyday like normal, full time drivers with some even having their 'own' route's! Management would not honor anything that was agreed upon in the grievance hearings and even thumbed their noses at the decision from the higher level of the grievance panels. They were doing pretty much what they wanted to do and the local union and Hoffa was letting them. The IBT should have taken us right back out as soon as all this crap had started up and stayed out this time until management would agree to cease all the harassment, but remember back to the comments that Hoffa had made during the strike of 1997. He didn't believe in the strike and there was no way in hell he was going to do anything drastic like that, especially after UPS management had been caught by the government for contributing funds to his election campaign back in 1996, as reported in the news.

Management had without a doubt created a hit list during the strike, which judging from the harassment I was experiencing daily, only backed up our claim. The management in Huntsville was using every dirty, underhanded trick they could think of to try and break us.

Life was a living hell for those of us during the first couple of months after the strike. I dreaded the thought of work. I was sick from the whole deal. The constant abuse by management was taking its toll on my health and my family.

I had unknowingly continued to withdraw further from my family and after eleven months, I still didn't have a real relationship with my daughter like I should have...like I wanted to have. My marriage began to suffer as well, even after numerous attempts of Lesley trying to signal me that there was a problem, not with just me, but with us... and our family. I just sank that much deeper in to a depression, which was being fed daily by the management of UPS. I continued to become disgusted with my job and lashed out more at those whom I loved the most.

I began to have more frequent problems with the intensity and frequency of the pain within the joints of my hands and fingers. They were beginning to hurt more and more every night after work, which required that they be massaged and popped constantly if I was going to get any sort of relief. I would also try taking Tylenol to help try and take the edge off of the pain, but my knees continued to ache at night, waking me up a lot of nights with pain that was, at times, unbearable with some times I would wake up in the morning being unable to stand with all of my weight on my feet.

After re-visiting my family doctor and discussing with him my work regimen, he said that it was no wonder I was experiencing this. His advice was to find another line of work or expect an increase of symptoms with another twenty years of service under these conditions, and then I'd really be broken down. The climbing in and out of the package car 200 times a day or more, having to step down two and a half feet with weight in excess of fifty pounds or more. Just stop and think of the shock and stress that having to do this daily puts on your joints. I was just twenty-six years old at the time and I had known several drivers who had to have surgery on their knees from this abuse of their bodies over the past thirty years. Several had been through divorces and all of them of them had missed out on seeing their children grow up. Is this what I had to look forward to?

The next major blow I personally dealt to management came in the form of my request and follow through on the disbanding of the CHSP, or safety committee, in Huntsville. Huntsville's safety history was a joke and still is. There had been several safety issues and work place incidents brought up and I had even filed grievances on several concerns involving safety in our center.

The management and the local union would hold the local level hearings to discuss these safety grievances and as usual, the management would agree to follow the ruling from the committee and the next thing you'd know is they'd be right back doing the same thing again. Management talked a good game, but we could never get them to play ball.

The whole CHSP, or Comprehensive Health and Safety Program, which involved the participation of hourly employees is nothing but a sham. I'll go into it a little deeper in a later chapter but to make a long story short, I disbanded it and no one participated in the CHSP in Huntsville.

This is when I had received word from other supervisors that I had established several high-ranking enemies within the corporate management level of UPS. The CHSP seemed to be managements pride and joy.

I went in to Davey's office to tell him the news about his safety program and there was a pretty hot exchange of words and threats made to me, but I was going to stand my ground. I thought it was the best thing to do. I had hoped that my actions would send a message to the 'big boys' over in Atlanta that we, the members of Teamsters Local 402, were going to stand our ground on this issue.

Davey remained with us all through the rest of the year. Upper management was cracking down hard on him and like the old saying goes...it was rolling down hill. The rides were constant and although they had finally given up on me for the time being, although they still brought me into the office at least two days out of the week, because of running over allowed. All that would take place then was that Davey would tell me he needed my help, but it was a little too late for that now. Everyone had rebelled against Davey, and we, the stewards, were the eyes and voices of the member's rage. Davey began to plead with us on a daily basis to please help him out and how we were still ranked towards the bottom of the list by center ranking. Dick was coming down hard on him for being unable to break our spirit and rumors began to surface that Davey was on his way out if he couldn't get us "in line".

The Huntsville center was making a name for itself during some high level meetings at corporate and we were labeled as being a 'militant' center, and now Huntsville had claimed the status of being the worst center in the District in regard to labor relations. If we stood up for our rights and tried to enforce the contract we were tagged as being a militant, and a rogue center.

Upper brass had decided to replace Davey after he and Dick had a falling out, after Davey went to Lenny with the ultimatum, "Either move me, or I quit."

Lenny, the Alabama District manager, busted Davey down to a lower, less 'prestigious' position and sent him one of our sister centers in north Alabama. I was glad to finally get rid of him. He had been a major problem that seemed to taint Huntsville. Maybe we would get someone who would work with us and not against us.

We had become so militant and unruly in the eyes of management that we received word that top managers had decided to send in their hard-core, "hired gun" to straighten us out. We, in fact, were in for a battle like we had never seen. He was coming that next Monday and were told to prepare for hell by all the supervisors who had ever worked with him.

They relished in the thought that this "man" would be able to break Huntsville. They didn't know us as well as they thought.

Chapter 13

"Thursday 8:55 a.m. The Little Colonel gets into it with a driver on the west belt and lunges into him trying to instigate a fight. This man is out of control and he must be stopped."

The "Little Colonel", as he is known as in the world of UPS was, as a Huntsville driver put it, a mean, unhappy man. This was putting it mildly as to describe the person who would single handily terrorize everyone in Huntsville during his ruthless rule. He was a bully, but like many cowardly, insecure managers...used the company as his muscle and backbone.

He would be, without a doubt, the worst manager I would have to face so far, and by far the dirtiest too. Combined with his henchman, Smitty, they would put Huntsville through some of the worst times we had ever seen. But ultimately, in the end, his less than conventional ways and ruthless tactics coupled with the strong will of the Teamsters in Huntsville would in fact be his undoing.

Up to now the intensity of harassment and levels of intimidation that was being conducted by the management, through Davey was in itself unbearable, but in the end...we did prevail.

The daily stress with being a center manager working in Huntsville and then having to work for men like Dick and Lenny, coupled with the unbreakable spirit of the drivers was in fact Davey's down fall. Davey remained at our sister center as a supervisor for a little over a year and then was moved to another center in the Alabama district.

Before I ever actually met the Colonel, I had heard a lot of stories about his "career" while in UPS management from several drivers and employees, both hourly and management personal, all of whom held very little respect for him ... and most of them hated him.

From the rumor mills inside UPS it was evident of the intentions the Colonel had for us, in regard to the Teamster employees in Huntsville. The Colonel was in fact being sent to bring Huntsville in line by any means necessary. He was given some questionable latitude by corporate to exercise his best judgment to achieve their desired results...including going outside the realm of the labor agreement.

Both centers in Huntsville were still ranked at the bottom of the list, because Davey had been unable to achieve the desired results Lenny wanted so bad, and with the recent results of the 'employee opinion survey' coming back with negative results that too had given the management in   Huntsville a black eye as well.

We were fingered as being the root of the problem, when in fact it was the draconian style of ruthless management and intimidation that had placed Huntsville at the bottom of the list. All of that was about to change or so they thought.

The Colonel arrived at the building just before the morning PCM and he was brought in during our meeting and was introduced by Dick. There was no fan fare, no red carpets, and after the world famous biscuit revolt of 1997, no food either. I feel that Dick did this to obtain maximum effect to let us know that top management was taking off the gloves. The Colonel didn't receive a warm welcome from anybody. All the older drivers had worked for him, or with him, at some point in their careers and they disliked him very, very much. The Colonel went through his spiel about how he was planning to turn Huntsville around with or without our help, and by the end of the year...Huntsville would be on top of the list in rankings. I wasn't impressed at all by him and his dime store speech and judging from the happiness of Smitty while just merely being in the Colonel's presence I smelled a rat for sure.

Before the conclusion of the PCM that morning he told me in front of everyone that he wanted to meet with the stewards individually, the next morning, and for us to report to work an hour early.

The next morning I arrived to work early and after punching in I went to the Colonel's office door and knocked.

"Come in," he answered and I walked into the office and stood in front of his desk. "Close the door and take a seat for me please," the Colonel said. I turned and closed the door and sat down in front of his desk. The Colonel held out his hand and introduced himself to me.

I reluctantly shook his hand, and replied," James Earls."

"I've heard a lot about you here lately, James," he said while leaning back in his chair and trying to cross one of his legs. He put his hands behind his head and tried to look really relaxed but I could tell that he was acting a little anxious.

I sat there looking at him, analyzing him for his weaknesses and possible strong points. Nothing was said for a few seconds and finally I mustered, "All good I hope?"

"I heard that you were a strong union man and had a little influence in Huntsville," he replied, as he leaned the chair back a little further with the chair creaking loudly sounding as if it was about to break.

"I've heard a lot about you too Colonel." I said.

"All good I hope?" He asked in return, while cracking a smile.

"Not much of it," I replied, as the smile left his face along with a little color too from my answer.

The Colonel reached across his desk and grabbed a half full, plastic soft drink bottle and removed the lid and spat in it. While he put the lid back on and returning to his relaxed position he proceeded to tell me what he wanted to do in Huntsville in regard to making it a better place to work. I thought that it all sounded good, but I've heard this same song before and I didn't trust him enough, in fact I didn't trust any of them. I needed to see something positive from him before I would even begin imagining trusting him. He continued describing his conquests and accomplishments during his twenty some odd years while at UPS. He was displaying an air of cockiness and arrogance while telling his little stories. I sat there for the whole time it took him to tell me his story, sitting un-amused and not very impressed, and finally when he was finished he asked me, "What would it take to accomplish this on his part."

I sat there and looked at him in the eyes and thought for a minute. "Was management wanting to call a truce to their abusive labor policy campaign finally or is this a trap?" I thought to myself while trying to make a quick reading of this question. "Treat my drivers right, follow the contract and call off the dog's." I replied.

He sat there just rocking back and forth in his chair, not saying a word only squinting his eyes and grimacing while studying me. I think this was a test of wills and whether or not I was going to be a submissive subject and blink first. Finally, after what seemed like minutes, a knock on the door came and he broke his stare and told them to come in while keeping his eyes on me. It was his little thug, Smitty.

Smitty was carrying several employees' folders, which contained our records, with mine visibly placed on top. Smitty placed them on his desk and looked down at me and smiled. I crossed my eyes at him and the smile quickly left his face and he turned towards the Colonel. "How good of a driver is Mr. Earls, Smitty?" The Colonel asked.

I thought that Smitty was going to explode from just the mere excitement of being able to degrade me. "He's one of the worst in the center, Colonel." Smitty replied, in a rather stomach turning tone.

The Colonel leaned over and picked up my file and opened it. "It seems that Mr. Earls may need a little help at becoming successful Smitty," He said as he grinned slightly.

I knew right then where this was headed. It wasn't going to be anything but an old fashioned pissing contest now and the only thing that results from a pissing contest is that both sets of feet just get wet...but if that's the way he wanted it, then so be it. I couldn't help but to take a jab at them and asked, "Is that worse in the east center as a union driver or worst than a UPS manager who wanted to be a union driver...but couldn't make it?' I said. The Colonel looked at me and stood up. I was almost as tall as he was while still sitting down.

"James I look forward to working with you," he said then excused me and I stood up and thanked him for his time and walked out of his office with Smitty closing the door. I left out of the offices and walked out into the building where some of the drivers were waiting on me to come out.

"What went on in there?" One of them asked.

"I'm not for sure, but I think he tried to intimidate me I guess and maybe tried to and find out where I stood on certain issue and things. Just watch out because it looks like he's going to be hunting heads." I said to them all as we went to work.

Immediately off the bat there was a serious problem, which involved Abel, who had now been promoted into feeders full time. This is a prime example of management's labor policy's set of double standards, which at times discriminates against employees.

Abel had taken out a tractor that was supposed to have been 'red tagged', meaning taken out of service, and it was not to be driven by ANYONE due to safety problems, but it was mistakenly placed in the line up for drivers to use.

The problem with Abel's tractor was that the fifth wheel, the mechanism that secures the trailer to the tractor, was broken. When you hooked up to the trailer it felt like it was 'locked' whenever you tugged on it with the tractor. Abel had climbed out after hooking up to the trailer to manually and visually inspect the fifth wheel to make sure that the locking jaw had come around the shank of the trailer and that the keeper pin was out, and in this case it was. Abel proceeded to carry the trailer to a business to exchange the empty one he had for another which was full of packages. He left the center and traveled about four miles, and all of a sudden the trailer came unhooked from the tractor and dropped off onto the highway as he was driving. The trailer, luckily, had swerved over into someone's yard and destroyed only their mailbox. Abel called the new center manager of the Huntsville building, the Colonel along with his little stooge Smitty, and several other supervisors came out to the site to investigate the incident and to take pictures.

Abel was immediately taken out of service pending the outcome of the investigation, and then he was later discharged under the labor agreement. Abel filed a grievance to protest his discharge and sat back waiting for Matt and the local union to do its thing.

The management carried the tractor down to Birmingham, to the automotive department, to have the fifth wheel placed on a device to check and see if it had functioned properly during this incident. It was rumored that the fifth wheel wouldn't lock after numerous attempts by the management to get it to lock. Finally after 'slamming' the device into the fifth wheel only then did it lock. They now had 'driver error' on the top of their list. By now Abel was growing restless and made a crucial 'revelation' to all parties involved that expedited the rehiring of him.

What management did not know until he called them and told them was that after dropping the trailer he got out and looked at the fifth wheel which was damaged. He then had begun to search the ground around the accident and found numerous broken and damaged parts that belonged to the fifth wheel. After management learned of this, they began to back peddle as if the world itself was coming to an end.

In fact, this proved without a doubt, it was faulty equipment, and if it wasn't for Abel's quick thinking, after the accident, to search the ground and find those broken pieces...chances are he would've never been back...ever.

One of the problems I had with this situation was that Abel was automatically found guilty and discharged before the conclusion of the investigation considering their was some doubt to begin with, whereas in our contract we are supposed to be "innocent" until proven guilty...which was clearly not the case here due in fact that the investigation performed by their 'competent' automotive management personnel failed to produce ANY finding's of 'missing and broken' parts. Did they even know what they were doing or did they know, and try to railroad this driver in an attempt to reduce any 'liability' from the accident? You decide. Drivers from other, 'less troublesome and passive', centers have done the same thing, and all they had received was being taken out of service for a few days, but they were ALLOWED to work thus missing no pay. It clearly was a display in the discriminatory and injustices of the managements labor relation's policy towards some of its employees.

The next problem I had with this was that the tractor itself was taken to Birmingham, Alabama, to be inspected by management without the presence of a local union representative or a designate to make sure that the integrity of the investigation was being upheld.

If Abel had not looked for and kept the broken parts to the fifth wheel, what then could have prevented management from lying and saying that the fifth wheel was okay and that it was driver error? Nothing.

Next, I had a problem that management failed to call the police and get a D.O.T compliance officer out there to fill out a report on the accident. They may have broken the law themselves for failing to do this since it involved a commercial motor vehicle and the accident happened on a public road, which involved collateral damage.

The reason why management had done this will remain unknown. Maybe they knew before hand that they had royally screwed up by sending him out in a tractor that was unsafe and if an officer came out to write a report they might not have been able to explain why the vehicle was on the road to begin with.

Abel got his job back but without any back pay if you can believe it although it wasn't even his fault. Matt and the local union should have been there when the inspection was being conducted. This was usual for Matt and the local union, meaning never being there when a member needed their help.

After the Colonel had settled in, and things were kind of eerily calm, I had the opportunity to change routes when it came time for a new bid.

I had been on the Downtown route now for about four years and thought it would probably be a good time to come off it. I had had so many problems out of the past three center managers with not being able to run scratch on it in just about the whole four years of being on it. I didn't need any trouble out of the Colonel because of the route.

I had been on the new route before, covering vacations for the driver then, and I liked it a lot. There were similarities between it and my old downtown route in relation to the amount of business stops it was dispatched with and I liked the residential stops more, because the houses were only a short distance off the road.

I could get down there and hustle them off, because I had been used to killing myself on my old residential stops, the Covemont section, and this would be a welcome change.

Everything was working out well after my transition. It took a couple of days for the customers to get used to my way of servicing them. I tried to conform to what they were used to and the way their old driver had taken care of them and even had a few try to take advantage of me.

One customer comes immediately to mind. The lady owned a copier business and received C.O.D's just about every day. Every time I would go in there they'd never have the money and wanted me to come back later in the afternoon when I made the pick up next door to them and they'd then try to have the money. Well this went on for several days and finally I had enough of it. This was costing me a lot of time to which I didn't get any credit, as far as time allowance, for the second, and sometimes, the third attempt. I finally just didn't go back that afternoon. Well the next day the lady comes unglued. I explained to her that for now on there would only be one attempt made, per day, on her packages and they needed to have the money for the C.O.D or I'd send it back after I made the third attempt. Needless to say that this didn't sit too well with her, because she called in a complaint on me.

After discussing the matter with the Colonel he sided with her and made me out to be the bad guy. I asked the Colonel how many attempts we were supposed to make on the packages a day which he told me just one. That's all I needed to know. I delivered again to her the next morning and once again it was the same old bull. "I need to run to the bank, will you wait?" was the common request from her. I told her that I couldn't wait that I had other customers who need their packages too. After telling her this she became extremely pissed off. I just loaded up her things and left. After I stopped for lunch, Smitty paged me wanting to know what happened and that her husband was trying to find me with the money to get the packages. I told Smitty to tell the husband he could catch me as I came back up the other side of the Parkway if he wanted to pay for his packages. As I'm delivering up the other side of the highway the husband pulls in front of me and blocks me in. After a minute or two of a heated cussing out by him I give him his packages and he leaves. When I arrive back to the center that evening they had called in a complaint on me and as a result the Colonel gives me a warning letter for what I had done, which was to work as I had been instructed. I didn't say anything to the Colonel about it because I was going on vacation the next week. This was on a Friday I believe. Before coming back to work I went to the store and bought myself a micro cassette recorder to carry with me the next time I had to deliver anything to her.

I returned from vacation, and later that morning I delivered to her again. Only this time I had a recorder with me and I cut it on right before I walked into the business. As I was in there she talked to me like I was a dog. She swore up and down that I had delivered to her last week, which was impossible because I was on vacation, and had cost her lots of money for not coming back by there to make a second attempt on the C.O.D's and on and on and on. I never said a word at all...nothing. When it was all said and done I walked out and cut the recorder off knowing what was going to happen that evening. Sure enough, that evening the lady called in another complaint in on me citing that I had cussed her and threatened her husband. Smitty was salivating at the mouth because of this. He thought I would get discharged for this latest complaint.

I was asked to come in into the office that very evening and Alvin was in there with the Colonel waiting on me to get back to the building. The Colonel went through his spiel about what the customer had said and how unprofessional I was and a disgrace to wear the UPS uniform and so on. I just sat back letting him dig himself a hole. Finally after I had enough, "I have something to say about that if you don't mind," I replied as I reached into my pocket and sat the recorder out on the desk. "I have something that might clear this whole thing up," I said to the Colonel as I switched it on.

The tape began playing the whole incident, and it plainly showed how the lady had lied on me. The Colonel and Smitty just stood there with a stupid look on their faces. I had shot down their little scheme and they didn't know what to do, and before it was all said and done they had to withdraw all of the complaints and discipline from my record.

They were going to take the word of that lady over me, and if not for the recorder, I would have more than likely been suspended for my 'alleged actions' involving that customer. This would be, but one, of many incidents involving the Colonel over similar things of this nature.

It was a matter of time now before the Colonel and son would grow tired of me finishing early everyday and going home at a decent time. I was getting off and leaving the building around 5:45-6:00 p.m. I was enjoying it and for a change I was running under allowed on the route by at least twenty minutes everyday. No reason to be dragged into the office you'd think. Think again.

After the incident with the 'less than honest lady' I went into work one morning when after checking my load, while still being on the dock, and I noticed that I had a section of my residential delivery stops missing. I asked a supervisor what was going on, and he told me that Smitty had instructed him to pull about twenty-five stops off in that particular section, and load in its place some apartment stops instead. Those stops were not on the truck when I had bid on it in the first place or I wouldn't have bid on the route to start with. This upset me tremendously. I, for once, since the failed team concept scheme, had been getting home in plenty of time to sit down and eat dinner with my loved ones, like a family and had begun spending more time with Mattie who was now a year old, and they were going to throw a wrench in the whole thing. Smitty came bopping down the dock and walked right up to my truck and peered in.

"By the way we moved some of your stops to Jeff and gave you 'Golf Road" instead," Smitty replied gleefully.

"For how long?" I asked.

"Till we take them off," He said as he smiled and walked off.

It took everything I had to keep from cussing him out that morning, but I just bit my tongue instead and loaded up my overnights and left the building to start my day.

When I came to the apartments that I now had instead of my original residential stops I lost all kinds of time. No one was ever home to sign for them, and most of the offices wouldn't sign for their resident's packages.

I was now arriving back to the building at around 6:30, and by the time I checked out, and drove home it was 7:20-7:30. I had lost almost two hours of family time by just management pulling that stunt to screw me over. It didn't make sense for me to deliver those and with the coming of the time change in the fall, it would become a concern for my very life.

The apartments they had given me were located in a high crime area, which had had three murders and countless robberies of delivery people in the past few years. Now I was going to have to deliver these stops in the evening after dark.

I immediately filed a grievance to protest this new concern for my safety, but the management and the local union didn't see any problem with it and turned my grievance down. I went on and tried to do the best I could with the apartments, but I began to run over allowed right off the bat and then the Colonel slowly increased the number of stops I was being dispatched with, which was slowly making it impossible for me to finish in time.

That was a new window of opportunity for management to once again start harassing me about running over allowed. I raised the question again several times in the office about how I was not running over allowed before they put those apartments on me, and now with them I was running over everyday. The Colonel's reply was that "I was intentionally running over allowed in a feeble attempt to have the apartments removed and give me back my original stops instead." They were crazy. Hell I just couldn't get done, because the apartments were killing me. With the increased number of paid send again's, known as undeliverable packages, rising daily and coupled with me running over allowed more and more each day, I received word that Smitty was going to ride with me on the following Monday. I really didn't mind a supervisor riding, I just didn't want him to ride, but maybe now he'll see how difficult it was for me to get the apartments delivered and hopefully take them back off of me.

I reported to work on time that next morning and right after the PCM Smitty had his clipboard in hand and told me that he was going to ride with me to see "what my problem" was. I didn't really think anything about it, but now there was a problem before I had even walked out of the PCM with all the drivers. I knew right then that it was 'my fault', and I had lost any chance of getting a 'fair' ride before I had even stepped onto the car.

When we arrived to deliver the apartments for that afternoon, Smitty asked me if I knew to go to at least two different neighbors if the consignee wasn't home.

I said, "yes," and that I had been doing it all along, except if I suspected or knew that the package was a high value item like a computer, VCR or something along that nature.

I started delivering the apartments and when the 'two neighbor' routine wasn't working, Smitty realized that I had been justified for bringing all of those "send-again's" back to the building each night, and he then 'modified' the rules.

"I want you to check with four or five residents if you have to try and get rid of these packages," he said. I just shook my head, but complied. We wound up walking across to other complexes as we tried to find a place to leave the packages.

Instead of the two minutes per undeliverable stop that I was allowed it was taking me sometimes five minutes per stop as we walked aimlessly door to door looking for someone to sign for the packages. It was really stupid.

We completed the route and arrived later back to the center that night later than if I would have been by myself. I couldn't wait to see the OR for this ride the next morning.

The next morning after arriving at work I walked straight to the east center office, and began to look for the previous days OR that would contain the answer to my question of how much time I had run over allowed with Smitty riding on car with me.

I began to search on the desktop in the office and it wasn't out there. None of the reports were. They were always out in view for everyone to see how they had done the day before. I asked a clerk where the reports were and she said that the Colonel had instructed her not to let anyone see it them.

I was called into the office after the PCM that morning and was instructed by the Colonel that I had demonstrated that I could do the job, and although I never actually got to see the OR, the Colonel told me that I had done a better job.

"Better job at what?" I asked, but no answer.

The Colonel was telling only half of the truth. I had done a better job at bringing back fewer packages that were undeliverable, but I had in fact ran over allowed worse than ever by having to do it. Management would never disclose this and although I filed several grievances requesting the information along with asking for a copy of the OR so I could verify the production numbers myself, but I never would get a copy of it although I had previously been guaranteed a copy of it by the labor manager for the Alabama District.

The summer months didn't affect me much because now that I was feeder qualified I got to cover feeder vacations and thankfully I didn't have to mess with the Colonel and son.

Toward the end of the summer I would be forced back onto the package car, after feeder vacations were dying down, and back onto my old route, and in the meantime, the Colonel had imposed the curfew of 6:30 p.m back on us with specific instructions to call in and 'speak to a supervisor' if we saw that we were going to be unable to make it back to the building in time to beat the curfew.

The Colonel had yet been able to get the pre-load down on time, just as with Davey, and it was getting close to peak season. We were still having a problem with getting out of the building on time, and once again we began experiencing the same problem with the Colonel as we did with Davey and all the others. With leaving the building sometimes after 9:30 a.m and then factoring in the imposed curfew of 6:30 p.m it was impossible to complete our day without having to go back out and finish delivering.

The Colonel decided to combat this by putting supervisors on car with the 'problem' drivers and dragging them into the office everyday and disciplining them. It was ruthless. He would make Davey's reign look like a nun's convention or something. He was proving to be relentless in his quest to 'bring Huntsville in line' and with help from Smitty they would step up their efforts in terrorizing the whole center.

Chapter 14

"8:57 a.m: Smitty comes running out and jumps into the truck yelling for me to hurry up and lets go. Needless to say when the smoke cleared I was the only one left standing because he had ran off to get his 'daddy'".

People were beginning to crack and we were losing them and their support. Some of the drivers couldn't handle the stress of going into the office everyday and having their jobs threatened for petty things that seemed out of their control.

The Colonel and Smitty were ruthless and clearly on a mission. I had received a couple of warning letters, that were later thrown out, for getting into verbal fights with both of them in the office over some of these drivers from the way the Colonel would talk to them while in there discussing the OR. He'd treat them without respect and the minute that happened here, the Colonel and I would go at one another. I knew that the drivers he had in there were good at their jobs and I knew that they were doing their jobs. I had had enough of it.

I called Matt, over at the union hall, and told him something had to be done about the Little Colonel. "Well give me a chance to call Hembry," or "Well you know how the Colonel is," is all he'd have to say about the way we were being treated. I was fed up with the way this cracker head was doing us. Something had to be done and done soon. He was out of control.

I held a parking lot union meeting one morning and discussed with all of the drivers about what was going on with the "Little Colonel and gang", and what needed to be done to put a stop to it or at least...try.

"We need to start filing grievances every time these two screw up," I said. "Not just the stewards or the person it affects...but everyone," I said.

We all agreed that's what we were going to do. Before the meeting had ended that morning in the parking lot, I told everyone that it was extremely important that we all stopped to take our meal period as it was stated, and required, in the contract. Most everyone had agreed, but unless we all would agree to do it and stick together on this, it wouldn't work. I did manage to tell everyone that as stewards we could press the issue and make the management force all of the drivers to take their lunch because the contract supported this course of action. I didn't want to do this because I knew that management would then manipulate the language in a way that would be harmful to the drivers, because the local union would allow it to happen and I didn't want to go this route unless it was just absolutely necessary.

The problem was that the Colonel had most of the new drivers, and even some less senior drivers as well, so scared of being fired that they were going out and running all day and skipping their lunch and giving it back to the company.

This is one of the areas of the contract that management does not care to push the enforcement of. The language reads as follows:

"ARTICLE 54: *The employee shall be entitled to and required to take a lunch period of one hour. Failure to take and properly record the required meal period may be cause for disciplinary action.*"

The dilemma was with me having been suspended and issued warning letters in the past for taking too much lunch, and for 'failing to properly record my meal period,' now the management was allowing the drivers to do the same thing except the other way around. Management only allowed this to happen because it was saving them money plus also getting the pick up volume back earlier to be processed.

The company was, and still is, making a killing on this practice nationwide.

I had gone in the office to represent several drivers whom had had their routes covered by cover drivers while they had been on vacation. When they would come back to work they'd be expected to run the same numbers as the cover drivers from the previous week, which, they couldn't. I'd then request to view the time cards of the cover drivers to see if they had even stopped to take their lunch, which my request were always denied. The reason why I asked to view the time cards was to see if they had stopped to take their meal break, which it they failed to take any lunch it would have a negative effect on the 'regular' drivers ability to run the same production numbers of the cover driver. Here's why... Take for example the normal driver delivers his route and runs over allowed by thirty minutes a day then when the cover driver runs it, they run under 30 minutes a day on the same route. Then say that the cover driver was proven to had failed to take their lunch period, per the contract, which then becomes a 60 minute subtraction to their 30 minutes of under allowed time, (-30 minutes under allowed time + 60 minute meal period = (+) 30 minutes over allowed time), which would put them at 30 minutes over allowed, just like the normal driver who stops and takes his lunch. I had requested numerous times to view the time cards to see if this was the case, which I knew it was after asking the cover drivers, while investigating a grievance filed by the driver in question. My request would be denied and thrown out in the grievance procedure.

It seemed that our 'old guard" infested local union wasn't too interested in rocking the boat. What in the hell were they there for? It started to become clearer each time that we lost 'winnable' grievances that the Local 402 officers were more interested in defending the rights of the management than that of the members.

Management had theses people scared and it was becoming a major problem that was out of control. I finally had enough of the drivers that were taking their lunch being disciplined for following the contract and then the management patting the ones who wasn't taking their lunch on the back.

DATE GRIEVANCE FILED: 9-1-98

EXPLAIN GRIEVANCE: *Management wants us to have our pick up volume in by 6:30 p.m. With us getting out late and the paid day still high, drivers are not taking their full one-hour lunch on the road and before the eighth hour. Many are giving their lunches to the company or taking it back at the building.*

REMEDY SOUGHT: *Make drivers take their lunch.*

The local union had become inept to deal with our needs and that's when I first decided to consider a run against Matt in the upcoming local union election.

During the summer of 1998 while making a delivery, I backed up to the dock and opened the back to the truck. I stepped up on the dock and rang the buzzer, to notify the worker inside of my presence, and stepped back down into the truck. The stop at where I was delivering was loaded in the rear section of the floor of the truck. I bent down and started picking the packages up that varied in size and weight and began placing them on the dock. Finally the one that was left on the bottom of the pile was a fairly good size package. I looked at the top of it and didn't see anything out of the ordinary about it. I squatted down to pick it up and pop! Something popped in my back. I fell to my knees in pain. The man who worked in the shipping and receiving looked at me and asked if I needed him to call someone. I said yes for him to call my supervisor and ask for Smitty. He ran to the phone and called UPS.

After about three minutes or so, Smitty came to the phone and asked to speak to me directly. The worker pulled the phone out to the truck and I spoke to Smitty.

He began to ask me what I had done wrong and if I was really hurt or just needed to rest. "I can't stand up straight Smitty,' I screamed into the phone.

"Can you make it until you get back tonight if I send you some help?" He asked.

"If you don't come and get me and carry me to the doctor I'm going to call an ambulance and cause a scene," I replied in pain.

"I'm on my way," he said slamming the phone down.

I asked John, the dockworker to carry the package in and weigh it. John couldn't lift it and had to get another worker to help him carry it in. They carried it to the scales they used to weigh their outbound shipments. "168 pounds!" John yelled to me.

UPS only allowed a maximum of 150 pounds to be shipped through their system. How did this get through UPS's system, not that it mattered now since I was injured?

Smitty finally showed up, with a replacement driver, about 45 minutes later. He didn't say a word other than to get in his truck. On the way over he asked me what had happened and I told him and gave the information off of the package. I still couldn't sit up straight and had to lean over the whole way to the clinic.

Once I arrived I filled out paperwork and was then sent back to see the doctor and come to find out, I had only pulled a muscle in my back, and I was given a shot and prescribed something for the inflammation, and then placed on a light duty restriction for a few days. After the shot had kicked in, I could begin to straighten back up, but it was still very painful to do so, as I walked on out to the reception area where Smitty was on the phone to the Colonel. I received my paperwork and was handed my work release and was sent home.

On the way back to the center nothing was said at all between the two of us, and it was a long fifteen-minute drive back to the building. I was sent home for the day and paid the routine eight hours pay although I had only worked about five hours. That's the way it worked. Up to this point, in regard to injuries that I had sustained so far while at UPS, I had two pulled groin muscles, one torn forearm muscle from moving a dolly, one scratched eye from dirt flying around inside the truck while driving, one neck strain and two strained stomach muscles all in just ten years time. I sat at home that night in pain and unable to sleep.

I awoke very stiff the next morning when I was getting dressed to report to work. Although I wasn't going to be able to drive a package car, I still could do some other work around in the building just to get my eight hours in. I wasn't going to be out long enough to qualify for workman's comp, but I really couldn't afford just to sit around at my expense and not draw anything.

I put my browns on and drove on down to the center. I walked in and like anybody who was ever hurt, everyone came up to see how I was doing and to find out what happened. After all that was over I went and knocked on the Colonel's door and there was no answer. I walked back out into the center and here he came bopping down the building spitting tobacco juice all over the floor. I thought to myself, "How disgusting," as he walked towards me and then rudely passed me by as if I wasn't even there. This really pissed me off and managed to set the tone for our little meeting that was to come between him and me.

I followed him on into his office, and I stood in front of his desk. He asked me to sit but I declined and told him, "I'm ready to work."

"Ready to work?" He asked looking puzzled.

"Yeah, you know...so I can get my eight hours in," I said smartly.

"You can't drive as far as I remember," he snapped.

"I didn't say anything about driving Colonel, I'm here to pick up trash and answer phones.' I replied confidently.

By now the Colonel had begun to dig around on his desk looking for my release from the company doctor. When he finally found it he said to me, "It says here that you're on a 25 pound weight restriction and unable to work. I don't have anything around here for you to do James," he said while sitting the release form back on his desk.

Leaning against the wall I said, "I can plant flowers just as good as the next guy."

The Colonel leaned back in his seat and wiped his mouth off that had some spit running out the corner of it and said, "I'm not going to work you."

"Colonel you can either pay me now or later, and I want you to remember that you worked two injured drivers earlier and had them planting flowers to get their eight hours in." I replied.

"File the grievance," he popped off in a smart alec tone. So I pulled out the grievance right there on the spot. I figured this would be his position while at home the night before, and decided as a precaution to go ahead and fill out the grievance in advance. I had already punched it on the clock to make it official with the date and he read over it and told me that I had to leave the property. I turned and walked out.

Two weeks later, when the local level hearing was held to discuss my grievance on this issue...I won. Management had to pay me eight hours pay for those days and Hembry reamed the Colonel after we left. The top managers don't like paying out grievances on anything especially something as stupid as this was which was the Colonels own fault.

The harassment and intimidation began to increase even more and it seemed that the stewards were the only thing standing in his way of really turning the heat up in Huntsville.

Harry told me that he had heard the Colonel tell Smitty during one of their meetings that he'd never seen a steward like me and didn't know quite how to handle me. I found this to be a compliment.

Several drivers had since retired after the Colonel's arrival, vacating several routes and once again I had the opportunity to move off of this crap route and move to one that had a good time allowance.

The strange thing about the move was I found out that as soon as I came off of the "Golf Road" route, the Colonel pulled off all of those apartments that I had been complaining about for several months that had been causing me to run over allowed, and moved them to another driver. That told me right then that he had only put those stops on me to harass me and to cause me to run over allowed.

Well, anyway, I wasn't on that sorry route anymore so it didn't matter, and I was getting a new route, one that I knew, but I didn't bother to tell the Colonel that. I decided to play dumb, and this time they were going to have to train me and whatever numbers I ran with them on car with me, and those production numbers would be what I would be held to.

Well the routes were to be 'officially' vacated with the new drivers on them by the following Monday. When that Monday came I was looking forward to the change of scenery and all of the new places to eat that were on my new route.

On Monday morning I found out during the PCM that Smitty was going to train me on the route. This was great because he had never been on it and didn't even know where it was. With him being from out of town he had no knowledge of the area. When I found this out I really played dumb.

After the PCM, I was walking out of the meeting toward the truck, which was parked on the inside of the building and just outside the customer counter door, and Smitty started right in on me.

"You're walking too slow let's go," he said, while snapping his fingers. I stopped in my tracks, and asked what his problem was?

"I don't have a problem, but you're not going to jerk me around today James." He said. I walked straight to the Colonels office and walked in on him with Smitty in tow. The Colonel stopped what he was doing and took off his glasses and looked up and asked me what I wanted.

"If this is the way this day's going to be I am going to file a grievance to keep him off of the truck." I replied in an upset tone.

"File the grievance, he's riding with you today or you can go home," the Colonel said as he began writing again.

I turned and walked back to the truck with Smitty clearing his throat annoyingly the whole way back. I stepped up on the dock and looked inside. I had a pretty good idea of where I was going but I wasn't about to let on. I started going through my overnight packages, which were piled out behind my truck, like Harry had trained me to do.

"What are you doing now?" Smitty asked.

"I'm going through my airs." I replied.

"You don't do that back here. Carry them around to the front and set them up outside." Smitty commanded. I knew if I would do this that more than likely I would have some in there that didn't belong to me but he was only interested in getting me to pull out of the building which would've then put me on my 'on road' time and would've taken me off of the preloads time...his time, which would only have a negative effect on my over allowed for that day...a day with him riding!

I had just about twenty overnight packages or so. It took me three trips to carry them all around to the cab and set them behind the door.

I followed Smitty's orders and closed the rear door and climbed up into the seat while he fidgeted with his jump seat. It seemed that it wasn't working right and wouldn't come down so he could sit on it.

"I'll just stand," he replied

"No you won't either. If you're going with me on the road you'll have a seat belt on or you won't go." I said smiling.

"You're joking right?" He asked in disbelief.

"Try me and see," I replied.

He jumped out of the truck and jerked the seat out and traded it with a car parked beside me. This one worked and he sat down and buckled up. As we pulled out of the building he put his sunglasses on and put another dip in his mouth. "Like father, like son," I thought to myself while sounding my horn. I still had all of those overnight packages to sort through and I just had a gut feeling that some of them weren't mine. I hoped they weren't.

As I pulled out I was sure to perform a thorough pre-trip inspection of everything on the truck checking to make sure that everything on the truck was working properly. Most of the drivers had left by now and I opened the bulkhead door and took my arm and shoved a space out in the shelf to put the three tote boxes full of overnight packages in. I began sitting up the packages the best I could and at times calling out to Smitty to find out if something belonged to me or someone else. Smitty pulled out a piece of paper and looked over it and would answer yes or no if something belonged to us.

I began finding one, and then two of them that didn't belong to me. I wanted to tell him that I had found some packages that weren't mine, but decided to wait until I had finished sorting them all. When I had finished setting them up, I told Smitty that I had found about six stops that didn't belong to me, but in fact belonged to the driver beside me instead.

"Can we get them?" He asked.

"I don't know the route remember, that's your call not mine," I replied.

Smitty turned really red from his sudden rise in blood pressure and he asked me whom they belonged to.

"I don't know," I replied, although I knew.

Smitty ran back into the center to see if any other driver was in there that could run them for us.

He came back out and asked, "Would you have a problem if a supervisor got these?"

"No," I replied, pausing for a second, "I could use the money." I answered.

He knew right then what I meant. If he used a supervisor to deliver them, when I could have, I would surely file a grievance and after the last one they lost to me the Colonel didn't need another ass chewing like he received from Hembry.

"We'll get them, let's go!" Smitty said excitedly, and I put them back into the proper location in the shelf and shut the door and we were off. By now, I had been scoring 96% on my methods, which meant two things. One I was good at them and two...I've been ridden with a lot by management. I knew the methods like the back of my hand, and I was going to use them today more than ever. I pulled out on to the road and drove up to the light. We sat there a few minutes and turned left onto the Parkway, which had a posted speed limit of 50 miles an hour, and brother, was I going to drive it.

The time was now about 9:15 and we had roughly an hour to deliver twenty-three some odd stops, once we got on area, and I knew that we weren't going to make service on some of them but hey, it wasn't my problem. Smitty called the shot on that.

Well, anyway I proceeded to drive down the Parkway watching my speed and adjusting it accordingly to the posted signs. I noticed, out of the corner of my eye, Smitty looking at his watch then leaning over to see how fast I was going which was the speed limit. He continued to do this several more times and then finally asked, "What are you doing? Let's go...we've got to go."

"Go where?" I asked, knowing that he was asking me to speed up a little since we were running behind. "Are you asking me to drive unsafe and speed Smitty?" I asked.

"I'm telling you to quit dragging around and go! We have to get all of the air's off by 10:30." Smitty replied franticly.

It was around 10:50 a.m when I delivered my last overnight package. I had about nine late, all a result of Smitty's poor judgment, and that was nine he was going to have to answer to Dick for the next morning and quite possibly refund those nine late air's out of his own pocket to the customers. He had become extremely perturbed with me after that although if he had allowed me to do my job like I had been trained to do in the first place, then this wouldn't have happened, but no, he wanted to be a wise guy about it and it cost him nine service failures.

I started delivering my ground stops at around 11:00 a.m and Smitty started right in on me. "You've got to use the handrail whenever you enter or exit the vehicle James okay?" He said. I didn't say a word. Finally, he was telling me to "grab the handrail" before I even had a chance to and often was in the process of grabbing the handrail as he said it.

Finally lunch came around, and after delivering a little strip mall I chose to go ahead and stop at a restaurant that was there in front of the shopping center. I turned the truck around and started towards the restaurant and backed into a parking space and shut the car down.

"What are you doing now?" Smitty asked in a disgusted tone.

"I do get a lunch you know," I said, as I stood up to unlock the bulkhead door to get my wallet from back there.

"I wanted to finish delivering the rest of this section before we stopped," he said.

I tossed him the keys and said, "You go ahead and deliver it, just be back in forty five minutes to pick me up," while reaching for my wallet and climbing out.

He handed me the keys back and replied, "Never mind."

We walked into the restaurant and he offered to buy me my lunch. "I've got a job and I don't need any help at buying my lunch," I said, as I paid for my order. I didn't want him or the Colonel to buy me a thing, I mean here they were screwing with me day in, and day out, and then they wanted to buy me my lunch...yeah right. Well my number was called for my order to be picked up, I headed for a table toward the front of the restaurant where I could watch and see who was coming in and out of the place. It was pretty well packed and seats were limited, and I had decided early on that I wasn't going to allow Smitty the honor of sharing a table with me to eat so I began to spread out everything I had brought into the place with me, my newspapers and books and so on. When I finished spreading everything out, I barely had room enough to eat on the table, and had to arrange the things a time or two for myself. Smitty finally came strolling up to my table and looked around and asked me where he was going to sit?

"I don't know...but not with me." I replied, as customers in the place had begun to stop eating and observe us and here came the throat clearing and grunting noises.

"You...you're joking right?" He asked nervously while stammering.

"No, I'm not JOKING." I replied "I can't keep you from riding with me today, but I can keep you from eating with me today," I finished. I thought he was going to break down and cry right then. People had begun whispering to one another and pointing indiscreetly at him and laughing quietly. He moved out of my way and sat down at a table beside me.

After about a couple of minutes of silence he began asking me personal questions and my family and etc..."I can't talk and eat at the same time Smitty it gives me indigestion." I replied, while lightly tapping my chest with the back of my fist. He sulled up like a kid and didn't speak to me until after lunch. I guess he never had a driver refuse to eat with him before and it was a shock to him. All I can say is welcome to Huntsville Jack!

As we left the restaurant I walked on out ahead of him and climbed up in the truck and put my wallet away. Smitty had to go to the bathroom and he was taking his sweet time in there and after about ten minutes or so, on their time, he came strolling out of the restaurant picking his teeth with a toothpick. I had the motor running and he walked up to the steps of the car and walked in and sat down.

"Uh, hum..." I said, drawing a look of ignorance from Smitty.

I sat there looking at him with him looking back at me...not knowing what I was wanting. Finally after a few seconds he said, "What?'

"Whenever you enter or exit MY package car you need to use the handrail Smitty. I'm responsible to make sure you are safe while out here in my care and I'd hate to see you fall out and get hurt and then get a warning letter or something for failing to work safe." I replied in a smart and meaningful tone.

I thought he was going to pop a 'roid' or something. He didn't say anything to me after that, hell he wouldn't even look at me in the face for the rest of the day.

The rest of the day, after that little incident at the restaurant went smooth with Smitty sitting over in the seat the whole time and never saying a word to me other than something that was business related. I was happy because that's the way I wanted it anyway. I still had fifteen minutes of my lunch left and decided to stop at a gas station and take it inside where they had a little deli later in the afternoon. I was about finished with my route and I decided to go ahead and stop there before running the residential stops that were left in the shelf. The day went well without a hitch and we returned back to the building.

The next morning I came to work earlier than normal to try and get a look at the OR before the Colonel hid it. I walked into the office and caught Smitty off guard and asked him to see the OR from yesterday. Smitty reached down onto his desk and snatched up a stack of papers and began rolling them up.

"Is that the OR there in your hand?" I asked.

"Yeah James, but you can't see it." He replied and stuck it in his back pocket. This immediately threw up a flag and I asked, "Why?"

"The Colonel said not to let any driver see it without clearing it first with him." Smitty said while trying to get around me and go outside in to the building. What in the world was he trying to hide? Unless...unless we had done really bad that day and had run way over allowed and if this was the case then there was no way they wanted me to see those production numbers for that day when Smitty was training me. This would wind up cutting their own throats in the process.

I followed Smitty on out into the building and around to the Colonels office. Smitty had already gone in and closed the door. I walked on in and knocked on the door. No answer. I knocked a little louder. Still no answer. Finally I looked down on the floor, and in-between the floor and the door I noticed that the light that was on inside the office caused some movement of the shadows across the floor and I knew that there were at least two people in there.

"I know y'all are in there...I can here your heavy panting, and..." I replied while gently tapping on the door and dancing around in a little three stooges style jig. The clerks in the office said they were both in there as they laughed hysterically at my antics. I gave up on this after a few more attempts to get them to unlock the door and I walked on out.

I mingled with the other drivers for a while and then we walked up to the customer counter to attend the daily PCM. After the meeting we were excused and I walked back down to the check in counter to get some supplies. I picked up a few things for my customers and made the walk back to my truck on the dock. When I started to step up on the dock I found Smitty standing there blocking my way, and he had his back to me. "Excuse me please," I said. He glanced over his shoulder a little to see if it was I and continued to stand there blocking my path.

"EXCUSE ME!" PLEASE!" I screamed out. This time everyone stopped what they were doing and turned to see what was going on. Smitty moved out of my way this time and as I passed him he was a solid red color, and he began grunting and clearing his throat. I believe he wanted me to bump into him so he could say that I was trying to provoke a fight with him. This wouldn't be the first time the "The Colonel and gang" would use this tactic. It would happen several more times with various other drivers in the upcoming months.

Well the local union and management later met and heard the grievance that I filed for the excessive rides, and it was agreed upon by both parties that management would not ride with me anymore until I was given a chance to learn more of my route. I had won another battle for the good guys.

Several drivers had been getting hurt quite frequently and management had stepped up their policy of rewarding injuries with discipline. Quite a few drivers had been given warning letters for getting injured. All of the injuries were avoidable in management's eyes, but with the line of work we do, a person was bound to become injured sooner or later.

This, in my opinion, was nothing more than an 'illegal' attempt, in violation of the OSHA Act, to discourage the reporting of injuries by the employees of UPS. The way this little 'game' works is that management has posters all of the building citing that it is your right and responsibility to report all injuries to your supervisor. It's the law. Then, when a driver reports an injury, management conducts an 'investigation' of how and why the employee had injured himself. Then they decide that one of their 'broad language' work place safety rules had been broken. For example...say that a person was walking inside the building and walked through a portion of the building that had a poorly lit walkway due from the negligence of management failing to replace a light bulb. Then that employee slip's and fall's on say...a black crayon that blended in with the shadows on the floor and couldn't be seen without a "properly functioning light". When the employee slip's they break their hand in the fall. Then, after management had 'investigated' the accident they then came back and ruled that the employee had violated the work place safety rule of "failing to keep their eyes ahead of their work" and issues him a warning letter, after...the key word here is 'after' they call in the injury and report it to the injury hotline.

The act of discouraging employees comes into play now. Other employees, then see that this injured employee has received a warning letter for 'reporting' an injury and the next time they get hurt they are then less likely to report it to a supervisor and just elect to tough it out and wait for it to heal...even at times making the injury worse due to their reluctance, and fear of reporting it and choose to work on. It is the 'psychological' effect of this part of UPS's labor policy that thwarts an already high OSHA reportable injury rate from skyrocketing even higher. It's against Federal law for an employer to take reprisal against an employee for the act of reporting an injury but the grey area is that they technically do not do this, although the 'end' result of their actions has a detrimental and lasting effect on the other employees. Their labor policy's point is well taken. This would later happen again only this time... management would cross the line with a driver.

One prime example of this involved a driver by the name of Joy who had sustained an injury a few weeks earlier which resulted in him 'losing' time from work, called a lost time injury.

All of the injuries are reported to OSHA, which then determines if a particular center is high in injuries then they could send in an inspector to find out what the problem is that is causing all of these injuries which management DOES NOT want this type of inspection at all, and uses every means at their disposal to keep the injury frequency down.

Well this driver had managed to cut their finger pretty bad on a piece of cardboard, and I'd have to say that for a paper cut it was pretty bad. It bled for a little while and he walked over to me and asked if I would walk over with him when he told Smitty about it, who happened to be the only supervisor there that night.

"I need to report this in case it gets infected." Joy said.

Smitty stopped what he was doing and looked it over and asked, "Haven't you been out with an injury?"

"Yeah, about three weeks ago," Joy replied.

"You can report it and we can call it in but I want to tell you that you'll probably get a suspension for it." Smitty replied.

What is this man to do? He has hurt himself on the job and by law he had the right and responsibility to report it, but now after Smitty telling Joy that he'd be disciplined...what do you think happened? Joy elected not to report it and went home. What I didn't know, at the time, was that Smitty had just broken a Federal Law and if I had known this then I would have filed a grievance and then called the Regional Office of OSHA and reported this 'threat of retaliation' that had just happened which was directed towards Joy.

The Colonel had begun on a campaign to hold everyone accountable in the Huntsville east center, through the discipline procedure if anyone worked past the set curfew of 6:30 p.m and there was not anymore of this 'going back out mess," as the Colonel put it.

No longer was it just for us to have our volume back in by 6:30 you now had to be back and off of the clock by 6:30 p.m, not 6:31 but 6:30.

Now to make it a little more interesting Dick had decided to "re-adjust" the minimum and maximum numbers of stops that determined an eight-hour paid day for each route. Now Dick, who had again become a division manager and now had all of the centers in North Alabama, had raised the numbers by at least another five stops per route, and rarely ever did he lower the number of stops that determined a paid day. There had not been a time study conducted for the routes or any other 'official' study to justify this course of action other than the top management wanted to squeeze every ounce of production out of us that they could.

We were still having the problem of not being able to get out of the building and on the road due to poor management of the preload by the Colonel.

Imagine for a moment, we were scheduled to be on the road by 8:45 a.m. every morning but were leaving the building sometimes around 9:15 a.m., or later. If we were on the road by 8:45 then our eight hours would be up at, including a one-hour meal break, 5:45 p.m. This was forty-five minutes before the 6:30 curfew. Plenty of time, right? Yes in a perfect world it would be but now factor in us getting out 45 minutes late every-day, which, would have put us leaving at around 9:30 a.m., and then factor in a one-hour lunch on top of that, which then put us at 10:30 a.m. Then factor in a cut off time, meaning allowing yourself enough time drive back to the center from wherever you were to unload your airs, fuel your truck, back it on the dock, do your turn in, and be off of the clock by 6:30 p.m. Now all this time of driving back cost you roughly, depending on where you were 45 minutes, which would be subtracted off of the back end of your paid day, which meant you had to be finished with your route by 5:30 in order to make the drive back and finish your routine. What about delivering the packages? How much time does that leave you to deliver your eight hours worth of work? If we started delivering at 10:45 and had to be finish by 5:30, that leaves us a little under seven hours to deliver an eight hour route...but we forgot about the jump in stops of five additional stops, which cost a driver maybe twenty minutes, which then gave the driver about six and a half hours to deliver his eight hour route in a perfect world. Then enter into this final equation the numerous traffic tie up's, slow customers, having to wait your turn to be waited on, a lot of C.O.D's, and various other problems that arose daily that interfered with a driver who was out delivering their route...but were of the norm. This was real life and not just some paper fantasy world that management lived in and was a far cry from just a view on paper involving numbers.

Even with drivers skipping their lunch and giving this time back to management, they were still unable to finish their routes, and were having to call in for help everyday. We had drivers, who tried to finish their routes and tried to do the "whole" job, but were unable to, and then when they went over the 6:30 curfew...they were carried into the office the next morning and disciplined. Management was handing out warning letters and suspensions like candy. It was sickening to say the least.

Finally, during a PCM, after just about everyone had received a warning letter for working past the 6:30 curfew, the Colonel personally made the statement that under no circumstances was anyone to work over the 6:30 curfew. We already knew this. Why was he again restating his position? We would soon find out why.

So that afternoon several drivers pulled into the parking lot of the center at around 6:20 and with only ten minutes to complete their turn in, and punch out, they just parked their trucks in the parking lot, full of packages and airs and told a supervisor they'd have to get a part timer to unload and fuel it.

I had to go into the office the next couple of days with these drivers, because some of the re-load supervisor's were raising hell about it. Their part timers were having to take on this new found 'job' which was costing his operation an extra fifteen minutes of work per re-loader, and this was killing his sort. The reload couldn't spare any part timers to do this which caused the sort to go down late for that day, which in turned caused the loads to leave late, which caused the inbound loads to come in late, which then caused the preload to go down late, which then caused then drivers to get on the road late then the vicious cycle started all over again. The Colonel was either too stupid to realize that this curfew was costing him a lot of money, or was just mean as hell and didn't care.

He might have been saving a dime per driver due to the curfew, but it was costing him a dollar everywhere else in the long run. It was very, very, very bad business sense. This new 'policy' involving the curfew was not only costing Huntsville money but think of what it cost a hub to keep several dozen people on the clock waiting for a load out of Huntsville to arrive to be processed. It didn't make sense to me and I immediately ruled this out as just being a 'cost saving' measure but instead, was just part of the 'labor relations' policy of the management.

Drivers had now begun driving more 'aggressively', in other words "unsafe", to make the curfew and deliver everything they had, and with the added heat of a hot summer it was unsafe to their health. The running all day, skipping their lunches just to try and get done, but in most cases, they were unsuccessful, and were disciplined according to the Colonel's new policy. It was damned if you did and damned if you didn't.

After a couple more days of this new shift in policy I filed a grievance protesting this latest action, and demanded to be present while the grievance was heard at the local level hearing.

When the time came to hear the grievance I was called into the office and took a seat beside Matt, and in front of Hembry and the Colonel. I listened as management read the grievance and then I listened to Matt state his relaxed position and this hearing proved to be nothing more than a horse and pony show.

It was another perfect example of local 402's "passive representation" by the old guard officers of the local union. I had had enough of this crap and after the finished going through the motions I stood up and said, "This is nothing but a load of crap." They all stopped talking and just stared at me. I pulled out of my shirt pocket and unfolded several pieces of paper. I handed one to Matt and the other to Hembry, and they both read over it and then looked at me with a puzzled look on their faces.

"What's this for?" Matt asked.

"I'm fed up with losing every grievance we file and how you let management run over us while you sit on your butt and let it go on." I replied. I was to the point of tears I was so angry. "I've decided to get the National Labor Relations Board involved from here on out every time we 'lose' winnable grievances." I replied angrily.

Hembry sat up in his chair and had a look of amazement on his face. After I made that statement, Hembry seemed to do an about face. Little did they know that if the local union wasn't going to educate me in what my rights were, that I'd taken it upon myself and read everything I can get my hands on about what my work place and union rights were and learn how to use them for our advantage.

I had sat back down and Matt and Hembry looked at each other and from that moment on things began to change. Upper management had taken a different outlook on what was going on in Huntsville and vowed to try and ease up on us if indeed what we were claiming was going on. Nothing really came of it other than by now I had definitely decided to run against Matt in the upcoming local union election.

After several weeks management had slacked off a little, but the Colonel and son were still very much out of control. They had decided it was time for me to have another production ride, and at first I had a problem with it until I found out that Harry would be the one conducting it. At least I knew that he'd give me a fair shake.

Harry and I left the center the next morning about as usual and when I decided to stop for lunch, I let him buy it. I've always got along with Harry and never had a problem with him. During lunch Harry received a page from the center while we were eating. He excused himself and went to the pay phone in the restaurant and then returned looking very upset about something, but he never would say what happened. I asked him if everything was all right? He said yeah that it was the Colonel and he wanted to know how you were looking.

"And?" I asked.

Harry didn't answer and I could tell right away that something was said, or maybe an order was given by the Colonel that Harry didn't agree with.

I decided to cut lunch short and saved the remaining thirty minutes to take later on in the afternoon. We left the restaurant, and I was doing the same, in regard to the number of stops I had delivered the day before, performance with him riding with me than when I was alone. It was looking like with every passing hour that we were getting further and further behind. I had been having to call for help everyday and having to come in and unload and go back out and finish.

Since the last local hearing, the Colonel had eased the curfew now to allow for 'two-tripping' if necessary, and it was looking like one of those kinds of nights. I had finished with what I could deliver and pulled into the gas station to sit down in their deli and cool off. It had been a hot day today and I was looking forward to a much-needed breather. Harry followed me in and sat down in front of me a stared at his watch three or four times and began biting his fingernails. I knew something was going on here. I had been sitting there for about five minutes then he looked at his watch again and said, "Time to go."

"I've still got twenty-five minutes lunch left Harry," I replied.

"We've got to go," He said.

"The contract says I get an hour and I want to finish my hour now," I answered.

"I'm instructing you to get up and go back to work...now!" He screamed. I was shocked. This wasn't anything like Harry, but to keep from being insubordinate I followed as he directed and went back to work. I didn't need to be discharged for refusing to work when I got back to the building by the Colonel, so I gathered my things up and walked back out to the truck and left.

Harry sat over in the jump seat staring out of the door. He didn't say a word to me the whole way back in. Something was eating him up on the inside, but he wouldn't, or couldn't tell me what was going on. I arrived back to the building and unloaded my airs and of the packages that I had picked up that evening, I went back out to finish delivering my route only this time leaving Harry to stay at the building.

Before leaving though, Harry told me that I had scored a 94% rating on my methods and that I had done a good job no matter what was said in the office the next day and for me to remember that. Harry said that I had too much work on me and that he'd do what he could to lighten me up. This was sort of strange, I mean the comment about "no matter what is said", coming from Harry, and I began to really smell something rotten. I thought that finally I was going to receive some relief.

I did receive something all right...but it wasn't relief! It was a warning letter for running over allowed. I tried to explain to the Colonel what Harry had said and he wasn't interested in what Harry had told me and the Colonel wouldn't even allow me to bring Harry in the office to tell him first hand how well my ride had went. In all sense of reality I received about ten more stops on top of the load I already had. It was now more than impossible to get done.

During the week ending September 21, 1998, I had a three-day lock in ride that was conducted by Smitty. Management was now going to attempt to lock me in to whatever number I had performed with Smitty during that three-day ride. I'd seen this in the past but this was a new step for the management, even regarding me. They were gearing up to begin building their case against me so they could fire me.

I thought, in my opinion, that I had performed very well those three days with Smitty on car and in fact it was once again just like I had done everyday before. I was quite confident that I had demonstrated a good job and figured that I'd have the numbers to support it.

After the three days, Smitty called me into the office and we walked into the front office and I sat down as Smitty closed the door behind him. The Colonel was standing, as he liked to whenever he had the chance to look down at someone, and Alvin was beside me while Smitty stood by the Colonel with his arms behind his back and rocking on his heels.

"Let me get to the point James," the Colonel said. I was quite glad that it wasn't going to be a long drawn out affair because I didn't care to share the same room with them, because they both made me sick to just be around them. The Colonel looked over my ride and reviewed what was costing time and pointed out several things such as failing to call out "UPS" when entering a business, getting the check first on C.O.D's and so on. All of these were trivial things that if they all were added up cost me less than two minutes for the whole day. It was all they had on me and I agreed to work on correcting these problems just to humor them.

The Colonel pulled out a sheet of paper and said, "I want you to sign this James."

"I'm not signing anything Colonel." I replied, without even looking at it.

"You'll sign it or I'll fire you," he snapped back.

"You know you can't fire him for refusing to sign that Colonel," Alvin said.

"I'm instructing you sign this now!" The Colonel yelled out at me. By this time he had really pissed me off.

I stood up and said, "Let me spell it out for you," and started working my fingers like I was performing sign language. "I-AM-NOT-SIGNING-IT-

OKAY!" I said real slowly. Alvin asked what was on the paper and the Colonel handed him the paper as Alvin began taking his glasses out of his shirt pocket and began putting them on. Alvin began reading the form with his glasses on the end of his nose in his usual trademark fashion.

"No he's not signing this!" Alvin replied in a disgusted tone, and shaking his head no as he took off his glasses and folded them up and stuck them back into his shirt pocket. "I want to see the records from his ride," Alvin demanded. Smitty, who was grunting and clearing his throat like crazy now looked at the Colonel who nodded his head and handed them to the Colonel.

The Colonel opened them up and looked them over and said, "His new standard is eighteen stops an hour and 50/100'ths, or about thirty minutes, over allowed. This was set as my normal base line, or scratch, which meant if I ran only thirty minutes over allowed it would be the same as not running over allowed. If I ran, say, forty-five minutes over allowed then subtract thirty minutes from that forty-five and that would give me only fifteen minutes of 'actually' running over allowed.

What they were wanting me to sign was a form committing me to running eighteen stops an hour everyday regardless of what happened and I couldn't run no more than thirty minutes over allowed...period. If I did, for what ever reason, my fault, their fault, no fault, I could receive discipline up to and including...termination.

"I want you to sign this NOW!" The Colonel demanded again.

"What's it going to take to make you understand that I'm not going to sign it Colonel?" I asked.

After about three or four more times of this, the Colonel finally said for me to call the local union and he'd call Hembry that he had had enough of me and I was going to sign it one way or the other. He was crazy as all get out. I wasn't about to sign that form. Heck they wouldn't even let Alvin see the OR from those days of the ride so I filed a grievance.

DATE GRIEVANCE FILED: 9-21-98

EXPLAIN GRIEVANCE: *I was called into the office by the Colonel to review my production ride from (9-15)(9-16)(9-17). I was told that I demonstrated a good job by being 97% effective in methods. The areas that I needed to work on added up less than four minutes total. I was asked by the Colonel to commit to running 17 stops an hour and no more than 50/100 over allowed. I find this insulting and nothing more than a total disregard for the contract and me. I will not enter into an agreement with management, which has not been negotiated in the contract. I do the same thing everyday as outlined by Article 66 in regard to my physical condition. The management of this company wants me to commit to this when they can't commit to giving me a good load to work from. I've been on this route now for nine weeks and continue to have poor loads and pathetic excuses from management promising to correct this. I feel that I am being set up for a constructive discharge. I fear for my job and my health. I want this harassment to cease immediately.*

REMEDY SOUGHT: *Harassment to stop.*

I turned this grievance in the following day, and in turn I was handed a letter from management which read that I would be disciplined if I failed to perform the numbers that they wanted me to, although I hadn't signed anything saying that I would.

I called the local union hall and told Matt that I needed him to schedule a local hearing as soon as possible. I told him about the letter from management and he told me not to sign anything. I also told him that I wanted a copy of my records from when Smitty rode with me so I could see them to aid us in presenting our case during the local hearing to hear this particular grievance. Matt told me that he would take care of everything.

Now that this had happened Smitty and the Colonel decided to up my stop counts again. When Smitty had last rode with me, my heaviest day was only about 100 stops, but now they were sending me out with 115-120 stops. Why didn't they send me out this heavy when they conducted the production rides last week? So I turned and filed another grievance to protest this latest action by the Colonel and son.

DATE GRIEVANCE FILED: 9-24-98

EXPLAIN GRIEVANCE: *Management has stated that I must commit to running production numbers that are the same as when the supervisor rode with me. My heaviest day I had with them on car was no more than 100 stops. Today I had 116. I feel that this is harassment on their part.*

REMEDY SOUGHT: *Harassment to stop.*

Matt finally arranged for a local level hearing to be held and during this meeting I finally got to see my records and what I saw shocked me. I had managed to run an average of thirteen stops an hour and I was an average of about 1.2 hours over allowed.

"Where did you get your numbers you were trying to get me to sign for the other day?" I asked the Colonel, who just sat there not saying a word, and wouldn't even look at me.

"You wanted me to sign a commitment to run my BEST day." I said angrily, after realizing that I had been deceived. Hembry and Matt just sat there watching and listening. I was really upset from the whole ordeal. The outcome of the local resulted in me winning my grievances and a pledge from me that I would just try and do better. I agreed.

What the Colonel had done was instead of taking the average number of stops an hour that I had ran those three days, which were (eighteen stops an hour, twelve stops an hour and eleven stops an hour divided by the three days which would've netted thirteen stops an hour as an average), he then took the highest, and best number, which was eighteen, and used only it as what they wanted me to run whereas if he'd taken the average from those three days it would have been closer to about thirteen stops an hour, which was a far cry from my best of eighteen.

When it came to the amount of over allowed time, he did the same thing for it as well. I had ran about .50 over the first day, about 1.08 over the second and about 1.15 over for the third day and when these three days are divided by three to get an average allowance of over allowed resulted in .91 over, almost an hour, was my average and not the best day of .50 hours over allowed. I had caught him in his little game. This is how the majority of the management in this company is though. They are indeed professionals when it comes to manipulating the numbers.

The issue of the CHSP, or safety committee, had come around again and a driver, who had been designated by management to co-chair the hourly side, came to me to discuss possibly lifting the ban on participating. We talked about the pros and cons and finally all of the stewards reached an agreement that the CHSP would be reborn, but with one condition. If we started sliding back into the same routine, as before, then we'd pull the plug on it again. The driver told me that he would keep the stewards abreast of what was going on and if it became a problem as before I wouldn't have to pull the plug on it...he would. I believed him and knew that he would.

The safety committee was reborn again and the Colonel appointed Smitty to co-chair it for the company. It would only be a matter of time before it would be once again disbanded. Management sent the hourly co-chair to school and gave him the training as to the administrative side as well as the basic, fundamental operation of the CHSP. It was looking as if management was serious about safety this time and was following the contract for a change.

Management had not only taken a new position on safety, but was as well...was implementing a new attitude towards working safely company wide. Only time would tell of their sincerity.

Well after about two weeks after the rebirth it was back to business as usual. The Colonel had chosen several drivers to stay in the building to work on CHSP related projects and the Colonel, like Davey, had failed to observe seniority. Not only did he not observe seniority, but also he divided the drivers, who were staying in the building, routes up amongst all of the other drivers, which was causing everyone else to work late every night. This caused a major problem with all of the drivers who were now doing these other drivers jobs for them, while they stayed in the building those days. I carried the problem to the Colonel and he saw nothing wrong with it, and I tried to explain to him that the problem was that he had cut out two full time drivers' routes just to work in the building.

The problem with this is that if management cuts a route out they cannot run cover drivers with full time drivers technically laid off for the day, since they had no routes to run, without violating the contract. Those full time drivers couldn't stay in the building as long as management was planning to use cover drivers for those days. Now if the management wasn't going to use ANY cover drivers for those days that the two routes were cut out then everything would've been okay as long as they observed seniority at determining who would stay in the building to perform CHSP work. This had all the makings of what Davey had began doing, and I decided right then to put a stop to it before it got out of control. The real kicker came when the driver, who management had sent to school, and was the co-chair for the hourly, came to me and told me that he had quit the CHSP program earlier in the week. When I asked him why he simply said that it was nothing but a joke and only a horse and pony show to pacify Liberty Mutual and OSHA. Safety wasn't a top priority...only production.

DATE GRIEVANCE FILED: 9-24-98

EXPLAIN GRIEVANCE: *Two full time drivers stayed in the building to work on safety and seniority wasn't observed. Many drivers had to work*

more than 9.5 hours as a result of this action.
REMEDY SOUGHT: *Disband safety program.*

This time I demanded that the local union put an end to this practice, but that too would, become another battle that I would later wage.

It was becoming even clearer from the local union that management was growing tired of me and Matt told me after the local hearing concerning this latest grievance, about the CHSP committee, that I needed to ease up on the company. I was causing too many problems and I was also beginning to hear that the Colonel may have been given the nod from the top brass to try and terminate my employment...any way that he could.

The frequency and types of harassment geared to just me increased everyday. I was being brought into the office for everything now. My name was honestly being called out everyday single day during the PCM to report to the office after the meeting.

As retaliation for the "CHSP" grievance I filed a few days ago, I was called to report to the office concerning an incident on September 29, 1998, just four days after the grievance was filed for failing to put a service cross on a package.

This was later thrown out due to the fact that Smitty had failed to 'properly' check the package for my service cross, because the package had two address labels on it, one on the top and one on the bottom, and I had indeed written a service cross on the bottom. Smitty went ahead anyway and gave me warning letter for it anyway, although he had no case, just because the Colonel had told him to. This is what I was dealing with on a daily basis, and it was going to only get worse in the days ahead...

Chapter 15

"9:12 A.M: I can barely hold my head up and I don't know how I'm going to make it through today. I went to the doctor yesterday and she tells me that I've got Acute Bronchitis, and here comes Smitty with a clipboard. Please Lord not another ride...not today?"

Things only worsened in Huntsville after an increased number of drivers were being called into the office for taking excessive breaks, after management had started once again on the "bathroom" kick, and begun cracking down on anyone whose records showed an "unsubstantial" and excessive amount of time between stops.

The Colonel had instructed Smitty, and the other supervisors, to closely review the delivery records of any driver who was running over allowed. They were looking for a lapse in time in between stops that were not ordinary. In other words, what they were doing was that they were going over them with a fine tooth comb.

Say, for example, that a driver had delivered ten stops total for a shopping mall. They would then check to see what time had been stamped on each stop, which the DIAD automatically stamps the time on each stop once a stop is "stop completed", or closed out, and if there was an 'unexplainable' time lapse in between each of the stops then the Colonel would question the driver as to why it would've had taken the extra time to deliver this particular stop.

For example say that those ten stops all received one small package each, which should have taken no more than two minutes, or so to deliver and complete each stop. Then theoretically each of the ten stops should have only two minutes or so separating them, but say there was a time lapse of five minutes between one of the stops. Then that alone would allegedly throw up a 'red flag'.

What the management was concerned with now is the possibility of the act of 'stealing time' was being committed by the driver. Although, if you went to the restroom that could explain the lapse in time between the stops. The Colonel wasn't interested in hearing this logical explanation and this was the common reply from everyone that had been questioned concerning instances like this.

The 'Little Colonel and gang' had begun surveillance of all drivers who were 'tagged' as stealing time, and it was as if they were everywhere watching you. I would at times be out delivering on Airport Road and I would be coming out of a business, after just completing a stop, and look up and Smitty and the Colonel would be parked off in the distance watching me. Other drivers began to report sightings of these two and people were growing very tired of it.

The pressure was steadily being placed on the local union to put a stop to this and as always, nothing would be done. We called a parking lot union meeting for one morning and instructed everyone what management had begun doing, what their possible intentions were and for everyone to be on alert and most important of all, to just do their jobs.

What management may have been looking for was just another way to thin out the ranks of the highly paid full timers and replace them with lower paid part timer drivers...just plain and simple economics.

Many employees had worked while being sick over the years and coming in barely able to walk, much less being able to run eleven-hour days with the flu and various other ailments. You would think that management would have cut some slack on these drivers who came in and tried "to help them out", and who often worked when they should have been in the hospital...don't hold your breath. In some cases management persuaded the drivers to come in, when they called the center to report they were sick and wouldn't be at work, and they'd opt to cut their routes down, or put somebody on the car with them, but this would only happen maybe, one time out of a hundred.

UPS management viewed us all as just a number, a soulless, emotionless machine. Management didn't care if you were on your deathbed and very, very rarely turned a blind eye to this policy. There was no excuse for failing to run production in the eyes of management who often were heard citing the, "We have a business to run" philosophy for their hard heartedness and ruthlessness.

This was the case that involved me in October of 1998. There had been a sudden, drastic change of the weather, and it had cooled off rather quickly, and in turn...it had made several of us drivers sick. I had had a cold now for about two weeks, but continued to work due to the fact that unless you had any "sick days" marked on the calendar, called option days, you weren't allowed any time off, no matter what the reason was...period. I hadn't any days left to use, because I had to use them all with my daughter, who at the time was having seizures and required me to accompany my wife to carry her to several medical specialist out of town.

The Colonel had begun suspending the drivers who were calling in sick, and was requiring everyone out to bring a doctors excuse back with them before he'd let them return to work or they'd receive discipline for their "excessive absences." I was notified that I was due for another D.O.T physical and by the time I was getting off at night I was unable to go to the company doctor to get my D.O.T physical.

I asked Smitty if I could go before work one morning and get my physical. It wasn't that big of a deal and chances were good that probably I wouldn't even be late. Smitty went to the Colonel and the Colonel said no.

I had made my mind up that I wasn't going to go on my personal time, during the weekend, and I was just going to let my D.O.T physical card expire, and then I couldn't legally drive that day, and then they'd have to let me go get my physical. They'd then be short one driver, and maybe even screwed for the day if I came in on a Monday morning without a physical, and they'd have no choice but to take me out of service until I received a new physical card. I decided that I'd probably need to leave a paper trail in case management tried to discipline me for failing to obtain a physical after letting my old card expire, so I submitted my request in writing to the Colonel, in accordance with the contract, and my request was denied once again. I was told that I could go on Saturday to Decatur Alabama, which was an hour away, and wait for a company doctor to see me. The Colonel had let several of the "rump kissers" off to go and get their physicals several days before I submitted my request, but he was unable to accommodate me. I don't think so.

I had became a lot sicker over the weekend and I hadn't felt like working at all that last week much less the one coming up. Smitty had brought me into the office every morning that week wanting to know why I was running over allowed, which I told him that I was sick, which from my appearance...couldn't be denied.

"We still expect you to do your job James, we do have a business to run," Smitty said to me, while chewing me out for running over allowed. I left, after another threat of a warning letter was made, and went out to deliver my route and I later became extremely ill during the course of the day, and was unable to continue. I called Smitty from a business stop at 4800 Whitesburg, and I was about two hours behind after not being able to finish. I couldn't go on any more.

Smitty brought out a part timer in another package car and told me to drive back to the center after saying, "If you think you can make it that far", in a very spiteful tone. I gathered up my personal belongings and drove on back to the center and went home.

The next morning I decided to go ahead and report to work and try to go out and run my route. Lesley tried to get me to call in sick, but I explained to her about what the Colonel's new policy was, and that I had to go to work or face being suspended or fired. Lesley couldn't believe it and I had to literally take the phone out of her hands, because she was going to call in and give Smitty a piece of her mind.

I arrived at work and was barely able to stand. I was extremely, extremely sick. I was having difficulty breathing and was running a fever.

Right after the PCM, I finished wrapping my truck up, loading everything in it, and pulled out into the parking lot to perform my pre-trip inspection, and that's when Smitty came running out and jumped into the truck and pulled the jump seat down on the passenger side while threw his clipboard up on the dash of the truck.

"What are you doing?" I asked.

"You were almost two hours over allowed the other day, and I'm going to do a production ride today." He replied.

"Heck no, heck no you're not either!" I yelled at him. I was too sick to have worked the last few days and was in no shape for a production ride today. I could barely even hold my head up much less perform as a machine and run like hell all day to pacify them. I lost it. I was sick and he pushed me up to the edge.

"I want to go home today, I'm too sick to work." I replied.

"Hell, every time I turn around y'all are riding with me, and I'm starting to get tired of it." I replied, as I slowly became upset.

"Are you telling me you're too sick to work?" Smitty asked after becoming upset with me.

"Yes, and I'm going home," I replied, while starting to stand up and collected my belongings. He jumped out of the truck and yelled at me that

I had better get my physical today too. I drove to their company doctor and received my physical and then drove to my personal doctor who, after examining me and x-raying my chest diagnosed me as having Acute Bronchitis. I hope that this was sick enough for management as I left the doctors office and carried my doctors excuse straight to the Colonel and threw it on his desk, not even looking at him or even talking.

"Hey James, wait a minute," he yelled.

"I'll see you Monday, Colonel," I replied, as I walked out of his office. I took the rest of the week off to try and get better.

I filed a grievance to protest this harassment and also that my load had still not been corrected as agreed upon by the management during the local hearing from the grievance I had filed several weeks before, because my loader was still killing me. I continued to find packages very late in the afternoon that I had already delivered earlier that the morning, and sometimes I had to go back by the same business several times a day. I wasn't getting any extra credit for this stop and it wasn't counted as a new stop, it only counted as a "duplicate" stop, as I had been directed by the Colonel to count it as.

On October 20, 1998 with the high number of mis-loads I was having everyday, Smitty decided to conduct another production ride on me. During this day I had over eighteen mis-loads, which was costing me well over an hour of time, that was going towards my over allowed time, after since I had been instructed to count it only as a duplicate stop instead of it as a new stop. I would wind up delivering about 100 stops for this day but in reality, after counting the mis-load, I had delivered well over 118 stops, but only received credit for 100 stops in regard to my over allowed time.

Management's argument was that I was getting credit for the extra miles that it took me to go back and redeliver the mis-loaded stops, but this was nothing but a "sham" itself. This argument might have worked if I was maybe on a rural route and drove 200 miles a day, but my route was so condensed, within a one mile square, that I was probably picking up a little over a minute or two versus the hour I was losing in having to back track to deliver that package so I wouldn't have a missed piece, which would have then netted me a warning letter as well, and It was clearly in a no win situation either way you looked at it.

Every time that I would stop and use the bathroom, Smitty would write down on his pad showing what time I had stopped to go to the bathroom, and how long I was in there for.

I had decided then that anytime, from here on out, that I stopped to use the bathroom, that I would write down in my daily journal, that I now kept to document everything I did including what mis-load's I had, and if I lost any time...I would write that down as well noting where, when and how long I had stopped for. If I stopped to use the bathroom, I'd record the time, place and whether it was number one or number two. It had gotten that bad. Smitty and the Colonel where watching me like a hawk and I didn't trust them at all.

DATE GRIEVANCE FILED: 10-20-98

EXPLAIN GRIEVANCE: *I reported for work on Oct. 15-16, sick with a real bad cold. I was harassed by Smitty and feel that I am being singled out* *for a possible discharge. I feel that I am having excessive rides.*

REMEDY SOUGHT: *Relocate problem manager and supervisor, and for the harassment to stop.*

This time, along with my usual request, as a solution and remedy to resolve the grievance I carried it to the next level. I had asked for the relocation of the Colonel and Smitty as part of what it would take to resolve this grievance. As a safe measure, I went ahead and filed an unfair Labor Practice charge against management with the N.L.R.B and had bypassed the local union on this before mentioning it, and this pissed both sides off to no end. If I had not known hell yet...it was sure enough coming now.

The picket camp in Huntsville during the 1997 Nationwide strike against UPS.
Photo courtesy of Huntsville driver, Mike Goodman

The Author, his daughter, and a member of the N.A.L.C. #462.

Local 402 Teamsters heading out to conduct a "rolling picket" during the 1997 Nationwide strike.

A local 402 Teamster, and a IPA pilot during the 1997 Nationwide strike.

Local 402 Teamsters picketing Huntsville just prior to the Teamster being hit by a UPS package car during the 1997 Nationwide strike.

Photo courtesy of Huntsville driver, Mike Goodman

The angry mob that began gathering right after a Huntsville Teamster was struck by a pakage car that was driven by a UPS supervisor.

Photo courtesy of Huntsville driver, Mike Goodman

The UPS supervisor being questioned by Huntsville City police about the incident of hitting the Teamster with the vehicle.

Photo courtesy of Huntsville driver, Mike Goodman

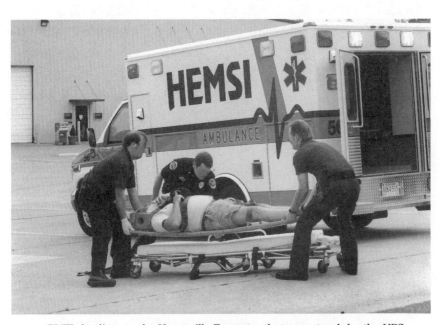

EMT's loading up the Huntsville Teamster that was struck by the UPS supervisor during the 1997 Nationwide strike.

Photo courtesy of Huntsville driver, Mike Goodman

A photo of the Author walking with the N.A.L.C. Branch #462 during their informational picket.

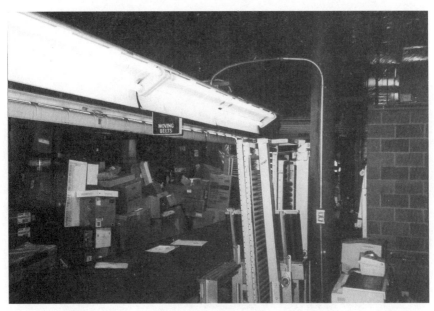

An example of a typical egress violation, and a serious safety hazard during the Huntsville preload.

A photo of a typical "badly" loaded package car of the Author during the "Little Colonel" regime.

The Author hand billing PPG employees during the 1999 organizing campaign.

Photo of the August 1999 rally that resulted in the Authors discharge.

A photo of a Huntsville City police officer on patrol at UPS in Huntsville after the Author was discharged in August, 1999.

Chapter 16

"8:55 a.m: I went into the office to defend a Teamster accused of sexual harassment. He was questioned and treated like a criminal by a loss prevention manager. After it was all said and done... they had the wrong man."

The next major incident that would happen involved the world famous 'in-house' version of a cross between the Keystone Cops and dysfunctional version of a type of a wanna be Gestapo squad, known as loss prevention, or commonly referred to as L.P.

On the morning of November 5, 1998, during the morning PCM my name, along with several other drivers, was called out and we were all told to report to the office. When the last driver was called into the office the Colonel asked us to follow him upstairs that we had a serious problem to discuss.

I looked at the driver in question, named Otis, as he looked back at me and shrugged his shoulders, while looking puzzled. The Colonel went on upstairs to the office and we followed behind him slowly climbing the stairs.

"Do you have any idea what you did?" I asked Otis.

"Man I don't know?" He replied.

We were soon to find out though. We finished the climb up the stairs and turned to go into the office and the Colonel was standing in the door holding it open like an usher, and we walked on past him and entered into the small back office. We weren't going to be the only participants in this labor discussion.

As we entered into the office, I saw that one of managements L.P supervisors was seated behind a desk and he asked us both to take seats in front of him. I glanced over at Otis as I sat down, and saw that he still had a puzzled look on his face. The Colonel took a seat beside Fredrick, the L.P supervisor.

This is one situation, as a steward, that I did not like to encounter. When I had to go into the office to represent a Teamster and you walk in and see one of these guys, an L.P, you would be at a severe disadvantage. The disadvantage would come from being blindsided, and being caught totally off guard, and not knowing what kind of case and evidence the management had against the person you were in the office with. Management doesn't share this information or even make it known that an investigation is being conducted due to the fact that it would severely jeopardize the "integrity", and I say that loosely, of their investigation.

Immediately I go into the defensive mode as I see this supervisor. This is one time you have to know the contract and some basic understanding of what rights you, and the accused have in regard to Labor Law, and you must be prepared to fight tooth and nail because this persons job is more than likely on the line.

Fredrick starts off, before the main questioning, by saying something that really makes me sick to my stomach. They treat you like they are your lost long brother or something and try to mislead the accused into the questioning by giving or presenting a false sense of security to them, which this in turn, may cause the accused to lower their guard, and they then become somewhat relaxed and feel as if there was some sort of comrade with these managers. Then when they ask them a question concerning why they're in there in the first place then they're caught off guard, and then have to try and get a hold on their mental state. It was a mental game that they play with people in the office. They were slick...no doubt.

"How are you doing today?" Fredrick asked Otis while smiling.

"Fine," Otis replied.

"How's your family?" Fredrick asked.

"Uh...fine." Otis answered nervously.

"Everything going okay on your route Otis?" Fredrick asked, while placing his hands on top of the desk.

"Yeah, as far as I know Fredrick." Otis answered, while looking at me and then at the Colonel who was sitting beside Fredrick, spitting in a cup.

"Let me get to the reason why I have you in here Otis," Fredrick replied, as he pulled out some papers from a file. Otis had already scooted up to the edge of his seat and was bouncing his leg, like when you get nervous, ninety to nothing as he sat there anxiously waiting to find out what was going on.

"Do you deliver 617 Clinton Ave?" Fredrick asked.

"Yes," replied Otis.

"Do you know a certain female who works in the front office?" He asked.

"Yeah," Otis answered.

I knew right then where Fredrick was going with this. This was an attempt at pinning a sexual harassment complaint on this driver. I have known Otis for several years and worked closely with him downtown. He was one of the three downtown drivers. I knew that he was married to a beautiful woman and had several wonderful children, and I knew that this was nothing but a load of crap.

"When do you make your deliveries?" Fredrick asked.

"In the morning," answered Otis.

"Who signs for the packages?" Fredrick asked.

"This lady in the front office," he answered.

"Did you see or talk to her on this date?" Fredrick asked.

"Yes," he answered.

I immediately jumped in and interrupted the line of questioning. This action caused the Colonel to stand up and tell me that I needed to wait until Fredrick was finished questioning him.

"I will not sit here and let Fredrick lead him into a false admission by systematically asking him questions," I said. "Either you tell him what you want with him or this meeting is over until the local union can be called, do you understand?" I replied, as my blood began to boil while pointing at Fredrick.

I'd seen this tactic before and decided to immediately put a stop to it before they had a chance to continue and apply this time proven tactic of theirs. This tactic they use is a very sneaky, under handed and was a very manipulative way to coax enough information out of a person to justify a "Just Cause Discharge" which the questions themselves are often times too broad, and the answers from the 'suspects' themselves are then broad, but then management has enough to go on and then they'd render a decision to discharge the person. It's textbook.

First management brings you into the office, like with Otis, and ask you personal questions regarding your personal life and how your family is, like in a casual conversation.

This is done to 'win' over your trust and counter acts whatever anxieties or reservations 'you' may be experiencing at talking to them or in disclosing certain things relevant to the line of questioning. They attempt to portray to you that they are your friends and that they care about you and want you to 'trust them'.

Then next step was to lead this person into a line of questioning that is not exactly to the point. Management is attempting to, while volunteering very few facts in most cases, let you walk into "self incrimination".

The majority of these investigations do not always involve serious offenses, such as the "cardinal sins" that are outlined in our contract.

The management lets you 'build' the case for them against yourself, by the selective questions they ask you and through your own admissions, that this incident could have possibly taken place with no real concrete proof. They then discharge you for "just cause" and then it has to be resolved through the grievance procedure. The local union then has the financial burden and task of proving you innocent after you've been found "guilty" in the early stages of the investigation.

Managements case is made, because of the type of broad question's they ask you leave very little room for interpretation by the panel, or the National Grievance Committee, to exonerate you of the charges, You have in fact unknowingly cut your own throat.

Fredrick looked at the Colonel and then at me and told Otis why he was in the office. "Otis, we had a female customer call in and say that you had made some inappropriate sexual comments towards her, and that you had touched her in a way that made her feel uncomfortable," Fredrick replied.

Otis was shocked. I was shocked as well. This didn't sound like something he was capable of doing.

"You've got to be kidding." I said.

"We're not kidding James, we take this kind of complaint seriously, that's a heavy liability on us," the Colonel replied, while spitting at the garbage can, but hitting the wall and floor instead.

"You've got the wrong man," Otis yelled out while quite visibly shaken.

"Well you just said that you were the only one who delivered, and made pick ups didn't you?" Fredrick asked, while beginning to become agitated.

I jumped up and broke right in. "No he didn't say that Fredrick," I said, while cutting Otis off who had become visibly upset. I couldn't blame him though, considering this grave accusation that was being made by the management.

"There are two drivers that go by there. One in the morning, who was Otis, and another one later in the afternoon to make the pick ups," I said. I knew this because I had done this routine while on one of the downtown routes for four years.

Fredrick had a look of puzzlement and surprise on his face as he looked at the Colonel who then asked, "Who's the other driver?"

"You figure it out G-man." I said angrily. This had not only upset Otis, but me too as well.

"You people bring this man up here and subject him to the humiliation of this senseless and unsubstantiated accusation." I replied, while scolding them.

The Colonel had now stood up as well and he didn't even have the gall to apologize to Otis for the mistake.

"You're excused," the Colonel replied. Otis and I both stood up to walk out of the office and it took everything I had to keep Otis from stomping a mud hole in both of them.

Come to find out the other driver 'in question', had turned down several request from the lady to go out with her, and it was he who had refused HER advances. The lady later made the confession to another driver saying that she had called in on him in an attempt to try and get him fired, and that she had lied about everything in the first place. To the best of my knowledge, all of the charges were later dropped against the other driver.

I could see though how it could have been an easy mistake to get Otis and the other driver confused. L.P.'s high level of professionalism and top notch investigative practices by these department store detective rejects had netted them nothing. It would have been an easy case to solve, in regard to having the right driver from the very beginning.

The fact of whether or not they had the right man would have been as easy as checking the skin color. One driver was an African American and the other was a Caucasian. Go figure.

As we left the office and began walking down the stairs the Colonel called me back into the office. I told Otis that I would talk to him later on today sometime and turned to walk back up the stairs. I went back into the office and the Colonel closed the door behind me. The Colonel and Fredrick began to try and explain that they indeed had made a mistake and they both had failed to get all of the facts before bringing Otis in the office.

"Will you talk to Otis for us and try to smooth everything over?' The Colonel asked.

"I'm not smoothing over anything. Y'all need to get your crap straight before you drag someone else into the office," I replied angrily, and asked if that was all they wanted and walked out.

This was far from being over and would pick right back up that evening when I returned to the building.

Otis was waiting for me to come in that night and he asked me for some grievance papers. I walked upstairs to my locker and retrieved several out of my locker for him, and for myself as well. When I walked back downstairs I was standing around talking to Otis and several other drivers about what had happened that morning up in the office when Fredrick came walking by us and smiled. I took that as a lack of respect, and as if he had the 'power' to do anything he wanted to do and there wasn't anything we could do on our own to protest it. He was wrong and I was going to make sure he understood that this type of behavior wasn't going to fly in Huntsville. We all turned and watched him walk into the Huntsville east office as the door shut behind him.

"What's his last name?" I asked.

No one knew. I decided that I too was going to file a grievance as well for the way management had conducted that botched investigation that morning, and how they had falsely accused a Teamster brother by conducting one of their usual half ass investigations.

I walked over to the office door and looked through the window and noticed that Fredrick was standing in there cutting up with several other supervisors. I couldn't make out what they were saying, but I could tell they were laughing it up well about something.

I stepped back when I saw that Smitty was about to walk out, and when he came outside I asked him what Fredrick's last name was.

"Victoriason?" He replied curiously as I wrote it down on the back of my delivery notices and started to walk off.

"Why do you want to know that for James?" Smitty asked.

I never stopped walking and just said, "Take care of your own business," and walked back up to the counter and began writing the grievance out.

Smitty turned and ran back into the east office and then Fredrick came out and walked by me as I stood there writing the grievance out. I could feel his stare as he slowly walked by me and rounded the corner. I never looked at him and continued to write the grievance out.

I completed filling the grievance out and by now several other drivers had come in from delivering the routes and one of those drivers approached me for some insurance forms.

"They're in the west office," I replied, and told the driver to follow me over to the office and I'd get him a couple.

When I walked into the west office I noticed that several supervisors, including Fredrick, were in there and they all had stopped talking as soon as I walked in and began acting like they were all working. I noticed that Fredrick just happened to be sitting on the top of the filing cabinet that contained the insurance forms.

"I need to get in there if you don't mind getting down out of my way." I said.

Fredrick stepped down and stood beside the filing cabinet with his arms crossed sort of like in an act of defiance and intimidation.

I knew that it was only now a matter of time before "it" hit the fan. I opened the drawer and began thumbing through the forms until I found the form the driver wanted. I pulled several out of the jacket and handed them to the driver who quickly left the office after sensing something was about to go down. And as soon as he left there weren't any hourly witnesses in the west office, only supervisors, and a total of four.

"Why do you want to know my last name for James?" Fredrick asked in a smart and cold tone.

"No reason," I replied, while closing the file cabinet door.

"I want to know why you want to know my last name for," he replied in an increasingly upset tone.

"You'll find out soon enough," I replied, while staring at him in his eyes.

Tom, a west center supervisor, had nevously lit another cigarette, and was feverishly working on his computer and evidently not wanting to get involved. The other two had decided to hang around and wanted to see what was going to unfold, and they both grabbed two seats beside Tom. Evidently from their actions and interest this was no doubt a planned encounter.

"Let me tell you something James, I don't have to tell you my name." Fredrick replied, while stepping closer to me.

"That's where you're wrong neighbor!" I replied, growing mad myself from this encounter. "Judging from the way you handled yourself this morning Fredrick, you don't know the contract either." I said. "You're supposed to wear a name tag while on duty. Didn't you know that? Its on page fifty-four." I replied in a sarcastic tone.

"You know James," Fredrick said. "I thought I knew you...I thought I really knew you," he replied, while attempting to intimidate me. "Now I know where I stand with you James..." Fredrick replied in a slow and cold tone.

I took offense to this immediately. "What are you saying Fredrick?" I asked sarcastically.

"I just like to know where I stand with people, that's all James." He sneered.

"Are you threatening me?" I asked angrily and walked over closer to him. I turned to one of the supervisors who were still in the office and was watching this whole thing unfold, and then asked him if Fredrick was threatening me. The supervisor had totally changed his mind now, and he didn't want any part of this and threw up his hands and waved them to let me know that he didn't want to get involved.

"Tom, is he threatening me?" I asked, while putting on a dramatic act. Tom just stood up and walked out of the office not saying a word at first.

"I don't know anything." Tom replied, as the door shut.

"What happened to you guy's?" I asked the other two supervisors who were left in the office with Fredrick and me. They weren't saying anything now.

"I thought you boy's wanted to hang around for the show?" I asked again and I still didn't draw a response from either one of them. The one supervisor who liked to shoot his mouth off about everything little thing that I did decided he wasn't enjoying the show anymore and walked on out of the office. This left just left Fredrick, the other supervisor and then me.

"If I was threatening you, you'd know it big boy," Fredrick popped off. That was what I was waiting for. It was on now and I came unglued. This is when the last supervisor got up and left. It was now just Fredrick and I.

Now that the office was empty, and there weren't any witnesses, I walked right over to his face, nose to nose and we got it on. After a minute or so of me blazing his butt he saw that this had quickly got out of hand, and after he saw that he wasn't going to be able to intimidate and bully me, he then told me to just go home. I walked out of the office and my blood pressure had gone through the roof, but at least I had proved my point.

I wasn't worried about getting disciplined for this latest fight, because first, I was off of the clock, second, I was trying to go home, third, he had threatened me, fourth, none of the other members of management had prevented it from happening, fifth, I wasn't afforded a steward. Sixth, I had the contract to fall back on regarding the 'name tag' issue and seventh...there were no witnesses. It would be my word against his, and besides...he was looking at, at least two unfair labor practice charges, and four grievances if he chose to make an issue out of it, but he chose the best thing to do and just let it go.

DATE GRIEVANCE FILED: 11-6-98
EXPLAIN GRIEVANCE: *On the morning of 11-5-98, I was called into the office to represent a driver named Otis. I was met by L.P and the Colonel. This driver was wrongfully accused and subjected to harassing interrogation and had been humiliated and embarrassed. This driver was later proven during the meeting to have been the wrong one on question.*
REMEDY SOUGHT: *Relocation of problem managers and supervisors along with a written apology from L.P.*

DATE GRIEVANCE FILED: 11-6-98
EXPLAIN GRIEVANCE: *I was threatened and subjected to an unwanted confrontation by Fredrick, a L.P supervisor, concerning him wearing his name tag. I was not afforded Union representation. I feel for my job and my health.*
REMEDY SOUGHT: *Charge with N.L.R.B and to terminate this L.P supervisor.*

DATE GRIEVANCE FILED: 11-6-98
EXPLAIN GRIEVANCE: *L.P supervisor needs to wear I.D nametag while on duty.*
REMEDY SOUGHT: *Management personnel to wear nametags.*

Two days after this confrontation with the loss prevention supervisor an incident happened that involved a personal package that belonged to me.

I had my Federal Firearms License at the time, and had a little gun business on the side selling firearms. I had waited to pay for a C.O.D on the last day before it was to be sent back to the shipper.

I came in late that evening and I had left the package that contained the firearm in the Huntsville east office, and I walked in there to get it after finishing my work day. I had finally received payment from the person who ordered it, and during the course of my day, I had stopped at my bank and purchased a cashiers check to pay for the C.O.D.

It was late when I came back in, and the mailbag had already left Huntsville on the Montgomery trailer. This bag contained all of the checks and other paper work in them that were to be processed in Montgomery.

I walked into the office and Smitty was still there working on something and I told him that I had some C.O.D tags to turn in, and I told him that I was carrying my gun home and that I had recorded my address into my DIAD as another stop for record purposes only.

Well, a couple of days later, I came into work and was immediately asked to report to the office. I was instructed by the Colonel to go ahead and punch in, although I was about twenty-five minutes early. I thought this was kind of odd, and when I walked into the office and saw that Alvin was sitting in there waiting for me along with guess who...Fredrick, I knew something shady was about to transpire. I sat down beside Alvin and Fredrick immediately began to ask we why I had failed to turn in any cash for a C.O.D that was 'missing' funds.

It seems that all Birmingham had received from me in respect to "my" C.O.D was just the paper tag showing the amount to be collected, and that was it. It seems that there wasn't any money turned in for the package and management wanted to know why I didn't turn in any money that night, and Fredrick was leading the charge for the company. Fredrick began to ask where the money was, and boy was he laying it on thick! It was a rather expensive firearm, around $1200 and Fredrick was beginning to imply that I had stolen the firearm.

I stood up in the office, and then everyone stopped what they were saying and they all just looked at me as I began to take my wallet out. Alvin sat there not saying a thing, almost as if he was just there to observe and knew what I was doing. I pulled from my wallet a piece of folded up paper, and I began to slowly unfold it, while the Colonel and Fredrick still looked on, and then I held it up for everyone to see. I had got into the habit of making copies of my own checks, and those of customers (after blacking out the account numbers) as well, including certified checks that I had purchased after collecting large amounts of C.O.D money during the day while running my route. I would then punch every copy I had made on the time clock showing the time and date. Management had become notorious for 'losing' checks, and then forcing drivers to pay for the C.O.D's, and with having been burned in the past on C.O.D's, I wasn't about to fall victim again. I don't think management was too interested in collecting their money in this case. They were looking for a discharge instead.

I had, as usual the night before turning in my C.O.D money and checks, made a copy of the $1200 certified check along with the C.O.D tag along side it with the C.O.D tag control number written on the check as well, just as a precaution. I then punched the copy on the time clock as proof that I had collected the check for later, like now, if a need arose.

I handed the paper to Alvin so he could see it and he handed it back to me, and then Fredrick asked me if he could have the paper, to which I declined.

Alvin just sat there grinning at Fredrick, and not saying a word.

"You can have a copy of it," I said, and started to hand it to him but then stopped, while still gripping the paper tightly. "I want you to understand that this is my personal property and I want this original paper back. Do you understand me?" I said.

"Yeah," Fredrick replied, in a disgusted tone as I let go of the paper so he could go and make a copy of it. After he returned with my paper we both were excused.

If I had not done that, and had lost the receipt I more than likely would have been fired for stealing, or at least had to repay the $1200 out of my own pocket.

So what happened to the check? I don't truthfully know, but I find it interesting that Smitty was still at work when I arrived late that night, and Smitty knew that I had a C.O.D to pay for, and then the check just 'mysteriously' vanished? It could have happened? I know that I had the check, because I made a copy of it, and stamped it on the time clock right before I punched out for the night and left to go home. I remember folding the check around the C.O.D, like I always had done, and placing the checks into my turn-in envelope. With the mail bags on their way to Montgomery then someone, a member of management, would've have had to take my turn in envelope and secure it until the next day and Smitty was the only one there. All evidence seemed to point to...well I'm not going to say, because I don't know for sure, so I'll let you decide for yourself.

As far as the two grievances went that I had filed resulted in that any unknown manager that came to Huntsville 'HAD' to wear a nametag while in the building. It was only a very short time after this grievance that management in Huntsville purchased name tags for all of us and told us that we had to wear them, and if we didn't that we'd be disciplined. What was good for the goose is good for the gander...I guess.

The other grievance was bargained down, as usual by Matt and the local union. So much for trying to fight for our workplace rights when our own local union wouldn't support and defend them themselves. I was about to attempt to change that.

The nominations for the local union election were coming up and I was preparing to run against Matt and hopefully defeat him. I was going to not only fight Matt and try to beat him, but it was beginning to look like I was going to have to fight management as well, which had now taken an interest in the local union election.

Chapter 17

"8:47 A.M: I had to call the Huntsville city police department after management stole my campaign signs and destroyed them. I'm going to have the managers arrested for theft of property."

I had become somewhat disillusioned with the way the local union was being run and the total lack of interest shown in protecting and defending our rights as Teamster's that was constantly being demonstrated by the actions of Matt and the other 'old guard' officers. The local union had begun putting the word out that I was indeed going to run against Matt in the upcoming local union elections in late November of 1998, and several people in the union became 'concerned' with my decision.

I would have my first heated verbal exchange voicing my displeasure with Matt after an incident, involving another member after the member was sold out during a grievance hearing by Matt, which would be the catalyst for the upcoming weeks in regard to the way my campaign would be conducted, and what obstacles I would have to try and overcome to try and achieve my goal.

My goal was simple. I wanted to restore the power back into the hands of all the members, and to restore the pride, integrity and honor back into the local union. I wanted to start holding companies accountable for the way they abused our members and enforce the contract to preserve and defend work place and union rights.

Before the nomination meeting was scheduled I had a little visit from Matt whom tried to persuade me not to run against him. He wanted me to run as a Trustee on a slate with him instead, and the other officers of whom, but a few, was "old guard". Needless to say after I told him what I thought of him and his offer he didn't hang around long...because I had told him to go to...well you know where.

Over the last three months I had a total of about sixteen rides, twelve of which were "lock in" production rides, and the everyday hell from the "Little Colonel Regime" was growing very old.

I had met with Josey and several other key people from the Huntsville center and we all laid out a game plan on how my election campaign would be conducted.

I had asked Abel to run with me for the position of local president and he accepted my offer, and Josey had pretty much become the unofficial coordinator of the campaign and immediately began laying out what we needed to do.

We decided to begin hitting every work site we could, that we knew of, that was in the local.

One mistake that I made in the beginning was to mainly rely on only the UPS member's vote. I had made a name for myself as being a "hard liner" towards UPS management, and I arrogantly thought that this in itself, would be enough to ensure victory, but really I was stupid to not know the whole dynamics that were involved in actually conducting a union election.

As a result, Josey thought it would be a good idea for me to call T.D.U, Teamsters for a Democratic Union, and I talked to a representative of theirs named Tim after I had followed Josey's advice, and Tim and I talked several more times over the next couple of weeks about what I needed to do. Tim told me several good things that I needed to do and he'd even sent me some information on how to conduct an election at no cost to me.

I was arrogant and stupid, though, and decided not to follow his advice, and I thought that I could just hit a few key places and that alone would win me the election.

I tried calling two of the existing officers on the local union executive board to see if they were interested in running on a slate with Abel and me, and evidently they weren't, because they would never return our calls to them, and come to find out they were all loyal to Matt and had decided to do their own thing.

We all made the trip over to the union hall the day of the nominations, and we both stood before the membership and accepted the nominations, and it was now official. We we're running against the old guard establishment.

Abel and I had begun going around to the various workplace sites that were in our local, and began meeting with key people in various plants trying to spread our campaign, and to be seen in person while we were out campaigning. We never could get the addresses to all the work sites, or what times to catch people during work shift changes. Matt wasn't about to help us with our legal rights to this information, and our ignorance wasn't going to do anything but help Matt. We struggled for a week or so and tried to get the handbills, that contained information about our platform, out by hand to all the work sites we knew of.

In the meanwhile we both still had to work our regular jobs. Abel would get off of work at around 4:00 a.m, after making a run to the Whites Creek hub, in Nashville Tennessee, and I would be waiting at the building to pick him up and we'd load up our signs and head to various work place sites. I was still on package car and I could only stay out for a few hours then I'd have to go to work that morning. I had made about two-dozen signs and we sat them out in front of several job sites and especially in front of all four centers in North Alabama that were in our local union.

Management had finally come to terms with the fact that they might actually have to deal with me, the lunatic fanatic, and they were scared as it was beginning to look like I was going to win.

Local managers were conducting polls within each of the centers to test the waters on how everyone was going to vote, and a supervisor, who in no longer with the company, confirmed that this was in fact going on. The supervisor, who wished to remain anonymous, said that management was terrified that I might win.

Management wasn't going to try and influence members in voting because they knew that I would be watching for that, and then I would nail their butts to the wall with a complaint to the U.S Department of Labor and the N.L.R.B, so they had other plans to 'interfere' with this union election.

I would leave from my house a little earlier than usual every morning, during the campaign, and drive to the Huntsville center to straighten my signs up. I had about eight signs total, and one pretty good size plywood sign that I had made from materials that were left over from the strike, which I sat out in the ground front of the center in Huntsville.

It was also election time for Federal Government offices as well, and those candidates had their signs out too, with the whole road in front of the building, both sides, being covered up with signs.

As I turned the corner off of the highway onto Winchester Road, and as I made my way towards the center I would check to make sure my signs were still up as I drove in front of the building to see if any of them had blown down during the night.

Only this time all of them were gone, even the plywood sign that I had anchored into the ground was gone too, and I knew right away that management must have done something with them. I went ballistic. I mean I totally lost it. I parked my truck and jumped out and went inside to find out what happened to them. I looked for the Colonel and found him in the east center's office, and I walked on in and slammed the door behind me.

"Where's my signs at Colonel?" I asked him angrily. I noticed right off that he was acting suspicious. Very suspicious. I knew he was mixed up in it someway. "I'm not going to ask you again Colonel, where are my signs!" I repeated. By now I was sure enough on a short fuse and it wouldn't have taken much for me to go off in the office right then. Smitty poked his head in the door, and asked the Colonel if everything was all right.

"The best thing you can do right know is mind your own business," I said, while giving him an evil look. He could tell that I was on the edge of going off. He slipped on in and never said another word and walked over and stood behind the Colonel.

"James, I haven't seen your signs," the Colonel replied. I knew he was lying, because the little goof wouldn't even look at me in the eyes. I walked on out knowing somebody must have seen something.

I walked back up towards where I had parked my truck at, which was just outside the building, when I heard my name being called. As I turned around and began looking for who was calling me, I heard my name again and looked over and it was a loader on the east belt.

"Did you find your signs?" He asked.

"No why?" I replied.

He looked around and then stepped into the rear of his package car, just out of view in case someone would be watching him talk to me.

He hung his head out and scanned the area looking for a supervisor and said, "I saw two supervisors go out front and pull them up and then carry them around back."

I thanked him and assured him that I wouldn't mention his name, and walked out to the back of the building where the dumpster was. I slid the door to the dumpster open and looked inside, and there they were. Whoever had put the plywood sign in the dumpster must have just thrown it in, because it had broken in half, and all the other signs had been torn in half, and weren't in any shape to be used. I had managed to let my temper almost get the best of me, and I wasn't thinking too clearly now.

I had become over run with emotions, and I knew what I would've liked to do, but what I was thinking about doing to them would only land me in jail, so I thought for a moment and I then decided on how I was going to handle it. I walked back into the office where the Colonel was still working in, and picked up the phone. He was pretending to ignore me, but I knew he would be listening to me. I dialed the phone and waited for an answer on the other end.

"No m'am, there's no emergency. I need as police officer to come to the corner of Winchester Road and Meridian Street at John's store." I said calmly.

The Colonel had now stopped what he was doing and had a look of fear on his face while he listened to my conversation with the dispatcher. I finished the call and hung the phone up. I didn't say a word to him at all, and I just turned and walked out.

I walked back up towards the front of the building, and on my way I ran into the two supervisors who had been the ones to pull up my signs and destroy them, and they immediately began telling me that they were sorry and pleaded with me not to call the police on them. They continued to tell me that they were sorry for what they had done and only had done what they were told to do. I stopped walking and asked them who told them to destroy my property.

"The Colonel did, James." He replied. That's all I wanted to know.

I drove on up to the store, which was about 100 yards from the center, and waited in the parking lot for the police to arrive. After a few minutes or so, I saw a patrol car approaching and I stepped on out of my vehicle and waved at him. The officer got out of his car and asked me what was going on? I explained to him about how management had stolen my signs and destroyed my property and so on.

"Mr. Earls are you sure you want to do this?" The officer asked. "I mean, you know if you follow through with this that they may try and retaliate against you for doing this," he finished.

"They've been trying to fire me now for almost two years officer. I can handle it." I replied, as he proceeded to fill out a report. I gave him the names of all the management personnel involved. During this several drivers had passed by us on their way to the center and I waived at them as they looked on.

"What can I have done to them officer?" I asked.

"Well Mr. Earls I'll tell you sir. What they have done is no different than if they'd walked right into this store here and had taken a two-cent piece of candy. It's third degree theft sir." The officer replied, while calling in the report for a case number.

"Is there any legal recourse for me to enact?' I asked.

"Come down this afternoon to the police station and pick up a copy of this report, and then go to the Magistrates office and swear out a warrant against them for their arrest." He said.

That was what I was hoping to hear. I thanked the officer and jumped into my truck and took off back to the center, and as I walked in, I was swarmed with people wanting to know what was going on.

"Not right now," I said, as I made my way to the Colonel's office. I opened the door and looked around and no was in there. I turned and walked up to the edge of the dock and leaned forward looking down the belt for the Colonel, and I didn't see him. I finally found out from a part timer that the Colonel might be upstairs with Dick. I hadn't known that Dick was here, but this had started to make things a lot clearer, so I walked on upstairs and knocked on the door.

"Come in," Dick replied.

"Dick we seem to have a problem," I said, and he stopped what he was doing and looked at me.

"I don't know if you're aware or not of the THEFT of my property this morning by certain members of management in this facility?" I said very slow and sarcastically.

"No, James I wasn't, but that's between you and the Colonel," he replied. I stopped and thought for a moment. If he wasn't aware of the problem then how did he know that the Colonel was involved and not some other member of management? I knew right then that he knew more about it than he was letting on.

"That's okay Dick..." I said, as I slowly walked to the door.

"If I don't have those signs back up by this afternoon when I get in from my route...I will leave as soon as I get done, and drive downtown and have warrants sworn out for everyone who was involved...you do understand me...don't you Dick?" I asked in a very cold and demanding tone.

He was in no position to negotiate, because he knew that I was crazy enough to follow through with it and that I'd have them all arrested for theft. I didn't give him the chance to respond, and opened the door, and walked back down the steps.

"The Colonel is in his office," a part timer said, as he walked by me never stopping or looking back. I turned around and walked back to the Colonel's office, and opened the door as he was standing in there on the phone, and as soon as I came into the office he hung up. I stepped on in and locked the door so Smitty, or anyone else couldn't walk in on me and hear what I was about to tell the Colonel.

"Colonel you're nothing but a lying piece of crap...but you already know that don't you?' I asked, while walking around over to where he was now sitting. "I want you to know that I have witnesses that are willing to say you're the one who ordered the signs to be stolen and destroyed." I said in a smart-ass tone.

"I...I...I didn't steal anything." He stuttered out.

"Well let me put it to you like this Colonel," I replied. "I have already had two witnesses to come forward to state that they had seen two of your supervisors pull up and carry my signs around to the back of the building, and ANOTHER witness just came forward to tell me that you approached him trying to get him to do it, but he refused to participate because he knew that it was illegal." I replied.

"I don't know what you're talking about James..." The Colonel replied.

"If I don't have those signs up just like the one's you destroyed by this afternoon when I get back...I will have the police pick all of you up and haul your asses to jail! Do you understand me Colonel?" I asked.

"...James they weren't the best looking things and Dick didn't want them junking up the place." He said realizing that I was going to follow through with what I was threatening.

"I'm glad you told me Dick was involved too Colonel," I said smiling. "This afternoon!" I said and walked on out the door through a small mob that had gathered after witnessing the earlier verbal exchange between Jake and me about how the Colonel had told him to steal my signs.

I attended the morning PCM and it was a very tense one for management and the Colonel was not in it, which was very...very unusual. The meeting went without a hitch and I walked back up to the counter to retrieve my personal belongings, which I had left there by mistake during the confusion this morning. I started to turn and leave and the Colonel was walking up to me. I looked in his hands and I noticed that he had a notebook and pen as he placed them on the counter beside me.

"Draw out your signs for me, and what they said on them...please." He said.

I sat my things back down on the counter and proceeded to draw and write the dimensions of the plywood sign down on the paper. I made sure that he understood that I wanted the "EXACT" same dimensions, same thickness of the wood, size of the letters and the same color of paint. I handed him the figures and he turned and went into this office, and I left that morning with a feeling of victory.

When I returned that evening, as I made the turn and was coming down Winchester road in my package car, I noticed that they had followed my demands right down to the very last one. I turned up into the entrance and noticed that management had made me one of the most beautiful plywood signs that I had ever laid my eyes on. It was some work of art and it was quite beautiful. Heck, it was even better than the one I had originally had made. I walked into the building and the Colonel immediately came up to me and asked me if I had seen the signs.

"Yeah, they look great Colonel." I replied smiling.

"Is this over now?" He asked solemnly.

"It is if you want it to be Colonel...that depends on you." I replied, while staring at him in the eyes. The Colonel turned and walked back to his office and shut the door.

I would later find out that management had paid two hourly employees to stay and make the signs and to paint them. Management knew that I meant business, and I would've had them arrested during the preload or when the drivers where present for optimum shock value. I would have honestly done it if I didn't have my signs back out by that night.

This one incident would concrete my existence in the eyes of corporate UPS management as one of the most hated stewards in the Southeastern United States, and one of the most hated in the Alabama District.

It had been well over a year now since the strike and management had still failed to put the first installment of the 10,000 "new" jobs on as they had agreed to in the labor agreement between the Teamsters and themselves. We, in Huntsville, had now had around six full time drivers retire and they were not replaced by promoting the part time employees. The volume was still there, and the management decided to just cut the routes back with a newfound policy that they implemented called "remote delivery".

UPS was making money hand over fist, and management was deceiving the union in the process by saying that they still hadn't met pre-strike level volume and so on, and Hoffa was buying it all.

What remote delivery was is that management would take and divide a rural route in half. Then management would create an "A" side and a "B" side of the route that would be delivered on alternating days. By doing this, it would allow an 'accumulation' of two days worth of delivery volume to collect to "justify" for the delivery services into a 'remote', or rural customers area. Management would then pull all of the packages off of the truck that fell into the "A" day and place them under the belt, while going out and delivering the "B" side of the route, and then the next day...do just the opposite.

We would have enough volume for four or five routes left in the east center everyday, and this wasn't counting the volume that was left in the west center. This was doing nothing but costing us Teamster jobs and taking the word "Service" out of our name.

The work was there, but management did this as a result of their 'logic' to save money. It was half true, though their intentions were not solely just to save money in the minuscule sense. The Big Picture was that they were going to save money...lots of money, up front, by 'failing' to put on the replacement drivers and through the combining of the routes.

Take for example the cost saving avenue this presented for management by taking an existing ten routes with ten full time drivers who had been running the routes for over the last two years. Then say that five of the full time drivers retire, which theoretically five part time employees "SHOULD HAVE" been promoted into the ranks of the full time driving force to replace those five drivers that have retired... right? Wrong.

Why should management replace those five full time driver slots with five newly promoted part timers when they can now, under the remote delivery plan, downsize the routes, and use the existing cover drivers to deliver the routes. And thus management was saving a ton of money from this.

They were saving the money by eliminating the hiring of five full time drivers at full time wages and benefits, and replacing them with savings associated from the use of the "PART TIME" cover drivers, such as on vacation pay, and pension contributions, and so forth, and then by rolling the ten routes down into nine through the 'remote delivery' scheme. By cutting out one package car route they've eliminated more than just a Teamster job and salary, but the allocation of the package car itself, and also rest of the cost that is associated with operating a package car on the road everyday, such as insurance, fuel, up-keep, maintenance and so on.

Management would then continue to implement the A and B side plan by dividing the routes up, and this would technically eliminate another two routes by combining and creating separate 'new' routes to handle the A and B delivery system all being delivered by the same driver.

I would later experience this first hand again as a 'temporary' employee of Kryspy Kreme doughnuts. They too had eliminated four routes by using this same device only they called it something different. That still wound up costing them four full time jobs and put the work on the other drivers and they'd go out and delivery two routes on the "A" and "B" days.

Why didn't someone do something? The truth is we tried.

I personally filed numerous grievances to protest this and the local union failed to see anything wrong with it, or either they just didn't care to do anything about it, which if they had chose to do something about it, their actions would have actually 'rocked' the boat for once.

So, technically, what was there to complain about other than management had failed to replace those drivers who had retired? So what...we weren't going to lose anyone, but the problem was that we weren't going to gain anyone either.

The drawback that affected us as members of a union was the loss of new members dues money. If management wasn't going to replace those five full time drivers then the local was losing, not only the revenue from five newly hired members off the street which was about $27.00 a month in dues each, but also the increase in dues from each of the newly "promoted" five full time drivers which would have doubled their union dues to $42.00 a month each. By just allowing the management to get away with this practice alone had cost our cash strapped local over $3200.00 a year in lost dues revenue, and if this practice was nationwide with a loss of 10,000 jobs due to retirements, through this same practice, could be costing local unions nationwide a total of over $3.2 million a year in lost dues money and thousands of new members. Surely they knew this? Why didn't they act? Simple...it was five little words...Hoffa. Think back to when he had alledgedly received money from UPS during his campaign in 1996. He may have been simply returning a favor.

The next problem I had with this practice was how it affected the reputation of the company and the perception of "US" through the customer's eyes. We had been known and founded, as a company, as a dependable delivery service that led the industry, and that other companies tried desperately to measure up to. We had a defined time in-transit schedule that customers could depend on everyday like clockwork, but now with this idiotic remote delivery scheme in place, it was damaging the image and credibility of the company as a reliable and dedicated service provider that set the standards for others to follow.

Customers had begun comparing us to RPS, which at the time had questionable delivery reliability, and one that was commonly associated with being below "UPS's" standards, and this troubled us all.

We brought this to managements attention during the daily PCM's, but they weren't interested in that at all and blamed it all on corporate. They only wanted that dollar, and this dollar would come at the expense of the reputation that the company founders had achieved from over the last ninety some odd years.

Complaints began to come in by the dozens, and we even encouraged customers to call in National Complaints against management in Huntsville on having their boxes sit in the building on their "odd" day if they fell into the category that required that "odd" section to be held for a later delivery. It was always taught to me that we NEVER, EVER brought back anyone's packages that could have been delivered, but here we were having hundred's of 'deliverable' packages just sit under the belt everyday. Some of these packages that sat under the belts everyday some people made their living by...and they just sat there. I personally had been disciplined, in the past, along with the majority of the drivers at some time in their careers, for bringing back "missed packages" and now the management was allowing this practice to happen everyday.

This practice would continue for several more months before being finally eliminated altogether, but the price had been paid. It was a blemish on our impeccable reputation, and the cost was greed by the upper management and board of directors. It was also an enormous act of hypocrisy on the part of management who were now talking out both sides of their mouths.

This was another one of the ways that management had undermined the contract, and deceived the Union into allowing the remote delivery scheme to continue. I have a hard time believing that the Hoffa couldn't have known the harm that this practice was causing and how it was preventing management from full filling their first installment of the promised 10,000 jobs, which was 2,000 for the first year, by years end. Surely he knew?

Chapter 18

"8:46 A.M: The Colonel jumps in my face screaming at the top of his lungs for me to shut up. I tell him to get out of my face. Everyone stops what they're doing to see what they thought was turning into a fist fight."

A local level hearing was scheduled toward the end of the month of November and the Colonel had pulled Smitty off of the truck with me for a week or so, until just right before the hearings.

I was still continuing to run over allowed everyday, and I still had to call in for help everyday, and the Colonel finally decided to just have another driver meet me everyday to help me make my deliveries. Why didn't he just lighten me back up to what I originally had? Because this would have meant that he was wrong and had indeed been persecuting me.

This move by him wasn't anything but an admission that my route had way too much work on it, and if this weren't the case, then why would he dispatch another driver to meet and take work off of me everyday?

I attended that morning PCM, and after the meeting I walked back up to the check in counter, in front of the east office, to pick up my DIAD, and other personal affects, and then I walked over to the dock and I stepped up onto it and began walking down to my truck, which had been moved again, and it was now parked about half way down the belt.

As I walked down the belt a driver asked me what I thought about everything that was currently going on in Huntsville, and I replied, "Another day in the salt mines and one less day in hell. I didn't see that the Colonel was standing on the dock beside the belt in front of me, and when he heard what I had said he spun around and jumped into my face and began screaming and spitting all over the place like a rabid dog. I mean he was literally screaming at the top of his lungs. At first I was taken by surprise, but once I regained my senses after the initial shock of what was happening I jumped off into his crap with both feet. Everyone on the whole belt stopped what they were doing and was watching what was beginning to unfold right in front of them.

"Don't you ever talk about this company again do you understand me!" He screamed while in my face.

"Who the hell do you think you are screaming at me like a damn idiot!" I screamed back in his face and now there was less than an inch separating us.

"Don't you let me hear you talk about this company ever again," he replied, while backing up out of my face. Oh no, he wasn't about to get off that easy.

I jumped right back into his face and said, "Let me tell you something you little jerk, I can talk about this company anyway I want...I earned it!"

The Colonel had realized that he had screwed up royally by showing his butt in front of all the drivers on the belt that morning. That incident literally made me sick. I walked on down to my truck with everyone staring at me and standing there shocked from what they had just witnessed. He had overstepped his boundaries and I was going to be sure to make his life a living hell for as long as he remained in Huntsville.

I left out on my route that morning, really in no shape to work. I felt like going home after that incident. My blood pressure was through the roof. "No...No I'm not going home," I said to myself over and over. "I'm not going to let these people win. That's what they want me to do." I thought to myself. I wasn't about to let them think that I was even thinking of cracking.

All this did was to harden my resolve and increase the stakes in the game that we were playing.

I had stopped while on my route at the bank that I used to deposit my paycheck, and this was on a Thursday, and I had my check so I decided to go ahead and get it out of the way as I pulled up to the bank entrance and stopped. I reached over to my DIAD and punched over onto mealtime, and I was on my personal time now so the Colonel couldn't say anything to me about stopping, although I had a stop for the bank anyway.

I walked into the bank and made my way on up to the counter as I began talking to the ladies who were the bank's tellers, and whom I knew them all well by now and had a good customer relationship with them. Into the transaction Mary said to me, "James someone's in your truck." I turned and ran out of the bank, leaving my money with her, to where my truck was parked and noticed that the Colonel and Smitty were up in my truck.

The Colonel was standing just inside the bulkhead door like he was blocking the view for Smitty, who was in the rear of the truck going through my load and checking various packages.

"What are you doing here?" I asked.

"We own the truck don't we?" The Colonel popped off.

"While it's out here I own it Colonel and you have no business going through it when I'm not out here." I replied angrily.

"I don't see it that way James," the Colonel replied.

"I have my personal money out here along with C.O.D money that I keep back here," I said, as I picked up my wallet and began going through it to make sure all of my money was still there.

"What do you want Colonel?" I asked, while tossing my wallet back onto the shelf.

"I want you to answer me why is it we can do a load audit on you one day and you have a good load, and then the next day you can have a bad load? Do I need to get out here and ride with you?' He said as Smitty was still rummaging through the shelves.

"What's he looking for?" I asked the Colonel.

The Colonel turned and glanced over his shoulder at Smitty and replied, "He's checking to see what the problem is James, and why you can't ever get done."

The Colonel spat out the other side of the truck with a little juice hitting my seat.

"DO YOU MIND NOT SPITTING ON MY SEAT COLONEL?" I said in an

agitated tone.

"Colonel it looks like he's got a lot left," Smitty said to the Colonel.

"What do you think I lie to you when I call for help everyday?' I asked Smitty who was now standing behind the Colonel.

"I'm getting tired of having to deal with you about this everyday." The Colonel said.

"Well I'll tell you what Colonel...Here's a jump seat and I'm sure you've got a set of browns...why don't YOU get out here and see what the real world is like and fix the problem like a real manager instead of hiding in an office all day and just talking about it." I replied. I had called him out now.

"Oh I can fix the problem," the Colonel replied as he stepped out of the truck being followed closely by Smitty.

I didn't say a word and just stared at the Colonel with a go to hell look on my face. Smitty turned back to look at me and I winked at him which caused him to roll his eyes and frown. They both got into the Colonel's van and left after telling me that they'd send me some help later on in the day. I was sent help that day as usual, but I began to question what those two were really up that day.

Were they out there to plant drugs on me?

Were they out there to plant something that was 'allegedly' stolen from UPS?

I decided then that they were going to change their tactics in trying to get rid of me, and I really didn't trust them now as I was becoming concerned for my job. So I decided to go ahead and file a grievance concerning this latest incident to document what they had done to me.

DATE GRIEVANCE FILED: 11-13-98

EXPLAIN GRIEVANCE: *The Colonel jumped into my face screaming at me. I find this very unprofessional and I fear that this could have led to a physical confrontation. This manager is unfit to hold the position he has. He needs to be severely disciplined and investigated.*

REMEDY SOUGHT: *Termination of this manager and an investigation along with a written apology.*

DATE GRIEVANCE FILED: 11-13-98

EXPLAIN GRIEVANCE: *While at 4806 Whitesburg Drive, I returned to my package car and found the Colonel and Smitty behind the bulkhead door going through my load. I've had poor loads except on the days they ride with me. I request to be present when they are going through my car. If something came up stolen then I'd be held responsible for it and I fear that they may try and plant something on me.*

REMEDY SOUGHT: *Terminate managers involved or at least relocate them both. No more rides from management until my load is fixed. Stay out of cars without drivers being present.*

The Colonel was now very much out of control, and he actually thought he could continue on his reign of terrorizing the Teamsters of the Huntsville center while remaining untouchable, but little did the idiot know that he was losing the support of the UPS's upper management during the local level hearings?

During one of these local hearings it was becoming apparent that the Colonel had in fact over stepped his boundaries on more than one occasion, and he was being ridiculed by non other than the Alabama District labor manager, Hembry, who had now begun withdrawing support for the Colonel's radical agenda, and during these meetings Hembry began to inquire further into the conduct of this maniacal center manager.

The Colonel's reign of terror would now include into its ruthless wake, several more incidents involving questionable behavior.

One incident involved a driver from the west center in Huntsville named Bob. Bob and the Colonel had engaged in an argument while upon they were both still on the belt and the Colonel intentionally bumped into him in an attempt to instigate a physical confrontation. Bob filed a grievance about the incident, which only added fuel to the fire.

I had decided to start campaigning grievances from everyone in an attempt to undermine support for the Huntsville management team, and we would eventually unleash a campaign of terror on the "Little Colonel Regime" that would rival their own campaign, which they were currently raging against us.

One of the last major incidents that involved the Colonel, and was just another example of his ignorance and total lack of respect for humanity and the contract happened as I was called into the office one morning concerning a 'labor crisis', just after the PCM, and it involved an east center driver named Chad.

Chad was an eight-year employee who had worked mainly as a reloader prior to becoming a cover driver, and was a no non-sense type of person and I knew that he had no love for management, like the majority of us in Huntsville, and he didn't take anything off them either.

The Colonel walked right up the belt that morning and told me that he needed me right away in the office, and as I walked in, I saw Chad sitting in there.

"What's going on in here?" I asked.

"James, I've instructed Chad to take off his knee brace." The Colonel said sounding upset. I looked down at Chad's knee and saw that he had a rather large brace on it.

"I have a doctors excuse, James." Chad said as he handed me the doctors excuse, and I began reading over it and finally handed it the Colonel.

"What's the problem with him wearing the brace Colonel if he's got an excuse?" I asked the Colonel as he was reading over the excuse.

"It's not part of the uniform." The Colonel replied.

"Is that it, or is it you don't want to tarnish the precious image of this company in the eyes of the public and make people realize that maybe we do really get hurt around here?" I asked sarcastically.

"Chad, you have a choice...either you take the brace off or you can go home," the Colonel replied. Chad leaned over and picked up his satchel, and he began to walk out the door. The Colonel went ape crap.

He followed Chad outside into the building screaming at him, "If you leave now you're fired. Do you understand me?" People had begun stopping what they were doing and turned to see what all the yelling was about.

"Colonel we need to take this back inside the office," I said, as I held the door open for both of them to walk back in.

I was trying to diffuse a potential confrontation that had all the makings to turn even nastier than it currently had become at any given moment. I managed to put whatever ill feelings I had towards the Colonel aside for the moment, and I just tried to concentrate on trying to work out a solution that would benefit both parties.

"James, instruct Chad to take the brace off now." The Colonel said to me.

"You know that I can't tell him to do that Colonel...he doesn't work for me. And besides I wouldn't tell him to do that anyway." I replied shocked from his request.

"James, call Matt right now and put him on the speaker phone," the Colonel demanded.

I walked over to the phone and dialed the number to the local union and Matt answered. I asked him to hold on while the Colonel put him on the speakerphone.

I explained to Matt what was going on and I asked Matt what needed to be done. Matt 'hee hawed' around, and like always ...gave in to the management and to the Colonel, and then he gave Chad a choice, after just discussing the matter over with Matt. The solution was that if Chad was going to wear the brace that he had to wear his long pants over it.

This was impossible to do, because the brace was too large to fit comfortably under his pants.

Chad reluctantly opted to just take the brace off, but did so under extreme protest. If Chad had a doctors excuse then I felt that Matt should've have taken the position that Chad should be allowed to wear the brace, but in usual fashion, Matt made Chad adhere to the Colonel's demands.

Chad went on to work that morning without the brace and by the end of the day his knee would blow out, which caused him to fall and break his wrist.

Management had once again put the image of the company before the health and safety of its employees, which would wind up costing them a lawsuit from Chad, and all because of this one little wannabe man...the Colonel.

I had immediately filed a grievance to view the OR of the drivers who had been covering my route for the week that I was off on vacation, after I had found out that a total of three different drivers had covered my route the whole week.

I then began to inquire to them individually, before the PCM that morning, and I asked them how well each of them had done, and they all told me that that they had run more than an hour over allowed.

Now, if four drivers had all run over allowed on the same route, and then chances were that there was a problem with the route and not the driver...right? Wrong.

I was once again refused access to the OR, which as a steward, I had the right to see, and Smitty replied to me that he couldn't remember how well the other drivers had done, but I knew that he was lying through his teeth.

"Can't you pull them up on the computer Smitty?' I asked.

"No, we can't go in there and change the timecards," he replied.

"I'm not asking you to change the time cards Smitty, I just want to see how much over allowed the other drivers ran." I replied.

"I can't do that." He nervously replied.

"Can't or won't?' I asked.

"You need to take this up with the Colonel, James." Smitty replied as he walked out of the office. I wasn't going to talk to the Colonel about it. I'd simply file a grievance.

DATE GRIEVANCE FILED: 11-23-98

EXPLAIN GRIEVANCE: *On 11-23-98, I requested to view the Operations Report, OR, for the Huntsville East Center. I want to see how the other drivers did who ran my route (27D) while I was on vacation for the week ending 11-20-98.*

REMEDY SOUGHT: *Relocation of these problem managers and compliance from this date on. I want charges filed with the N.L.R.B.*

The election results would come back in, and Abel and I had both lost. Management was relieved that we had lost, which meant that they had another three years with the 'Old Guard" officers of Local 402, which meant that management could continue to dictate local union labor policy, and they now had the guarantee of another three years of "passive representation" from Matt.

Management had now increased the level of personal hell they were going to put me through knowing now that they didn't have to worry about any retaliation from me since I had just lost the election.

I was called into the office one evening, shortly after the election results came in, and was told that there would be some changes in my route. I was having a bulk stop taken off of me, which this one stop in particular had been costing me roughly fifty minutes a day to deliver it, and I wouldn't be picking up anything to replace it. I was excited.

Finally, I thought to myself, now I would be able to run under allowed and I was very eager to go to work the next morning to prove to them that it was the route, and not the driver that was the problem.

I reported for work the next morning and after I attended the morning PCM, I began going through my load to make sure that they hadn't put anything else on me after removing the bulk stop. I saw that there wasn't anything extra in the shelves either, and I was now raring to go.

I went out and performed on my route just like I had been doing everyday for the last four months, and to top it off, I had been given a new loader, who was a veteran of four years and only worked on the pre-load, and I had a fantastic load along with just the right amount of work. It was in fact...a perfect day. I was able to finish the day without having to call in for help and I arrived back to the building well before the curfew. I knew in my heart that I had performed "a perfect, textbook day" and I was looking forward to viewing the OR the following morning to see how well I had actually done.

I arrived to work the next day expecting to be called into the office to be told by the Colonel that I had done a great job and that all this would finally be over.

My expectations were right. I had my name called to report to their office during the PCM and I was really looking forward to seeing the results from the previous day. I walked on up to the office and looked through the little window that was in the door, and noticed that Marsha, the part timer's steward was sitting in the office. I thought to myself, "Why would she be in here for," as I knocked on the door and walked on in? Smitty walked in right behind me along with the Colonel and he asked me to take a seat.

I sat down and looked at Marsha who shrugged her shoulders indicating to me that she didn't know what was going on.

I was now the only steward in the Huntsville building who handled all of the package car drivers, about 75 drivers, because Ronnie, a driver for the west center, who had taken over as chief steward for them, after Alvin retired, only to resign about three weeks later, after seeing how Matt and the local union would leave you out on a limb by yourself when you dealt with management.

I sat down and was waiting for the praises to begin spewing from their mouths.

"James we did an audit on your records last night, and we found that you had failed to properly record a business name in the proper place on the records."

I was disappointed as my heart began to sink. "Did you audit anyone else's records?" I asked, while wiping my face with my hand in a display of disgust towards them.

"We're not worried about other people right now James," the Colonel replied. I had now put my head in my hands, and I began to rub my face in a frantic attempt to curb the swelling anger inside.

"What did I do?" I asked, while sitting back up and letting out a long sigh.

The Colonel handed me a copy of my delivery records from the day before and I began to search them.

"Where is it?" I asked angrily.

He pointed his pen to a section on one stop that showed that I had abbreviated a consignee's name instead of spelling it out.

"Is this it?" I asked. "Is this the best that you two can muster Colonel?" I asked as my voice began to rise and become shaky from the rush of adrenalin that had begun to flow through my veins. I was trying very, very hard to contain myself. I wasn't going to give in and let them have the luxury of another confrontation.

"That's all we could find James at the moment," the Colonel replied, sort of grinning.

"James, I want you to know that you'll be receiving a warning letter for this incident, and I expect you to follow the methods like you've been trained to use...next time." The Colonel replied, as Smitty handed me a copy of the warning letter.

I looked it over and then stood up and tore it in half and threw it in the garbage.

Smitty stepped back behind the Colonel, while Marsha looked on in shock. This was beginning to get out of control. "How did I do yesterday Colonel?" I asked angrily.

"I don't have a copy of the report right now James," he replied sarcastically.

"You mean to tell me you don't have a copy of the OR, after y'all have been dragging me in the office everyday for the last year with copies of everything but my birth certificate and now...conveniently you don't have a copy of the OR for me to see. That's a bunch of bull and you know it!" I said angrily, as I was beginning to become unglued and it was becoming ever so difficult to try and contain my temper.

"James, go to work!" The Colonel popped off. I walked outside, back into the building and stepped up onto the dock and I began walking down to where my truck was parked, but the truck was missing. I didn't have the same loader as yesterday loading it, and it had been moved to the other side of the belt, and I noticed that my old loader was back loading it again. I walked all the way around to the other side of the belt and looked inside, and saw that it was a total wreck, and it was a mess. My heart just sank lower, and I was about ready to just give in.

I began loading what was left stacked out behind it when Smitty came walking up to me wanting me to sign a form saying that I had received the warning letter that I had torn up while in the office. I stopped what I was doing and just stared at him with a dumb look on my face, and he turned and walked off grunting and clearing his throat.

I had a package for one of my residential stops, and as I went to place it in the shelf, I noticed that all of those particular stops were missing. I then dug around in the shelf some more and I noticed that they all were gone. "This is strange," I thought, and I then looked down and saw about five tote boxes full of packages in the floor section of the truck. It was a split. I started going through the packages and reading the address labels...it was the Golf Road apartments.

"What the hell is this crap?" I screamed out.

"SMITTY!" I screamed aloud.

He came walking back up to me, and the other drivers were still loading their trucks, but were watching and listening to Smitty and me as they worked.

"What is this?" I asked, while pointing to the tote boxes that were in the floor of my truck.

"We pulled about twenty stops out of your residential's and gave you thirty stops in Golf Road."

"Why in the hell would you do something that stupid for?" I asked angrily. "Why would you do this knowing that I ...wouldn't ...get done?" I started to say, but slowly finished after it became clear to me now what they were up to.

Smitty just stood there with his hands up shrugging his shoulders. I turned my back and stopped what I was doing and just took several deep breaths to try and calm down, as he walked off, while I threw the rest of the packages into the shelf and left the building. My day was shot to hell. I was so disgusted and upset from this experience that I had to call in sick the next day.

I was unknowingly slipping further and further into a depression, and it was beginning to take a more dramatic, and defined toll on my wife and daughter. I had all but totally withdrawn from my family, and all I wanted to do when I was off was to sleep. I didn't want to have anything to do with anybody. Management was apparently winning the war.

I wouldn't find out until later in the week that the 'perfect day' that I had run for them just a few days earlier, I had actually ran under allowed for them. I had exceeded the number of stops they wanted me to run, and had in fact done the job they wanted me to do, but that's not what they wanted. They wanted to torment me as much as they could by changing my route so I would once again, start running over allowed. Only this time, that latest screwed up split in Golf Road would only increase my over allowed time, and I had once again begun having to start calling the center everyday for help.

The twenty stops they had taken off of me were where I made up time if I was running behind for that day. I could run those twenty stops off in about forty-five minutes, but now, with the Golf Road apartments back on me it was once again taking me almost two hours just to run them all. I had gained the hour of over allowed back, even though the bulk stop was still off. And I was right back to square one.

Management wasn't interested in "making me successful" and helping me to achieve their production demands. They were out to force me to quit or to fire me, but I wasn't going to quit, and I wasn't about let this sawed off dwarf get the best of me. I filed a grievance to protest this latest incident.

DATE GRIEVANCE FILED: 11-30-98

EXPLAIN GRIEVANCE: *I was issued a warning letter for an audit on my records, to which I was the only driver audited. My route was changed into a way that would prevent me from running under allowed, after I had demonstrated that I could run under allowed by improving my load and reducing the number of stops that I'm being dispatched with, which I feel is nothing but harassment. I feel that this is nothing but discrimination and harassment.*

REMEDY SOUGHT: *Harassment to immediately cease, my route changed back and I want the load fixed. I want the termination of both the manager and supervisor of the Huntsville east center.*

On the morning of December 5, 1998, during the preload shift a part timer had got injured from an 'over 70' package, meaning a package that weighed over seventy pounds, that had been placed on the top belt, which in turn came crashing down the slide on the west belt onto an unsuspecting victim. The package had managed to injure the girl's arm, which required medical attention, and after an examination by Smitty who was now saying that she was okay and that it was probably just sprained, and that she could finish the sort. Smitty and I immediately got into a huge fight over this part timer while we were still out on the belt. It seems that he only wanted her to stay and finish the shift, because he didn't have anybody to replace her with, and to wait and go to the doctor after the sort went down. This wasn't going to fly with me and after the smoke cleared from our huge fight right there on the belt, he had a part time supervisor carry the girl on to the emergency room.

After the girl left, to go to the doctor, Smitty and I got into it again about running these dangerous packages through the system. He told me that it would take too long, and cost too much time to shuttle these packages around to the heads of the belt and it was more 'economical' to continue doing it the same way that they had been doing. Economics versus safety...it seemed that the dollar beat out safety once again. We'll just see Mr. Smitty!

DATE GRIEVANCE FILED: 12-5-98

EXPLAIN GRIEVANCE: *I instructed Smitty that 'over 70' packages were coming down the top belt. He showed no interest in following through my request to investigate. This management team has no concern for safety. I witnessed and followed the progress of several "over 70" packages through the system in the building.*

REMEDY SOUGHT: *Safety training and mandatory awareness of managers to comply. Redirect over 70's through the use of carts.*

Crap hit the fan after I filed this grievance. I had overwhelming evidence to support our claim that the CHSP, or safety committee, was just a front to the insurance company and OSHA, and that it wasn't anything but a bull crap sham.

Evidently management didn't care too much for the safety of its employees, and the Colonel caught hell from the upper brass on this one, and retaliation against me for filing this grievance was just days away.

I managed to lay low for the rest of the morning after filing the grievance until it was time for me to start work. After the PCM I had walked to my truck to begin loading the packages that were still stacked up behind it, and that's when Smitty came walking up behind me and surprised me.

"What is this crap?" He asked.

"What are you talking about?" I asked, while playing dumb.

"This... I 'm sick and tired of you filing grievances everyday," he said while waving the grievance around with his voice getting louder and louder between grunts.

"You'd better step back out of my face Smitty and lower your voice or you're going to have a major problem with me." I said growing angry.

"This...this is nothing but a bunch of lies," he blurted out almost to the point of crying.

"Lies! Have you discussed with the pre loaders about the over 70 problem?" I demanded to know.

He wouldn't answer me.

"Yeah that's what I thought," I said as I turned my back to him and started loading the packages again.

"I'm not finished with you yet!" He yelled out at me being almost to the point of crying.

I dropped the packages that I had in my arms and walked right up to his face.

"I'm done with YOU until we have a local. Do you understand me...SIR?" I replied.

He turned and ran off to get the Colonel like a little kid to tell on the big union bully.

It seemed after this little ordeal that they were the ones who were beginning to crack, due in part to the constant bombardment of grievances from us everyday, and from our strong resolve was finally beginning to take a toll on them, and our plan was working. They were visibly beginning to crumble from the stress caused by the Teamsters in the building, and I decided not to let up one bit, so I filed another grievance against Smitty for the way he had talked to me that morning.

DATE GRIEVANCE FILED: 12-2-98

EXPLAIN GRIEVANCE: *I had previously filed a grievance concerning over 70's coming down the top belt, which created a serious safety hazard. I gave the grievances to Smitty and was later approached by him before leaving the building. He confronted me in an abusive and degrading tone. I find this nothing more than harassment.*

REMEDY SOUGHT: *Terminate manger and supervisor.*

Smitty wasn't speaking to me now and he wouldn't even look at me. It was well into peak season now and I was not given a helper to help with the added volume increase on my route.

I didn't mind though because I adopted a new attitude.

I figured that the more work I had on me to deliver...the longer it would take to deliver it, thus making me more money.

I came in early on the night of December 3, 1998 and I was instructed by the Colonel to go down to south Huntsville to meet with several drivers, and Smitty, to pick up their pick up volume, because they were going to have to stay out late that night and finish delivering their routes and would be unable to make the long drive back to the building without going over twelve hours for the day.

I drove on down to Bruno's grocery store in south Huntsville to meet with all the drivers in the parking lot of the store.

All the drivers had congregated in the southeast corner of the lot, and when I came rolling up on them, I could immediately sense that something was wrong.

I had about ten minutes of meal left, and when I stepped out of the truck a driver named Jimmy came walking up to me, and he began telling me that Smitty had cussed at him and they both had gotten into a huge fight right before I arrived.

I walked on over to where Smitty was working, in the back of a package car, and asked him what was going on. He never acknowledged that I was even alive. Jimmy then asked me if I had any grievance papers on me, and I replied that I did, and I walked on over to my truck to retrieve him a few. I climbed up into the truck and slid the bulkhead door open, and began digging around in my tub for my stash of papers. I managed to find him two that were somewhat wrinkled up, and I walked back over to where he was standing, and I made sure that Smitty saw me hand them to him, after I told him that I'd collect them from him the next day, and to be sure to just write it out as a harassment grievance against Smitty. It would go well with the one I had just filed on him the day before.

Smitty looked up as I handed him the grievance papers, and he put his head back down acting as if he didn't see us and continued working in the shelf.

When I arrived back to the building I began doing my turn in for the day and then Smitty came walking up behind me and walked up right beside where I was standing and leaned over on the counter.

"You know, James...I try to help Jimmy out every time he comes to me," Smitty replied slowly, and as if he was hinting at something.

I stopped what I was doing and looked right at Smitty.

"If I see any grievance papers from him about what happened out there tonight...I'll make sure he never gets off of work again to take care of his problems with his wife and kids," Smitty said and he walked off.

What a sorry piece of feces this little $%^% was. I couldn't believe what I had just heard come out from the mouth of this low life piece of scum. He was blackmailing this driver in an attempt to 'coerce' him into not filing a grievance. This was not only against the contract, but against the law as well. This pissed me off to no end. "Jimmy wouldn't have to worry about any retaliation for filing a grievance, because I'd be the one to file it for him!" I thought to myself.

Jimmy was having marriage problems and was trying to get custody of his kids, and he needed time off to go to the lawyer and to court, and this was driving Jimmy crazy from this whole personal ordeal, and now management was going to try and black mail him, and use his personal problems against him, in an attempt to discourage a grievance he was planning to file to protest the abuse from his supervisor. I wasn't going to stand for it one bit, so I went ahead and filed the grievance on behalf of the members of Huntsville, because this one incident in fact, affected us all. The grievance was later heard and Smitty was made to apologize, now whether or not he did is a different story.

I was asked the next morning, by the new west center manager, named Gordon, to come in and represent a part timer in the office. I asked why didn't they just use Marsha, who was the part timers steward? This case was going to be something out of the norm and the part timer had specifically demanded me.

I followed Gordon on into the office where the part timer was already sitting in a seat waiting for me to arrive, and I noticed that Fredrick was sitting on the file cabinet in the corner of the office and he stood up as I walked in. Fredrick offered me the chair from behind Gordon's desk, but I declined his offer and chose to stand.

I'd rather stand eye-to-eye with them rather than sit and look up to them, because I had always found this to be sort of demeaning to have them look down at me.

I wondered exactly what they had on this young man, and as usual I had no way to prepare for a defense, because I had no idea what the charge were. I was thrust again into a case involving someone's job without any knowledge of the circumstances involved.

Fredrick sat a package on the corner of Gordon's desk and he began the meeting.

"Melvin did you deliver a package to 'so and so' address on this date?" Fredrick asked Melvin.

"Yes sir," he replied nervously.

"Did you make contact with the customer at this address?" Fredrick asked.

"No sir." Melvin replied.

"Can you explain to me what happened in your own words?" Fredrick asked Melvin, while picking up his pen and paper.

"Yes sir," Melvin replied nervously, and he began telling us all what had happened for this particular stop on this date. Melvin explained that he simply stopped to make a routine delivery, and when he walked up to the door to leave the package he noticed that the door had a note on it telling him to carry it across the street, and to leave it at a neighbors house. He said he followed the instructions on the note and then he left.

Fredrick sat there writing all of this down and when Melvin finished, Fredrick just sat there chewing on the end of his pen while staring at Melvin. He was looking as if he was contemplating management's next move, and I just rolled my eyes.

Melvin looked up at me with a very scared look on his face, and I winked at him to try and reassure him that everything was going to be okay. After about a minute or so Fredrick stood up and asked Melvin, "Did you collect any money for this package at this stop?"

"No sir!" Melvin replied surprised.

"Are you sure?" Fredrick asked again.

"He answered no, Fredrick." I replied.

"James, I'm asking him the questions," Fredrick snapped back, while looking at Gordon who was just standing there and not saying a word to anyone.

"You've asked him that question already...you need to move on to the next one Fredrick." I snapped back.

Fredrick was trying to trip this guy up by taking advantage of his anxiety. I've seen it a dozen times before. I wasn't going to let him manipulate this frightened employee into making a "coached" confession by continually asking him the same questions over and over. I jumped right in immediately as this tactic began and by doing this I intentionally slowed the tempo of the meeting back down to where I wanted it and not to where the management wanted it.

I walked over to where Gordon was standing and then Gordon handed me a copy of his delivery records while pointing to the times that were stamped on his records which showed what time he had completed this stop and had delivered the next one. The time stamp on his delivery records between stops was only a minute apart, and the distance between the two stops was several mile's, which theoretically he should've had several minutes lapse between each stop, but his records wasn't showing any lapse. I immediately saw that they were going after this man for not only the package, but for this time lapse. They were laying the groundwork for a dishonesty discharge for falsifying his records.

Fredrick began to increase the pressure on Melvin by raising his voice in the next question he posed to Melvin, but before Melvin could say anything I stepped in.

"Let me tell you something here Fredrick...you're not going to talk to this Teamster like that. Do you understand me? Either you'll talk to this man like man or this meeting is over until you can get Matt over here. I'm not going to put up with it!" I said as I walked back over in front of Fredrick.

Fredrick didn't say a word. He just looked at me with a look of hatred and lowered his voice.

"Did you collect any money for this package? Maybe a C.O.D?"

Fredrick asked in a more gentler and polite tone.

Melvin sat up in his seat now after realizing that they were accusing him of stealing. "No I didn't," he replied looking puzzled at me.

"The customer said you collected $100.00 from them as a C.O.D for the package." Fredrick replied.

"I didn't collect any money from nobody." He replied angrily.

"Why would the customer lie and make it up?" Fredrick asked.

Before Melvin could answer I asked Fredrick, "Why would MARVIN want to lie and make it up for?" I had just turned the tables on Fredrick. He didn't know how to answer that question. He just stood there with a look of ignorance on his face. Gordon was still just standing there, not saying a word or getting involved.

"I'm asking Melvin a question James so stay out of it!" Fredrick replied in a rude tone.

"I will not stay out of it Fredrick, it's my job to get involved like this and you need to get that through your head." I replied angrily. "Get to the point Fredrick, why have you got this man in here?" I asked. I had just shot to hell his plan of methodically milking an admission out of this guy whether he did or not. I wasn't going to sit back and allow him to strong arm this Teamster into a confession for something that he evidently didn't do.

"Melvin did you collect $100.00 on this package?" Fredrick asked.

"He said no Fredrick," I answered for Melvin

"I'm not talking to you," Fredrick said growing tired of me interrupting him.

"You've asked this man that question already Fredrick, maybe you need to write it down on your little pad so you'll remember it." I replied sarcastically.

Fredrick had begun getting upset with me, but I didn't care. If he didn't like the way things were going or couldn't handle me one on one maybe he should have called in some more of his L.P goons to help him out.

"The customer says you collected $100.00 from them. Can you explain this?" Fredrick asked smartly.

"They're lying, I didn't collect any money for that package." Melvin answered nervously.

Fredrick turned around to retrieve a copy of Melvin's delivery records from the day before. Fredrick looked through them for a couple of seconds, and then he turned back around to us with them in his hands.

"Do you even remember delivering this stop on that morning?" Fredrick asked Melvin sarcastically.

"Yes," Melvin replied.

"Do you remember what stop you delivered after that?" Fredrick asked.

"Yes," Melvin answered.

"What was it?" Colby asked.

"It was 'so and so'." Melvin answered.

"How far away was this stop from your last one?' Fredrick asked.

"Uh...about four or five miles I guess." Melvin answered.

"How long would it have taken you to drive from here to there in minutes?" Before I could tell Melvin to say he didn't know, he blurted out, "six or seven minutes maybe." I didn't want him to answer that questions that way, because I knew what the next question was going to be.

"Explain to me how you can drive...let's see...you said..." Fredrick said while reviewing his notes. "Four or five miles... in less than one minute. How is this possible if it takes..." Fredrick said while once again reviewing his notes. "In your own words...six or seven minutes."

"Melvin was shocked. He sat there trying to think of a way to explain it, but he couldn't.

"I can't." He replied.

This is when Fredrick began to come in for the kill. Fredrick thought that he had Melvin on the 'time thing' here, and he knew that his case concerning the C.O.D money was weak, so he thought that if he could nail him on this act of dishonesty for falsify his records, it would possibly cast a shadow over Melvin's integrity, and then make him look like he was a liar, and then his C.O.D case would fall right into place as well. It was a good plan only I wasn't going to let him enjoy it for long.

I asked Gordon to see the package that was in question as Fredrick sat there grinning and thinking he had this man where he wanted him. I examined the package for a couple of seconds.

"Fredrick let me ask you a question if I may...after all this man's job is on the line." I replied, and got a nod from Fredrick.

"Who's saying he collected on this package?" I asked.

"The customer who accepted the package for the neighbor," he replied.

"Gordon...is Melvin a good driver? I mean has he been trained in the methods of sheeting up packages and C.O.D collection procedures and such?" I asked drawing the attention of Melvin.

"Yeah he's a good driver and yes, he's been trained." Gordon replied.

"Can I see the complaint?" I asked. Gordon handed me a copy of the complaint and I looked over it...examining everything on it very closely. "May I see the delivery records again Gordon?" I asked and Gordon handed them to me. I began to look for the stop in question and saw that he had sheeted the package up as not having any C.O.D amount to be collected. I then opened the invoice on the package and examined it as well. They all just stood there waiting for me to finish.

"Is the customer at the original address and the customer at the alternate address related?" I asked.

"Yeah," Fredrick replied curiously.

"What did the note on the door of the customer that the package was addressed to say?" I asked Fredrick.

"It said to leave it at the sons house next door." Fredrick replied.

"Oh... I see," I replied sarcastically trying to insert some doubt into what I was driving at.

"Fredrick don't you find it odd that this kind of complaint would arise from two separate customers who just happened to be related?" I asked. Fredrick didn't know how to answer. I had now inserted some doubt, no matter how little it was perceived, into his investigation. Fredrick wasn't too used to this and he didn't know just how to handle me.

I could tell on his face, in his eyes...that he was losing confidence in the strength of his case and I smelled blood.

"Did you examine this package Fredrick?" I asked.

"Yes," he replied.

"This is the package that had the alleged C.O.D tag on it...right?" I asked.

"Yeah James." Fredrick replied.

Melvin and Gordon were both tuned into everything that I was saying and doing.

"You did inspect "THIS" package?" I asked again trying to make him upset a little.

"I done told you yes!" He answered angrily. It had worked, and he had become pretty agitated by now, and I knew that he wouldn't be thinking too clearly now.

I held the package up in front of everyone and spun it around exposing all the sides of the package. It was a small package...probably six inches by six inches.

If this package had a C.O.D tag on it like you're saying, then where is it?" I asked while handing it back to Fredrick.

"I didn't say that it did have a C.O.D tag on it James." Fredrick replied upset.

"Whoa...whoa...hold on now Fredrick. You just said that this was the package that you inspected with the C.O.D tag on it." I replied. "Didn't he Gordon?" I asked Gordon who just shook his head in disbelief and let out a long sigh and replied, "yeah."

Fredrick didn't know what to do now. He'd just sabotaged his own case.

"Show me where the tag is Fredrick?" I asked in a demanding tone.

Fredrick just sat there. "Maybe he tore it off James." He replied angrily.

"Show me where the missing layer of cardboard is that would have been left on the box as a result of him tearing the tag off." I demanded.

Fredrick couldn't, because it didn't exist, and because with the kind of adhesive that is used to put the C.O.D tags on the packages it makes it virtually impossible to just pull the tag off by itself without pulling the top layer of card board off as well. There was no evidence of this ever happening, or even that someone had attempted to cut the tag off of it which would have left tell tale signs of missing cardboard.

"Where's the missing cardboard Fredrick?" I asked again, demanding to know.

No answer.

"Have you examined this invoice as well as you have the package?" I asked, while holding the invoice up for all to see. "Show me where the C.O.D charges are reflected on this invoice Fredrick." I asked.

There weren't any on it.

"Let me see if I have this whole thing understood here guys...we have two customers who are related, and who are claiming that poor old Melvin here collected $100.00 from them wrongfully. You've stated that Melvin is a good driver, and he has been trained on the proper C.O.D methods, and his records do not reflect a C.O.D amount on them, and there is no evidence of C.O.D charges on the invoice, and no evidence of a missing or torn off C.O.D tag from off of the package...in other words you have nothing on this man concerning this package...NOTHING!" I replied angrily.

They didn't know what to do. That's when they shifted to the "time lapse in between stops" part of their case.

"I can explain that too," I replied.

"I'm sure that with Melvin being found, by management just now, of being a good driver and he was in fact, and without a doubt, using the methods while making these deliveries..." I said while pausing and looking at Melvin. "Right Melvin?" I said, while nodding my head yes to him.

"Yes I did," Melvin answered, while shaking his head yes and mimicking me.

"Then when this fine, and properly trained driver stopped at this address, and while he was walking up to the door he's sheeting the package up, like he had been trained to do, and as he then turns, after making the delivery, and walks back toward his truck continuing to punch the next stop's address into the DIAD...but he fails to realize that the DIAD had cut off on him on his way back to the truck, and before he can close out the stop to this address first. He then unknowingly thinks that he has typed all this information in, and that the previous stopped was closed out, but in reality it was still active. You may ask why didn't he visually check to see if the stop was completed? The answer is simple...he kept his eyes ahead of his work area, while he was walking, and if he would have looked down to check his DIAD he would've had to take his eyes off of his walk path thus rendering him vulnerable to tripping hazards. He was working as he was trained to do by the methods which is to work safe...right?" I replied.

They just sat there not saying a word with their mouths dropped open.

"Then when Melvin gets to the next stop, which is what Fredrick if you could check your notes for me...five or six minutes away, he then arrives at the NEXT stop and finally realizes that his previous stop hadn't been closed out, so he then "stop completes it", which as we all know...stamps a time on his record. Then Melvin types in the next stop and closes it out within.... lets say...one minute and then the next stop gets stamped with either the same time or within a one minute lapse." I finished saying.

The room was silent. I had just foiled his attempt to discharge this man for dishonesty and theft. Management had nothing on this man, and I had managed to save this Teamsters job and Fredrick's hatred and discontent for me had grown to monstrous proportion, because I had made a mockery of him and his comic book detective practices twice now.

This wouldn't be the only example of management failing to investigate it cases against its employees, though the next time would happen two days later only this time...involving me.

Chapter 19

"The Colonel and I get into a full blown confrontation in front of the customers and I begin taking off my shirt demanding him to either fire me or get off of my back."

Peak season was in full bloom in the Huntsville building and as usual some new routes were being cut-in in an attempt to take some of the workload off of the heavy volume drivers. The Colonel was still being relentless in his pursuit to increase production and he was still cracking down on those of us who were running over allowed.

On the morning of December 4, 1998, as I was exiting the customer counter, in front of the building, just immediately following the morning PCM, I was met by the Colonel and Smitty who were both standing outside the door waiting for me to emerge.

I walked on out, and the Colonel said, "I need to see you and Joseph for a minute James."

I stepped on over to where he was standing which was in front of several west center package cars that were still being loaded in to by the preload. We all were standing in front of the huge door that was the main entrance and exit into the building with the wind blowing right into the building, and it was rather cold and dreary day outside. It was around 9:00 a.m and customers had begun lining up outside the building waiting for the customer counter to open so they could ship their Christmas packages.

Smitty was standing beside the Colonel and I noticed that he was holding several pieces of paper.

"Did you go by and make the pick up on Spring Valley yesterday?" He asked me coldly while not waiting for Joseph to show up to represent me.

"Yeah," I replied.

The Colonel looked at Smitty and he then held out his hand as Smitty handed him one of the papers that he was holding, and he began reading it to me. It was a complaint. The customer at that address had called in a complaint on me and said that I had failed to come by her house and to make her pick up the other day. I knew that the customer ran a business out of her house and was scheduled for a pick up everyday...but I also knew that I had gone by there to make an attempt.

"James I'm going to ask you one more time," The Colonel said, while gradually raising his voice and talking to me as if I was a two-year-old kid or something in front of the customers.

"Did you go by there?" He asked, as customers began to look and listen to what was going on between us.

"I told you that I did Colonel." I replied.

"No you didn't go by there," he replied again as his voice began to rise. "I-went-by-there," I answered slowly.

"I don't believe that you did," he replied, and he had really screwed up now. He had humiliated me in front of the customers that were lined up in front of us and they were standing there watching the whole incident unfold before their eyes.

I took a few steps toward him and got right up in his face. "Don't you ever call me a liar again. Do you understand me?" I said in a very loud voice. I had lost my cool, and I had become very upset, and I felt that I had every right to be mad, because he was standing there calling me a liar, while on one of his power trips and trying to make me out to be a second-class servant or something right in front of the customers. But the craziest thing about it all was that he actually thought I was going to stand there and take it. The little man was very, very wrong. I started hammering him and we broke out into a huge fight right there in front of the customers. Smitty jumped in with the Colonel and now they were trying to tag team me. I put that little rat Smitty in his place right off the bat and he backed out of the fight and began licking his wounds after it became too much for him to handle.

"James step in here now." The Colonel replied after taking a tongue lashing in front of the customers and he had opened the door to the customer counter back up and stood there propping it open and directed me to go inside.

Joseph had walked in by now and was trying to calm me down. I had been pushed by this little wannabe of a man for several months now and I had enough, and I was willing to lose my job that morning.

"James you need to calm down," the Colonel replied.

"Calm down hell...you stand out there and accuse me of lying in front of everybody and you think I wouldn't get upset about that?" I screamed at him. I had snapped. I had been pushed and pushed until I couldn't be pushed anymore. They had started all this in the first place and now I was prepared to finish it.

"Let me tell you right now!" I said as I started unbuttoning my shirt. "Either you fire me right now or you get off of my ass!" I screamed at them, as they just stood there not knowing what to do. I meant what I was saying as I took my brown shirt off and threw it up on the counter, while Joseph was still trying to calm me down, but I had enough of this.

"James we'll talk about this later," The Colonel said and they walked out of the room.

I was upset to say the least. That was the closest I have ever came to crossing over the line. They had been pushing me for several months and I finally had enough of their crap. When I walked out of the customer counter that morning and was heading towards my truck, I thought I was going to black out. I had one of the worst headaches that I had ever had in my life. I thought my head was going to explode. I was in no shape to drive but it wasn't over yet.

I stepped up onto the dock and Smitty came walking up to me again. He began clearing his throat and grunting uncontrollably and looking over his shoulder.

"Would you mind stopping that please? It gets on my nerves, Smitty."

I said to him and my request embarrassed him. Heck, all that grunting and throat clearing was nerve racking.

"James, uh...uh, I need to ask you...hm...hm...what happened to you yesterday?" He asked nervously.

I had stopped loading my truck and stood there with a look of disgust and a display of annoyance.

"WHAT ARE YOU TALKING ABOUT NOW SMITTY?" I replied in a hateful and slow tone.

"Well, uh...you were an hour over allowed yesterday and I need to know why James," He replied, as I looked past him and noticed that the Colonel was standing at the other end of the dock watching everything that was going on between Smitty and I.

"Evidently you have a selective memory, Smitty." I replied, as I tried to maintain my temper, but I could feel the anger beginning to swell once again. Joseph had looked up after several drivers hollered at him and he walked down to where we were.

"Smitty why in the hell don't you leave this man alone?" Joseph replied.

Smitty ignored him and tried to muffle his throat clearing and grunting.

"I...I need to know what happened to you James. That's all." He said.

"Well let me explain it for you then Smitty," I replied, as I sat down the package that I was holding and stepped over a little closer to him.

"Okay Smitty, I ran into a construction project on the way down to my route and lost about ten minutes in traffic. Next I had to call for help because once again...I had too much work to get done and as a result of having to call you for help I had to wait for the driver in the parking lot of Ryan's for about...twenty-five minutes. Then after that meeting my DIAD went out and I had to go start using the paper delivery records. When I finished with what I had left I ran into a wreck on the Parkway and had to detour around it to make it back before the curfew. But most important of all Smitty and maybe you 'forgot', when I did make it back to the building you personally made me re-enter all of the delivery information that I had written down on the paper records from that day, and had to enter it into another DIAD board, and that sir...took me roughly an hour to do!" I finished saying in a very upset and perturbed tone.

He stood there looking at me, not knowing what to say. I had just explained to him and had accounted for every bit of the hour I was over allowed.

"I need you to try and do better today okay? I need your help." He said. I just stood there looking at him and shaking my head. "I need you to sign this saying that I covered this with you." He said while handing me the piece of the paper.

"Sure I will Smitty," I replied, and I took the paper from him and walked into the rear of my truck and placed it in the shelf so I could write on it. He was shocked. He stood there with a 'deer in the headlights' kind of look on his face, as I scribbled on it and handed it back to him. He thanked me and turned around and managed to walk about four feet and then he stopped.

He read it and turned around and said, "S. It?"

"Yeah, shove it!" I replied, and turned around and finished loading my truck and left out for the day.

The next morning I was called into the office. I was told that I was going to receive two warning letters, one for missing the pick up and the other for failing to show my employer 'dignity and respect'.

Dignity and respect...what do they know about dignity and respect? They accused me of lying in front of customers and then they instigate a confrontation, then they verbally abuse and degrade me and the most shocking part of it all was that they expected me just to stand there, and take the verbal assault and abuse, and not stand up for myself, and then when I did defend myself...they wanted to discipline me for failing to show THEM dignity and respect. That's one of the biggest hypocrisies of this management. Upon learning of my two warning letter's I went ahead and filed the necessary grievances to protest this latest actions by management.

DATE GRIEVANCE FILED: 12-4-98

EXPLAIN GRIEVANCE: *I was accused of lying by the Colonel and Smitty concerning an alleged missed pick up. I was subjected to not only humiliating but also very abusive treatment as well from management. I was not at first afforded a union steward.*

REMEDY SOUGHT: *Withdraw warning letters and terminate center manager and supervisor.*

I turned the grievance in that night, and it was later heard in a local hearing a few days later. Before the local hearing was held I had called Matt over at the local union, and told him to tell Hembry that I wanted to see a copy of my delivery records for this particular day in question. When the local hearing started, Hembry dispatched the Colonel down stairs to get them.

"What's going on up here James?" Hembry asked.

"He's out of control Hembry." I replied.

"Tell me what happened that day James," he replied. I sat there and told him everything that happened and how he made me out to be a liar. After a couple of minutes the Colonel returned and knocked on the door.

"Hold on a minute." Hembry yelled out loud.

"When this meeting is over I want to talk to you two some more okay." Hembry asked, and we both agreed to hang around after the meeting was closed.

"Come on in," Hembry replied, as the Colonel stepped inside the office and shut the door.

The Colonel handed Hembry the records and then Hembry handed them to Matt and then to me. Hembry asked the Colonel what had happened and as usual he told a totally different story, which was altogether different than what had actually happened that morning in front of the customers.

"Did James go by there and make the pick up?" Hembry asked the Colonel.

"No he didn't," the Colonel replied, as he spit into a cup which then caused Hembry to frown.

222

I had had time to check and see if I had made a delivery stop to her that day, and I had in fact done so, and there it was in black and white...stamped on my records by the DIAD at 2:45 p.m. I then looked on over to my pick up records and verified the time at which I had made the pick up which would have also been stamped with the time as well.

It read 2:45 p.m.

It was showing the same time as when I had delivered to her. I pointed this out to Matt who had now sat up in his chair and placed his glasses on his face to read what I was showing him.

Hembry and the Colonel just sat over in their seats patiently waiting for us to get finished examining the records.

"Explain then Hembry, how James' record's show a delivery time of 2:45 p.m, and pick up time of 2:45, all at the same time?" Matt asked, while tossing the records back onto the desk in front of Hembry. Hembry picked up the records and began looking over them, and then looked at the Colonel whose face had turned a solid color of red. Hembry finished reading the records, and took off his glasses, and began wiping his eyes with his head hung down in disgust.

"Colonel did you check his records?" Asked Hembry while sighing out loud.

"Not...all of...them," he replied slowly, while sliding down in his seat a little.

"James I'm throwing out your warning letters, and I apologize for any inconvenience that this might have caused you," Hembry replied.

I was shocked. Heck, this was a first. Here we had a company labor man apologizing for the actions of a cracker head like the Colonel. I didn't know how to take it, and we sat there just looking at each other in total disbelief.

"Colonel, that's all I need with you," Hembry said to the Colonel, and he sent him on out of the office. We all watched the Colonel walk out with his tail between his legs and we waited until we finally heard the outside door shut.

"I don't know what I'm going to do with him?" Hembry said while tossing his glasses on top of his desk and letting out a long sigh. "If he screws up much more..." Hembry replied, while standing up to put his suit coat back on, and then he began gathering up the papers on his desk and placed them into his briefcase.

"He was like this everywhere he was...I don't know what else we can do?" Hembry replied, sounding somewhat perplexed and throwing his hands up in the air.

"What do you think we should do James?' He asked as he closed his briefcase.

"I think you should fire him." I replied coldly.

"Would you want to be fired James?" Hembry stopped and asked me.

"He's been trying to fire me for the past five months and putting me through a living hell Hembry. I don't feel a bit sorry for the goof, and I figure that he gets what he deserves." I replied.

The meeting came to a close that morning, and I left there with the sense that upper management was beginning to get tired of the Colonel's unorthodox tactics as much as we were.

We were averaging about twelve grievances a week on him and Smitty, where as the new west center manager, Gordon, had failed to have a single one, to my knowledge, filed against him or any of his supervisors. It was a dark contrast indeed.

The Colonel's demise had begun, and he was too stupid to realize it. It would only be a matter of time now before he'd either be ousted, or replaced. The Colonel was slowly beginning to lose control over the center and the wheels of fate had begun to roll. It would only be a matter of time now.

Chapter 20

"8:46 a.m: I catch a member of management in my truck, I think I've caught the person who was planting next day airs in the load in an attempt to fire me."

I had continued to file grievances pretty much every other day to protest the conditions of my load and for the outrageously high number of stops that I was being dispatched with everyday, but there was some good news from all of this...I no longer had to call into the center everyday for them to send a driver out to help me. They just dispatched a driver everyday to meet me. I found this to be really stupid and nothing more than to show me that no matter how stupid they looked, and how ignorant their actions were, they weren't going to acknowledge that I had too much work for me to deliver in the 'time frame' they wanted it done in. It was impossible to do.

Harry had ridden with me earlier in the week, and he decided that the Golf Road apartments needed to come off and I once again was given back my original residential's. Harry went on further to say that day, that I was doing a good job and that he appreciated the fact that I was trying. He even went as far as to tell me that there was no real reason, or 'need' for him to be out riding with me other than the fact the Colonel wanted it.

Smitty had been gone for the last couple of days and I really liked working for Harry. I never really had a problem with Harry, although there were times that we tied up and said things to one another, but we always managed to work things out and apologize to one another and neither of us ever held a grudge against the other.

After leaving the building on January 13, 1999, with one of the worst loads in the history of my career, I had fought with Smitty and the Colonel about the condition of my load before I had left the building, which proved to be nothing but a waste of time trying to argue with those two imbeciles.

I drove on down to Airport Road and I began delivering my route and after I finished delivering my over night packages for this day I decided to stop and sort the whole truck out. I was in the parking lot of a drug store I opened the bulkhead door and saw that everything had pretty much spilled out onto the floor of the package car, so I decided to go into the drug store and buy a disposable camera and take a picture of the load I had been dispatched with for that day for future use during any grievance hearings.

I came back out to the truck, after buying the camera, and opened the rear door of the truck, and packages fell out into the parking lot with several of them bursting open and spilling their contents onto the ground. I had what I wanted. I wanted Hembry and Matt to see what I had to contend with everyday, and what I had had to work with for the last five months or so while on this route.

How could management expect me to go out and deliver the packages like they wanted me too when they couldn't even put me good load on the truck?

Needless to say, I struggled that whole day as well, and the next morning I was called back into the office, and asked again by the dynamic duo as to why I was over allowed. I didn't say a word. I just sat there...expressionless, and let them run through their dime store routine. I would simply file a grievance, or more like several grievances, in fact...a record total of eight for that day.

DATE GRIEVANCE FILED: 1-13-99
EXPLAIN GRIEVANCE: *I've filed several grievances and after a Local hearing was held it was settled that my load would be fixed. Nothing is being done to ensure that I have a good load on the truck. I feel that this is another example of management's failure to bargain in good faith.*
REMEDY SOUGHT: *Charge with NLRB.*

DATE GRIEVANCE FILED: 1-13-99
EXPLAIN GRIEVANCE: *I've requested to see copies of the OR of the drivers who covered my route and how well they performed. A previous grievance had been filed and the management agreed to let me see the OR. This is nothing but failure to bargain in good faith.*
REMEDY SOUGHT: *Charge with the NLRB*

DATE GRIEVANCE FILED: 1-13-99
EXPLAIN GRIEVANCE: *I asked Smitty to come and view my load on this day, to which he replied he didn't have time. I feel that this is nothing more than harassment.*
REMEDY SOUGHT: *Discharge managers and a charge with the NLRB.*

DATE GRIEVANCE FILED: 1-13-99
EXPLAIN GRIEVANCE: *Management used independent contractors to pull empty trailers to Memphis Tennessee because of a trailer shortage. I was available to work.*
REMEDY SOUGHT: *Thirty hours pay at double's rate.*

The other four grievances that day, included in the total eight, pertained to various other minor contract violations, but I chose to include them as well because the Colonel had given three of my drivers in the east center warning letters for not having their shoes shined, and even gave one to a driver for having his sleeves rolled up.

When the grievances were heard, I showed the pictures of my load to Hembry, and he tried to dispute the credibility of the picture, citing that he couldn't see the truck number in the picture, and that it could have been anyone's truck. I thought this was a very pathetic, but typical, attempt to discredit my evidence, but he knew that he had nowhere to go with it. Hembry had had about enough of the Colonel that morning and truth be known...every since the Colonel came to Huntsville.

Hembry instructed the Colonel to show me by weeks end, everything that I wanted to see, in regard to the OR, and he promised that I would be able to have access to whatever I wanted in the future that applied to what I was looking for.

The Colonel agreed to do this in front of all of us and the grievance was settled including that there would be no more rides for until the load was fixed, and the Colonel assured Hembry that come tomorrow morning...my load would be fixed.

After the conclusion of the local meeting that morning with Hembry, the outcome didn't help the Colonel's self esteem any. He knew that we were up there talking about him again after he was asked to leave by Hembry, and the Colonel was even beginning to make it known, through rumors started by Smitty, that he thought we all were plotting and conspiring against him. This is when he decided to try and get rid of me by any way he could...even if it was unethical.

I had still been complaining about the load and had even reminded the Colonel numerous times about what he had 'agreed' to do during the last local, and I made it clear to him that his actions now would dictate whether or not I'd choose to 're-instate' the grievance that I had withdrawn during the last local meeting. He reluctantly pulled off my loader, the one who was killing me, and moved me up to the front of the belt so that Marsha could load it. I was very happy once I heard the news.

Finally, I was going to have a perfect load, because Marsha was the best there was. She had the most years of service with UPS on the whole belt...probably more than all the pre-loaders combined, and another thing, she was a part time union steward, which that in itself wouldn't do anything but help me.

I had managed to decrease my over allowed time every since Harry had taken all of Golf Road off of me. Now with Marsha putting perfect loads on me, I should be able to run scratch, or possibly under allowed for a change, which should get these two stooges off of my case. I was being sent out with about 90 stops now, and all but a very few apartments that were in my original residential's, and those were a far cry from the hellhole on Golf Road. I had also got to where I no longer had to have a driver meet me everyday and was finishing my route well before the 6:30 p.m curfew.

This is what management had wanted from me for the past five, or so months and finally I was going to be able to give it to them. When I walked up to my truck to start work, after the PCM, the door was shut and inside was a perfect load. It was textbook and I didn't have to load a thing! I thanked Marsha and told her that I appreciated the good job she was doing and she went out of her way to make sure I knew where everything was that she had loaded out of the way. This made my day that much easier.

Man this was great. I mean, no more having to go back to the same place two and three times a day after finding packages misloaded in the shelf, everything was nice and neat and in the right place, but all of this was going to be short lived.

Smitty came walking up to the truck with a clipboard in his hand and asked Marsha how many stops were on me, and so on.

Marsha began telling him what was on there and he asked her how many stops were in Golf Road.

"Golf Road isn't on here Smitty," she replied.

He stopped reading and looked up at her and said, "Why not?"

She told him that no one had told her to put them back on me, and that Harry had written down what was to be loaded on my truck.

Smitty looked at me, and smiled.

He didn't know anything about the rides that Harry had conducted while he was away for those couple of days, and Smitty literally took off running into the Colonel's office and after a minute or so they both came to the edge of the dock and stepped up on it, while I was just standing there and waiting for something to happen while talking to Marsha.

"Why aren't these stops on him Marsha?" The Colonel asked in a smart tone.

"I told Smitty that I loaded what Harry told me to load." She replied.

"James doesn't work for Harry, Marsha...he works for me," the Colonel said in a derogatory tone.

"That's between you and Harry, Colonel," Marsha replied, while sticking her marker behind her ear and placing her hand on her hip.

"Pull all of those residential's off right now and give him..." He said while pausing and looking at the clipboard. "Pull all of them off and give him all of Golf Road." The Colonel said.

"How many in Golf Road, Colonel? There may be forty or fifty stops in there." She asked.

"I said all of them!" He snapped back.

"Whatever," she replied, while rolling her eyes and began pulling off every one of my residential stops and to replace them with Golf Road.

She pulled off about twenty-five stops and Smitty had the other loader pull all of Golf Road off of his driver to send to me.

I counted the stops as I placed them in the shelf and there were almost forty stops in that split. I had gained about three hours of work after losing forty-five minutes work, at the most, from the loss of my original residential's.

My day was once again shot to hell, and I would wind up having to call for help again later that day, and the cycle had started all over again.

Then, mysteriously, my days began to take a new twist to them. I still had Marsha loading me who rarely ever made a mistake, but during the course of my day I began finding a couple of over night packages loaded in my load, which had been stuck behind and under packages, scattered throughout the truck.

These were the packages that had to be delivered by 10:30 a.m. I would find one stuck in the load well after the 10:30 commitment time, and after finding it, I had to call back to the center and tell them that I had found an overnight package in my load, and that it was going to be delivered late, and when this happened the loader would get into trouble the next morning, and possibly even receive some sort of discipline for loading it in the load, which was a big no-no.

I was called into the office the next day and asked about why I had ran over allowed, and why I had delivered a Next Day Air late.

While I tried to explain to the Colonel that I had found it in the load, Smitty brought Marsha in and they began questioning her about the air that had been loaded in my load.

She knew nothing about it, and at first, she said it was just a mistake and took the punishment for it.

The next day I found another over night package stuck in the load, which was just thrown in the back of the shelf behind a package that I wouldn't find until later that evening. I had only stumbled across this one by accident right before noon only because the Colonel had instructed every driver to stop at 3:00 p.m, and go through their whole truck to see if we had any misloads.

So I would stop everyday and go through the whole truck looking for packages that were out of place, and for ones that didn't belong to me, and after I would find a misloaded package, I'd write it down in my personal journal.

With Marsha loading the truck I was reluctant at first, and felt that I really didn't have to do this, but now with finding another Next Day Air in the load after 2:00 p.m for the third day in a row, I thought that it would be a good idea to sort the whole truck earlier than usual just to cover my butt.

I called the center and told a supervisor that I had found another air in the load, and they told me to go ahead and break trace, and to deliver it right then, because the customer had been calling the center looking for it and raising cane about it.

The next morning I was called back into the office and once again the Colonel interrogated me as to why this had been loaded in the load.

I explained to him that I didn't load it, but he wouldn't listen and he really showed his butt in the office that morning. I found it strange that Marsha had loaded yet another one in the load again the very next day. Once again she received a warning letter for her actions and she just couldn't understand how she was doing this.

Smitty had to take off for two days, and those two days while he was gone I didn't find any more Next Day Airs in the load, but after Smitty came back to work I found another in the load that very day.

I was called into the office again that morning, and was asked about my over allowed hours and received a warning letter for failing to work as instructed, or actually for running over allowed, and then asked again about the late air, then Marsha was brought into the office, as well, and they questioned her in front of me as to why the air had been loaded. She knew nothing about this and the Colonel threatened to suspend her from work, for loading the air.

I had Smitty ride with me the following day and what do you know? I didn't have a Next Day in the load.

I began to find this a little too coincidental.

I met with Marsha early the next morning and she told me to write down on a separate sheet of paper a list of all the addresses of the Next Day Airs packages that I delivered and how many for the same stop and so on and that she would do the same as she loaded them and we'd see if our list jived together the next day.

We both agreed to did this and sure enough that afternoon I found another Next Day Air in the load. I called the package in and when Smitty answered the phone he immediately started in on me about how he was tired of this and for me to come into work early the next morning that they wanted to talk to me about this problem. The next morning I went to the office as he instructed me to do, and I waited for Smitty to show up. I went ahead and came in to work at 5:30 a.m that morning, and I just sat in the office. I knew that Smitty didn't arrive until 7:30 a.m, but he failed to inform me as of what time to come in so I decided I was going to make me a couple of hours of over time that morning and just sat in the office.

He finally came in and when he saw me sitting there he told me that I was going to have to wait until the Colonel arrived to which I replied, "Fine," so I sat there for about another thirty minutes, at time and a half, and when the Colonel walked in he told Smitty to go get Marsha.

It was now about 8:15 a.m and most of the drivers had arrived for work and then Marsha walked into the east center's office and began taking her gloves off, and tossed them onto the top of the counter, as she sat down. I sat beside her, and Smitty came back into the office and the show got under way.

"Marsha, did you load that air on James' car yesterday?" The Colonel asked.

"No," she answered.

"So neither one of you loaded it onto the car then? Well since neither of you loaded it onto the car yesterday then I'm going to suspend both of you for two days, that way I'll get the right one who loaded it." The Colonel replied.

Marsha and I just looked at each other in amazement and I knew immediately what this little turd was trying to do. He was trying to cause a riff between Marsha and me.

"I want a full time steward in here right now to represent me." I demanded.

"No, you'll use Marsha, James." The Colonel replied, while spitting into a cup.

"I have the right to choose whom I want to represent me in the office and I want a full time job steward." I replied in an increasingly angrier tone.

"You're not going to get one," he said, and pulled out some papers from a clipboard. "We audited you records yesterday James, and found that you failed to put the name of a business on your delivery records. I'm going to have to give you a warning letter, because you've been trained in how to properly sheet up a package," he said and handed me a copy of the warning letter.

I stood up and ripped it to pieces and threw it on the floor.

I was extremely upset. Smitty had become concerned by my actions just then and slid behind the Colonel.

"You'll also be getting a warning letter for missing the Next Day Air, and also for failing to work as instructed as well James," he replied.

We were dismissed and Marsha was almost in tears. "You need to keep that between you and him. Leave me out of it." She replied and walked off.

Before I left, I met with her in the front of my truck, out of everyone's view, and we pulled our list out and checked the total number of Next Day Airs she loaded against the number I had delivered. They didn't match up. I had delivered two more than she had written down. Everything was there except for the two that I found later in the day.

We both looked at each other and said Smitty.

I knew right then that he was probably loading the packages on me while she wasn't looking. I had the feeling that I was being set up. Marsha and I kept on writing down what was loaded and every day I continued to find misloads. I had begun to take pictures of them immediately after that meeting with the Colonel and Smitty. I would snap a photo of them while they were still in the shelf.

One morning I decided to come in early to stake the car out, and to try and catch the one who was possibly planting the airs in the load after learning from two drivers that they had seen Smitty in my truck pretty much everyday, and they both told me that when they confronted Smitty about what he was inside my truck, he told them that he was doing a load audit.

"Load audit my butt," I thought, as I began thinking of a way to catch him in the act, because I knew that he was probably the one was planting the airs on my truck, and he was doing it under the excuse of that he was "conducting a load audit."

I came in early the next morning and sat in another car, in the west center, across the east belt where I could see my truck clearly. No one had seen me come I and I sat in the floorboard of the package car waiting and watching for something to happen.

When they called a break for the part timers, they all went to the break area that was in the rear of the building and no one was around the trucks. After a minute or so I saw Smitty come out of the east office and look at his watch and then he leaned around the trucks and was apparently looking down the belt. He turned and briskly walked around the trucks and down to the other end of the belt and disappeared.

I climbed out of the cab of the car and walked around to the other end of the belt and walked under the slides and came up on my trucks blind side.

I stopped and listened very carefully...I could hear someone in the truck.

I jumped up on the belt and stepped into the rear of the truck. Smitty was in there.

"What are you doing?" I asked startling him.

He began stuttering and grunting.

"I-I-I-I'm just checking your load to see if you have any airs in it." He replied nervously.

"The airs haven't even ran yet Smitty," I replied. He couldn't think of a thing to say. He just stood there looking at me in utter shock.

"I had better not find anymore airs in the load after today, Smitty. Do you understand me?" I asked.

He began clearing his throat uncontrollably. He walked past me while I was still standing in the rear of the truck. I turned and watched him hurry off of the belt and disappear. I may have caught the little rat in the act. From that day forward I never again had any more Next Day Airs loaded in the load while Marsha was loading my truck. We had evidently foiled their plan.

Everyday was more of the same. I was dragged into the office and asked why I was running over allowed. I had another two rides from Smitty, and I had managed to do better both times, even though I had a lot more stops and more packages on the day's he rode with me than I did on the other day's when I was by myself. Something didn't seem right.

When the Colonel had reviewed my production rides performance I mysteriously had done better than when they hadn't ridden with me. I couldn't explain this. I began to think and I had found it funny that every time they rode with me I seemed to do better.

I would receive another warning letter the next time I ran over allowed for once again, "Failing to work as instructed."

When the Colonel reviewed this with me he pointed out that, "With Smitty on car you ran forty five minutes over versus 1.7 hours over by yourself, and you managed to run eighteen stops an hour versus the fourteen by yourself."

Whenever Chester or Harry rode with me I always had done a perfect job, and they both found that I just had too much work to deliver, but whenever Smitty rode with me, my stops on road went up and my over allowed came down. I didn't do anything any different. Really I didn't. I couldn't explain it.

Until...after I had received another warning letter for running over allowed.

The morning after the meeting with the Colonel, I just "happened" to run across a copy of my time cards for the previous week, which included the two days that Smitty had ridden with me.

I sat down and really examined them closely. Everything was the same on each of the days except when on the days Smitty rode with me I did better. Once again I didn't do anything any different in fact...I would probably be a little slower from using all of the methods correctly. With this in mind I should have done a little worse than when they weren't riding with me, but this wasn't the case.

I sat there in the east office looking over my timecards and then suddenly something strange caught my eye. It was my pay code.

UPS has several different pay codes that you enter into your DIAD every time you do something outside your normal classification outside part of your daily routine so they know what department to charge the hours to. Everything has a pay code. My pay code was six, which meant that I was a package car driver and would be taking a full one hour lunch and that I would be working at least eight hours for that given day.

I had "code sixes" everyday except for the days that Smitty rode with me and on the days that he rode with me I had "code 64" instead of the code six on my timecard, and I know that I didn't change it.

"What is this?" I thought to myself.

I asked Chester what it was, and he sort of blew me off. He just said that it was just something management put in to let payroll know that you had a rider for that day.

I knew right then that I may have figured out their little game. I couldn't wait for the Colonel and Smitty to come to work that morning.

When they both arrived I was naturally called back into the office, as usual, for running over allowed. I let them run through their usual spiel and at the end I asked, "I want you to pull my time card from yesterday. Can you do that?"

"Sure we can...why?" The Colonel asked while looking over at Smitty who shrugged his shoulders.

"I want you to change my pay code from a code Six to a code 64." I asked politely.

The Colonel sat up in his seat and Smitty looked at him.

I knew right then judging from both their reaction's they knew that I had found out about their little game and what management uses to possibly manipulate the numbers when they performed production rides.

"Code 64?" The Colonel said.

"Yeah, I want to see what my number's look like after you change my pay code from a code six, to a code 64," I said.

"James, that's just to let payroll know that one of us had ridden with you for the day," he replied.

"Colonel, why do they care in the first place, whether or not you rode with me for that day?" You don't get paid from my time card do you? I mean…it's not like that code changes my allowances or anything…does it?" I asked calmly.

The Colonel was beginning to become very, very evasive of the subject.

"We can't change the time cards once they've been transmitted," he replied.

"I find that to be a load of crap Colonel!" I popped off. "Someone has changed my time cards and my pay code those two days, because I know for a fact that I had entered a code six for both those days."

The Colonel didn't say a word or even spit, which was quite unusual for him.

I could tell right then that he was extremely uncomfortable about something.

"I want to know who changed my time cards for those two days?" I asked angrily. No answer came.

"I demand to know… right now who changed my time cards without my permission or do I have to call Fredrick and loss prevention and tell him that someone in Huntsville is playing with the timecards." After I said this, the Colonel began singing like a bird.

"I did," the Colonel replied, in a low voice.

"Who authorized you to change my time cards?" I asked.

"I don't need authorization from anybody James." The Colonel snapped back.

"When it comes to changing my time cards, and when the change could possibly affect my numbers you do!" I replied, while Smitty sat over there with his big mouth shut.

"Colonel, if it's no big deal…then just change the codes back to code sixes and let me see what the numbers look like afterward." I asked.

He wouldn't do it.

I was immediately excused to go to work. After bringing this to their attention the rides ceased. I decided to go ahead and file a grievance just as a precaution to document and protest the latest actions of the Colonel.

DATE GRIEVANCE FILED: 1-18-99

EXPLAIN GRIEVANCE: *I feel that the management in Huntsville is manipulating the numbers in attempt to create a case and fire me. I am* *constantly being singled out and held to a higher standard due to the fact that I'm a union steward. I find this is nothing more than discrimination and harassment.*

REMEDY SOUGHT: *Termination of managers and for the local union to immediately file a charge with the NLRB.*

I received all three warning letters and a two-day suspension just right before the local level hearing was held to discuss these new grievances.

I had called Matt over at the union hall and gave him an ultimatum to either file an Unfair Labor Practice charge against management, or face one himself if he failed to act and allowed this to continue. My threat to nail his ass left him no choice...so he wisely chose to file a charge on behalf of Teamsters Local 402.

Matt included at my direction, illegal surveillance, illegal harassment, illegal discipline and illegal auditing without cause. I had management by the feet now.

When the local level hearing took place that morning management had no leverage to bargain with. I had evidence of management possibly being the one's who were planting the airs on me, and then there was the code 64 issue, and the constant refusal of the Colonel to bargain in good faith didn't help them out much and left them very little room to bargain in.

Hembry wouldn't even let the Colonel attend the meeting, and in that office was just Hembry, Matt and myself.

"What would it take to settle this NLRB charge and these grievances James?" Hembry asked while sighing.

"Get rid of the Colonel," I replied sternly.

Hembry sat back and rubbed his eyes and face with his hand in a display of disgust. I've been trying to find someplace to take him, but every department I talk to hates him and doesn't want him." He replied.

"Why don't y'all just fire him Hembry?" I asked.

"We can't do that." Hembry answered.

"Why? Because he has something on somebody up high?" I asked. Hembry just looked at me and grinned.

"Or is it because he has numerous lawsuits, and about 100 grievances against him?" "What more do you need Hembry? This man is a walking liability and he's going to wind up costing this company a lot of money because of his stupid mistakes." I replied.

"We know, we know but we can't find anywhere to put him. I.E, Plant Engineering, Quality Control no body wants him." Hembry replied.

"Well the only way that this is going to get resolved is to get that little creep out of Huntsville," I said. I wasn't going to budge an inch on this.

Hembry looked at Matt, and all Matt said was, "This is between you and James here, Hembry," and just sat back as Hembry and I worked out the deal to rid Huntsville of the Colonel.

"If you'll give me a few weeks James, I promise to have him out of here and...I don't know where, but somewhere." Hembry replied.

"I'll withdraw my grievances and the NLRB charge under good faith, but if he doesn't leave and you crawfish on me, I'm going to blow this thing totally out of proportion." I said.

"Okay then James...it's agreed that you'll give me a few weeks to do something?" He asked.

"Agreed," I replied.

"Anything else then?" Hembry asked while gathering up his papers.

"What about Smitty?" I asked.

"Don't press your luck," Hembry answered while laughing and shaking his head.

We then all sat around and debated why he was like the way he was. The Colonel had come to Huntsville to break our spirit and beat us down as a "hired gun"... and was supposedly the "BEST" in the business. Huntsville had surely now became to be known as the "worst" center when it came to labor relations and union solidarity in the eyes of all Alabama management. Every Supervisor who had learned that they were going to be assigned to Huntsville pleaded to be sent elsewhere.

I had gained a reputation for being a hard-core steward and my name had begun getting around even more in the whole southeast whenever Huntsville and labor relations were discussed.

The Colonel stayed almost four weeks after the crucial meeting with Hembry had ended, and he was sent back to one of our sister centers in north Alabama with his tail between his legs.

We would wind up getting another center manager to take the Colonel's place from another of our sister center's, whose name was Antonio.

Smitty remained with us, and after the Colonel had left we intensified our efforts to make his life in Huntsville a living and miserable hell as much as we could. Smitty had no friends, at least on the hourly side...that was for sure. Everyone hated him. He was like a vicious dog that had had all its teeth pulled and had been neutered. Now that the Colonel was gone, he tried to make amends with everyone that he had crapped on since he had come to Huntsville, but this only had infuriated everyone and the worse it then became for him to try and survive in Huntsville, because no one helped him out with anything, including his fellow managers, and anytime he screwed up, no matter how small, we'd unleash an avalanche of grievances on him. He was beginning to crack from this intense pressure that we all were placing on him, but we refused to let up one bit.

He was nothing but an outcast among his own kind. Even the other supervisors tried to screw him over every chance they got. Smitty was going around the building moping and depressed, and finally the Colonel was able to get him transferred back with him. He was once again...back in hog heaven.

On the morning that Smitty told us he was leaving, during the PCM, everyone became ecstatic and began clapping, yelling and whistling. It was really embarrassing and humiliating for him. It had to have been. Piss on him though, he got exactly what he deserved.

The next couple of weeks were a real turn around. We hadn't had a bit of problems out of neither one of the "new" center managers. They were easy to work things out with and it was a welcome and strange change. I had not had to file a grievance for anything for several months.

After a few weeks, I managed to go full time into feeders and no longer had the headache and pressure of working for the center anymore. It was like working for a totally different company. I managed to be able to bid on a run up to the hub at the Whites Creek facility, in Nashville Tennessee and enjoyed the change of pace. I worked only eight hours a day now and I knew pretty much what time I would get off of every morning. I loved it.

I was notified that the District Manager, who was still Robert, wanted to hold a first ever meeting with all of the head stewards in North Alabama. I was told that I was going to have to go and Gordon, the west center manager, was worried that I'd show out, but I told him not to worry that I'd be good boy and behave.

The meeting was held at a hotel in Huntsville and all of the department heads for the Alabama District attended, as well as all of the stewards for north Alabama.

It was a joke. The whole meeting was nothing but a union bashing session about how we had caused the strike, and how much we had cost the company money and business and so on. Finally, after I had enough of this crap, I stuck my two-cent's in, and I then tied up with Robert, the Alabama District Manager, over his union bashing and finger pointing. Things went down hill pretty quickly after we got into it. I tried to shoot down every lie they told, but one thing that bothered me tremendously was when I asked Robert about the way they determine punishment for the employees.

He told us all that it all depended on how many 'credits' they had in the bank.

I questioned him about this "credit in the bank" thing, and he said that if an employee does something to benefit the company they then get an 'imaginary credit' deposited into their "imaginary bank account". If the employee does something bad then they have 'credits' taken out, and the number of credits that remain in the account determined the level and type of discipline they then receive. In other words he was saying that the employee themselves are judged rather than their offenses. That's why no one ever gets the same kind of discipline for committing the same offenses. Take Abel's case for example...when he dropped the trailer and was fired whereas, several drivers out of the Birmingham Alabama facility, who committed the same offense, only received warning letters with no time off. The Birmingham driver was a butt kisser whereas Abel was not. Where's the justice in that. This was truly despicable, but still stands true...even today.

The mentality of the District Manager and his 'little credit in the bank' involves and embraces a little known system of what is called "Procedural Justice" and is a little more complex and cynical than it first appears.

It's been argued that there are six different procedural justice rules that managers use in making judgment's of fairness: A uniformed application over time and persons; bias suppression, the removal of any conflicting personal feelings geared toward the grievant; the truthfulness that the decision was based on actual and truthful information; correctability, allowing for the modification of decisions; representatives of the concerns from of all recipient groups; and ethically based on prevailing moral or ethical standards.

But UPS's management applies a distorted and perverted view of procedural justice, and they do not fear to invoke, and use it during any stage of the disciplinary procedure. As demonstrated by their actions in the past it could be understood as follows: (1) unequal application over times and persons. With each new regime that rises to power, they bring with them too their own set of rules, and then they implement how their rules will be applied. One example of this is the many different variances of labor policy with each new center manager we ever received in Huntsville over the last ten years with the Colonel being the extreme part of the spectrum whereas, Eliza was on the other end; (2) being unable to suppress any bias, and fail to remove any conflicting personal feelings geared toward the grievant. An example of this is the retaliation by UPS management towards those who file grievances against them to protest any abusive treatment that was committed against the grievant by these same managers, whom are the same ones who determine punishment for the employees at a later time if the need arises, just like in the case of Smitty illegally coercing the member who was going to file a harassment grievance against him, but then retracted it after Smitty threatened to make it hard on him to get off to fight for custody of his two very young children. These managers proved without a doubt that there was no way they could suppress any feelings when they used those same feelings to manipulate employees into giving them what they want and desire; (3) unfair decisions that are based on lies and misinformation. An example of this is when Davey had repeatedly lied about the numerous contractual conversations to end the abuse of the cover drivers to Hembry and Matt during a local hearing. Another example is when the Colonel refused to include in my performance evaluations the truth regarding how bad I had been doing while a member of management had ridden with me and then tried to cover it up and attempted to lie about it after he was caught; (4) there is only a modification of a decision if it only benefits the management; (5) unethically based decisions depending on prevailing profit driven standards. There is no better example of this than when UPS management refused to cart around the over seventy packages and decided that it was cheaper to just place them on the belts and run the risk injuring an innocent employee. The moral thing for them to have done would be to cart the over seventies around which would've eliminated, or greatly reduced the likelihood of injury, but the rewards outweighed the risk, with the rewards being in the reduction of any extra cost of taking three minutes just to cart the heavyweight packages around to prevent injuries, and the risk being that the odds were high enough that the package would more than likely make it through the system without injuring someone which in this particular case it wasn't, and the young Teamster member was injured as a result of their decision to save dollar.

Any violation of any of these rules by management can lead to an employee's perception and belief that they have become a victim of procedural injustice. This is the way it's supposed to work in order for the employees to perceive that there is integrity and honesty in the system.

Researchers have found in studies that an employees perception of their "defined" justice system plays a direct role on the impact regarding their satisfaction with their employment involving all level of management personnel and this has been found to be an important attribute in the development of their organizational attitudes and creates their attitudes towards authorities figures in the company hierarchy structure.

One of the negative and lasting effects that can be caused from "unfair" procedures is the powerful effect that they threaten ones self esteem, indicates that one is not a valuable person, and suggest that the decision maker (management) regards that person (employee) as an inferior human being.

This perception of this principle by UPS top management can be substantiated and supported due in part to the comment made by a top level manager from corporate UPS during the nationwide strike of 1997 while he was conducting a press interview, to which UPS's management representative called the Teamster employees, "Gutless, little nobody's". That statement alone should establish the base perception of how we are regarded in the eyes of UPS's management and how they deal with us on any level of interaction.

When dealing with any form or level of management in any unionized industry, one has to realize that there is more at play than just a common written contract that both parties are supposed to adhere to, and quiet commonly, not only does that written contract get violated, but also an unknown contract does as well, called a 'psychological contract', which it too has a much more definitive and defined impact on the relationship between the employer and the union member than the latter one does.

It doesn't matter whether the contract is a written one or an 'unwritten one', they are both "promises" that then will be an exchange for something else in return, and these contracts are the foundation of any core labor relations policy.

"A psychological contract is distinct from both a formal (a labor agreement) and an implied contract. A psychological contract is an individual's beliefs about the terms and conditions of an agreement to which that individual is party to, (Rousseau, 1989.)"

"Whenever a psychological contract violation occurs it produces a specific form of distributive injustice that may have unique and intense attitudinal, behavioral, and emotional reactions for the parties involved (Rousseau, 1989; Rousseau & Parks, 1993)."

The intense reactions following a psychological contract violation also emanate from receiving treatment that is inconsistent with standards of law, good faith dealing, contracts, and general standards of right and wrong. A common reaction to an employer's violation of a psychological contract is lowered trust and a sense of betrayal, which cannot be so easily repaired, and the violation subjects the relationship to a form of trauma in which the factors that led to the emergence of a relationship (through a labor agreement), such as trust and good faith, are undermined, as well as every aspect that is involved in the mechanics of production are too, negatively affected as a result of this violation.

One historic example of a "trusting" psychological contract being violated by UPS management was during their attempt to implement the team concept though deceiving and manipulating their employees, and then followed with their retribution, and punishment for our lack of willingness and participation to undermine and destroy the union from within that soon followed.

Is it beginning to make sense now, and that there is more involved here than just a simple perceived contract violation by just mean and nasty managers? There is a reason why we feel the way we do towards them…you just have to stop and think outside the box for a moment to realize what is actually going on here at UPS.

As of April 1999, profits at UPS are strong, and climbing. Business, in fact, has never looked better for the 90-year-old company. But while UPS publicly lauds employees for working "very hard to rebuild" the company after the 15-day labor strike in mid-1997, top management has been working very hard, too—to renege on its promise to turn part time work into full-time jobs.

The five-year contract UPS signed included an agreement to create full-time jobs by combining existing part time-positions. But 18 months later and $1.2 billion richer, UPS has yet to make the first installment of 2,000 full time jobs.

Nothing has changed in regard to the sentiment of the regard of the company in the eyes of the part time employees. Many are saying that if it were left up to them we'd be back on the streets. On the other hand, much has changed—and all for the better for UPS.

UPS totaled $6.16 billion in revenue for the third quarter of 1998, up from the $4.81 billion in 1997, which was affected by the strike. UPS also reported profits of $449 million for the third quarter of 1998 and daily package volume is now at 10.9 million, compared to 11 million just before the strike.

Despite the gains, UPS continues to drag its feet and the International union has taken the company into arbitration. Hearings are planned for Feb. 24 and March 4.

UPS' tactics to avoid honoring its commitment to part time employees included claims that low package volume prevented the creation of more full time jobs. However, UPS is moving virtually the same amount of parcels as before the strike. And during the holiday season, UPS announced it expected a record volume of deliveries. Record profits could result when fourth-quarter tallies are announced next month. UPS' revenue for the first three quarters of pre-strike 1996 was $16.4 billion. Revenue soared to $18.1 billion for the same three quarters last year.

Chapter 21

"Oh my God! My chest is tightening up and I think I'm going to black out. I've got to get the feeder off the road before I wreck. I manage to stumble to a phone and call an ambulance...I think I'm having a heart attack."

Everything was going pretty well during the summer of 1999 with no major problems occurring in Huntsville after getting rid of both the Colonel and Smitty. In the meantime I had been asked by Matt to assist him in organizing a local plant here in Huntsville named PPG. Pittsburgh Plate and Glass manufactured aircraft windows and ballistic glass for airlines and security services.

I had been helping Matt for several weeks out at PPG, and I had been pretty much running the organizing campaign for the local union. I managed to put any hard feelings that I might have been feeling at the time against Matt, and chose to organize this plant to help the members out, because it would mean a lot for our local to have these fine people come in and be with us. I had been pretty high profile with all the PPG employees, and they all looked up to me and trusted me because they had heard about my reputation as being a hardliner with UPS's management from several of my co-workers who were friends with some of them at the plant.

Little did I know that I was about to embark on a journey of betrayal that had all started with just my simple refusal to succumb to old guard politics.

After one afternoon of hand-billing the PPG plant, after everyone had left, Matt asked me to walk over with him, and climb into his car for a minute to cool off, that he had something he wanted to talk to me about. As we made our way back across the highway, and climbed into his Lincoln we closed the doors and he cranked the air conditioner up on high. Matt sat there for a minute or so, thinking to himself, while I sat over in the passenger side while working on pointing the vents toward my face in attempt to try and get cooled off. After a minute or so of sitting there, staring out the window he started the conversation off.

"James I want you to know that when this union goes in over here that we will probably need another business agent to handle these people and even possibly the members at UPS in Huntsville." He said

I sat there trying to cool off from the sweltering heat from having to stand on the hot pavement in front of the plant for two hours.

"Yeah, well you know as well as I do that everyone here at PPG wants me to represent them" I replied, while wiping my face.

"I know." He answered while looking out the window at passing traffic.

I was excited about the proposal. Why shouldn't I be? I was finally nally going to be able to use my 'labor relations skills' that I had acquired from dealing with UPS's management people. And most important of all...I was going to make sure every way that I could that PPG didn't turn into another UPS.

"James..." Matt said.

"Yeah Matt," I answered, while still daydreaming about the business agent offer, and wiping my forehead off.

"I know you're probably going to run against me in the next election aren't you?" Matt asked nervously, while he fidgeted with his pen.

I felt kind of uneasy about this question, because I didn't want to screw this business agent thing up by telling him something to piss him off, and answered him "I haven't decided yet Matt," I replied, hoping he'd catch the hint and just drop it.

"Hell I know you're going to run and you'll probably beat me too" he replied, sounding a little more curious now.

I knew inside that I stood a good chance of beating him especially with the ways things were looking with PPG. He knew it as well, but I wasn't going to play into that. Not yet. "Well I don't know about that Matt." I replied.

Matt sat over in his seat and he began fidgeting a little more like he had something he wanted to say, but just didn't know just how to approach it.

"James I need just one more year after this term to be able to retire, and draw my pension," he said, while sounding pathetic.

"What is he trying to do? Play on my pity for him?" I thought, but I didn't say anything at the moment. I knew that when Matt had ran against and beat Huey several contracts ago that if he quit or was ever defeated that he couldn't come back to UPS and finish out his time, whereas under the new contract that covers me, I can. Simply put if he was defeated, by anyone, in the next election he'd be out of a job, and it could wind up affecting his pension dramatically. It was IMPORTANT that he was in office one way or another for one more term.

I continued to sit there and looked over at him expecting him to say what he had to say and quit this kiddy game of going back and forth.

"James if I hire you to be the business agent here in Huntsville I would like you to hire me for the same position that you'd have here if you beat me in the next election. I need just a little more time so I can get a little more money on my pension." Matt said waiting for my answer.

I sat there not knowing what to say. I knew right then what this was. This was nothing more than 'old guard' union politics, to which I despised with a passion this type of politics within our union. We had enough of this crap going on with Hoffa and his cronies on the International level, and we sure in hell didn't need it in our local like it was going on in local 612. I sat back in the seat and let out a sigh and looked out the window for a moment thinking of a way to delicately handle this situation.

We had now gone from hiring me without strings attached based solely on my merit to a new position of scratch my back and I'll scratch yours.

"Matt I'll have to think about it," I replied, and wiped my face off again.

"Well think about it and let me know what you've decided," Matt re-

I had finally decided to go ahead and tell Matt during one of the meetings just prior to the union certification election, which was scheduled on August 12, 1999, that I wasn't interested in the 'little deal' he was trying to cook up, and at first he didn't seem to take the news real well, but then he played it off like it was no big deal, but the other people there with us could tell that it in fact bothered him, after I told him that I wasn't interested in doing it and that it sounded shady.

One reason was I didn't want to associate myself with anything like that or him. It had the potential to ruin me politically over the next few years, and besides... it was old guard style, underhanded, back room politics anyway, and I simply wanted no part of it. I wasn't going to worry about how he felt about my decision too much, because back at UPS there was a major problem brewing in regards to safety.

Josey had been called into the office several times over the past few weeks, because he was taking "TOO LONG" to pre-trip his feeder equipment and build his set of trailers with management claiming that he was exceeding the 'allotted' thirty-minutes that they "ALLOWED" a feeder driver to pre-trip and build his set. Josey was checking everything on the equipment in accordance to D.O.T's standards, and he was following the rules established by the Federal Government and not management's quick build standards, which cut the inspection down somewhat.

Josey was going to stand his ground on this serious issue and he should had, because if he had failed to inspect a piece of the equipment, and if it had failed while he was out on the road then he could be held responsible for failing to properly pre-trip his equipment and then he would stand to be disciplined.

This was just another example of management trying to cut cost, and time at the expense of the driver's, and the public's safety. Even though Josey had been fighting with management for several days and after having filed several grievances, management tried to get one up on him.

Josey came into work one afternoon and noticed that the trailers he had been dispatched with to carry over to Atlanta had been put together and were ready for him to just hook up to and go. After he asked around about who had built his loads he had found out that a part timer had put the equipment together that morning and that they had been sitting out in front of the center all day.

Josey was instructed to hook up to them and to pull them straight to the Pleasantdale hub in Atlanta...no questions asked. So what does he do? He goes out there, and breaks them down, and then he inspects them and then puts them back together again which wound up costing management an extra twenty minutes or so by him doing this on top of his initial thirty minute allowance. They were pissed as they stood out on the yard and watched him do this, but they wisely elected not to say anything to him about what he had done.

I always thought that this was sort of stupid and irresponsible on managements part, because the driver was responsible for the equipment, and was responsible to make sure that the equipment that was being taken out on the road for that day was in a safe and dependable condition.

Josey was well within his rights to refuse to take the equipment out without first 'properly' inspecting the equipment.

It wound up that after management had started coming down hard on Josey about the pre-trip issue, Josey finally had a D.O.T enforcement officer that he knew pay the Huntsville managers a little visit one afternoon, and they didn't like what Uncle Sam had to tell Uncle Buster.

In the meanwhile Petey had started doing the same thing in support of Josey, and Abel and I soon followed suit. Soon the over allowed time in Huntsville skyrocketed in regard to the amount of time we were spending on the yard every night. Finally one of our supervisor's was dispatched to Huntsville, from Birmingham Alabama, to find out what our problem was, and the problem was soon to escalate into a full-blown ordeal.

I was called into the office on the evening of April 19, 1999, by Walt, our group supervisor, and he wanted to know why it was taking me over thirty minutes to pre-trip and leave the yard every night. I explained to him that in order for me to do a proper pre-trip I had to do this, that, and so on.

"You'll have to learn to do it in thirty minutes," he replied.

He had taken on a cold and disrespectful tone and demeanor by now, and I could tell real fast where this was going.

"I'll red tag the equipment before I take something out on the road that is not safe," I answered. Right then after uttering those two words, "red tag"...crap hit the fan, and we got into one rather large fight, with only the two of us being in the office, I asked for a steward, but was told that I wouldn't be getting one, and with him denying me my right to union representation he had become fair game since I was then "forced" to once again defend myself. I then unloaded both barrels on him. After he saw that he wasn't going to get anywhere with the pre-trip issue he was in a hurry to end the meeting as soon as possible, but he had one other item to discuss with me.

"One other order of business I need to cover with you James," he said. "You get one hour for meal," he replied, while looking over some papers. "Why do you show stopping for three minutes here, and then another two minutes later in the day after you've already taken your one hour meal?" He asked.

"I had to stop and urinate," I replied sarcastically.

"You cannot stop after you've had your one hour meal," he replied.

"What do you suggest I do Walt?" I asked.

"Either use it during your break time or hold it." He replied.

"I tell you what Walt..." I said while standing up. "I'm going to stop anytime I want to use the bathroom whether I have any break left or not," I popped off.

"Well, I'm instr...." He started to say.

"Just fire me for pissing and let's see where it goes then Walt," I finished for him and I walked out of the office.

DATE GRIEVANCE FILED: 4-19-99

EXPLAIN GRIEVANCE: *I was called into the office by Walt to discuss taking my meal and the pre-trip allowance. During the conversation I tried to explain to him that I couldn't achieve the on yard allowance. I was denied union representation after I requested it. He was very rude and disrespectful to me and I was forced to defend myself.*

but I wasn't doing it for personal gratification, but rather I was doing it for the cause. Hell I was proud that Huntsville had the reputation of being hard core. Now maybe they'd back off of my drivers some and just let us do our job without having to play these Mickey Mouse games with management anymore.

I was still chief steward over both centers representing all of the package car drivers, and helping with the part timers whenever the need arose. Josey had all the feeder drivers and mechanics and he didn't need any help at all with them.

I was still learning a lot from him. Abel was helping both of us, and he was still as active in leading the Huntsville building as Josey and I were. Abel was very different than me, maybe because he had a cooler head than I did. He was more geared toward the feeder language in the contract, but could hold his own whenever another member needed him in the office, and with all of us being in Huntsville, we were finally being respected and extremely well represented, and everyone was pleased except for corporate management.

A couple of days after being fired for pulling the wrong load back, I was forced into yet another confrontation with two managers and a supervisor over the pre-tripping of my equipment. It seemed that one member of management wasn't enough to 'talk' to me, so they decided that it would be best if all three of them took me on at once. I was still very stressed out from the other day, and the mere sight of these three cracker heads only seemed to make things worse. It was sort of like walking home from school, when you were a kid, and saw that three school bullies were blocking the only path that led to your house, and you knew deep down inside that you were going to have to scrap it out with them in order to be able to get home, and there was no avoiding it. It was that kind of feeling. When it was all said and done nothing was accomplished on their part. It was a senseless waste of time and, once again, I was not afforded union representation due to their claim that "no discipline was to come of the ensuing conversation". Well in that case I stood there waiting for them to say something, which could've been interpreted by me, as a provocation to a confrontation, and like always it was only a matter of time before it would come, and when it did come...I became unglued and it was on. The best I could tell, they weren't used to anything like I was giving them out in the parking lot, because I had two of them stuttering and stammering and the other one just stood there in silence. So much for the big, bad management bullies.

When they finally threw in the towel, and when I was told to leave, I could barely walk straight from the ordeal. My head was throbbing and my chest was tight and hurting very much due to the fact that I had just become extremely upset from what had just transpired between us. Maybe this is what they wanted? I felt that they were trying to get me to take a swing at them, but I was too smart for that. I did take advantage of the situation after they 'drew first blood' and I hammered their butt's relentlessly.

I tried to collect myself, and calm down, but it was getting harder and harder to do so.

I started work right after the fight, and headed out to the 'Creek with two trailers. I managed to make it up to a little town that was just across the state line, when I started getting tunnel vision, and seeing spots, and began swerving all over the road. I honestly felt that I was going to black out. My mouth became very dry and I began to perspire a lot. I hadn't ever felt this way before. My shoulder began to hurt and the first thing I thought was heart attack.

I managed to pull the truck over at a gas station and called the Huntsville center and spoke to Gordon. I told him what was going on and that I had called an ambulance, because I thought I was having a heart attack, and all he said to me was that he asked me where I was. and then he told me to hide the keys on the tractor, and that he'd send someone up there to get the truck. I told him that I was going to Fayetteville, Tennessee's emergency room and I told him I had to go as I heard the siren came closer. He never even asked me one time if I was going to die...he was only interested in the trailer making the sort on time.

When the EMT's arrived they loaded me up and sped me to the emergency room with sirens blaring. When I arrived in the emergency room they immediately began hooking me up to several machines, and drawing blood, and so on. The hospital had to call Lesley, because management didn't, to tell her that I was in the hospital and that I was okay. Management was still only concerned with getting the load up to Nashville in time to make the sort. Lesley finally showed up and we were given the news that it was probably just high blood pressure, which at the time that I was admitted was very, very high, and they made me stay there for a couple of more hours until they could finally get it under control. I was surprised that management didn't come to the hospital and fire me for abandoning my vehicle, because I have heard of it happening in the past to other drivers, but the saddest part of all was that management did not call one time to check and see if I was alive or dead. It was in fact later the next day, after reporting to work, when I was finally asked by one of them if I was okay and able to drive, because they needed to know if they needed to run someone else through to get my loads. They then requested a copy of the doctor's report to make sure that I had in fact been in the hospital to begin with, and not just laying out for the night.

I returned to work and everything was very low key. I found out that I was scheduled to have a local hearing concerning my discharge for June 25, 1999.

On June 25, 1999, I returned from making my run from Whites Creek and I waited a couple of minutes in the building for all of the key players that were going to discuss my discharge to arrive. As I sat over in the break area drinking a coke in walked William, the feeder manager for north Alabama, and Hembry both carrying their briefcases, and as usual, Matt hadn't shown up yet and it looked like he was going to be late once again.

As they both disappeared, I walked on over to the slides, where the sorters were still working, and I looked down the long, east belt as the sorters continued to put packages on it, and I stood there watching the packages on the belt as they made the slow monotonous crawl down to the other end. I often stood there watching, and trying to catch supervisors working, while they didn't have a clue that I was watching them from my hidden vantage point.

Hembry came back out of the office and came over to where I was standing and surprised me. I turned to greet him and shook his hand. He then asked me to follow him outside for a minute so we could talk in private, so I followed him on outside and we stood by the back door for a couple of seconds, as I noticed that he was acting sort of strange.

"James you're going to have to ease up on us a little," he said out of the blue.

Playing dumb I asked, "What do you mean Hembry?"

He kind of chuckled to himself and crossed his arms. It was drizzling rain ever so lightly and it was rather foggy that morning.

"James you know what I mean." He replied.

"Are you talking about..." I said, while pausing in an attempt to try and draw him out into revealing a little more of what he was driving at, because I wanted to make sure that we were both on the same page before answering him.

"I'm talking about all the grievances here lately and especially the one you filed on Robert...of all people. Do you know how much heat I took for that one? Jeez...how many people do you think I've heard grievances from that were filed against District Managers? None! Yours was the first one that I had ever even heard of that an employee had filed like that." He said excitedly. I shifted my weight to the other leg and crossed my arms while wanting to hear more from him. I looked over his shoulder and Hembry turned to see what it was that I was looking at. It was just a driver, who was staring at us both, as he was walking up to where we were standing to go into the back door. Hembry and I moved a little further down to get out of the way of the back door.

"James...you've got another twenty years or so left here to work, don't you?" He asked.

"What's that got to do with anything Hembry?" I said suspecting a possible threat, and Hembry could tell right away what I was that I was thinking and immediately began to calm me down.

"All I'm saying James is that I can't keep going out on a limb for you," Hembry replied. I was surprised and interested in finding out soon what he was trying to say.

"What do you mean out on a limb for me?" I asked.

"You're starting to get a lot of attention over in Atlanta, James," he answered.

"I guess that means that I'm doing my job as a steward here in Huntsville doesn't it Hembry?" I replied proudly, as I rocked back and forth on my heels.

"That kind of attention you don't need," he answered. "Corporate managers know your name now and they're asking me and my boss what's going on over here in Huntsville. What am I supposed to tell them James?' He asked.

"Tell them the truth Hembry. Tell them that over here in Huntsville we enforce the contract." I replied.

"James, I moved the Colonel like I said I would didn't I?" He asked.

"Yeah, but this discharge for me pulling the wrong load isn't anything, but a crock and you know it Hembry." I replied.

"What will it take to settle all this right now?" Hembry asked.

"Withdraw the discharge and issue me a warning letter like the contract says to do. I mean you're going to have to do that anyway right?" I asked.

"All right then." He replied.

"James I know you believe in what you're doing, but don't do something stupid and be a martyr to these people." He replied.

The discharge would be bargained down after Hembry put on a little show in the office to make it all look 'authentic' after our little meeting out back, and reduced it down to just a warning letter, and then everything was settled...or so it seemed. This would be the beginning to a crisis that was soon to come for management in Huntsville.

Chapter 22

"August 11, 1999: I notice that there are three Huntsville city police cars parked behind the building with another one parked out front as I arrived to work this evening. I wonder if they've finally caught the people who's been stealing packages from inside the building and are going to arrest them?"

The organizing campaign at PPG was going extremely well and I was really enjoying working and performing the organizing duties for the local union, and besides I was learning a lot about the other areas of the union as well. On later in the week, I was later brought in the office and questioned about whether or not I had worn a set of 'browns' down to the PPG plant while standing outside and hand billing their employees during one afternoon, and I told them that I had worn a shirt down there from time to time, and that was about it, to the best of my memory.

I was working my regular job during the week and I was still working for the local union for about 30 hours a week, as well, during the afternoons before I started work, and on the weekends. I was pretty stretched with my time and once again had managed to push Lesley and Mattie to the side while allowing this campaign to take precedence over every other thing in my life.

I had learned from a clerk, back at the center, who had had taken a call from a representative of PPG who was asking a lot of questions about me in regard to what kind of person I was, and what kind of employee I was as well.

The clerk became uncomfortable with some of the questions that were being asked by the PPG caller, and she referred them to the Antonio, the east center manager who stayed on the phone with him for a while, because she sat there in the office and watched the line until it became came clear again.

She went on to tell me that someone from PPG called pretty much everyday, and that they had been calling pretty regularly every since the organizing campaign was kicked off back way back in early May of 1999. Once I learned of this I brought it to Matt's attention with the concern that UPS management may be divulging personal and confidential information about me to them. Matt assured me that this sort of activity was common and he told me that he'd call the center and discuss this concern with the management in Huntsville. Nothing else was ever brought up again about PPG calling the center after I told Matt that I wanted it to stop. Management brought me back into the office one evening, before I was scheduled to start work, and asked me if I had been picketing with the U.S Postal Letter Carriers, or the N.A.L.C branch 462, while wearing a UPS shirt? I told management that it was none of their business what I did while I was on vacation and I just left it at that. It seemed that they were only interested in the bad press they could receive if customers saw a UPS driver out picketing with one of their competitors, the U.S Postal Service.

The National Association of Letter Carriers Union's contract was coming up for negotiation and I had been invited to join and walk with them while they conducted an informational picket outside their stations. I told Lew, their President that I would be honored to walk with them and I that I would proudly carry a sign in support of our brothers of organized labor.

I hadn't forgot about the tremendous help and support they all gave to us back during the strike of 1997, and I wanted desperately to return the favor, although this wouldn't even begin to pay them back for the help they had given us during that turbulent time. The N.A.L.C had special signs made up just for us, the Teamster members, to carry, (see photo insert), that read, "UPS Drivers support letter carriers", and I had asked several other Teamsters to join me and walk with these fine people. Abel and Josey, and even Matt walked with them along with several other Teamsters from our building. I mean...here we were "competitive enemies" walking together in support of one another for a common cause. It was all over the news that evening and it was great. I was able to drive to several different stations located throughout Huntsville and tried to walk at every one of their picket lines that I could for that one day.

Meanwhile, back at UPS...the issue arose again with Walt concerning the bathroom breaks that I was still taking. I had had enough of that crap from him so when I got home that morning I constructed a homemade urinal for a tractor and sent it to the Birmingham feeder office with a note saying that if they'd back me financially I'd go in to a partnership with them and they could place one in every tractor, which then they could save millions!

What I had done was I had taken an empty three liter plastic coke bottle and connected a two foot long garden hose with a funnel taped to the end of it. I then took a coat hanger and fashioned a toilet paper holder, and hung a roll of toilet paper on it along with a copy of UPS' magazine affixed to it as well. This contraption was held to the seat of the tractor via two bungee cords. The driver then could urinate in it while driving, and the driver would never have to worry about ever having to stop again to urinate. It looked great. After I sent that contraption to the management in Birmingham the bathroom issue never arose again.

August 6, 1999 (Friday), I came into work that night, after attending a small birthday party at home to celebrate my thirtieth birthday, and walked into the center only to learn that one of our feeder drivers had been fired earlier that morning for dishonesty, or as management claimed for allegedly falsifying his records. When I heard the news I knew immediately that this allegation was nothing but a bald face lie, and that there was no way in the world that it could've been true.

This was nothing but a classic case of the pot calling the kettle black. You see...several weeks earlier, I had to have a little discussion with the east center manager, Antonio, about a complaint that I had received from some of the east center package car drivers concerning the fact that the Huntsville managers were ordering all of the east center drivers to enter an 8:55 a.m leave building time into their DIAD's regardless of what time they left the building.

In essence, this too was nothing but a clear cut example of management forcing these drivers to falsify their records, and we were now getting into an area now that involved a serious question of ethics, so when I confronted Antonio about the practice, he reluctantly agreed to stop it altogether.

Since then, I had learned that this practice had started back up and I decided to file a grievance to protest this act.

The problem I had with this practice is two fold. First, it involved the drivers falsifying their records and entering a false leave building time just to make the preloads numbers look good, because Huntsville management was still unable to get the preload down on time and this was a serious question involving ethics; and second, the time that the driver's were showing as having left the building, which was 8:55 a.m, wasn't being credited to their on-road hours which only did one thing to them, and that was to drive their over allowed time up. In fact the majority of the drivers were leaving the building well after 9:10 a.m, and even some drivers...later than that. These drivers were having to start their routes twenty-five to thirty minutes in the hole everyday before they had even left the building and never received any credit for that negative time.

Then to top it all off, the managers were bringing these same drivers into the office the next day and were disciplining them for running over allowed, and yes...even including the ones who were running just twenty minutes over. The management were actually punishing these drivers for running over, when in fact, in some of the cases it was the management who were the ones causing them to run over everyday in the first place, just from the drivers being forced to falsify the records, when in fact it was the management that had ordered them to put in the false leave building times to begin with.

If the drivers would have been allowed to enter their correct leave building times in the first place, then the result would have affected most of their over allowed time dramatically, and would've brought them back to running either scratch or under allowed, but by doing this would've meant that the local managers would've have had to explain to the big wheel's as to why there were still unable to get the preload down on time. They were doing this, because instead of the managers charging all of that time back to the pre-load it was easier to cover up their mismanagement of the preload operation by putting the burden on the drivers, and then forcing them to try and make up the time of managements incompetence.

I wasn't about to sit still and allow this atrocity to continue. I immediately sat down and wrote the grievance out and handed it to Antonio, but come to find out this hadn't been Antonio's call. I had learned from another steward from the Florence Alabama center, named Ted, who had filed a group grievance to protest the very same thing that was happening in their center. That told me right away that this wasn't just an isolated incident, and that it must have been orchestrated on a level higher than the center management team, but that still didn't make it right.

Management had fired so many drivers, and management personal in the past for doctoring the numbers, which is any way you care to look at it...an act of dishonesty, which is a cardinal sin under our labor contract.

How was it all right now that a member of management from   Birmingham or even higher to authorize the practice, which was now plaguing the Huntsville, and Florence centers?

Several weeks earlier, before the driver was fired, and after the center had started back with this practice, Abel and I were out on the yard, and I motioned to Abel for him to come over to where I was standing.

Abel walked on over to where I was, and asked me in his usual fashion, "What's up nut's?"

I told him that I had asked Fredrick, a loss prevention supervisor, to come outside, that I had wanted to talk to him about something that was going on in Huntsville. I wanted Abel to be a witness so that Fredrick couldn't come back and say that I had threatened him, or something else along that line as Fredrick came into view and began making his way over to where we were standing.

"You wanted to see me James?" Fredrick asked.

"Yeah, I need to ask you a hypothetical question," I replied.

"Okay shoot," he replied. "Fredrick, take for instance you had a driver that say...enters the wrong time into his DIAD on purpose to make his over all time for the day look good." I said, with him becoming increasingly interested in what I was saying. "What would you call that?" I asked.

"That's dishonesty," he replied.

"What would you do if a driver had done that?" I asked.

"I'd fire him on the spot," he replied. "Is that going on here James?" He asked.

"Yeah," I replied, while looking over at Abel who looked at me and grinned.

Abel couldn't keep quiet any longer. "You've got managers in this building doing that right now, who are forcing drivers to put in wrong leave building times," he replied, while pointing towards the center.

"In this center?" Fredrick asked while looking puzzled.

"Heck yeah in this center." Abel replied, as I nodded my head yes as Fredrick looked at me to support Abel's claim.

"Are you sure?" Fredrick asked.

"Yeah, I'd like you to look into it for us," I said while smiling.

"Oh I will...don't you worry about that," he said and walked away.

I knew in the past that center managers had been fired, or they had been busted down and demoted for playing with the numbers and timecards. This should become very interesting in the next couple of days.

The following Monday, Fredrick was back in Huntsville on some other business, and he seemed to have been avoiding me most of the night, until I finally cornered him up and asked him to come back outside again. Abel was out there on the yard and he walked back over to be with me again as a witness, and I asked Fredrick how the investigation was coming along.

"The best thing you can do is to forget about it James," Fredrick replied sternly.

"What do you mean forget about it Fredrick?" I asked angrily.

"Just forget about it," he said while walking off to go back into the building.

I knew right then that there was a different set of standards for upper managers than for lower managers, who had been disciplined for the same offences, and were in the same boat with us. The "big boy's" could get away with whatever they wanted to do and think that they were above the contract and untouchable. This is when I filed the grievance to protest this action.

DATE OF GRIEVANCE: 7-12-99

EXPLAIN GRIEVANCE: *Management had directed the package car drivers to enter false leave building times. We the drivers of the Huntsville east center do hereby protest this dishonest act and demand that this practice cease immediately.*

REMEDY SOUGHT: *Termination of all managers involved for this unethical and dishonest act.*

As soon as I could get all of the facts regarding the drivers discharge, I learned that Friday evening, August 6, 1999, that all the driver had done was to not go by and make a pick up, and that he had closed the stop out, showing that he made the pick up, while another driver had told him earlier in the day not to go by there that he'd make it for him, but management wasn't too interested in hearing about this new information and they fired him on the spot and sent him on home. He could be classified as one of those kinds of drivers, like myself, who didn't have any "credits in the bank."

I went ahead and punched in, on August 6, 1999, and noticed that Antonio, Fredrick and Ricky, who was the number two man in Alabama, were all standing around together in the middle of the building, talking and having a good old time about something.

I walked right up to where they were and interrupted their little celebration, as a small crowd of drivers had begun to gather in front of the DIAD station and were watching and anticipating fireworks.

After all, one of our own had been unjustly fired, and I guess it could've been understood that I was maybe the eye of the storm for everybody. As I came walking up to them, Fredrick nodded over towards me, and then they all stopped talking and they all turned to look at me, and then Ricky stuck out his hand for me to shake.

"I'll have to pass," I replied, while refusing to shake his hand, and I asked them if they had fired the driver for dishonesty, and Antonio popped off that he was fired for falsifying his records.

"Fredrick I expect you to fire him and him," I said while pointing at Ricky and Antonio. "They've both committed an act of dishonesty, and I expect you to fire Robert as well, or you haven't seen hell that compares to what is coming if you don't!" I said, and turned and walked off, leaving all three of them standing there looking at each other in total shock and disbelief.

Ricky and the others continued to stand there speechless for a couple of minutes. I didn't give them an opportunity to respond. I went directly into the office and called the UPS Integrity Hotline and reported the incident to corporate. I made two separate reports that evening and was given a case number along with a "call back date" for each incident. I went ahead as well and filled out several grievances to protest the wrongful discharge of my driver.

I never received a call, or any sort of notification about the ethics complaints that I had filed concerning the management ordering the falsifying of the drivers records. In fact, when I later called to check on the status of the investigation, concerning the integrity problem, I never received an acknowledgement that my case even existed. I asked the caseworker about my case number who said that the case no longer existed. I found this to be rather strange that they couldn't explain to me why this had happened. I asked to fill out another compliant and was then instructed to discuss it with the Division Manager for my district. I knew right then that this was much bigger than I had imagined.

The driver wasn't back to work that following Monday morning, so I met the drivers that morning and handed out a handbill that was announcing a meeting that I was going to call for the next morning on Tuesday, August 10, 1999. Everyone took one as they pulled onto the property, and most all agreed to attend the meeting, and the stage was being set for a major confrontation.

I reported to work that Monday night, and Gordon called me into the office and he held up a copy of the handbill that I had passed out that morning. I managed to leave several of them laying around so they could find them with ease and have a copy for themselves so they wouldn't have to resort to taking one that belonged to a driver.

"What's going on with this James?" Gordon asked.

"Nothing that we can't handle Gordon," I replied coldly.

"We don't need this right now James, everything is going smooth here in Huntsville." He replied.

"It's going smooth in your center, but explain to me why you didn't speak up about this dishonesty issue earlier when I came to you several weeks ago about what was going on in the east center." I asked while becoming upset.

I didn't get an answer. "Just be careful," he replied, as I walked on out of his office and started work. I left out of Huntsville to make my run up to Whites Creek that evening, and came back on time that Tuesday morning. After I finished breaking my loads down I walked on into the center to punch out and was going try and get a couple of hours of sleep out in my truck until the meeting started. It was around 5:00 a.m and I had roughly two hours to kill, so I walked over and told the shifter to come out and knock on my window in about an hour and a half and I handed him a coke for agreeing to do the favor for me.

As I was starting to walk outside, a preload supervisor, named Wendel, came up and asked Abel if he'd mind helping him for a couple of hours and Abel turned it down, because he was tired and then offered it to me. I told Wendel that I could help him out for a couple of hours, but I had to leave at 7:00 a.m, because I had something important to do this morning. He agreed to work me until 7:00 and then he promised turn me loose so I could take care of my business. I loaded two package cars for him and when 6:45 came rolling around, they called a break for the preload operation and it shut down for ten minutes. I walked on over to the office, and looked inside, and saw that Wendel was on the phone as I knocked on the door and opened it to wave by to him to let him know that I was leaving.

Wendel held up his finger indicating for me to hold on a minute, that he had something to tell me. I was tired from being on the road all night, and was looking forward to getting this meeting over with and going home and go to bed. I stood there and he hung the phone up and asked me to step into the office.

"James that was Hembry and he instructed me to tell you not to leave until the sort was over," he replied.

"No...I told you that I'd work until 7:00 Wendel," I replied, while becoming annoyed.

"Hembry said if you leave that you will be fired for abandoning your job," He replied.

This had really pissed me off, and I knew right then that Hembry was trying to prevent me from holding that meeting, as I looked at my watch and saw that it was 6:55 a.m. I left the office and walked over to the shop area and looked for their phone. I knew how I could get out of this.

I picked up the phone and called the feeder department in Birmingham and I hoped that a supervisor would be there.

"Hello, Birmingham feeders this is Barbara speaking," a familiar voice said.

"Barbara this is James Earls in Huntsville...is Walt in?" I asked hurriedly.

"No he's not, but Terry is," she replied.

"Let me speak to Terry," I asked, and then asked her to stay on the phone to act as a witness for me, and Barbara agreed to do so.

"Birmingham feeders, Terry speaking," he replied.

"Terry this is James Earls in Huntsville I'm having a problem," I said.

"What's going on James?" He asked.

"Terry, Wendel asked me if I'd help him out on the preload for an hour or so and now they won't let me go and I'm really tired," I replied while laying it on thick.

"Whose they?" Terry asked.

"Hembry," I replied.

"You don't work for Hembry or Wendel. You go home right now James," he replied angrily.

"Are you instructing me to go home Terry?" I asked.

"Yes, I'm instructing you to go home," Terry answered, and I hung the phone up and I began walking out of the shop towards where everyone had congregated.

Break was now almost over as I walked over to where Wendel was standing. He was leaning up against the coke machine and I started out the back door with my car keys in my hand.

"Where are you going?" He asked.

"Terry said I work for feeders and not for you or Hembry. If you have a problem with it you need to call feeders," I said, as the door swung open. He began to panic, because Hembry had told him to keep me there working until after the drivers started. Wendel took off running to the office as the door closed behind me.

I drove my pick up truck around to the front of the building to where everyone had already gathered waiting for me. I climbed out of my truck and took out several signs that I had made from over the weekend, which denounced management's double standards towards the black drivers who had been wrongly singled out and discharged for what I felt were for racial reasons, and various other 'friendly' signs, careful not to say anything that could "harm" UPS to where I could be held accountable.

I started the meeting off, and the fired driver was present as I discussed how the company was abusing us and what we needed to do to combat their efforts. I discussed the firing of the driver, as well as the status of the PPG campaign, and let everyone know that the PPG union certification election was scheduled in just two days.

Wendel came out to the corner of the building and began writing down all the names of the drivers who were attending the parking lot union meeting and everyone began shooting him birds and calling him names. Another supervisor then appeared with a camera, and began taking pictures of everyone who was out there, which was illegal surveillance, and was a violation of the National Labor Relations Act.

During the fired driver's speech, and in between me trying to prevent trouble between the Teamsters and the management, Hembry came flying into the parking lot and sped to the rear of the building as he stared at us all.

Now I knew why he wanted to keep me working on the pre-load...until he arrived. What was going on was that he was on the road to Huntsville from Birmingham, when he made the call, to try and put a stop to our meeting. I decided it was time to move the meeting from where we currently were at due to Wendel interfering with us and trying to cause trouble. I told everyone to gather up everything we had, and that we were moving up to the store on the corner so we could finish our rally.

Everyone gathered up the signs and started walking up the sidewalk towards the store when Hembry and Antonio came walking rather quickly out of the center calling my name out loud. I stopped walking, as well as everyone else, and turned to see what they wanted.

Hembry came walking right up to the edge of the property and motioned for me to come over to where they both were standing.

I walked over to them, and Hembry asked me what I was doing.

"We're having a union meeting Hembry," I replied.

"I'm instructing you stop immediately James!" He said in an extremely upset tone, and out of breath.

"Stop what?" I asked.

"I want you to know that you're violating the contract James," he said nervously.

"How do you figure that, Hembry?" I asked, while everyone watched closely.

"If I have to, James, I'll get a court order and make you stop," he said as his voice began to crack from the stress.

"Last time I looked Hembry...this was still America." I replied smartly, while looking around.

"James, with Antonio as my witness, I'm instructing you to stop this illegal picket right now." He said very nervously and I noticed that he was visibly shaken from what was going on here with this meeting.

"Hembry...this isn't a picket. We're just having a meeting." I replied.

"I've called both the International and the local union and they both said that they haven't authorized this picket James," he replied.

This was the moment of truth in my career as a labor union leader. Was I going to cave in to managements demands, and call everyone back into the building and lose any respect that I had from not only the drivers out there, but from myself as well? If I turned back now, I'd never be looked at the same way again by any of them. It was one of the most important decisions of my life...

"I'm not stopping, because we're well within our rights to be out here Hembry. Do what you have to." I replied, and I then motioned for everyone to continue walking up to the corner. They both turned and jogged back towards the center and disappeared inside.

We all walked up to the corner of the highway in a little grassy area right out front of a gas station. We went ahead and held our meeting, with several members standing on the side of the road to support the fired driver while he held up a sign demanding his reinstatement.

Harry came driving up to the intersection, and hung out the window of his personal vehicle, and began to snap Polaroid pictures of us while yelling at us, "I'm sorry." After a few more minutes, Hembry and Antonio reappeared, and they pulled into the parking lot where we were assembled. They both sat there in Hembry's car, writing down all of our names down and taking more pictures. It was getting close to 8:00 a.m. now, and I didn't want anyone to be late so I called the meeting to an end and sent everyone back down to the center, and I then started on my trip home.

When I reported to work that evening nothing was said to me about anything. Not a single word. Not even a hello. Wednesday was sure to be a different story.

I reported to work on Wednesday, August 11, 1999, a little earlier than usual in anticipation that something might be going to happen for us having the rally the other day, and when I pulled into the parking lot I immediately noticed a police car sitting at the entrance just as you came onto the property, and as I drove around to the back of the building to park, there were three more police cars there as well.

I didn't think anything of it, and thought that maybe they had caught the people who had been stealing packages from us on the inside.

I parked my truck around back, and walked on inside, and punched in. It was fifteen minutes or so before I was scheduled to start work so I walked around to the east center's office, and walked on inside and I saw that Chester was busy typing on the computer, and he had only stopped long enough to check to see who had walked into the office.

"Chester, what's up with all of the cop cars?" I asked.

"I don't know? Why what's up?" he replied, as he continued to type.

"I guess they caught the thieves, and are going to take them to jail tonight." I replied.

He didn't say anything and continued typing.

I started work and went on outside on the yard to look for my tractor. It was a humid night and it looked like it might rain.

About 7:05 p.m, Jeb, the assistant steward, came out and told me that Hembry wanted to see me in the office upstairs. I stopped what I was doing and began walking back towards the building. I figured that they were there to give me a warning letter for the meeting or something along those lines. Little did I know what was waiting for me up in the office.

I walked on in and saw that Hembry was accompanied with Ricky, and they asked us to take a seat.

"James we need to talk to you about the other day." Hembry replied.

"Okay." I answered while smiling and nodding my head yes as Jeb sat over in the corner watching everything.

"James...who was responsible for the picket the other day?" He asked.

"There wasn't any picket to my knowledge Hembry." I replied sarcastically. I had talked to Matt that morning and he didn't say a word to me about this meeting that was taking place now.

"I'm talking about what happened on Tuesday, James." He replied coldly. Jeb just sat there not saying anything and Ricky was leaning over in his chair with his hands in a praying position up to his mouth.

The dialog between Hembry and me went back and forth several times and finally I said, "If you're going to punish me, do it so I can go to work Hembry."

Hembry looked and Ricky, and Ricky began to take his hands away from his mouth and took a deep breath.

"James you are discharged under Article 51, Section 4 of the contract and are no longer employed with UPS," He said. I was shocked. Heck, the worst I should have received was just a warning letter according to the contract.

"How can you fire me when this isn't even a cardinal sin?" I asked.

"No discussion...I need your keys to the building and your uniforms immediately," Ricky replied.

I was floored. I stood up shocked and walked out to my truck to get their keys and while I was outside they both had walked down stairs from the office, and just stood at the base of the stairs. I had noticed that the police officers were out of their cars now and were standing beside their vehicles. I walked back into the building, and people began gathering around Hembry and Ricky, after hearing of my discharge, as I walked back in with my key to the building. I tossed the key at Ricky and he didn't make any attempt to catch it, and he just let it drop onto the floor and it made a loud ringing sound.

I turned and walked upstairs to my locker and took out every stitch of uniforms, and dirty old socks that I had in my locker, and walked back down to the bottom of the stairs, and literally threw all of my uniforms on them and told them what to do with them.

They both just stood there with solemn looks on their faces not saying anything. I then ripped my shirt off with buttons flying everywhere and threw it on Ricky and told him what I thought of him, and how they had done me and everyone else for the past ten years of my life.

They both just stood there not saying a word at all. The other drivers just stood there as well. I then turned and walked out of the building Abel was coming up the side of the building and pulled up beside me as I was walking to my truck to leave and asked me what was going on.

I told them that they had fired me and he couldn't believe it either. Abel just sat there stunned as well for a minute or so. I mean here I was standing there half naked in the parking lot, and I was on the verge of going ballistic.

Abel managed to calm me down and I immediately filled out a grievance to protest my discharge and he turned it in right then. I left the center to make the longest drive of my life back home to tell Lesley that I was no longer employed at UPS.

On the way home all I could think of was how management had done me and how this was an all time low...even for them. When I got home I told Lesley what had happened, she couldn't believe it either.

What was I going to do now? How long would I be out of work for? I figured I'd be out just a day or two to teach me a lesson like before. At least I had the union to fall back on...right?

I managed to get a hold of Matt that evening and I was still very upset from the whole thing and I was extremely nervous from not knowing what to expect, or how long I'd be out. Matt couldn't believe what management had done, and a very strange conversation soon followed. Only time would tell.

Chapter 23

"I'm on my way to Athens Alabama to meet with an individual that has some information about the local unions involvement with my discharge. I don't know really what to expect, so I decided to carry my .38 pistol with me just in case the meeting takes a turn for the worst.

Little had I realized that I was about to undertake the worst struggle of my life. I had unknowingly embarked on voyage that would be filled with heartache, grief and pain, which would prove to be more than I have ever known on this earth during my lifetime. This voyage would test every belief I had not only in myself, God, and family, but last, the very institution I had defended and sacrificed my job for...The Teamsters union.

My journey of betrayal by the union had all started two months earlier with Matt back in the summer 1999 during the PPG campaign. I would later learn that there was more involved in my discharge from UPS rather than just the simple 'perceived' contract violation that both the company and local union were portraying. I had yet to realize that betrayal came in many different forms, and that those forms are not always in the guise of a company.

The following morning, after being fired from UPS, I arrived at PPG to begin sitting out the "vote yes", and other pro-union signs, up and down along the highway that ran in front of PPG where all their employees had to pass to enter the plant. Shortly after sitting all the signs out, Matt finally showed up, and he pulled in across the highway and parked in the Golden Flake potato chip company parking lot. He walked across the highway while dodging traffic, and I asked him once again, as we turned to begin the walk up the long drive that led into the parking lot of PPG, about how he thought the vote would turn out today. He was still very optimistic, and he said that he felt it would go in, but it would be a close vote. When we finally made up to the ramp that led into the plant entrance, PPG management had hung banners, and signs all up along the walkway and on the fence, asking the employees to vote no to the union. We walked on in the plant, and stopped to check in with the guard who asked us to wait in the lobby while he notified the PPG officials of our arrival.

Shortly, after a couple of minutes of waiting in the lobby, Carlson, the principle 'bad guy' of the company, came out to meet us and to carry us back to where the election would be conducted. Carlson finally introduced himself to Matt shaking his hand and Matt then introduced me to him. Carlson extended his hand to greet me, and I said that I'd pass, which did nothing but piss him off, but what did I care.

We turned and walked down the hall following behind Carlson while he tried to make small talk. The room where the election was going to be conducted was used as a conference room at the PPG site, and there were several tables already sat up for the 'appointed' observers to the election to use to tabulate the votes on at the end of the voting.

Matt and I walked into the room and were met by several of the PPG managers, and company attorneys who were there to represent the company during the election, and to voice any complaints during the course of the voting, or during the tabulation of the votes. The National Labor Relations Board officer, Leon, was there as well and he was busily working to get everything set up as Matt introduced me to him. Leon was all business, and very professional, and was cordial, but he remained focused on his job at hand. He would be the one supervising the election to make sure that neither side would break any laws. Leon began setting up the little voting booths that were very crude, but effective, in design to permit the voters to cast their ballots in total secrecy.

Employees began lining up in two separate hallways that entered the room on opposite ends and as they walked into the room, they would show their I.D badge, and then their name would be checked off from the Excelsior list to verify their eligibility as part of the bargaining unit to vote. The voting lasted several hours, and we stood there the whole time watching and waiting. There was so much tension in the air that you could almost cut it with a knife.

PPG had a lot to lose, because there hadn't been a union in this plant for some time, and they especially didn't want the Teamsters in there.

Most of the employees there were very doubtful of the outcome, and many had just about abandoned any hope of winning, but I tried to remain optimistic. The PPG in-plant organizing committee had given so much, and I had sacrificed a lot as well. I had been threatened by one of the 'vote-no' employees to be run over by a car, as well as other threats, and the intimidation from PPG calling UPS on me, everything, but it had reached the end, or so I thought. After several grueling hours and careful tabulation the verdict was finally in. In a scene similar to Norma Ray the tension was unbearable as the final tally was read. The union was voted in.

We had defeated the company and the pro union supporters began hollering and clapping, and I felt relieved. The hard work finally paid off. We were all overwhelmed with joy. The PPG attorneys and plant management just turned and walked out of the room never saying a thing.

We walked out back outside the plant and the news crews had already gathered outside the plant gates, and immediately began interviewing people as they came out. Although the victory at PPG was overshadowed by my discharge, I had managed to escape from reality if only for a brief time, and returned to 'life' after I called Lesley at home to tell her the news. She was glad of our victory, but I could tell that she was worried about our situation, and I told her what Matt had told me that I'd probably be back the following Monday morning, and not to worry about it. Several of the PPG people, along with Matt, wanted to go and celebrate and Matt told us all that he'd buy the first round. We all left to meet at a local restaurant in Huntsville, The Rack, and I stopped to call Lesley back to ask her to come down to celebrate with us, and after a few minutes of heavy coaxing, she reluctantly agreed to do so, and I went on outside to wait for her out in front of the restaurant.

People were still coming in, and they began walking up to thank me for my help, and everything that we had done for them. It felt good to be appreciated for a change for doing something positive with the union. That was something that I rarely had experienced whenever I went into the office with someone at UPS. I was hardly ever thanked, but that was my job, and just part of it I guess. Matt had pulled in and parked as I waited by my car, and I noticed that Matt was standing down on the other end of the parking lot while talking on his cell phone, and I walked on down to where he was. When he hung his phone up he shook my hand and said. "James thanks for everything."

"Well I'm just glad it's over." I replied

"We just now have to get them a contract but I don't see a problem with that." Matt replied.

"Matt...have you talked to Hembry yet?" I asked.

"No not yet James, but I'll try again right quick and see if I can find out anything," he said reaching into his pocket pulling out his phone, and began calling Hembry's office in Birmingham. Matt asked if Hembry was in, and left a voice mail for him to call him as soon as possible.

"Matt when my wife gets here, tell her that everything's going to be okay and for her not to worry." I asked.

"Aw she shouldn't worry about it." He replied confidently

After a few minutes Lesley pulled into the lot and parked beside me. She got out, and I could immediately tell that she was upset.

This discharge had her worried, and me too, but I tried not to let it show and I tried to express my confidence in getting back to work Monday, and gave her a hug and a kiss, and told her that we had won. She was less than enthusiastic about it. Matt came walking up to us, and I introduced them as I walked off winking at Matt, and I went on inside the restaurant to call Abel at home to tell him the news, and I could see out the door as I dialed Abel's number that Matt was talking to Lesley trying to reassure her that it was going to be okay. I couldn't get a hold of Abel and I just left him a message, and walked back out and asked them if everything was all right. Matt said not to worry that he'd buy us dinner tonight and we walked on inside.

Marty, Donna and several others had reserved us several tables and were already busy tying one on. We all sat down at the table with Marty, whom I had became good friends with, and ordered us a drink. People were still coming in and thanking me, and Matt, and it was a very upbeat party. When we ordered our food, Marty asked Matt "When do you think James would be back to work?"

Matt replied, "probably Monday morning."

"Why did they fire him for anyway?" she asked.

Matt didn't act quite right, and tried to blow it off by replying," they're just pissed at him for helping y'all."

"Do you think I'll be back Monday Matt?" I asked.

"Sure, I don't see this lasting long." Matt replied.

"What if it does?" I asked, feeling a little unsure of his confidence.

"I'm telling you not to worry." He replied.

I looked at Lesley who still had her doubts and I went ahead and asked Matt, "What if I don't? Do I need to go ahead and withdraw from the union?"

"No, no there's no need for that." He replied.

"If I don't have any money coming in I can't afford to pay the dues Matt." I said, trying to illicit a response in an attempt to reassure both Lesley and I.

"James I'll make sure your dues get paid, even if the union has to pay them." Matt replied.

By now there were two dozen or more PPG employees at the gathering, and somehow the local news station found out they were here and sent over a crew to interview some people and Donna and Sandy stepped in and went on camera to discuss the victory. After forty-five minutes or so Lesley and I left and went home. It just wasn't the same. I was nervous about the whole thing. This time it felt strange. I had been fired just three weeks earlier and this was the third time that I had been fired total, but I felt very different about it this time.

I decided to go to the center that Thursday morning, two days after being fired, to pick up my checks, and I had been told the night before that UPS management had hired off duty Huntsville city police officers to guard the building twenty-four hours a day, because the management in Huntsville was fearful that I'd return to 'go postal' on them for firing me. Management knew that I was a gun dealer and that I had a rather large arsenal at the time of firearms, but honestly the thought never entered into my mind, and it only proved to me, and the others, that they were indeed afraid of what they did to people. I found it amusing and quite flattering to be honest that they'd be this worried about me.

I pulled onto the parking lot in my beat up, light tan Ford truck and noticed a police officer parked right in front of the entrance to UPS. I pulled right on in and parked my truck right beside him and climbed out with a basket containing the rest of my uniforms, and other company memento's that I had at home from over the years.

"Are you Mr. Earls?" The officer asked.

"Yes sir, I'm just here to turn in my uniforms and get my paychecks sir, that's all." I replied VERY respectfully to the policeman.

"They figured you'd be coming down today." He replied, while situating his utility belt.

"You're not going to cause any trouble are you Mr. Earls?" The policeman asked.

"No sir, I have a three hundred dollar radio in one of their tractors, and some personal effects in my locker and my paychecks officer." I replied anxiously.

We began the walk up to the building and he began casually asking me what had happened to warrant this. I explained to him what happened and when I finished he stopped me and replied, "You've got to be kidding?" While rolling his eyes.

We entered the large opening to the building and he asked me to stop and stay right where I was, and I stopped where he told me to, while holding my basket. I noticed that most of the people that were there at the time began congregating inside the building and were watching Antonio as he walked up towards where we were standing. When he finally made it up to us he stopped a short distance from the policeman.

"I want my checks and my radio Antonio." I replied.

"We want our uniforms first." He replied, with his voice cracking.

"You're not getting a damn thing until I get my checks." I replied, as the anger began to swell.

Antonio stood there drawing a puff from his cigarette and replied, "You're not going to get your checks until we can mail them to you."

"I want my checks now because I've seen people with them in their shirt pockets Antonio." I replied.

"Well You..." He started to say and that's when the policeman interrupted him.

"If you have Mr. Earls' paychecks you need to go get them right now." The policeman said to Antonio. Antonio turned and stormed off to retrieve my checks.

"I don't see how you work for the people?" The officer said, after Antonio left.

"I used to have to contend with this sort of horse crap on a daily basis from these people." I replied as I saw Antonio coming back towards us.

He handed them to me and grinned. That flew all over me.

"We want our uniforms now James." Antonio replied.

I worked as instructed. I dumped them all out onto the floor and kicked them on him and scattered the rest over the oily floor, and that's when the policeman pulled me over to the side and told me if I did that again that he'd arrest me for disorderly conduct while winking his eye, and I took the gracious hint that he was giving me. Antonio then went into his speech of how I was not wanted back on the property ever again. The policeman relayed the message and asked me if I understood.

I replied, "Yes sir."

We walked on out to another police car that had been called, as back up to this one, and we both stood over by the right side of the car as Antonio followed us out. I told the policeman that they still had my radio, and he said that he'd give management just 24 hours to get it to me or he'd be back to get it for me himself.

I was pleased with the way the whole thing had unfolded. It had shown the extent, to others, as to the nature of management, and the fear they harbored inside of its employees from years of rampant abuse. Management would manage to keep a policeman on the property for the next seven days, twenty-four hours a day, out of fear of some sort of retaliation from me.

When I called back over to the local on Friday, I finally got a hold of Matt and asked him if he'd talked to Hembry, and he said that Hembry still didn't want to talk about it just yet.

"What the hell was there to talk about?" I asked while getting upset.

"I don't know James this is strange." Matt replied.

"Contractually they couldn't fire me for this Matt then answer me why am I not working until they have a local to hear my discharge?" I asked perturbed.

"I don't have any answers for you I'm sorry." He said nervously.

"Matt I need to work. Do you understand that? I need to work." I said in a loud tone.

"I can get you a job working on a pipeline in Jasper, Alabama if you want it?" He asked.

"Yeah I need it, what would I do?" I asked although not really caring what it was.

"You'd be a driver for a one-ton crew cab truck hauling equipment and workers." He replied.

"How much does it pay?" I asked.

"Fifteen dollars an hour plus all the overtime you want. They work six days a week, and a lot of them boys make $1200 a week," he replied, as if he was trying to sell me on the idea.

"I'll take it." I replied. I had no choice. I figured I'd work there for a week at the most and then come back to UPS after making a little spending money on the side, so it was really no big deal to me at the time.

"When can you start?" Matt asked.

"Well...how about next Wednesday?" I answered. This would give me a little time to get my affairs in order, and also I was hoping to stall a little bit figuring UPS would bring me back before I started.

"Fine, give this guy called 'Oscar' a call. He's the steward out of local 612 handling the site for the Teamsters and I'll call local 612 to let them know the situation." Matt replied and he hung up.

For something that's not going to be that big of a deal, and now all of a sudden, he's offering me work right off the bat? That didn't seem right to me, and I began to wonder what was actually going on.

I called Oscar that following Monday and received directions to the construction site, which was about 85 miles one-way, and he told me where to report once I arrived on the site to find him.

That Wednesday morning, I had to get up at 3:00 a.m, and be on the road by no later than 3:30 a.m. to make it to Jasper by 5:30 a.m. It was rough getting up this early after being asleep, although I had been working nights driving feeders, it was still rough. I hadn't had to get up this early since I came off of the pre-load eight years ago.

I made the long drive and when I arrived I found a parking spot across the street of the site in a little gravel parking lot. I locked up my car and proceeded to cross the street. I began making my way up to several trailers that were used as offices as I walked through the masses of people that were congregating in front of the trailers. I noticed that there were a lot of people already there as I stepped from around the tanker truck. I hadn't seen that many people in one place. They were all standing in the center of the lot where they had parked a large tanker truck that was used for fueling the vehicles. I noticed that a knee-high wall of sandbags was surrounding the tanker and quite a few people were sitting on the bags and talking amongst themselves.

As I walked by the tanker I noticed several signs that were on the sandbags, which read, "STAY OFF SANDBAGS" and "NO SMOKING". Here they were though sitting on the bags, and several of them smoking cigarettes.

"What a bunch of idiots," I thought as I walked by heading to the office. I made my way over to the Teamster trailer and met with Oscar, and to my surprise he wasn't what I had expected. He was an older man and he looked like he had been ridden hard and put up wet.

"I'm James Earls." I replied, as Oscar stopped talking and stretched his hand out. He introduced himself, and asked me a couple of questions about what happened at UPS as I followed him over to another trailer. We talked a little on the way and we went up some stairs into the office. Oscar told me to talk with the lady behind the desk and she'd fix me right up. He left and I waited until my turn to meet her.

After five minutes, or so, she smiled and asked me to step up to the desk.

"I need you to fill this out right quick, and you'll need to give a urine sample for me." She replied, pausing and looking at me as if I was going to refuse to take one.

"Okay," I replied, and finished filling the paperwork out.

I finished filling the forms out and handed them back to her and she looked over them briefly and then she asked me, "Are you working on a permit?"

I didn't know what to say. "I don't think so" I replied, unsure of what she meant.

"Do you need to buy a book?" She asked.

Again I had no clue as to what she was saying. "I don't think so? Do I?" I asked.

"If you do we can have it deducted from your check every week." She said, while becoming a little perturbed with me.

I thought to myself that she must have meant union dues. I replied, "No my locals going to pay them for me," thinking back on Matt had said to me that my dues would be taken care of by him. She looked kind of puzzled at my response, and then asked me if I belonged to a Teamster local.

"Yes m'am Local 402." I replied.

"Maybe you need to talk to your steward to find out for sure what you need to do." She said.

I agreed that I would and she sent me over to the medical officer who carried me out to the port-a-john to urinate in a cup to check for any drug use. After giving my sample I walked back over to where Oscar was and asked him about the book and permit deal.

Oscar explained to me that people buy a permit to temporarily work on the job, because they were not members of any Teamster local, and the buying the book deal was the terminology for paying membership and initiation fees to join the Teamsters. I didn't need any of these because I already belonged to the Teamsters. I explained to Oscar about the deal that Matt had made me about paying my dues, and he told me that Matt was supposed to come over to the site in the next couple of days, and that he'd talk to him about the dues issue. I went on to work, and after a couple of days I asked Oscar if he'd talked to Matt, and he said yes and that everything was okay.

I worked for about two weeks and I still hadn't heard any word from UPS at all about my discharge and I was beginning to get pissed off about the deal. Most of the time a discharge rarely went over one week before they held a local to hear it. I called the local several times during the week asking Matt and Jamie if they had heard anything from UPS, and they'd heard nothing. I asked Matt what the deal was and he said that management wasn't interested in holding a local just yet.

"What do you mean not interested?" I asked, shouting into the phone.

"James they're acting strange about the whole deal. I haven't ever seen them act this way at all." He replied.

"Well hell Matt, what are you going to do now?" I demanded.

"Let's give them a couple of more days and I'll see if I can get something set up for a local." He replied, and hurried off the phone. He could tell I was upset and I could tell that he didn't want to fool with me right at the moment. I called Lesley to let her know that there hadn't been any news. It really didn't seem to bother her too much, and she tried to calm me down, and tried to reassure me that it probably wouldn't be too much longer until I heard something from UPS.

I continued to work a couple of more weeks, and I was still calling over to the local several times a week, and I got the same answer as always. "We haven't heard anything." I was growing really tired from no one not have any answers for me. Finally after about two months Matt came out to the job site, and met with me, and he told me that UPS had agreed to have a local level hearing, and that it would be held on the following Friday, at a neutral location, at the Pipe Fitters local union hall, which was just outside Huntsville in Madison, Alabama. I was figuring they'd offer me my job back with no back pay, and reduce it to a warning letter like they had given to everyone that had been out on the demonstration with me that morning.

I left the site the following Friday and made the drive up to the union hall and waited for Matt to show up who was once again...late as usual.

I was waiting in the lobby of the union hall and in walked Hembry and Antonio. As they filed by me, I stared at them both with a go to hell look as they went on into an office and sat down. Finally Matt came in and we made our way back to the office were they were seated, and as we walked on in, Matt shook their hands and when it came time for me to shake their hand I shook my head no, and sat down.

"James, you were discharged under Article 52 of the labor agreement for your illegal picket on august 11, 1999." Hembry replied, as he looked over a couple of papers.

"There wasn't any illegal picket Hembry." Matt replied.

"Well we seem to think so and I have pictures to prove it." Hembry popped back while Antonio just sat there like a little stooge.

"We have pictures as well, along with the signs Hembry," Matt replied, as he let out a long sigh.

"Can we see the signs Matt?" Hembry asked while appearing to be surprised.

Before Matt could say anything I answered for him, "No you may not see the signs!"

"James you cost us several accounts and a lot of business for that little stunt you pulled out there." Hembry said.

"Would that be one of the accounts that one of 'YOUR' account executives were going around and soliciting letters for, and for something the customer had no knowledge about." I said in a stern tone.

Hembry didn't know what to say. He didn't know that I had a driver get his customers to sign statements that UPS management had came out to their place of business, and were trying to get them to write a letter saying that the "illegal picket" we had conducted had hurt them and that they would no longer do business with UPS. Management couldn't get one letter from a customer to my knowledge, and the customers that they tried to get to write one...refused to. What management was doing was not only unethical, but illegal as well.

I would find out later, according to rumor, that one account did quit using UPS only after their unethical practice ended up backfiring on them, and costing UPS a couple of hundred thousand dollars, because the company they approached didn't know that the rally had even happened until UPS management told them about it. I never could prove it for sure, but management in Huntsville had rumored it to have had happened.

"Local 402 takes a position of a point of order that you did not give this man a warning letter before discharging him which is against the labor agreement." Matt replied.

"We have no intentions on bringing Mr. Earls back." Hembry replied, as he began collecting his things and putting them in his briefcase.

"Well I guess this will go to the panel then?" Matt asked.

"Yes it will." Hembry replied.

I sat there stewing over the whole thing and finally asked Hembry, "Explain to me why I'm not working pending the outcome of the grievance procedure since this is clearly not a 'cardinal sin', even if I was in the wrong Hembry?"

"James I'm not a liberty to discuss it any further." Hembry replied, while standing up.

"Well I want the money you owe me for my vacation for this past year, and try not to take so long on scheduling this to be heard by the panel" I demanded as they turned to walk out.

Once they left, I asked Matt what is going on, and he told me that I had pissed some boys from over in Atlanta off, meaning corporate, and that the man himself, the CEO of UPS, had ordered me fired immediately contract or no contract.

"I figured that they were going to deadlock it." Matt said.

"What do you mean deadlock it?" I asked not knowing for sure what was going on.

Matt explained it to me as a little maneuver one side uses to draw a matter out when an impasse is reached.

"What about Hoffa?" I asked.

"I've already spoken to Ken about your case and they're behind you one hundred percent." Matt said. Ken was the southern region vice president for the International Union, which meant that he had some stroke.

"What are they going to do?" I asked again waiting for him to answer my question instead of side stepping it.

"President Hoffa is aware of your case and they both assure me that they should have it worked out soon." Matt answered.

"How soon Matt? It's already been almost three months now, and were just getting around to the local hearing?" I asked sarcastically.

"It shouldn't be too much longer now," Matt replied.

"By the way James, I filed an unfair labor practice charge against UPS for this, and you should be contacted by a N.L.R.B board agent soon to discuss your case."

I still didn't feel any better. I knew though that if the N.L.R.B was getting involved that maybe that would give the union a little more leverage to bargain with and maybe then force UPS to go ahead and settle my case.

I continued to work on the pipeline, and the drive back and forth everyday was killing me. We were working eleven hours a day now, and including the time I spent on the road averaged out to be about fifteen hours a day. The time I dedicated to the pipeline meant very little time spent with Lesley and Mattie. I barely had enough time to sleep. I started to get a place to stay down there in Jasper, but I wanted to save all the money I could, because I didn't know how long I'd be out with UPS.

Several more weeks would pass and management was still holding to their guns. They were not intent on bringing me back. Joseph called me one Sunday evening to find out how I was doing and I told him tired.

"James...they've rumored that you wont ever be back." Joseph said, trying not to alarm me.

He didn't alarm me though, because I'd heard the same thing only from one of their own, which was a supervisor, who had been calling me frequently, and checking in on my family and me. This manager was also supplying me with what I wanted to know about what was going on in the center as far as how they were treating the employees, because I was still very worried about them.

"Yeah I know Joseph, that's what I've heard." I replied.

"We're trying to get a little money taken up for you, but I can't get hardly anybody to pitch in. I ashamed to say that some of the drivers are even saying that you've brought all this on yourself that they weren't going to give any money to you." He said while sounding disgusted.

"Well Joseph that's the way it's always been...you and I both know that." I replied, trying to calm Joseph down.

"But hell James, with Christmas coming up in a few weeks I'd figure they'd give something, even if it was only a dollar so you could buy your little girl some gifts." He replied angrily.

"It'll be a light Christmas Joseph, but don't worry about that. I've sold some of my things to come up with some money to buy her some stuff." I replied, while trying to reassure Joseph.

"There were several driver's that you'd gone in the office with in the past to fight for their jobs and they all turned their back on you, James." Joseph replied sounding even more upset.

"Well, what goes around...comes around Joseph. You know that. There'll be a day when one of them gets fired, or is out hurt then all of y'all need to remember what they said about me and what I had done for them, and not give them a single dime." I replied.

Joseph didn't say a word and let out a long sigh.

"How's everybody doing?" I asked.

"They're scared. We tried to hold a parking lot meeting the day after you were fired and no one would show up. We've even had a steward resign from out fear of getting fired too."

"What about Matt?" I asked growing frustrated.

"Hell we haven't even heard from that piece of crap since it all happened." Joseph replied.

"You mean to tell me that he's allowed UPS to destroy overnight the solidarity that we built?" I asked upset.

"Matt doesn't give a crap about us over here James. We've tried calling him but he won't return our calls." Joseph replied.

I talked to Joseph a little longer and he told me to give him a call if I needed anything. I thanked him and we hung up. I sat down in the chair, because by now, after learning of this development, I had become upset. I had been up pacing the floor after realizing that I was still very much interested in the well being of the members in Huntsville.

It had been several weeks since the local level hearing and I still had not received the checks that UPS owed me for my unused vacation. The amounts totaled in excess of $2000 and contractually (and I use that loosely with management) upon discharge they were supposed to pay the money they owed me the following pay period after my discharge.

It seems that management was holding out on paying me the money they owed me, and were trying to make it hard on my family. They had claimed they had discharged me under Article 52, although not for a 'cardinal sin', and were saying that since it wasn't a 'cardinal sin' they didn't have to pay me. Other words the language to pay me the money they owed didn't apply to me. In the other since then if this was the case that they were claiming, then I should had been allowed to work at UPS pending the outcome of the grievance procedure under language called 'innocent till proven guilty', and remain on the job. But this was not the case, and this clearly demonstrated that management had no respect for the contract, and were in fact acting quite typical of their nature, and were clearly bent on trying to break me.

After a day or two of trying to get a hold of Matt, I finally reached him, and I asked him why I haven't received my money yet, and he couldn't say anything other than I'll ask Hembry.

"Don't ask Hembry, Matt, you tell him I want my damn money or my job back." I replied, cutting Matt off.

Matt sat there on the other end not saying a word.

"Are you still there?" I asked perturbed.

"Yeah James," he replied.

"What's the word about the hearing at the national grievance committee?" I asked.

"It's been scheduled in a couple of weeks." Matt replied.

I could tell he was growing tired of me getting on his case about this, but I didn't care whether he liked it or not, because he worked for me.

"When did you find this out Matt?" I asked smartly.

"Uh...the other day." He replied.

"When were you going to let me know about it Matt?" I asked upset.

"I was going to give you a call in a couple of days." He replied.

"Am I going to have to go out there with you?" I asked knowing that I needed to, but the cost would have been close to seven hundred dollars, and that, was money that I did not have to spare.

"No... there will not be a need for it, because it looks like it's going to be deadlocked again only this time by the union." He replied.

I sat there for a minute thinking about the whole thing. Something wasn't making sense about the whole thing, but I couldn't just put my finger on it.

"Why are they going to deadlock it?" I asked.

"Well James they fired you out of compliance with the contract. The union is going to take a 'point of order' position and carry it to the deadlock committee." He replied.

"And…what's happened to Hoffa?" I asked.

"He's aware of it. I've talked to Richard Heck, the Teamster's small package director, and he's on top of it." Matt replied.

"Oh, by the way you need to give Leon a call to set up a time to meet so he can take you deposition." Matt finished.

We hung the phone up and I called the Birmingham, Alabama office of the National Labor Relations Board, and spoke with Leon, and we sat up a meeting for the following Friday in Cullman, Alabama.

I met with Leon in the presence of Matt, and Leon took my statement from the days that lead up to my discharge and the days since after my discharge. I told him everything that I knew about what UPS had done to me, as well as the PPG campaign and so on. I gave him copies of the pictures that I had taken during the meeting on August 11, 1999, and as well I showed him the actual signs that we used during the demonstration.

"I can't believe they are this stupid." Leon said while looking at the signs.

"What you mean" I asked.

"UPS knows better. They know they're going to have to put you back to work." He said.

I asked him what my chances were of getting my job back, and he told me not to worry about it. Regardless of what the outcome was in the grievance procedure, the N.L.R.B would force UPS to put me back to work if I received an unfavorable ruling during any part of the grievance procedure. He stated that what I had done out there that morning was protected under Federal Labor laws, and that I had without a doubt, engaged in 'protected concerted union activity'.

This was not a case of an illegal picket, work stoppage, slowdown or walkout like UPS was claiming. My case was nothing more than a 'political firing'.

How could the NLRB force UPS to put me back I asked? Leon explained to me that once the Regional Director of the N.L.R.B made a ruling, and if UPS refused to comply with their directive to reinstate me then it would wind up in Federal Court, and then go before a Federal Judge. Then if management was stupid enough not put you back to work, and refused to comply with the court order, then chances were that when the Federal Judge got finished with UPS…they could quite possible not be doing any business in the state of Alabama.

But, on the other hand management could drag this out for years by appealing the decisions. It could even possibly take up to ten years to come to an end, in an attempt to wait me out. When I heard this I became sick, because I knew that management had the money, and they didn't care for contracts, labor laws or anything.

Later in the week I received a call from Marty, from PPG, asking me what was going on with them. I was puzzled about her question?

"What do you mean going on?" I asked.

"Matt has not called us or anything, James. We hadn't even had a meeting since you had held one James, and people are beginning to ask me what's going on." She said while sounding upset with me.

"Give me a couple of days to try and get a hold of Matt, because Marty...I don't know what's going on. I honestly don't know." I replied, while trying to reassure her. We talked a little more before finally hanging up.

After a couple of days of trying to get a hold of Matt I finally got in touch with him.

"Matt, what's going on with PPG?" I asked.

"Well... not good news James." He answered while sighing loudly.

"Why? What's going on?" I asked.

"PPG has filed several charges that some illegal things had went on during the campaign and they have appealed the election." Matt said.

"What things?" I asked puzzled.

"Well they're claiming that you called an employee and threatened him with violence if he didn't vote yes." Matt said.

"That's bull crap Matt and you know!" I replied angrily.

"I never threatened anyone Matt." I replied.

"The only thing that I know that was even close was on their part when that 'no vote' of theirs threatened to run over me with her car. How about that?" I replied, while becoming very upset from the accusation.

"You'll have to meet with the N.L.R.B within the next two weeks to give another deposition concerning this accusation." He said.

"That's fine. You just tell me when and where Matt." I snapped back.

This was a typical tactic for a company that had just lost a union campaign to do. They would have an employee, or several employees mysteriously come forward citing union threats, intimidation and coercion, all of which are 'illegal' under the law, especially during an organizing campaign. PPG had had an employee to come forward that cited this very thing. Then what they'll do is call for another election, and then would spend tens of thousands of dollars on outside or "in-house" consultants specializing in counter-union organizing drives, and engage into another full-blown blitz. Then they stood a better chance of winning the election due in part by playing on the 'sympathy' of the fence straddles to the claim of union intimidation was the only way the union was voted in. Then the ones who voted yes in the last election, and were the fence riders, would more than likely vote no just out of spite to the union. It's happened dozens of times and even Martin Jay Levitt, famed author and former professional union buster, has written about similar union busting practices, and PPG was following the textbook on this one.

Several days passed and I finally received a call from the NLRB. It was Leon and he called me to try and set up a time for another meeting to take my PPG deposition.

I met with Leon and he asked me what I knew about an individual named Byron Jones, not his real last name, and a certain telephone conversation on a day just prior to the election.

I explained as follows: *I had been receiving calls from several employees in regard to general questions about the union and how it functioned and so on. I remember talking to this individual right before I had to go to work because I was eating dinner. I took the time out to answer his questions. He asked me the basics about Alabama being a right to work state, open and closed shop, stewards and then asked me about striking. It seemed that*

*there was a rumor floating around that we would force them to go on strike.
I explained to him that that was not true and that it was in fact a lie I explained to him about the mechanics that were involved to call a strike and
what was involved. I paid particular interest in explaining to him that he, a
member and his fellow members would have to vote on calling a strike and
then, and only then could the Teamsters call a strike provided that the majority of the members voted to do so. He then asked me what I thought about
scabs. I told him that 'personally' I have no use for the people but by law
there was nothing I could do. I went on further to explain to him that the
union could fine him or throw him out for scabbing, but I would not, and did
not encourage violence against anyone if someone chose to scab. As being a
steward it was my responsibility to protect that persons rights as well, even
though I didn't want to, but I had to. I told him that I would fight just as much
for his right not to join a union as well as his right to join.*

I asked Leon about what was said by the plaintiff, and Leon couldn't
go into detail, but told me not to worry about it. I went back to work that
day after meeting with Leon, and I called Matt on his cell phone and told
him that the people at PPG wanted to hold a meeting, and that they wanted
to start going over contract proposals, and I felt that we needed to keep
portraying as much of a positive image as we could, regardless of this
temporary setback.

Matt told me to go ahead and handle it, because he was going to be
out of town for the next couple of days to handle some other union business. I called Marty and told her to pick a day and to call me back. They
decided on Thursday, and I asked Oscar if I could be off, and he told me
that there wouldn't be any problem at letting me go to the meeting.

I worked on some contract language for them on my free time by
taking it out of my own contract book and rewording it to fit them. I liked
a lot of the language in the UPS contract book, but the language was too
broad, and could be interpreted by the company to tailor it in a way to fit
their need. I simply closed the loopholes.

I met with the PPG employees at the I.B.E.W union hall in Huntsville,
after Marty and several others hand-billed the plant letting everyone know
about the meeting.

We had a good attendance, one of the largest turnouts yet. I asked
that Marty sit with me at the front while I conducted the meeting, because
I wanted her to take notes and question me about anything she was unsure of. I provided several of the people there with what copies of the
proposal I could afford to have run off.

The meeting went well, and it seemed to rebuild their interest, their
faith and they finally saw something positive coming out of their efforts. It
had been several weeks now without any word from Matt, and I tried to do
some damage control, not to cover for him, because the truth was I was
just as upset about it as they were. I was trying to protect the local and
squash any perception of inadequacies anyone might be feeling at the
moment towards the union and it commitment to them. We were still at a
very crucial point, and my actions and answers that day could very well
have caused the vote to sway the other way if indeed another election was
called for by the N.L.R.B. I stood firm, and told them that I would still be

committed to them, and that I would not allow anything to happen. I was then asked point blank by one of them about the charge against me concerning the 'threat' claim involving the PPG employee, and I immediately began to dispel any rumors that may be circulating and I simply told them the truth about had transpired between the plaintiff and me.

Matt returned from his trip, and I met with him on the pipeline and handed him a copy of what I had been working on regarding the contract proposal, and he looked shocked, as he opened it up and began to flip through it. I guess he was shocked that I had been so thorough with the meeting, but the question was...was he impressed or did he feel threatened? Only time would tell. I finally received my vacation checks from UPS only until after I had threatened to seek legal action if I didn't receive them.

Several weeks had passed again and Matt attended the National Grievance Committee meeting to hear my case, and just like he had said, the union deadlocked the case before UPS had the chance to. It was now going to the Deadlock Committee, which would hear the case in Tampa, Florida, and the meeting was set for January 2001. I was not going to be able to attend this meeting either, because it would prove to be nothing but a waste of time and money on my part, because my case was looking as if UPS was going force it to go before an arbitrator to be decided on. They were doing this because they knew they had no strength in their claims and were going to take a chance on a 'union hating' arbitrator to get the case and rule in their favor, and as well, it meant that UPS could draw my discharge out a little longer, thus hoping to make me and my family suffer even more.

I received another call from Marty, and she asked again what was going on with Matt. It seemed that Matt would not return any of her phone calls, and it looked as if he had lost interest, and was pushing them all to the side. I was getting to the point of running out of answers and excuses, so I finally gave her Matt's cell phone, and his home phone number, and told her to give him a call and to call me right back to let me know what was going on with the campaign. She tried calling him, but still couldn't get any reply. Every time she'd call the local union hall to talk to Matt about the campaign, Jamie would give her some lame excuse of Matt's whereabouts, and then tell her that he'd call her back, only he wouldn't. He was beginning to treat them like he had been treating us at UPS for years.

I received a call from Donna, later in the week, who had assisted Marty with the campaign, sometime in late 1999. It seemed that she was going to be discharged from PPG for hitting another employee. I had asked her what had happened, and she began to explain to me that another employee had taped a sign on her back and when she asked him to remove it some of her hair had become tangled in with the tape on the sign, and when the man removed the tape from her back it pulled some of her hair out along with it. She then turned and slapped the hell out of the guy, and then PPG's management brought her into the office and questioned her about the whole incident.

Donna sounded very distraught over the telephone, because she didn't know what to do about her problem. I began to try and calm her down by treating her like I would've Teamster member from the center. I asked her what did she say to them and she told me she said nothing. I then asked her if she admitted to anything? She replied no. I asked her if there were any witnesses. She said no. I then asked her what this guy was like that she had slapped and what kind of employee he was. She began to describe his work ethics to me, and I immediately picked up on the fact that he sounded very much like a company butt kisser, and a definite 'no' vote. I advised her not to say anything at all to anyone, because I was pretty sure they were going to fire her anyway regardless of what she said, and I didn't want her to help PPG build their case against her with her own incriminating statements. I told her to call Leon with NLRB and Matt first thing in the morning and to keep her mouth shut to anyone else.

I knew that PPG was splitting hairs in an attempt to weed out all the 'yes' votes against them and, besides, they had a reason now to discharge her and make it look like it wasn't retaliation against her for her involvement in the PPG union campaign, which would've been illegal. PPG would fire her in the next couple of days.

The impact from her discharge had an immediate effect on everyone as a whole. They all were beginning to feel threatened of losing their jobs for their involvement in the organizing campaign, and then...during the next couple of meetings, the attendance would be off dramatically, and without a doubt we were losing them.

Meanwhile back at UPS...the integrity, honor and responsibility of the top managers of UPS were being summed up in the following case, which should enlighten the reader about the level of professionalism we have to encounter with them on a daily basis.

November 9, 1999, the timing of the most anticipated IPO in recent years remains in question. What are the true underlying motives behind the historical offering that is being made by dominate player in the package delivery industry?

Late Tuesday evening, UPS Executives priced its offering at $50 a share, which is a dollar above the $47-$49 dollar range which was expected by Wall Street analyst. The IPO reflects an over 90% gain in price from the 25 ½ price for each share of the privately traded stock, which is held mostly by its managers. UPS is selling a 10% stake in the company, which this move translates into roughly 109.4 million shares which will net UPS somewhere in the neighborhood of $5.3 billion after expenses. This astronomical amount does not reflect the over allotment of 10.9 million shares that were ordered by the underwriters of the major investment banks on Wall Street worth an additional $547 million.

One evasive reason UPS representatives gave for the IPO was that the money was to be used for future acquisitions and expansions, and a secondary reason was to create a market for the stock held by its employees. UPS's managers were the only ones allowed to purchase the stock or compensated with stock, and only until 1995 were the hourly employees permitted to purchase the privately held stock during its 97-year history. UPS claims that 65,000 of its 125,000 shareholders are hourly employees, but UPS, in usual fashion, will not disclose what percentage of its 564 million shares are owned by the hourly employees. Hourly employees are restricted to buying 42,500 shares, with many of the hourly employees being unable to purchase any substantial amount at one time.

It seems though that the only portfolio's that will truly prosper from this deal is the eight current and former UPS top executives. Evidently the big winners in this game will not be the lowly hourly employees who wear the "browns" and who drive the trucks and sort the package's in the hubs and centers.

UPS will take a portion of the takings and buy back the current holdings of stock from its current shareholders. But it seems that the stock, which UPS is offering to the public only holds 1/10th the voting power of the currently held stock of its managers, and I find this rather odd.

One major problem that UPS's executives might have is explaining about the recent ruling that forced UPS to set aside $1.442 billion to pay its penalties and back taxes to the IRS. Maybe UPS's managers aren't wanting to tell the who story behind why possible the IPO came to exist in the first place...

During the 1980's many different corporations chose to become self insured, which only stands to reason that it is very economical feasible for them to do in part because it maintains a sort of control over the liability expenditures that they may encounter. Of these companies like Hertz, Avis and even UPS who participated in this "self insuring" policy came under fire by state insurance officials with threats of potentially costly regulations. On February 24, 1983 a rather devious, and unscrupulous birth was about to take place whose cost of creation would later run into the billions of dollars if the scheme was exposed, but the rewards then were well worth the later risk as you will see, which will have the makings of one of the largest tax fines in history that had ever been levied against a U.S corporation for tax evasion.

At the offices of a well-known insurance brokerage firm in Briarcliff Manor New York were several of United Parcel Services top executives who were accompanied by an attorney. During the top-secret meeting the plan for an unholy generator of profits was outlined, and subsequently it was created in the formation of a foreign company, which wouldn't be owned directly by the U.S Corporation thus rendering it unaccountable to United States corporate income taxes. On June 28, 1983 as an end result of that initial meeting came the birth of UPSINCO Ltd, which was incorporated in Bermuda as a wholly owned subsidiary of United Parcel Service with UPS owning almost 1/6 of its stock. Then on November 12, 1983 the UPS Board of Directors changed its name to Over Sea's Partners Limited, or as it is commonly known as...OPL.

The new venture's untapped sources of revenue was going to derive from the insurance that was being charged to every customer who declared an "Excess Value Charge", or ECV, on their packages at the time of shipment with UPS. This ECV assessment of $ .25 per each increment of $100 declared value was going to prove to be a monstrous avenue for making an ungodly amount of revenue for UPS's top executives. In just 1983 alone, UPS declared $69.9 million in this new found source of revenue, but only claimed $21.4 million in damage and loss claims, which in turn left UPS's management with a "pre-tax", and I use that loosely, profit of $48.5 million dollars. It seemed that UPS's top thinkers had found a nitch for creating unrestrained wealth with a little 'creative' thinking and a profitable future...that is until Uncle Sam caught up with them. As fate would have it their "innocence and ignorant" argument would fall on deaf ears as Judge Ruwe, who was once a former IRS director of its tax litigation division in the 1980's during the height of the tax shelter era was drawn as their judge to oversee the United States case against UPS.

According to U.S Tax court Judge Robert P. Ruwe in 1999, that 'questionable' creation that was born 1983 wasn't as innocent as it seemed on the surface and as many of those involved were claiming. In the three-year-old tax case against UPS that dates all the way back to the 1983 tax year Judge Ruwe makes a statement about the type of transactions UPS made and UPS's involvement with OPL, which he says, "Sham transactions lacking in economic substance."

UPS's knowledge that this scheme could be later called into question first arose during the initial IRS investigation into the UPS-OPL venture back in 1983-1984, after UPS was questioned about the suspicious deductions that it claimed. It seems that UPS had set aside $230 million to "COVER ANY POTENTIAL TAX LIABILITY FOR THAT FIRST YEAR". If this was an accidental, an innocent mistake then why would they set aside this plethora of money to cover any LIABILITY that they may encounter in the future. Could that liability that they spoke about been the possibility of getting caught for not paying their share of their taxes? You decide.

In detailed court documents the United States strong case against UPS displays an intricate look inside the scheme of how a large and respected carrier, such as UPS, operated in the areas of insurances and Excess Value Charges, or EVC's. What was claimed by the Untied States was that UPS had illegally "Doctored" its tax deductions by charging customers three times more than competitive market prices for comparative insurance coverage on packages with declared values of more than $100, although UPS management denied any such overcharge to the customer.

Another area of concern for the U.S Government was the way in which UPS's employees were selling EVC without being properly licensed as insurance brokers. Judge Ruwe was concerned at this revelation, which was highlighted in court documents involving the cross examination, and questioning of the head manager of UPS's insurance department who was one of the key players present at the Briarcliff Manor meeting when the OPL scheme was concocted, and the testimony of Theodore J. Kletnick, & the lead IRS attorney in the case against UPS.

The EVC charges in question resulted in nearly $65 million of improper deductions being claimed by UPS, while they inflated the profits from OPL, which if you remember were not required to pay income taxes in the United States. According to Judge Ruwe it is highly unlikely that a smart corporation like UPS would sell itself out of more than $100 million in revenue without "completely" analyzing the issue.

Another major concern was the fact that UPS was selling EVC Insurance without even knowing if it was permissible under each states insurance laws. My question is, if they were unsure of the legality then why not ask a professional about it? I believe that they knew about it well in advance and decided to make as much money as they could until they finally got caught.

U.S Judge Ruwe noted that it was legal to arrange business activities in a way to reduce paying taxes, but against the law to engage in transactions whose primary purpose was to reduce its income taxes in the United States by illegitimate business purposes.

The twenty-five cent premium that UPS charged the customer for each increment in a $100 declared value of a package was ruled as additional income for UPS. The IRS argued successfully that UPS never fully accounted for the income tax on the EVC charges which netted UPS $77.7 million after paying out only $22.1 million after taking in $99.8 million in EVC premiums.

When UPS's expert witness, a professor from Wharton School of Business at the University of Pennsylvania was asked about whether or not the 25 cent/ $100 ECV charge made sense for UPS if the money it was taking in wasn't being paid to an insurer that UPS controlled? The expert witness testified, "It would be a rather strange business decision to basically give off that profit to an outsider."

One thing that Judge Ruwe refused to accept was the level of responsibility that UPS, National Union and OPL incurred. UPS stated that the EVC claim payments from 1979 to 1989 didn't exceed 40% of the total EVC revenue. But the Tax court found otherwise...It was found that UPS received $208 million in EVC charges from customers, but only paid out $77 million in claims for the 1989 year, which gives them a $131 million profit, and gives UPS a substantial profit ratio of a whopping 67%, which is a far cry from the 40% UPS claimed to have never exceeded. In Judge Ruwes ruling, he stated, "As a result, the level of risk, if any, that was shifted from UPS to NUF and OPL was insignificant." U.S Judge Ruwe found that National Union was only a "front" to the scheme, because it funneled the ECV money to OPL primarily to get around the United States tax consequences.

Although UPS's top executives dispute the interpretation of their true intentions by Judge Ruwe, he ruled that UPS only set up the OPL arrangement to illegally hide income from the U.S Government, to which UPS management denied any wrong doing to the end.

After the U.S Court found that UPS had charged its customers three times the market price for declared valued revenue was sure to draw some attention from major shippers and customers who may be seeking refunds. When UPS officials were asked if they sat aside any additional money to cover potential lawsuits from customers of givebacks concerning the legality of their overpricing customers their reply was simply, "Zero, none, zip chance of lawsuits by shippers." To the end UPS's spokesman still claimed that a lot of evidence was omitted at trial and that everyone may not have received a big picture of the evidence that was introduced at trial.

IRS officials were overwhelmed with the penalty portion levied against UPS in their tax case. The estimated overall tax liability owed by UPS could reach $1.76 billion, excluding some tax related benefits for interest from 1984-1999, after the $1.442 billion that was set aside in an after tax reserve. According to one IRS official, "The assessment of civil penalties in this case had the indicia of deceit."

This tax case has caused UPS to take an additional charge against its second quarter earnings of $1.442 billion. This recent charge filed with the Securities and Exchange Commission has wiped out its corporate profit for the first half of the year, which almost surely ensures that UPS will fall well short of matching last year's net income of $1.7 billion on $24.88

billion in revenue.

UPS is immediately changing the way it insures its packages, and UPS will no longer reinsure with its offspring companies by creating a U.S based company to take over the jobs of offering ECV's. UPS didn't want to face additional regulations from 50 state insurance commissions and the District of Columbia so they got out of the business altogether and the end result for OPL is that is was spun off from UPS and it's now a $1.3 billion company itself.

Even after being caught and punished for their scheme, the arrogance of UPS's top executives was truly and typically pathetic, but fitting of their style. UPS's spokesman continued to state that they didn't break the law by illegally trying to evade their responsibilities as a corporate citizen, although the U.S Tax court had found them guilty for their actions.

In typical spin fashion UPS's spokesman decided to make UPS the victim by blaming the court for besmirching the reputation of the company by continuously citing that it had built itself into the best carrier in the business by...excuse me for a moment...by treating people fairly and following the law. I'm sorry for that interruption but I almost became sick from it. It seems that they are suffering and living in extreme denial. But when they finally accepted the reality of having to pay the back taxes they were more concerned with the responsibility to the stockholders than to the responsibility to pay for their mistake. In my opinion an IRS official summed it all up in one statement, "this is another case of corporate greed getting its proper respect by the judicial system," and in my opinion this clearly, and without doubt establishes the character and integrity of those who have control of the corporation, which in typical UPS fashion all of this was kept out of the news and it is quite possible that the public still does not know the truth about this incident.

During the weeks of December 1999 I met up with Matt's brother in-law, Danny, whom began working on the pipeline as well. Danny had helped with the PPG campaign and I liked Danny a lot. We'd talk about the jobs he worked in the past and what was going on now with PPG, but he was concerned about the dwindling support of the PPG employees and agreed with me that Matt needed to do something about it before it was too late.

Christmas would come and pass and I had received word from Oscar that the pipeline job was coming to an end, and I had only about two more weeks worth of work left and after that I would be laid off. I hid that from Lesley until after Christmas, not wanting to ruin it for her, but I anguished with it during the holidays...I didn't know what I was going to do, and I was scared. Joseph had delivered about a thousand dollars that had been collected from everybody at the building, and Abel had collected some money as well, from some of the other feeder drivers from our sister centers. I used that money to try and pay what bills I could, and used what was leftover to buy Mattie some Christmas presents. Joseph managed to deliver Christmas for us that year and I'll never forget him for it, because without him there wouldn't have been much of a Christmas for my family. We only received one day off from the pipeline after we had been working seven days a week now, sometimes thirty-eight hours straight without ever leaving the truck. It was rough on us all.

I worked on the pipeline until January 7, 2000, and was laid off, I was now officially unemployed and there was no end in site with UPS. I had managed to save a little money while on the pipeline, and decided on taking a week or two off, and spend it with Lesley and Mattie. It had been almost four months of being away from them and I missed them both so very much.

On the morning that I was laid off, I received my final checks and I then drove straight to the local union to see about signing up for another job, and to put my name on the job list. I made the two-hour drive to Florence and walked in the office and found Jamie sitting at her desk on the phone. She looked up at me and waved and I took a seat waiting until she got off the phone. Several minutes passed and finally she hung up.

"How are you James?" she asked.

"Doing fine. Where's Matt?" I asked her while looking outside the window for his Lincoln.

"Oh, he's over at PPG today James meeting with them." She replied, while acting strangely.

"Oh really. What about?" I asked.

"It seems they had been complaining about wanting to have a meeting, and he went over to talk to them. I don't know what for. There's nothing we can do for them now, at least, not until we find out about those charges." She replied.

I sat there thinking why he didn't tell me about any meeting? If I had known about it I would've gone to it. He didn't have to tell me anything, but I figured it would have been nice to know. I went ahead and signed up on the job list, and asked her to tell Matt to give me a call as soon as he came in. I left there and went straight home. Later that evening Matt called me, and I told him I needed some work. He asked me if I had a Hazardous Material endorsement on my CDL, and I told him no, but I could get one.

Matt told me about a job that was going to be opening up was driving a dump truck on Redstone Arsenal Army base, here in Huntsville, for a clean up project that was about to get underway. I said that I'd be interested about it and he told me to call him back the next day.

The next day came and I called him right at 8:00 a.m at the local. He answered the phone, and we discussed what was going to be required for the job and that I was going to have to take a Hazardous Material training class to get certified to haul the materials, and the only class there was for this kind of training was going to be conducted at the Painters Union hall in Florence. That didn't matter to me, because I was used to a long drive everyday. The union hall was only a few blocks from ours so he called their local union's president and enrolled me into their class.

Matt had asked if I would mind Donna riding over with me that the job I would be getting actually needed someone to drive a little bus around as well. He was going to let Donna have that one. I said I didn't mind, and I called Donna and told her we could car pool if she liked.

I received my little card showing I was certified on February 13, 2000, and Donna and I drove up to the local union hall to let Matt know that we had just completed to the course and to find out about the job.

We walked in and Jamie was there, but as usual, Matt was not. We all made small talk and before leaving Jamie told me that I needed to catch up on paying my dues, because I was almost four months behind.

"No, I shouldn't be behind on them." I replied.

"James we haven't got a payment from you on them for sometime. I didn't remember you filling out a withdrawal card when you were fired...did you?" She asked.

"No Jamie I didn't, because Matt told me that he was going to pay them for me." I replied, referring back to our conversation on August 11, 1999.

"I don't know anything about that, you might ought to talk to Matt about it James" She replied nervously.

Something wasn't right here, because Jamie did the entire record keeping and she practically ran the local union office, and she was aware of everything that went on in the office, and in the union, because she was a local union officer who sat on the executive board. She knew everything. Everything but this, and I began to become very uneasy.

"Tell Matt to call me when he comes in that I have a serious problem with something." I replied.

I stewed over it the whole way home and I talked to Donna about the situation, and she remembered back to when Matt had told me that he'd pay my dues for me even if he had to himself. I waited by the phone that day and no call came, so I tried calling him on his cell phone the next day and still...there was no answer. I called Jamie at the local and told her to tell him to call me, and that if he didn't...that I was coming over there to talk to him in person, and she said that she'd relay the message to him.

While waiting for Matt to return my call I looked for my copy of the local 402 union bylaws, and looked up the section that would apply to me in regards to the non payment of dues, and there it was in black and white. "The outcome of anyone being late one month in dues will make such said person ineligible to run for office in any election." I said aloud as I read them. "That son of a bitch," I said to myself. He had just eliminated his main competition from the next election. The longer I waited for his call the madder I became. Finally Matt called me.

"Matt we seem to have a little problem about my dues," I replied, while shaking from the anger inside.

"Yeah that's what Jamie told me." He replied acting strange.

"Well?" I asked.

"Well What?" Matt answered in a smart tone.

"You do remember what you said to me about my dues don't you Matt?" I asked knowing his response before it came.

"No, what are you talking about?" He said, while sounding puzzled.

"You know what the hell I'm talking about Matt. You said that you'd pay my dues for me while I was out." I snapped back to him.

"I don't remember telling you that at all James. You know you needed to pay your dues while you were out." He replied.

"You piece of crap you." I said, and slammed down the phone.

I was so upset that it was a good thing that little coward wasn't in front of me. I would have stomped his brains out right there.

I could not believe what had just happened. I felt like such a fool. I couldn't believe that this little piece of crap had screwed me over like this.

I called the International Union and finally talked to Richard and Ken about what Matt had done and they told me that it was a local union affair.

"Local union affair my ass." I screamed at them and hung the phone up. Here this officer of the union, had violated several articles of the International Constitution, and this was only a local union affair? Bull! They should have jumped all over this. It was their job as union leaders, as Teamsters, to protect and defend my union rights, and me as a member from this sort of 'old guard' trick, but if the truth were known, they were probably mixed up in it too, because they were part of Hoffa's old guard regime.

I called Leon, with the NLRB, and explained to him what was going on, and he couldn't believe it. He said that he would call Matt to try and find out what was going on, but it really wasn't in his power to handle it. He then referred me to the Department of Labor, Office of Labor Management Standards, whom oversees union rights violations, and there was little they could do about it until a union election came up, and to make things worse, Matt put Jamie up to calling me to tell me that it would be a good idea if I stayed away from PPG, and their employees that I've done enough to jeopardize the campaign. Jamie and I would have a knock down drag out fight over this after I told her that Matt didn't do a damn thing for those people at PPG. Hell they couldn't ever get him on the phone when they needed him.

He was treating them just like he did us at UPS, and now that he got what he wanted, which was to get me out of the political arena, and he didn't need any backlash from Marty and the other PPG employees for screwing me over. Jamie proceeded to tell me that if I'd kept my mouth shut to that guy that none of this would've happened. She was in fact blaming the PPG appeal on me.

The truth of the matter was that she never got off of her fat butt to come down there and help us except for one time that we had a cookout and that was only to get some free food. None of the officers ever did anything except for a Trustee named Joey who showed up one time at a meeting with Matt to discuss his life history. They never did anything of substance. I had put that union in that plant, with the help of Marty and others, and now they were going to crap on me like that. Matt was losing the campaign from his neglect and lack of caring for the PPG employees, and he was in desperate need of a scapegoat in case he lost this election, so he found one...me.

The funny thing about Jamie was that when I had ran against Matt in the last election, and it looked like I was actually going to win, she talked about Matt like he was a dog. She said how sorry he was, how he was wasting money, and everything. Now she's defending him, and telling me how great he is and everything just like a lot of the Carey Supporters did after Carey was ruled ineligible and Hoffa was put in office. She's practically cussing me out. Finally I had enough and told her, "I hope I can run in the election so I can beat Matt and fire your deadbeat ass," and I hung up on her. I have never felt so betrayed in my whole life.

I called Henry who was local 402's vice president and explained to him what had happened about my dues, and he told me that Matt didn't have the power to pay my dues, and I told him that he did have the power to, and we talked for several more minutes about the problem, and he told me he would call me back later that evening. I waited for a few hours and he returned my call, and he said that Matt had told him that he didn't tell me that about paying my dues. I was feeling abandoned. I expected this from UPS management but not from my own union. I never saw it coming.

I immediately began to become extremely worried about whether or not Matt was doing anything at all in regards to my case. I began to wonder as well, as to whether or not he had a hand in my discharge and if he had been working in conjunction with UPS on this all along. A lot of things that were going on with my case weren't making sense to me.

I decided not to call Matt back, but instead I drove over to the local union hall and walk in on him unexpected. He'd have nowhere to run and hide. As I pulled off of Woodward Ave onto the street that the local union was located and there sat his Lincoln. I parked out front and walked on in and, Jamie looked at me and then back to Matt, who was sitting in his office, who then comes out to see who it was she looking at. Jamie didn't say a word to me, and Matt came out into the center office, and stood there nervously, and after I noticed that all the color had left his face he asked me to come into his office.

"I want to know when I'm going to start this new job?" I asked, while staring at him in the eyes, but he wouldn't look at me and just turned away.

Matt turned and walked back into his office and he asked me to take a seat. I walked in looking around and noticed we were alone and took a seat on a ratty old couch he had in his office.

"James I've been trying several times to call Scott who works for the construction company handling the project but I haven't been able to get him." Matt replied looking at Jamie as she came to a filing cabinet just outside the door.

"Jamie do you mind? This is personal," I said in a smart tone as she stood there eavesdropping to our conversation. This pissed her off, but I didn't want he nosy butt just standing there listening to me, because it was none of her business.

Jamie walked off cussing me under her breath, and I turned back to Matt a said, "How about trying now Matt...while I'm here?"

Matt leaned back up in his chair, and began shuffling papers around searching for the number. Finally he found it and called the guy, as I sat back into the couch crossing my leg and staring right at him while he dialed the number. What do you know? He got a hold of him. Matt talked to him about the project and talked out loud so I could he what he was telling him. According to the conversation, it would be another two to three weeks before he was going to need me. Matt hung up and I asked him about my case with UPS. It had already been heard and deadlocked again, which meant it was going before an arbitrator to be decided on. I didn't know what to say. He had failed to tell me again about my case so I decided right then that it would be best if I went ahead left before I did something he might have regretted.

I was so disgusted with the whole thing. The screwing I had received from the UPS managers, and now the lies from the union only compounded my frustration. I was ready to say the hell with it all and just walk away.

I just decided to lay low for a couple of weeks and signed up for my unemployment insurance and began drawing a whopping $180.00 a week from it. I had to fill out several applications for various job interviews that fit my qualifications.

One major problem I was going to have, was explaining a discharge from UPS and the circumstances involved. It wasn't looking good at all.

One job they gave me to follow up on was with Krispy Kreme doughnuts as a driver. I went down to the plant and met with the manager, but the job had already been filled.

Lesley had begun keeping three kids on the side to help try and supplement our income, because it had been over a month now since I had been laid off from the pipeline, and I was still unable to find any work. UPS was still dragging their feet on choosing an arbitrator, and although the union had evaluated and ranked the list supplied from the Federal Government, UPS had not. It seemed that it would be awhile longer before they could get around to it because Hembry was on vacation. This was a bunch of hogwash. UPS doesn't revolve around this one man. They could have already had it done but this was nothing more than another stalling tactic to drag this out even longer. I became very upset with Matt about the relaxed position that he was taking on this recent turn of events and he simply said it was out of his hands.

Our money had run out, and we were forced to vacate our house, because the bank was preparing to foreclose on it. This was very upsetting for us all. When moving out that last piece of furniture, I looked back on the time of bringing Mattie home from the hospital after running across the banners that I had put up in the yard to celebrate that joyous day, and I sat down inside and cried. We were leaving more than just a house. It was our home. Mattie's first Christmas was here. Mattie's first birthday, her first steps, her first snow.

We finished loading everything up, and before leaving I took one last walk through and I didn't want Lesley to see me cry. I could almost see Mattie walking through the hall, and see her crawling on the floor. It was one of the hardest things I had ever experienced.

"The door!" I said aloud. I cannot forget our bedroom door. They may get the house, but they won't get this door. I walked back outside to my truck and found a hammer and screwdriver and went back inside as Lesley asked me what I was doing, and I told her to just wait that I'd be right back. I walked back to our bedroom and closed the door. There it was etched on the back of the door.

We had marked on the door Mattie's growth for the past two years. I would've died for this door.

I took the screwdriver and placed it under the pin in the hinge and began to knock the pin upward. Finally the door came off and I put it to my side and carried it out and Lesley seemed relieved when I brought it out and began to cry. She'd forgotten all about it. We were moving into an apartment that was located in a rougher part of town, over near a housing project, but we managed to make the best with what we had, but I was still very unhappy. I was feeling very guilty for losing our home. I wanted more for Lesley and Mattie but I couldn't give them anything more than this. I felt ashamed.

After a week or so, I received an interesting phone call from Danny, Matt's brother in-law. He wanted me to meet with him, because he had something that might be of interest to me. I asked him just to tell me now but he declined and said, "Not over the phone."

I didn't have a problem meeting with Danny and I agreed to meet with him at a Cracker Barrel restaurant located in Athens Alabama, which would be sort of halfway between Huntsville and Florence.

I made the drive over that Tuesday morning, during the month of March 2000, and as I pulled around to the front of the restaurant I didn't notice Danny standing out front of the restaurant.

I went ahead and backed into a parking spot off to the side, and waited for Danny to arrive. Finally after a few minutes Danny pulled in across the parking lot and got out of his car and began looking around the parking lot. He didn't know what I was driving, and I decided to go ahead and wait a minute or two, and watch him to make sure that someone else wasn't with him, or in another car following him. I wasn't too trusting of anyone associated with the union now, and who knows if I was going to be jumped or what?

I had decided before leaving the house to carry my .38 pistol, careful not to let Lesley see it, as I tucked it in my pants, and covering it with my shirt just in case something was to happen during the meeting that was out of the ordinary. I was beginning to have suspicions that this could be a set up.

I remembered hearing about how cinder blocks had been thrown off overpasses, in Birmingham, and through the windshields of people running against the local 612 old guard family regime, and I was not going to take a chance. I honestly didn't know what to expect, but I felt better carrying the gun. I knew that Matt had questionable ties to certain people who were less 'sympathetic' to my plight, and were subject to help 'persuade' individuals in making decisions at the drop of a hat. I wasn't going to take an ass kicking from anybody.

I sat there crouched down in the seat for a few more moments, and I finally felt comfortable that no one had followed him, so I went ahead and got out and I walked over to where he was standing. I held out my hand, and he shook it and told me he was glad to see me. We went on inside and sat down at a table and ordered our food. I sat there waiting for Danny to 'start the show'.

Finally Danny looked at me and told me that he knew everything I wanted to know about my discharge. I sat there puzzled.

"What are you talking about...everything?" I asked bluntly.

"Everything." Danny replied.

"For instance?" I asked.

"It seemed you've not only pissed UPS off, but Hoffa, and the other big boys as well." He replied, while taking the wrapper off of his straw.

I didn't have a clue at all with what he was saying.

"Are you recording me James?" Danny asked, while leaning over the table and looking at my shirt.

"No I'm not Danny." I replied, hoping that he wouldn't notice the bulge being made from the gun.

"That little incident that got you fired back last year at UPS made Hoffa and the others look like a bunch of fools." He replied, while taking a sip of his drink.

"How did that make them look like fools?" I asked, still lost with what he was driving at.

"Stop and think for a minute James. Here a little 'pee on' like you has managed to do something that he has not been able to do. You all had united a group of people and they supported you. You were getting too much power in Huntsville. Hoffa knew it, UPS knew it, and Matt knew it." He replied.

"Danny we're only one building...a hundred or so people. What significance is that?" I asked smiling. It all sounded ridiculous.

"You're failing to what this could've led to." He replied, while looking at me.

I was failing to see what he was implying, because I had no idea what in the world he was talking about.

"It was no secret that everyone knew you was going to run again against Matt in the next election. They all knew that you'd probably win this time, and then you'd start holding UPS to the book, and then when the members in Local 612 saw how strong you were, and how you was enforcing the contract...they'd then want the same thing out of their officers. The union was scared that they might to have to finally start doing their job for a change. You've got more influence than you think James. The old guard doesn't want a reformer like you in control of a local union. Didn't you openly support, and campaign for Tom Leedham against Hoffa?" He replied.

"Yeah, why?" I asked.

"That should answer why Hoffa hasn't stepped in to stop all this?" Danny replied.

"It was all about politics." I said while sitting back in my seat. I had suspected it, but I didn't know for sure. How was he to know? I knew that he was Matt's brother-in-law, but was he sure about this?

"Exactly" Danny said out loud with several people looking at us.

"I don't know Danny it sounds a little far fetched to me." I said, while taking a sip of my tea.

"Ask your self this question then...why'd they fire you in the first place when everyone else only got warning letters. Didn't you find it strange that you were the only one fired? Hell...this is an open and shut case James. Why has it taken six months to get this far in the process and its still not resolved? You've should've been back to work the next day. Why hasn't Hoffa stepped in and forced UPS to put you back to work and now all of a sudden...this thing about your dues." He replied.

"What do you mean about my dues?" I asked sitting up now from this revelation. How did he know about my dues when I haven't told anyone outside about this?

"I know all about that too, James" He replied, as he sighed.

"What exactly do you know?" I asked, feeling the anger beginning to swell inside.

"I was on the yard one evening loading up some dynamite and Oscar came up to me, and said that he heard my brother in law, Matt, was going to run again. We began a discussion about who could possibly beat Matt. I told him yeah that he was and so were you. Oscar then told me that Matt was going to let you go suspended for the non payment of dues and that I'd better keep my mouth shut." He replied.

"You mean he said this to you" I asked in an upset tone.

"Yeah, I would have told you sooner, but I was afraid Matt wouldn't let me work. I need the insurance to pay for my wife's illness. I'm sorry James, I had no other choice." He replied.

I wasn't upset with him, but maybe this was what I had been looking for. Danny might be the one able to get this matter cleaned up and then I'd be able to run again. I sat at talked with Danny for about another hour. He told me about some of the unethical behavior that went on during the Coke strike, back room dealing on job sites and on the payment of work vehicles, questionable trips to Tunica, possibly stealing cable TV services and Matt getting his family members jobs, which was all just typical old guard behavior.

It seems that a lot of interesting things had been going on in our local for some time. I now just had to figure out how I could use this to my advantage.

I called Matt later on in the week and UPS still hadn't picked an arbitrator, and I told Matt that the next time I called he'd better have an answer for me, or there was going to be a problem.

I was actually the one having a problem. We had been unable to keep the payments up on Lesley's car and the bank came during the night and took it away from us with no warning at all. I had to go out and pay a twenty-five dollar fee to the repo-man just to be able to get our property out from inside the car, and the trunk. I had to find a job, and I wasn't having any luck and all of the jobs that I was being sent to, by the unemployment office, I could make just as much off of unemployment and stay home rather than work at these slave shops. If they had insurance, or something I would've jumped on it, but I still had about three months left on what insurance I had accumulated while working for the pipeline, and I was trying to be selective.

I went to Service Transport, a freight company, and answered an ad for a driver. I went to the interview and was asked about why I wasn't with UPS anymore, and I had to explain to him about the discharge and all he had to say was "Why didn't the union get my job back"? I left there upset. Why couldn't they get it back? I then realized I knew why, because they didn't want to.

Over the weekend I was looking through the want ads and saw that RPS was looking to hire a few package car drivers. I perked up. "I can do that," I thought. Sure I could, heck I did it for eight years. I knew the job. I still had my D.O.T physical card, and I was a safe driver, and I knew most of Huntsville. "This was a sure thing," I thought to myself.

I filled out the application and talked with a manager whom immediately didn't seem interested at all. I never got a call, and when I finally called them back...the job had been filled.

I knew then that it was because of one of two things. It was either the discharge, or my involvement in the Teamsters union, or both.

I decided that it was time to start working smarter and use the law to my favor, so I went ahead and filed an unfair labor practice charge against RPS and Federal Express for discrimination against me for my union involvement.

Everywhere else I went I was sure to wear my Teamster jacket and make it known that I was a member of the union. Every interview I went on and I felt that I was qualified for the job, and did not receive the job I filed a labor board charge.

Finally I went back to the unemployment office and noticed that Kryspy Kreme was looking for another driver. I decided to go over in person this time, and as I walked into the back of the building and went up to the window, I asked to see someone in charge of hiring. I had my Jacket on just in case.

An older gentleman then came out, and I handed him my paperwork from the unemployment office, and he looked over it, and he asked me about my previous employment, and why I was no longer with UPS, and I told him simply "a labor dispute," and left it at that. I noticed that he kept looking at my jacket, and finally I said to him that I wasn't interested in organizing his business...I just wanted a job.

He stood there and he told me to give him a day or so and that he'd call me back, so when I left there I went ahead and filled out another Labor Board complaint form, because I knew that it was going to be just like the others. I waited by the phone and finally the call came. I had the job. Shortly after receiving word from the NLRB that RPS and Fed-X had received the complaint they were interested in giving me a part time job, to which I declined.

I went ahead and went to work, riding with other driver's delivering doughnuts, learning the routes. I was going to be used for vacation coverage, but I was hoping to be back at UPS before they needed me.

Management and the union had finally reached an agreement on what arbitrator to use. They had a list of eleven and each would strike one off until there was only one left. I asked Matt what kind of person she was, and he said she was pretty fair. That didn't make me feel any better, because heck...I didn't trust him at all. I asked him when the date was set, and he told me they had been unable to get a hold of her, and that it all depended on her schedule. If she had something open on her book, then it could be soon or it could be several more months. Then the decision itself, after she heard my case, could take any where from a few days to a few months. I've been this far, and now I've got a job. I be damned if I give up now.

Matt and I would have several more falling outs after the date had been set for my hearing. It was to be set in May 2000.

I wasn't trusting Matt at all by now, and I had written him several times trying to get a copy of the letter he said that he supposedly sent to me concerning my dues back in February 2000, but I never received a copy of it. I had the right to the information, according to the local union bylaws, but Matt refused to let me have it.

I resorted to sending all of my future correspondence to the local union via certified mail to reduce any chance of something important being "accidentally" lost, and I also wanted to leave a good paper trail for later use. I managed to request a copy two more times and I still did not receive it. The last letter I sent them I requested not only a copy of the letter and a copy of their return receipt, but any and all information as well about the local union paying the dues for some of its officers, which was similar to my case.

It seemed that the local union might have paid the dues for Joey while he was out or something, and Matt may have paid them directly for him or so I had heard from Danny. Joey and Matt were best friends, and shared property on a lake around Florence. I never received a reply other than the receipt where Jamie had signed for my request. The union was denying my right to information and in the way it conducted it business.

I called Leon with the N.L.R.B and explained to him what Matt was doing and Matt's refusal to grant me access to the local unions records and books. What did he have to hide? Evidently he had a lot to hide.

I told Leon that I was afraid of Matt handling my case that he may try and sabotage it. Then Leon gave me his advice, "Be ready to present your case before the arbitrator." He replied.

I was shocked. Here this person was supposed to defend me, and now I had to worry about him selling me out me before the arbitrator, so I began to research similar cases at the Huntsville law library, and proceeded to build support for my case and gather evidence to support my position. Matt had first decided to represent me himself, rather than to use an attorney, because it was such a simple case. Hembry had begged him from the beginning to use an attorney but management couldn't use one unless the union agreed to do so first. Hembry was afraid, because he knew that he didn't have a case. Matt bragged about how he would tear Hembry apart and so on.

Two weeks before the date I was scheduled to go before the arbitrator, Matt called me, and told me he had changed his mind, and that he was going to turn it over to the local unions attorney to let her handle it.

I became extremely upset from this, and all of my suspicions were beginning to come true. All of a sudden here at the end, he turns it over to an attorney to handle my case who had no idea what was going on, and it was only just two weeks before it was to go to the hearing.

This wasn't enough time to get the affairs in order. I had had enough. I told Matt right then on the phone, "If I wind up losing my case I will sue your ass, and Hoffa's too. Do you understand me?" and hung up on him.

I managed to work one day at a time. It was the best I could. Some union I had was all I thought about, but I couldn't blame the union for this. It wasn't the unions fault...it was those fat, old guard sell out bastards up in the "Marble Palace" that were to blame. I had to remember that and remain focused on the business at hand.

Finally, I called Richard Heck up in Washington, D.C, and explained to him what Matt had done and once again, he blew me off. I managed to tell him that he and Hoffa could expect a lawsuit if they allowed Matt to lose my case and hung up on them.

Two days later, after the call to Richard, UPS wanted to meet with me and make an offer. I was excited about the news and looked forward to ending this nightmare. It seemed that my threats of suing Hoffa and Matt had paid off. Maybe I should have done this eight months ago and I'd been back to work then.

I met UPS management at the Pipe Fitters union hall, whom Hembry, Stanson and Walt represented UPS. Matt was with me, and I didn't speak a word hardly to him. Hembry handed me a copy of their terms and I looked over them and I didn't like them one bit. It was as if they were forcing me to admit that what I had done was wrong. I would receive my back pay and my discharge would be listed as a suspension on my records. I was tired, and I just wanted it to be over and to start trying to put my family and health back together. I reluctantly signed it.

If I had refused their offer and it went before the arbitrator and lost my case then that would've been it for the union. The N.L.R.B would've stepped in then, but who knows how long it would take. If I would've chose to fight it out then it would've been nothing but a gamble. It was finally over, and I was back at UPS.

I was scheduled to start back to work the following Monday and I went ahead quit Krispy Kreme that Tuesday and took the rest of the week off. I was very relieved to say the least and very happy it was over. It had been a very long and exhausting eight months, which had cost me a brief stay in the hospital along with a separation from my wife, which this discharge had resulted in me losing my house, cars and having to file bankruptcy...I felt that it was a terrible price, for a steward who believed in union reform and standing up for members and all of their rights, to have to pay...but this wasn't over, it was only beginning.

Chapter 24

"I've been back now for less than two days and management is start-ing back up on me, and they're once again trying to accuse me of falsifying my records. I thought all this was going to end...they leave me no choice now but to get the Federal Government involved now. Matt had lied and deceived me to take me out of the picture of politics all together and he is planning to get rid of me for good."

I had beaten the odds that were against me. Many fellow members wagered that I would not get my job back, and it was even in the casual conversation amongst the management at UPS with them often telling their employees, "He won't be back...ever!" But I had proved all of them wrong. I wasn't about to let UPS's management beat me, but the toll that it had taken on me, both physically and mentally, was exhausting, and I was at the worst state of health that I had ever been in my entire life. I was dead tired. I had...my wife had...and my little three year old daughter had, just been put through nine months of pure hell for no reason.

Certain manager's would later admit, that I had been wrongfully dis-charged and even some of the "key" players involved in the whole ordeal would later come to me and apologize for what they had did to my family and me.

I had done my job as a steward, but in the process I paid a terrible price for it as well. I had stood up for just one Teamster who had been unjustly discharged, and I in turn paid one of the ultimate prices in labor...it cost me my job and my family.

I felt a lot of things during this time, but the one feeling that I felt the most of was betrayal. Not by the members themselves, but by the very institution I was defending...the union, but I would deal with the old guard in my own way and at a later time of my choosing. I was adjusting to the thought of returning to UPS and I actually looked forward to completing that long, hard victory walk back into the Huntsville center.

I was planning to jump back in the saddle of being union steward as soon as I could, and I was looking forward to it, but that too would prove to be short lived.

After I had returned to UPS it was only a matter of time before I would have a run in with management. This was not of my choosing for I had decided to lay low for several months, and not try to be perceived as an instigator about anything. I was planning on being low key, because I knew that UPS was very pissed off at me after that they had lost their 'monumental' case against me. And I knew that they would be in fact gunning for me, and this first little incident would prove so.

Upon returning to UPS I decided to bump a less senior driver off of his run which was to the Montgomery Alabama hub. The first thing in store for me was a safety ride, which was to be conducted by the supervisor of our group, Walt. This was standard practice to all employees who had been out of service for any period of time due to injuries and even discharges.

When I reported for work that evening I went through the equipment pre-trip process and various other safety related things, and Walt was making sure that I had not forgotten how to 'safely' operate the feeder equipment. This took me a little longer than UPS' standards allowed, but Walt didn't say anything as I began to notice that he wanted to get on the road, and that he was becoming very anxious.

I finally got the equipment put together, and we left the yard in Huntsville bound for the Montgomery hub, which was almost four hours away.

Less than ten minutes into the trip Walt asked me something totally off the wall, and something that I wasn't expecting at all.

He led into it with the usual UPS technique of asking about my family, and I chose not to disclose anything about my current family situation, which wasn't good at the time, and simply said, "They're fine."

Walt then proceeded to ask me about what my plans were concerning union politics. He had unknowingly ventured into something where, in my book, he was not welcome.

What do they care about what I do in regard to my plans and future involvement in the union? It was none of his business and I began to smell a rat. So what did I do? I fed the rat a little cheese. I told him what I thought he wanted to hear knowing all along that the information I was pumping him up with would make it back to Hembry, and then to the appropriate people within the union.

I told Walt that I was possibly interested in running for office again, maybe on the International level as a vice president or even small package director, but at the moment, I just wanted to do my job and be left alone. He picked up on my tone and my evident lack of interest, and he just sat back and enjoyed the long ride.

Several days later I would come back into Huntsville pulling my loads from Montgomery, and after breaking the trailers down I walked inside to check out when a preload manager, named Don Woodson, the same supervisor who had run over Petey with a package car during the strike, approached me while I was standing at the turn in counter.

"James I need to talk to you about why you were late with the loads yesterday." Woodson said, while flipping through his clipboard.

"I wasn't late yesterday Don." I replied.

"I know you were late yesterday James, because I had written the time you arrived down on my sheet." He replied, with his face growing redder by the second.

I could tell he was beginning to become pissed, and I could also tell that he was looking for a confrontation.

"I don't care what your sheets show Woodson I wasn't late." I replied, while raising my voice, as Abel was standing over by the drink machines and watching the whole thing unfold.

"I want you to know I'm writing this down in your file that you were late." Woodson screamed out.

It was on then. We exchanged words back and forth, and I finally I just walked off. Abel stopped me, and asked me what was going on, and I explained to him what Don was saying, and he then walked over to find out what was going on. I stood over by the coke machine watching Abel talk to him, and finally after I had enough of sitting on the sidelines, I walked over to where they were standing.

"James this doesn't concern you." Woodson screamed out.

"The hell it doesn't!" I replied.

"You're not even a steward anymore now LEAVE." Woodson replied.

I was floored, and I didn't know what to say, because Matt hadn't told me anything about this and this was news to me. I walked away in shock.

I called Matt about this recent revelation, and he hee-hawed around and he never would give me a straight answer. He finally told me that he felt that it would be best if I lay low for a while, and tried not to cause any problems. I was disgusted after everything I had done for this local union he was going to strip away the privilege of being a steward. I wasn't about to take this sitting down.

I began to plan out how to combat this new turn of events. So as a safety measure I went ahead and filed a grievance about the "Woodson incident" along with two separate labor board charges, one against management and the other against the local union for failing to bargain in good faith.

I remembered back to the day that Hembry told me, as I signed the agreement, that this 'waging of war' was over, but I soon found out it was just beginning again after management had violated the cease fire truce between us, and I wasn't going to sit back and allow them to systematically set me up for a 'dishonesty' discharge for stealing time.

I immediately called the Birmingham Alabama feeder department and had copies of my time cards faxed up to me. I knew that these copies would show what time I had arrived in Huntsville, because I would have had to hit a button on my computer that would have stamped my 'finished work' time on the timecards...and there it was. My time card had shown 6:20 a.m. as the returning to building time, and not the time of 6:50 a.m. that Don was showing. I just kept this little bit of information to myself, at least until the local hearing.

When Matt received his copy of the charges from the N.L.R.B against him, he was rumored to have flipped out. He couldn't understand how all this had brought him into my charges against UPS. It was simple. He was failing to uphold and make management keep their word to leave me alone, and I decided early on that I was going to start holding him accountable as well, and that he was going to do his job. Management would come to withdraw their little 'notation' on my records after I revealed that the finished work time did not match the hand written time of Don. Matt managed to put on a good little show in the office in front of Hembry, but I knew that it was all just an act to deceive me into thinking that he was now going to fight for me, but honestly I didn't really care what Matt did now or in the future, because I was not going to withdraw either one of the charges against them both.

Later in the week I had received another call from Marty concerning how no one had heard from Matt or the local for months, and that everyone out there at PPG was beginning to lose interest, and the local was beginning to be perceived as if they didn't care one way or the other about finishing what they had started out with them in the summer of 1999. I called Jamie to find out what was going on, and why Matt wasn't doing anything for them. Needless to say, Jamie and I got into another very heated exchange of obscenities towards one another, because it seemed that the local was still blaming me for everything that was going on at PPG. It was my fault about the hearings. It was my fault because of the delays and the expenses incurred for them. I was costing the local union thousands of dollars, but the truth was that it was Matt, and the dead beat good for nothing old guard officers who were costing this local union the campaign, because they had been treating them just like he did us. They didn't care about any of them. The truth of the matter was that it was Matt's incompetent, old guard style, union dividing tactics, and his stranglehold on the local that was costing us all this money.

I had written to the local union, via certified mail, once again requesting a copy of the February 2000 letter that Matt claimed to have sent me concerning my dues along with some other information concerning the membership status of several members. It seemed that a member had telephoned over to the local union hall requesting information about my membership status, while I was discharged from UPS. Unknown to the old guard officers, I had secretly obtained two signed statements concerning this issue that both stated that it had happened.

There is a problem with this.

First of all, its no ones business what my status of being a member is; Second, the local union is not permitted to disclose the names of members that are contained on membership list except only during elections, and then only if you're a candidate, and I had a major problem with this, because they had violated the local union bylaws. After butting heads with Matt about the steward issue, he was claiming that the members in Huntsville had held an election and had elected new stewards, but I found out later in the week that there were no elections held in Huntsville while I was fired, and that he was lying through his teeth.

I had asked Joseph about the so-called steward elections, and he immediately said there was no election, and Joseph proceeded to tell me about a conversation between him and Matt, which had happened sometime during December of 1999, to which Matt had begged him to take over as steward until my return, and this was out of Matt's own mouth according to Joseph. He was wanting Joseph to temporary take over 'until my return', and Joseph agreed to do so, because they were without a steward, and only under this stipulation. I got Joseph to fill out a statement claiming that this conversation had occurred, along with several of the other stewards who had witnessed it.

I went ahead and petitioned the local union executive board for a special meeting to be called, and they agreed to hold one. In the meantime I had filed a complaint with OSHA and with the NLRB concerning the CHSP committee (safety committee) and its question of being legal, not only under the guidelines of the contract, but also under Federal Labor law as well.

My complaints with the committee were numerous, with some of the main ones being that it was not observing seniority rights and various other contract issues. The most alarming one of all was that they were discussing labor issues within the committee, and it had been rumored that some members of the CHSP were discouraging grievances in the committee, which this was not legal. I mean that's what we have a union for. Management had handpicked whom they wanted to chair the committee, and to represent the employees, and without a doubt it was, and is, 'employer dominated'. The special meeting would be called for the middle of July 2000.

During the few weeks leading up to the meeting, we all tried to solicit everyone we could, in regards to getting a verbal commitment to attend the meeting, because it would be extremely important for everyone to be there. I had prepared a list of complaints and questions, on my part, concerning various other by-law and IBT Constitution violations that were being perpetrated by the local union officers against the local 402 members.

We only had a commitment of about a dozen people from out of almost two hundred Huntsville workers, and this was a far cry from the numbers that I had hoped for, but it'd have to do.

In usual fashion the local union had scheduled the meeting to take place on a Sunday at our union hall in Muscle Shoals, instead of coming to Huntsville to meet with us, which was nothing but an old guard tactic.

You see...anytime the old guard local officers had to answer to us about something that they were doing which was questionable and we didn't like, they'd have the meeting in Muscle Shoals at the normal time, but whenever they wanted something to benefit their needs...they'd have the meeting in Huntsville at our convenience. This is a well-known old guard trick that Matt employed to his benefit, because he knew that very few people would travel the 75 miles to the union hall, at a time that was scheduled right after church. He was attempting to cut down on our numbers. He knew what he was doing.

We arrived at the union hall and parked out front waiting to see whom else would show up. I had ridden over with Abel, as always, and we arrived earlier than most everyone, but I noticed that several other key stewards from other centers were already there and inside talking to several different people of whom I didn't recognize. Abel and I sat there in his truck for a few more minutes until we saw Petey coming out of the hall, and that he was making his way to where we were parked. Abel rolled his window down as Petey came up and leaned inside the window.

"I think y'all better get in there." Petey said, while glancing over his shoulder towards the union hall.

"Why what's up?" Abel asked, while looking concerned.

"Ted just came in before you got here, and they carried him into the back room and shut the door." Petey replied.

I went ahead and climbed out and stretched a bit and then walked over to where Petey was standing. Abel had stepped out and finished rolling up the windows and locked his truck up.

"What do you think it is?" I asked Petey.

Petey turned his back towards the building so they couldn't see him talking.

"Something doesn't seem right. They all were in the office talking about you, and all the stuff you had stirred up since coming back to UPS, and then when y'all pulled in they took him on into the back." Petey replied.

"They who?" Abel asked.

"The executive board." Petey replied. I wasn't sure as what to expect, but I really didn't care, because I was ready for them. We walked on into the building and there were a few people in there. I knew most of them and I said hello to everybody. Several minutes passed and finally Matt came in the office to carry us on back into the meeting hall.

We all walked in and some of the officers were already sitting down at the tables that were sat up for us. We had about a dozen or more representatives from Huntsville, and we all sat at one end of the table with a few of us staggered on the sides of the room.

Most of the executive board members sat on the opposite end of the table, and I noticed that Ted, the steward from Florence, was sitting on the end with Matt, another feeder driver out of Florence who was a trustee named Charley, and some of the other officers. That sort of seemed a little strange to me, but I wasn't sure if I was just being paranoid a little more than usual as I began laying all of my notes, and records out on top of the table as Matt called the meeting to order.

I immediately raised my hand to be called upon, and I immediately began hammering his ass about several different things. I asked him why he had failed to give me a copy of the February 2000 letter they supposedly sent me, but he said he was still working on it.

"Working on it Matt? It's been almost five months now, and I would think you would keep better records than that." I replied.

"Well we do have a business to run here you know." Jamie replied in a smart tone.

"I'm talking to Matt and not you Jamie." I replied smiling.

I could tell this burned her up. "I would think you would keep better records than that Matt." I replied again, seeing him shift around in his chair.

"I need to see the books concerning the financial records and the dues payments of several members Matt." I replied, while looking right at him. He turned away and wouldn't look at me, and let out a long sigh.

I had read the local union bylaws and they stated that when I requested this information I would be granted access to everything except to the membership list, but that's not what I wanted to see. I just wanted to see if the local union had paid the dues for anyone, namely Joey a local 402 officer.

I also wanted to know if they had allowed Donna, the PPG worker, to attend the HazWopr class as a Teamster without actually being a member of the union, and if this has happened then we would have a real problem, because that would have meant that Matt would've violated the bylaws at least three times, but Matt sidestepped the question altogether with one of his usual off the wall answers.

"Answer his question Matt" Josey replied.

"What do you want to see James?" Matt replied sighing.

"I want to see what I have a right to see, Matt." I replied.

"James we need to know what you want so we can have it ready for you!" Jamie screamed out like a damn idiot.

"Mr. President, I request that you either calm Jamie down or appoint a warden and have her removed." I replied calmly.

Dwayne who was local 402's president looked up at me with the dumbest look on his face. He didn't have a clue as to what was going on, and he just sat there like a dummy.

"What?" He asked, while looking around the room.

"Either calm Jamie down, or remove her...Mr. President" I replied, in a sterner voice.

Matt put his hand on her shoulder, and Jamie looked at me with a go to hell look, as she threw her pen down on the table and crossed her arms and just stared at me. I found it rather amusing.

"James put in writing, and send it to me outlining what it is you want." Matt replied.

"No Matt I won't do that. I want to have access to the records as the bylaws allow me to have." I replied, while beginning to raise my voice.

Matt sat there looking at me not saying a word.

"Tell us what you want to see James. I don't see what the big deal is?" Joey replied. I turned and looked at Joey and then back at Matt.

"Put it in writing and send it to me, and then I'll let you see the books within fifteen days." Matt replied.

All the executive board members just sat there not saying a word. Dwayne who still had this dumb look on his face was clueless to what was going on. He was probably more interested in what flavor kool-aid they were going to drink after the meeting than what was going on right then. The executive board members were going to sit back and allow Matt to do this to us, not one of them spoke up to protest the fact that Matt was openly denying our rights.

If the truth were known they probably didn't know the bylaws that well, which was no excuse, and that they stated that any member had the right to inspect the books during the business week, and...without written notice. Matt didn't let us know that the IBT had conducted an audit of the books just a few weeks prior to this meeting, and that everything HAD to be in order. He was doing nothing but attempting to stonewall me, but he was playing into my plan, because I had achieved what I wanted from that particular question, which was his open denial of my rights, and now I had plenty of witnesses to it to back it up.

I moved on to my next concern, which was when the local had disclosed my membership status, while I was discharged, to an individual who had called over to the local to inquire about my membership status. The local had disclosed this information, which was against the bylaws, and quite possibly the law.

"I want to know why you told this person my membership status?" I asked.

"I don't see anything wrong with doing that James?" Matt replied.

"Yeah, we do it all the time." Jamie replied, as if trying to smooth it over.

I sat back in my seat not believing what I had just heard.

I flipped open my bylaw book and read the section out loud that pertained to this problem.

"And membership list shall not be copied or open for inspection to any individual." I said, while looking at Matt.

"I did not give you permission to do this now did I, Matt?" I asked, while looking right at him. I could see several executive board members shifting around, and some leaning on the table looking at Matt, and then to me.

"I need you to make an interpretation of this language now Mr. Secretary Treasurer." I replied in a loud voice.

Matt sat there not knowing what to do or say. This was the first time he'd been challenged formally to make an interpretation at the direction of a member.

Matt continued to sit there silent.

"Well?" I asked.

"I see no problem with it James." He replied, as I sat there scanning the faces of the board, waiting for one of them to step in and challenge him, but none came. I knew then that this was nothing but a waste of time.

"I need that interpretation in writing Mr. Secretary Treasurer...please." I replied sarcastically.

"Okay," he replied.

"I want to know what position the local union takes on the formation of the CHSP committees?" I asked, while getting a puzzled look from the executive board.

"As to what?" Matt replied.

"I want to know where this local stands on the position of the safety committees?" I replied again.

"I see no problem with them meeting?" Matt replied.

"You see no problem with the fact seniority isn't being observed. How about people who stay in the building who are being replaced with cover drivers to run their routes?" I replied, and ever so increasing my tone.

Matt sat there staring at his writing pad as if I was burdening him with this petty problem. This was in fact a clear, cut example of a basic, fundamental right of a union member being violated, which was workers seniority.

"I see no problem with it James" He replied.

I just sat there staring at him. I couldn't believe it. Here management was violating the contract on at least three separate articles of the contract, and the most sickening part of the whole thing was that they were bypassing the union by discouraging and pressuring employees not to file grievances. Management wasn't the only ones discouraging 'grievances', but management had recruited the members of the safety committee to 'talk' with the employees whom had any 'concern' about safety. They were using peer pressure to work this matter out, and statements like, "If you cared about safety you wouldn't file this," were said on more than one occasion in Huntsville to a grievant.

The Teamster members who sit on these committees fail to realize that with the way the CHSP is set up now, are only harming the membership as a whole. These members have no power whatsoever. They cannot even have a meeting in our center unless a member of management is present. Why is this? Heck, I thought that they were equally controlled? At least that's what management tells us.

The answer is simple really. It's an employer-dominated group. The

CHSP, at a location, is supposedly co-chaired by a member of the employees, and then by a member of management. "Co-chair" means 'equally' distributed power and responsibility, but this is not the case with UPS's CHSP. Management holds all the power and NOT ONE BIT of it is delegated to the hourly co-chair, unless it's to fill out a quick look audit form or other menial task that was once performed by a supervisor, but now the menial task has been shuffled onto an hourly employee to make it all look legit. Also none of the existing contract language from in our contract is being used to 'help persuade" management to actually provide us a safer place to work by invoking and using the established grievance procedure. We have the language already established to handle any safety concern and grievance, and once that language is invoked it would have the grievance heard through existing grievance machinery committees on the national level, and not in some little pathetic, Mickey Mouse committee like management advertises and controls on a substandard level.

"Matt how many safety grievances have you heard using the existing contract language?" I asked him, and sat waiting for his response.

"I haven't had any." He replied.

"Haven't had any or heard any?" I asked again wanting him to answer my question.

Matt sat there for a minute not saying anything. This is a simple question I thought to myself, and there was no reason for him to have to think of a response unless his response was to be a carefully orchestrated lie.

"I haven't had any that comes to mind." He answered nervously.

"That's a lie Matt." I replied.

"DON"T YOU SIT THERE AND CALL HIM A LIAR!" Jamie screamed out.

"Mr. President I've asked you before and this is the last time that I will ask you, either shut the recording secretary up, or remove her, because she will not disrupt this meeting." I said in a demanding tone.

Dwayne just looked around lost. He hadn't even followed what was going on.

"I'm the one who calls the meetings to order James not Dwayne" Matt replied.

"No sir you're not the one either, all you do is conduct the meeting. Under article so and so of the local union bylaws the President has the responsibility and AUTHORITY to maintain order and remove anyone who disrupts a meeting, not the Secretary Treasurer." I replied staring straight at him.

Matt didn't know what to say. No one did. They did not know the bylaws well enough to challenge me on this issue. There would be no challenge any of them just contempt, and nothing was said. Jamie was fit to be tied. She let out a disgusted sigh and just stared at the ceiling in disgust and began running her hands through her hair like a lunatic. I was controlling her with the power of the bylaws and she couldn't stand it. Power truly comes from knowledge, as I had just clearly demonstrated.

"Before I was so rudely interrupted by the unruly outburst of the recording secretary," I replied, while trying to draw her out again so I could have her thrown out of the meeting, "I have filed at least four separate grievances concerning safety issues" I replied, as I began pulling out copies of the safety grievances that I had filed in the past and tossed them on top of the table. Matt didn't say a word. No one did.

"You seem to have forgotten about these then...didn't you Matt," I replied, as I picked them back up and was holding them for everyone to see.

"I handle so many, James that I can't keep track of them all." He replied.

Matt had nowhere to go with this. He had no answers for us as to why he was allowing the despicable violation of member's rights to be carried out against his Teamsters that he works for and was supposed to fairly represent everyday.

"James are you saying you disagree with having a safe place to work?" Ted asked. I was disappointed by his question and didn't expect Ted to take this position, which is siding with the old guard.

"No, not in the least Ted." I replied, while cutting my eyes over towards him.

"Then what is it then?" Ted replied.

"These committees are violating members rights everyday Ted." I replied growing upset from his sarcasm and his attempt to make it look like I was unhappy about anything that was going on at UPS.

"I don't see how they are," Ted replied.

"Well maybe you need to invest in a contract book then Ted...I thought that with you being a steward you'd be up on this language a little better than that." I replied sarcastically.

"James what is it you just hope to accomplish here?" Joey asked.

I sat there for a minute thinking. I knew what I wanted to say, but if I said what I wanted to say it would probably get me thrown out of the meeting.

"I want this union's officers to start doing their job." I replied.

The saddest part of this whole thing was the fact that everyone on the executive board refused to act. They had the responsibility and duty to open an investigation into my allegations to this to see if, indeed what I was alleging was actually going on in our local. I had all the evidence they needed to remove Matt from office, but they simply didn't care enough about it and would not act, but by doing so would mean that they'd have to bring charges against one an all of them, which is something they weren't about to do.

The last topic I covered at the meeting was in regard to my removal as a steward.

"Matt I want to see a copy of the letter that you sent to UPS stating that I was no longer a steward." I asked. I had asked the same thing from management a few weeks earlier, with Walt, and I had even filed a grievance requesting it, but I had yet to hear anything on it. It was going on over a month now.

"I'll have to look for it James." Matt replied.

"I want to know why I'm no longer steward anymore Matt?" I asked.

"Josey's the feeder steward and Abel is his alternate." Matt replied. I sat there thinking how I wanted to handle this.

"What happened to me being the chief steward of the building like before I was fired?" I asked.

"We felt that there's not a need for a chief steward anymore James." Matt replied.

"You didn't seem to have a problem with it before, and I now find it quite funny that all of a sudden you don't need me." I replied angrily.

"They had an election James, and they voted for other people." Matt replied.

I had him right where I wanted him, because he knew that there hadn't been any election. Several of the people with me looked at me as if they were waiting for me to explode on him.

Not now. Not here. I had him stating this lie in front of several members of the executive board, and I would use this later on down the road.

"I find it very disrespectful as a member of this union for me to find this out from a member of UPS management instead of you Matt." I replied, while staring at him, but he still wouldn't look at me. He just sat there rolling a pen around with his fingers.

"Why would you want to even be a steward again after what happened to you?" Henry asked me.

"Why not?" I asked in return.

"UPS doesn't want to deal with you at all. Hell, they can't even stand the sight of you." Ted replied.

"I know I'd want someone in the office with me that could work things out with the management instead of someone with the reputation you have." Someone else replied.

"I'd be scared to have you in the office with me." Another said.

"I follow the contract and the law. There is no compromise with this company when someone's rights are being violated, and I don't sell members out while I'm in the office with them like some of these bastards do." I replied.

They wanted a butt kisser to be steward. They wanted someone to get in there and make deals with management instead of "bargaining in good faith" like one should. The truth is I had worked out discharges and suspensions, and I'd done this dozens of times in the past, but I didn't go around bragging about it like it was a trophy or something. It was my job, and what went on in the office...stayed in the office, and it was only between the people I was representing and me. I did not trade off grievances like the others did. I didn't believe in it, and I simply would not do it, because I felt that everyone's grievance was separate and it should be heard, and that alone gave me the reputation of being a hard head. As far as my 'verbal outburst' goes, I remained cordial and respectful until management crossed that line and verbally attacked one of my Teamsters. What was I to do? Just sit back and let management run over and beat my members down, while I sat idly by with the power and authority to intercede and defend my members rights? That's what Matt, Ted and the other old guard bastards wanted out of a steward. All I have to say about that is too bad, because my members deserve to be respected and they will be treated with respect while I was in the office representing them, and if they weren't, then ask management about the hell that would erupt out of me as soon as they started this crap up. It wasn't about to happen on my watch.

"Well I don't care about the rest of you, all I know is if I was going to be in the office battling management for my job, I'd want James in the office with me. At least I'd know he'd do a hell of a job in fighting for me unlike some of you bastards in here would do." Abel replied.

I looked over at him and I could tell that he was pissed off about what was going on.

Nothing else of substance was discussed after his statement to the old guard, and this whole thing proved to be nothing more than a waste of time, but I had achieved what I sat out to do. I had made aware to the entire executive board about what was going on between Matt, and me and how he had been violating my rights as a union member. When, and if I, decided to make my move I could include them into charges that I would file against the local as well for failing to carry out their respected duties as officer's of this union, and for failing to protect and preserve my rights which were guaranteed to me under the bylaws and the I.B.T constitution.

I talked with Abel on the way home about what had happened during the meeting, and we both decided to pay a little visit to the local on the following Monday, un announced of course, to view the books.

I carried over with us, that Monday morning, a micro tape recorder in my pocket, and I had asked Ronnie, a Huntsville feeder driver, to ride over with us as a precaution. I wanted plenty of witnesses just in case Jamie claimed that we had came over and started trouble in an attempt to get us thrown out of the union. I wasn't taking any chances with her, because I didn't trust her one bit.

We arrived over at the union hall and noticed that there were just three cars there. One was hers, and the other I didn't recognize, but I did see Matt's Lincoln parked on the side of the building.

"This should prove interesting," I replied.

"We don't want to get into a fight with them in here okay? If they deny us access then we'll leave right?" He replied, while looking at me with a stern look on his face.

"Yeah right," I replied, while cutting on the recorder and slipping it into my shirt pocket. We walked on into the office and Abel did the talking.

"Jamie is Matt here?" He asked.

"No...uh... he had to leave to take care of some business." She replied.

I looked out the side window and noticed that his car was gone. Matt had slipped out the back door and left as we were coming in the front. I laughed to myself about his cowardice.

"We'd like to look at the books Jamie." Abel asked, while standing at the edge of her desk.

"I can't let you do that Abel." She replied.

"Under section so and so we have the right to view the books Jamie." I replied, while stepping into the office.

"Matt told me not let you see them for now." She replied. She was unusually calm for some reason, and I wasn't sure why though.

"Jamie I'd like to know the membership status of a couple of members." I asked her staring in her eyes.

"James you know we can't do that. After all, last week you were making a big deal out of it...and now you want to do it." She replied, while cracking a smile.

"Let's go." Abel said walking out with Ronnie in tow.

"Those son of a bitches." I said out loud as we walked outside. I knew what was going on and they had an idea as to what I may be looking for, but they weren't quite sure.

Several weeks would pass and finally I received a subpoena from the attorneys who were representing PPG. They wanted some of my personal property, and copies of everything I had in regards to PPG and the campaign.

I reluctantly called Matt, and told him what I had received from PPG's attorneys, and he in turn called the attorney who was representing the local. Later that evening, I received a call from the union's lawyer who discussed with me what it was exactly that I was going to give them, in regard to their request. PPG wanted everything I had in relation to correspondence, letters, pamphlets, books, my computer, photos everything that related to the PPG campaign. She told me that she'd take care of it, and for me to just show up at the hearing that was scheduled in August of 2000.

I would be questioned about my role in the campaign, and if indeed I was a professional organizer whom was on the payroll of local 402 during the campaign. I was also going to be questioned about the so-called threat that I had allegedly made against the PPG employee as well. That had been pretty much settled and it had proven to be nothing but a false allegation, after they subpoenaed his phone records and it was shown that he had called me, instead of me calling him, which contradicted his initial claims.

The employee of PPG had an attendance problem as well, according to several PPG employees, and this helped shed a little light as to what might have motivated him to make up such a story like this, because it was really stupid, and it defied all common sense, because he was the only one who had filed a complaint against me for 'strong arming' him to vote yes.

I did not know what he looked like, who he was, and further more, there was no way I could have known if he didn't vote one way or the other. It was totally asinine to even entertain the thought of this even happening, and it only made PPG look very foolish.

I called Matt back, and told him to call Birmingham feeders, and to tell them that I needed Friday off to attend the hearing. I also told him that I expected him to bring me a check for the amount of wages that I was going to miss for the day, because I wasn't about to attend the hearing, and go up there on my own time. Not after what he pulled with me.

Monday arrived, and I showed up to the hearing, which was being held at the City of Huntsville's Municipal Building. I arrived early, and saw several of PPG's representatives in the lobby, and I decided to walk on into the concession area to buy myself a coke.

I walked on in, and I saw sitting at a little table, several of the PPG head managers and a little pee-on employee, who they sent out every time we hand billed to get several of the handbills to take back into PPG, and they were eating snacks and drinking cokes. They all stopped talking as I walked into the room and they all looked at me, and the little flunky recognized me right off.

I knew who she was, but I didn't know who the other three were who were sitting with her. I walked on by them and went up to a vending machine. As I stood in front of the machine, and looked into the glass, I could see their reflection in it, and I could watch them while my back was turned to them. I fiddled around with some change in my hand, as I watched them very carefully. I then saw the girl lean into the center of the table, and say something to them, which then caused all of them to turn around and look at me. I went ahead and bought me some chips and a drink, and I sat down at a table right behind them. I was facing the girl, and could see the others fairly well, but none of them would look at me except for the girl, so I decided to have a little fun with her. As I sat there I stared right at the girl, and I could tell that she knew that I was looking at her, and I could tell that she was becoming very uncomfortable. I continued to stare at her until she looked at me, and when she finally made eye contact with me...I winked at her. I thought she was going to crap on herself. She said something under her breath that caused one of the suits to turn and look at me, and I then blew him a kiss and smiled. I thought he was going to cry right there on the spot as he almost dropped his drink. After that, they all stood up, while being careful not to look at me, and put on their suit coats and walked on out of the concession area. I thought it was pretty funny, and finished my snack, and walked on over to the elevators.

I took the elevators up several flights to the room where the hearing was going to be conducted. It was a fairly large room, similar to a courtroom, and I noticed, as I entered, that several attorneys for PPG were on one side talking to the 'PPG suits', and on our side were our representatives. The hearing started with PPG challenging several people's presence in the room during questioning. They wanted us out, because they thought that our presence could influence testimony. The Judge agreed, and ordered us out until after we had testified then we could return if we wanted to. Only this didn't just apply to us though. The Judge ordered all of the PPG managers out as well, to which they attempted to argue, but to no avail, because their money and power didn't have any bearing on the judge's discretion.

The hearing finally got underway and several people were heard and their testimony was given concerning the campaign. I sat down there for about six hours and I was never called to testify. I was asked to meet with Matt and the attorney at the Hilton, which was about two blocks away, to discuss what I was going to say, and what type of questions I might be asked.

The hearing was closed for the day, and I met Matt and the lawyer in the lounge of the Hilton. We took our seats at a table and they ordered drinks, to which I declined their offer.

I went through everything about what I had said to the PPG liar, and whether or not if Matt paid me anything for organizing, and anything else I could think of.

There was one other thing though. There was something that the whole campaign could hinge on depending on the testimony of one individual...Donna's testimony about the slapping incident at PPG.

"If they ask me whether or not I know anything about the slapping incident I'll tell them everything I know." I said while looking at the lawyer.

"What do you mean?" She replied.

"She called me, and told me that she slapped him, and then she asked me what to do." I replied.

They sat there for a minute, taking a sip from their drinks, and not saying anything.

"I'm not going to offer the information up if they don't ask me, but if they do...I'm not going to perjure myself, and lie for anyone." I replied, trying to solicit a response.

"I don't think they'll ask you anything James." She replied, and after a few minutes of casual conversation I left and went home. I had time to go to work that night, but I didn't go, because I had told Matt that I hadn't slept any that day, and he told me just to take off, and that he'd have my check sent to me in a couple of days.

The hearing would wind up being postponed for a few more weeks, which turned into months due to the fact that the judge presiding over the hearings was in an accident and was unable to preside. The hearing was assigned to a new judge and this would mean that we would be starting the process all over again.

Matt had yet to return to PPG, and do anything of substance for those people. They all were about ready to say the hell with it all, and with him, when he finally decided to hold another meeting to discuss what was going on. Marty later told me that very few people had shown up to the meeting, and that the union had lost support, and it all was from Matt sitting on his dead ass, and not doing anything for them which wasn't going to fly with any of them. They demanded some sort of action and soon.

The action would come in the form of Marty being shunned with Donna and Sandy, a no vote who had jumped sides after the union had been voted in, being placed in charge of hand billing and running what was left of a fractured and dying campaign, and this action didn't sit too well with me, Marty, and most of everyone else at PPG, but I was in no position to do really do anything about it other than bring it before the executive board at the next meeting, but little good this would do.

I was getting complaints pretty steadily from people who despised Donna and Sandy for even being out there. It was almost as if it was a mockery, but it was usual fashion though on the part of Matt. We had done all the work and now that controversy surrounded him he put others in place to try and remove the questions and doubt. We were beginning to lose the campaign, and I felt that he was trying desperately to finish the job of sabotage by enlisting the help of these two individuals.

The local would attempt to take on another campaign with a company named Cinram, which was just a mile away from PPG, and in a stupid and costly move, he put Donna and Sandy out there at Cinram, helping him to try and get enough signatures to petition for an election. Nothing would ever come of it. Hell he couldn't even keep PPG taken care of. How was he going to manage this campaign as well by putting people in charge that had never, ever even been in a union? It didn't make sense. Matt hinted around to several people about asking me to help with organizing Cinram, but I told them hell no. It was his baby, and let him take care of it.

During the month of October, Matt would appoint, to the Huntsville building, two chief stewards. It was Josey and Marsha, and this move upset me a lot, because several months ago the executive board members were all so stern against it and now they thought it was a good idea. I don't know if it was intended to be a slap in the face to me or not, but I chose not to challenge the appointment, knowing all along that Josey would do a good job, so I just decided to let it pass.

The next hearing for PPG was coming up in February 2001, and I had received another subpoena for the next hearing. In the meantime I was still trying to obtain a copy of the February 2000 letter about my dues, and I still trying to gain access to the books, which Matt was still refusing to allow me. I had learned that Donna had gone to work for TVA, performing a Teamster job, and was working steady, while I was still trying to find out about her membership history and whether or not she was a member back in February 2000. The PPG hearing finally came, and it was held at a different location this time than before, but it was still in Huntsville.

I arrived to the hearing early that morning and as usual Matt had yet to arrive. The Attorney for the union was in the room discussing some things with the opposing counsel, and Donna was in the courtroom along with several others, and I was told that I couldn't come in. I didn't know why though, so I went back into the lobby to sit down. I sat out there for several minutes, and Matt finally showed up and walked by me, and headed back into the office.

I stood back up, and walked over to the door and peered in. I couldn't see anything at all, and I was beginning to grow impatient from all the waiting. I had heard through the grapevine that Donna might have testified that she did not slap the man, which would mean that they allowed her to give false testimony, but there would be no way to prove it. They could simply say that they believed what she had told them as to be the truth. Several other PPG employees had now began showing up to find out how things were going, as I told them that I didn't know, because they wouldn't tell me anything about the hearings. The union lawyer finally came out and pulled me over to the side, and she told me that Matt had made a deal to have another election in exchange for settling Donna's case. She received a little settlement from he discharge and went on her way. I became furious from this decision.

"They've sold y'all out," I screamed out with everyone looking at me. I could not believe that Matt would agree to have another election.

"You'll lose the election this time Matt." I replied angrily at him as he walked by me...never stopping to look at me as I screamed at him. He didn't say a word. He looked guilty as hell of something.

I asked him why he chose to allow PPG another election and his reply was to me, "I didn't want to put Donna through all that again, and the money Hoffa promised to fight PPG, never came."

"Through what?" I asked angrily.

"She's had a rough time these last few months, and she just couldn't handle going through all this again." He said and walked off.

"Please tell me that you didn't sacrifice 450 people just so you didn't have to inconvenience one person Matt. Is that it? What about the dozens of people who will probably lose their jobs now from supporting the union during the campaign? How about them?" I screamed out. "How noble of you." I continued to say as he walked off out of site.

"You sold out 450 people for one person. I can't believe you did that." I replied, still shocked as a police officer stepped around the corner to see what was going on. I was so disgusted I just left. I would later read about it in the paper the next day.

Marty called me that evening and she simply said, "Tell me he didn't do it James?"

What was I going to say? I told her everything I knew. "There's a bunch of guys out looking for Matt right now, and I hope they find him." She replied, while becoming upset.

"You know we're going to lose this next election." She replied.

I knew it, but I was so sick from the whole thing that had just happened, that I couldn't see straight. It was a matter of days, after the last hearing, that the whole PPG plant knew about what happened and what kind of deal Matt had made to sell them out. I had asked Matt for copies of the transcripts, and a copy of the final deal he made with PPG, but like everything else he refused to give it to me.

The new election at PPG was held again, and this time... the Teamsters had lost.

People had become so disgusted with the way Matt had been treating them, and with his lack of concern, and then coupled with their alleged sell out for Donna, were just some of the reasons that a lot of them voted no, figuring they had a better chance with the company rather than putting their trust in him, and the union, because at least with the company...they knew where they stood.

The local union would continue to place the blame on me after this pathetic loss, but in reality Matt was just trying to take the responsibility of losing the election off of his back. Jamie would continue with her lies about my involvement in the defeat of the union, and I would finally have to threaten legal action against the local union before she would finally stop.

Hoffa, Matt and the relaxed position of the old guard local union executive board had managed to cost several of the employees their jobs at PPG, and some would later be forced to quit who had been very pro-union, and was very vocal during the campaign. I was truly ashamed of what the old guard had done to the employees of PPG.

I called for another meeting with the local union executive board for the following month. I had had enough of what was going on in our local, and I had decided to go ahead and bring charges against Matt and several others on the board for violating and obstructing my rights as a member of the union. The charges ranged from denying members access to union records to failing to carry out their respected and sworn duties and obligations to the members.

I researched the local union bylaws and I.B.T Constitution and came up with more than a dozen charges against Matt, and the others had roughly three apiece. I was going to call for a trial before the membership of our local. I worked on the formal process, and with the line of questioning in relation to my evidence before attending the meeting that day. I had written to the local union about a dozen times over the past few months, via certified mail, requesting information to be used in building my case, but I never received a reply. I knew that they were getting the letters, because of the return receipts that I had received back from them that showed their signatures on the cards.

In the meantime I decided to file a formal complaint against Matt and some of the other local union officers with the Independent Review Board of the I.B.T.

The I.R.B is a separate entity of the I.B.T created by the courts, which is designed to investigate internal union corruption complaints filed by the members of the Teamsters Union.

I had typed about five pages of charges and statements outlining everything that had happened along with my evidence, and sent them to Mr. Carberry whom was the Chief Investigator of the I.R.B. I later received a letter from Mr. Carberry stating that he had received my complaints and that he would be conducting an investigation into my allegations. I was hoping that they'd come through for me.

Management wasn't screwing with me much at all during this time, and I in turn was going along with the flow of things. I welcomed the change with open arms. I hadn't decided if I was going to run for a local union office this coming up time, but I knew that the nominations to the convention were coming up in November, which was only three months away. I thought about it, and talked to Abel about us running as delegates to the IBT Convention.

We had heard that Matt and Joey were considering running which would mean they were only interested in a vacation at the member's expense, so I decided to go ahead and run.

I had a lot of business to try and get in order before the nominations, which I was still facing the suspension for the non-payment of dues back during my discharge. That was going to be a hard obstacle to overcome and beat, because Matt wasn't providing any information to help me, which was understandable. I mean...why would he want to help me cut his own throat? It wasn't looking good for me, and the only shot I had was to try and show his intent on eliminating me from the political scene for personal reasons.

I would have to file a complaint with the Office of the Election Administrator, whom oversees the Teamster International elections. The U.S Government established this position due to past corruption in Teamster politics as part of the consent decree by the U.S Government.

This process is pretty straightforward. I prepared a letter to the E.A, Mr. Wertheimer, citing my complaint and allegations, but decided to hold off for a few weeks, and send one more letter to Matt, in a last ditch attempt to try and get him to make a ruling on my eligibility. The bylaws stated that when a member requested a ruling on their eligibility to run in a local or International election they were to submit a letter to the secretary treasurer of their local union requesting a verification of eligibility. I fired a letter off to Matt requesting him to make a ruling.

I was thinking that maybe he'd be man enough, and just rule me eligible so I wouldn't have to drag this out through the process, but I was wrong. I wound up sending three more letters to Matt, and finally I had resorted to sending letters to the local union president, Dwayne, in an attempt to try and get him to force Matt to make a ruling on my eligibility.

The letter I finally received from Matt said that if he was to rule me eligible then a member could protest his decision, and I'd do the same, meaning to appeal it, if he ruled me ineligible.

That's what I wanted him to do, which was to just rule one way or the other so I could appeal it, if I had received a bad ruling from him, through the prescribed process that was outlined in the bylaws. He went on to say that it was probably best if I appealed directly to the election administrator and let them rule.

Little did I know that this was a bad idea, and just another old guard trick? I wrote it off as he was just trying to take the monkey off of his back if he ruled me eligible if someone raised hell about it.

I went ahead and sent the letter to the election administrator while attempting to get Matt to make a ruling on me in the meantime. I continued to write letters to Matt and the other officers to no avail.

I then went ahead and wrote a letter to IBT President Hoffa, keeping in mind that this was part of the appeals process that was outlined in our bylaws, and I explained to him what Matt had done to me, and how he was jerking me around, and not performing his duties as an officer. I sent Mr. Hoffa copies of everything I had to back my case up against Matt.

This proved to be nothing but a waste of time and only helped Hoffa's case against my eligibility. I later received the return receipt from where Hoffa had received the letter, but I would never receive an answer from him. It seemed that Mr. Hoffa wasn't too interested in preserving and defending members rights like in this case, unless of course they supported him, which I clearly didn't.

I went ahead and contacted the Department of Labor, Office of Labor Management Standards, who handles union corruption and I explained to them my situation. They advised me that I had to exhaust all of my appeals through the union first and then file a complaint with them within the allotted time frame allowed by law.

This time frame in which I had to act in was narrow, and I had a short window of time during the last appeal if I received an unfavorable ruling from the election administrator. So I began preparing for the worst-case scenario.

Several more weeks would pass, and finally I was contacted by a representative from the office of the Election Administrator and spoke to one of the caseworkers. She interviewed me over the phone, and after about an hour of talking and telling her what evidence I had, which included taped conversation, said she'd have to call the union and get their side and then she'd give me the ruling by her office.

I felt confident enough in my case that I would be ruled eligible, and it wouldn't be a problem for me to run. This matter was going to take a few weeks to complete, and in the mean time I had called a local union trustee and explained to him that Matt wouldn't rule on my eligibility, and he assured me he'd make Matt do his job and issue me a ruling.

Several days later I received a letter from Matt ruling that he had found me eligible to run. I finally received the news I was waiting for, and I immediately sat down and wrote out a letter to the representative from the E.A, and told her that I was ruled eligible by my local union to run in the election, and that I'd like to withdraw my request of them ruling on my eligibility.

I came home one evening shortly after mailing the letter, and found that the woman from the E.A had left a message on my answering machine, and that she was going to rule me ineligible to run in the upcoming election. I was floored. I called her immediately, and she answered her phone, and I blazed her about not having the decency to tell me in person and she apologized. I debated with her for what seemed like hours, and she said that she'd withdraw her decision pending her 'reevaluation ' of my circumstances. I still couldn't believe that she had found me ineligible to run, because I had plenty of evidence to back my claim up. I didn't know what to do next.

After a couple of days I received a letter in the mail from the election administrator. I was very eager to open it, and judging from the thickness of the envelope it might contain good news. I tore the end off and pulled the letters out and unfolded them, and as I read them all very carefully...my heart sank. They had found me ineligible. I was extremely disappointed. I looked at the other letters that was accompanying this one and began to read them.

As I began to read them I shook my head no. "No...this isn't what I told you," I said aloud.

I continued to read on through her statement of all the witnesses to my claim and it was a lie. Most of my testimony that I had given to her had been twisted, and even some things were put in there that I didn't even say. I read on through and got to Matt's testimony. My mouth dropped open.

The little bastard had stated to her that 'HE DID' tell me that he would make sure my dues were taken care of even if the local had to pay them. It went on to say that also, "I never told him to start paying his dues again once he went to work on the pipeline." He had told the lady a bunch of lies.

I finished reading the findings and I became enraged. The so-called 'impartial' election administrator had not only made just a simple ruling, but had ruled, and found me to be the perpetrator and had made Matt out to be the victim. The E.A had painted such a terrible picture of me and, to say the least, I was fit to be tied. I immediately stormed into the house and called the lady up on the phone and she answered. She arrogantly told me to appeal it after I had it out with her on the phone, and appeal it I would.

I appealed the decision to the E.A himself, Mr. Wertheimer who backed up her claim. I was running out of options and time. I decided to go ahead and exhaust all my appeals, which would then allow me to file a complaint with the Federal Government. I appealed the decision to the Appeals Master, who would schedule a hearing and allow me to present my case before him. I had a lot of work to do ahead of me and I immediately began to review word for word the findings of the election administrator and rebut their findings. This would take several days and many long hours to complete.

The local union had posted the election plan, which formally announced the time, and place where the nominations would occur. I was ready. I was going to go ahead and attend the meeting, and get nominated for the position of alternate delegate to the 2001 Teamsters Convention, after having changed my position to allow Abel to run as delegate for the Tom Leedham Slate in our local.

This political move was done so if Abel won enough votes in the election, and a Hoffa Slate member won as alternate delegate, we'd still have control over our Leedham reform votes for the convention.

I would go ahead and prepare for someone to challenge my eligibility right at the meeting once I was nominated and seconded by another member so I typed out a formal letter challenging anyone, who in turn, challenged the question of my eligibility. I chose to do this because I only had forty-eight hours to appeal the protest to the local union, which would then start that individual appeal process concerning the member's complaint of eligibility against me, and with Matt's reluctance to reply or even acknowledge having received my letters that I had mailed to him, I wasn't about to let this one ride on chance.

I had prepared a new set of charges to be filed, only this time instead of them solely being against Matt, I decided to go ahead and include two other local union officers as well. The charges outlined several bylaws violations, and I added a few extra to the original ones that I had already filed against Matt, prior to his recent confessions to the E.A about the 'dues incident', after he had lied about it to all of us for months.

In usual fashion I rode over with Abel to the local union hall, and while on the way over to the hall we discussed what might transpire once we got over here, and how we'd handle it if it happened. I told him to just hang around close to me after the nominations that I was going to request a meeting with the executive board directly after the nominations had been called closed.

We arrived at the local and there was a fair amount of people there already, which is usually the case with election nominations, and as we walked on into the union hall, you could feel the tension mount as we entered into the office. It was as if two notorious outlaws had entered a dusty little town in the old west.

Several members were around one of the desk, in the business office, talking amongst themselves as I looked around to see who was all there. I had heard that several others were going to run for the 'delegate' positions, but I didn't know for sure who, other than Matt and Joey, was actually going to run. Abel walked over to talk to some people as I went over to the file cabinets and leaned up against them. Dwayne walked by and said hello to me, and I nodded my head without saying anything to him. After a few minutes Abel came back over to where I was standing, and pulled me over into the corner. He was acting very anxious.

"You're not going to believe what I was just told." He replied anxiously.

"What is it?" I replied.

"Get this...so and so over there just told me that if you were nominated that Hoffa's going to protest your eligibility." Abel replied.

"Who told you this?" I asked, growing angry.

Abel turned and nodded his head toward two members who were standing over to themselves. I knew that they were tight with Matt is some areas, but they would have had no knowledge about what I was fighting the old guard about, unless Matt told them, and this would prove to me that their statements could be credible.

We still had several minutes before the meeting would officially begin and I told Abel that I wanted to talk to Henry and Charley, both were local union officers, by themselves.

Abel rounded them up, and asked them to join us in an office, and as they followed us in I shut the door behind them as several other old guard members looked on.

Henry sat down behind the desk and Charley stood beside him. I explained to him what we had just heard, and asked them point blank whether or not they knew anything about it. Neither did, because Henry was visibly concerned from it.

"What business does Hoffa have sticking his nose in this local? We run it not him." Henry replied in an upset tone.

I ran through what had transpired since I've last talked to him and he knew nothing about it. Matt had failed to let him in on what was going on between him and I. But it was all beginning to make sense.

"How the hell did Hoffa find out about it unless...Matt told him?" Henry replied. He was beginning to see that my claims were legit.

We were just a small Teamsters local in the south, but this election was important to Hoffa and his old guard administration. We were running on a Leedham reform slate whereas Matt and Joey were running on a Hoffa 'old guard' Slate, called the "no dues increase slate!".

The vote that we would have at the convention could possibly affect the control Hoffa would have on the union concerning several issues. Those issues we supported could loosen the stranglehold that Hoffa had on the membership, in the sense of language contained in the IBT Constitution, and if enough locals carried the Leedham Slate then there stood a good chance that we could've changed the IBT Constitution from the old guard style to a more democratic way of doing things.

Hoffa was sternly against this, and as time would show, local 402 wasn't the only local he was doing this in, and I wasn't the only 'Leedham' supporter that had to face the question of eligibility. Hoffa was feverishly engaged in an old guard scheme, because his very future could be at stake and every local he could gather support for him would help ensure his plans would unfold to carry us back twenty years and strip us of our rights to have a say in how our union was being governed.

The nominations would go off without incident, and although I was expecting someone to challenge my nomination, and had prepared an 'official' letter protesting that action, which would have started the whole process all over again, but nothing came though, and I was surprised and relieved as well.

After the nominations had concluded I walked over and asked Ted, the feeder steward from Florence, to hang around that I had something I wanted him to be a witness to. I then walked up to Henry, and asked him if he'd call the board together that I had something I wanted to tell them.

Everyone was mingling with the members talking, smoking and having a good time. Little did they know what was coming...

Finally, after most of everyone had left, Matt gathered all of the executive board member's around the table, and they all took their seats. The looks on their face's when I began to stand up to say what I had to say said it all for me. It was a look of disgust and contempt. I smiled a little on the inside, because I knew that I was about to exercise my power as a member of the union against the old guard establishment.

"Matt I wish to exercise my rights under so and so section of the local 402 Bylaws. I am serving you with notice of charges against you, Jamie and Dwayne." I stated as they looked on in total disbelief and shock.

"What kind of crap is this?" Joey replied, while standing up.

I didn't say a word. "Not yet," I thought to myself, while waiting for the others to reply.

Jamie became enraged, and put on such a good show that she had become so pissed she finally got up, and walked out of the meeting visibly shaken from the bombshell that I had just dropped on them. Dwayne was lost, and all he could muster is "What charges?" He hadn't a clue as to what had just happened.

Matt had taken the charges, and handed them to Joey who began to look over them. I hadn't seen these clowns that concerned ever.

We discussed, and debated the legitimacy of my charges, but they didn't have a leg to stand on.

Finally, I ended the meeting by saying, "I wish to defer the hearing until I give further notice." They all stood up, and left except for Charley, Myron and Henry.

Abel and Ted talked amongst themselves about what had just happened, and Charley and Henry asked me to step outside to discuss the matter of the charges. I talked to them, and explained what evidence I had, and how the trial would work and what their roles and responsibilities would be in ensuring that the integrity of it was maintained. This was all new for them, and as well as for me.

"Henry, since that Dwayne and Matt are on trial you'll assume the head role of the presiding senior officer by virtue of your office. You and the others will have to fill the vacancies of the three others with members from our local to try the case," I explained to them as they were still recovering from the shock of what had just happened. If Matt hadn't done what he did to me, and if the others hadn't just sit on their butts, and allowed it to happen, then we wouldn't be going through this.

I had wanted to bring charges against Joey as well, but by doing so would have jeopardized the integrity of the trial. By only bringing charges against three of the seven officers, the trial would stay in, and be conducted by the officers in the local union, whereas if I had brought charges against 'the majority' of the officers in the local union then the Teamsters Joint Council would have conducted the trial, and this I didn't want.

The integrity of the Council remained a question, and I couldn't chance an outright acquittal, and I feared this result, because the Joint Council President was an old guard officer and a Hoffa supporter, and with Hoffa already having displayed to me that he had no intentions in preserving and defending my rights, I wasn't stupid enough to put my trust in the Joint Council.

The question would arise that one of the remaining officers was considering pulling out from having to sit in the trial in an attempt to sabotage it, and as well, in an attempt to force it to go before the Joint Council, but I was ready for that. I had already drafted a letter to Matt and would later hand deliver it to him stating that if this happened that another member in 'OUR' local would have to replace the one officer who was withdrawing, and then they would not be able to transfer the hearing before the Joint Council. Matt didn't want this to go before the members, because it could cost him dearly.

Henry and Charley asked me to withdraw the charges, and to see if we could simply work it out. I had given the local union several chances to work it out and there was no interest then, so why should there be any now?

I declined the offer, and I was planning on holding off on the trial until the time limit for the charges would be close to expiring, which was one year, except for the charges concerning my dues which doesn't have a time limit.

I was saving this, as the local union election was next year, and it would still be well within the time limitations for the charges. I was planning to force the trial and attempt to have the Matt and the other officers suspended from the union, thus making all of the ineligible to run, and if nothing else, it could at least cloud the perception of his administration to the members, and at least cripple his ability to get votes.

Abel and I would campaign for the delegate election, and finally, I was scheduled to have a tele-conference hearing before the election appeals master.

I had prepared an outstanding defense and rebuttal of the claims and lies of the election administrator's findings. I was ready, but the hearing would be short lived.

The side for Hoffa, whom was permitted as a participant, stated the findings, and laid out one hell of a lie as an opening statement. Then the judge asked me for my statement.

Once I started into it he cut me off, and started drilling me about my dues.

The judge would not even let me state my side of the case as he had allowed Hoffa's thugs to do.

I saw that I was just getting railroaded. This went on for another minute, and finally I saw what was going on, and that this was nothing but a "kangaroo court". I knew I had lost my appeal, because I wasn't even given the chance to rebut their findings or even offered to make any kind of statement. He made his ruling right then, and without any testimony from me. Hoffa had won.

I figured I had nothing else to lose, and interrupted him while he was talking like he had done me so many times, and I blazed him like he had never had heard from anyone before. I called him everything under the sun, and told him what I thought about him as a judge and slammed the phone down.

I was sick from the rush of adrenalin and emotions I was feeling from this travesty, and I immediately filed a complaint with Department of Labor. I'd just turn it over to them and let them handle it.

Everything rocked along for several week's with nothing really happening. I managed to file another complaint with OSHA against management concerning the egress problem again. I made sure management knew I had been the one to do it, which in reality was of no surprise to them. I was growing concerned at the fact that several part timers had come up to me about the problem and how they were being brushed off by the co-chair of the hourly employees, Marsha, and nothing was ever really being done about it.

I was still trying to be low key in my involvement in the center, because I didn't have any 'recognized' authority, as a steward, and in turn, no power to intervene. A small number of preload employees had in the meantime tried to oust Marsha from being the preload steward amongst numerous complaints that she was 'failing to do her job', and being too 'in tune' with managements concerns instead of her members.

Marsha had obtained, in our opinion, a few perks that was outside the norm of the average employee, and that's when Josey and I, along with several others began to question what was really going on here. We decided not to allow any steward in this center to succumb the 'tantalizing' perks of management without a fight. For if we had, then it would only be a matter of time before the members would lose faith, what little they had left, and the grievance machinery would suffer and potentially 'break down' as well. It was already fragile from the years of neglect and abuse from the management and the old guard union, but it was all we had.

The coup attempt, within the preload, would prove to be unsuccessful, due to the fact that no one was really 'willing' to assume the role of steward out of fear of retaliation from management. Management had what they wanted, which was a steward who straddled the fence.

The CHSP problem would surface again after I learned of some things that were going on in the meetings that were quite questionable, so I decided to attend the meeting for myself to see if the allegations were in fact the truth.

I looked on the safety board and found the minutes from the last meeting, and I couldn't find a date anywhere on them, which showed the next meeting. I began asking Chasity Muller, another preload manager, every morning when the next meeting was, and I kept getting brushed off. I then sat down and wrote out a note to the west center manager, Gordon, to let him know that I was interested in attending the meeting. After all...the CHSP meeting was opened to ALL employees who wanted to attend, or so I thought.

I would later learn from a steward that a 'certain' manager had talked with him about me attending the meeting. I asked him what was said.

"Everybody, but you can attend." He replied.

"What do you mean, but me?" I asked curiously.

"They don't want you in there," He replied.

"Who told you this?" I asked wanting to know.

"Gordon did." He replied.

Several days passed after I talked with Josey, and one morning after completing my run I came in and asked Chasity when the next meeting was going to be held, and I was told that it had been already been held the previous day. I had them right where I wanted them. I caught her in the office, and began to question her about the posting of the meeting, and why I wasn't told about the date, I felt right off that she didn't want to deal with me, and I could tell she was beginning to fold. I explained to her that I felt I was being discriminated against and I intended on filing a grievance and several complaints to OSHA and the NLRB for retaliatory discrimination.

Antonio came right in after that little confrontation with Chasity and began trying to smooth it over. He explained to me that everybody was welcome to attend the meetings, and that the failure to post the date was just a mere oversight due to her being so busy with the preload and everything.

Abel, who was sitting in the office with me when this all went down, asked, "Why didn't you tell James when y'all were going to meet, Antonio?"

Antonio didn't have anywhere to go with it. He continue to reiterate that I was welcome to attend the meetings, but he thought that I didn't care enough to get involved, because of all the grievances I had filed because of all the safety violations, and that I thought that the committee was illegal and I had disbanded it twice in the past.

"Gordon said I couldn't attend the meetings, " I replied.

"I'm saying you can attend them if you like, James." Antonio replied, and walked out of the office. We didn't buy what he was trying to sell us, so I filed the grievances protesting the obvious discrimination. I never heard the outcome from them, but I was sure to attend the next meeting now that I had been "invited" by Antonio.

The next meeting was held the following month, and I was sure to attend it. The meeting started with Gordon speaking, whom had showed up to make sure that I didn't get out of hand, and I sat over in my seat and taking notes, and questioned several things that were going on. I soon found from his responses that the CHSP was still a joke.

They made light that a driver, who was a 'member' of the CHSP, and who had had two backing accidents in less than a few weeks apart, and they thought it was funny as they sat around the table and joked about it. I didn't find it funny, and the way they made light of this mans predicament made me sick...and while he was sitting there, no less. Management would fire him a few days later, after the meeting, for these accidents. I wonder how funny it was to the fired member of the CHSP then? I wonder if his wife and kids had the same laugh that management had that day during the meeting when he came home and told them that he had been fired from UPS? I doubt it!

After the meeting was adjourned I could tell that Chasity was relieved that it was finally over. Management thought I was going to derail the meeting and attempt to ban it again like I had done so many times before, but I wasn't interested in doing that...not yet.

Later on in the week Josey had arranged a meeting with Matt over in Huntsville, and it was the same old malarkey as always. We voiced our concerns, and he'd say that he was going to show up and put a stop to management working in our building. This was the same old routine. I was surprised though in one turn of events. Abel had resigned as steward and handed Matt his letter of resignation. Matt didn't show any interest, because that's one less 'fanatic' he had to contend with in Huntsville, and I'm sure management was going to be glad of Abel's resignation too. I told Matt during the meeting that he needed to find a replacement to Abel soon as possible, and not for him to drag it out several weeks without the feeder drivers having a steward. Matt said that he'd take care of it within the next two weeks. Two months would pass without Matt appointing anyone to take over after Abel had resigned.

Matt and Joey would wind up winning the election and they headed to Las Vegas to the Teamsters convention to support their old guard leader...Hoffa. What a waste of our money, but they'd at least get the paid vacation they so desired... at our expense.

I had decided to go ahead and run for the steward position if Matt was going to call for an election as I asked everyone if they would object to me being their steward, and the majority of all the feeder drivers were behind me. Only one problem though...UPS management didn't want me in there.

I had learned from a supervisor in the building that Matt had a little meeting in Huntsville with UPS management on May 24, 2001 to discuss several things, and one of which was their (UPS management) disapproval with him even considering appointing me as a steward again for Huntsville. Management was sternly against this, and it seemed that Matt had followed their advice.

Once we learned of this meeting we all became outraged, and Abel immediately began putting together a petition, which was calling for an election, or an appointment of me to be the feeder steward if I ran unopposed. An overwhelming majority of members signed it, but it seemed that this would be the first time in nine years that there wouldn't be a steward election held at a job site in our local. Matt was now facing a dilemma.

Although Matt had held elections at all the other sites, including at the center here in Huntsville, but all of a sudden he had a change in policy? Why was this? Could've it had been because of Hoffa's wishes or managements...or a combination of both? I found it to be just too coincidental especially after he had met with Gordon, the west center manager, in May 2001. Matt would continue to avoid the issue of this, which would drag on for several more weeks.

Chapter 25

"I am calling for a trusteeship of the Teamsters Union."
**-James Hoffa Junior, August 22, 1997
while on Larry King Live.**

Flashback...the Teamsters convention, 1996: While the Hoffa forces are out of control in an attempt to derail the reform movement and squash the voice of democracy within our union they are acting at the direction of a wolf clad in sheep's clothing...Hoffa junior. The unrelenting pounding on tables, the screaming and chanting that was conducted during the speeches of the Carey slate should be a shocking revelation of what lies in store for us once the old guard seizes power within the Marble palace once again.

Elements of Hoffa's platform that were published in whole during the October/November issue of *Teamster* magazine, (on page 31), describes just the opposite of his maniacal plan of deceit to once again entrench his foothold and establish the throne of the old guard, all this is being done as he deceives the membership, whom most are looking for a rebirth, and a reformation of the Teamsters...but it'll take more than just a famous name to reform this union as you will soon see.

Fast forward to the IBT Convention in 2001: The old guard desperately needs Hoffa's name and celebrity status, which will only be used as a means of deceit to achieve their personal and selfish ambitions which will all be at the expense of the members. Hoffa Jr., who had never worked a day in his life as a Teamster, and this one fact alone should've alarmed the members beforehand, and this revelation alone should've made them all to begin asking themselves what exactly it is that this former labor attorney, who's now chosen to run as the leader of the most powerful union in the Unites States, truly wants.

While as a candidate during the 1996 campaign, Hoffa Jr. repeatedly preached about a "Rank and File Bill of Rights", which he adamantly promised "Trusteeships free of political terror, and no mergers or break ups of local unions without first a membership vote to authorize such a action," but Hoffa's actions as the President has been a much, much different story altogether. Hoffa promised to; make UPS deliver the 10,000 new full time jobs that were won after a two week nationwide strike; Negotiate good contracts for Teamster Carhaulers; refuse to give money to anti-union politicians; balance the unions budget with no dues increase; cut and cap IBT officers salaries and perks; allow Teamsters the right to open debate and dissent; protect members' democratic rights; and continue the fight against union corruption. I have to admit that this all sounded good at the time, and it should've and this is what the members wanted and needed. That's the way that a true labor leader should sound, one who wants to tackle and address the core issues that have been plaguing, and slowly destroying our union from the decades of oppressive old guard style of governing and rule. But Hoffa is far from being the true union labor leader that he so desperately tries to portray...so it is wise not to be fooled by his two faced antics, which all depends on what crowd he is addressing at the time, because in reality... he is actually nothing more than a deliverer of union destruction, who has been cleverly wrapped in a famous name with no real desire to reform, and protect the very rights which guarantee us a strong union. For he is the new front man for the old guard...

Let's first address the issue of making UPS deliver us our 10,000 jobs by combining existing jobs. Although the creation of these jobs did not depend on increased volume or filling existing full time positions as they were vacated due to members retiring, but UPS's management had managed to have changed the rules in the middle of playing their game, and coupled with Hoffa's weak stance on this one issue only allowed UPS's management to run unrestrained on the UPS members by subcontracting out numerous feeder work and moving the loads by rail, and only until after intense pressure from the members at UPS did he finally do something about the issue, which was to cowardly turn the case over to be decided on by an independent arbitrator through the grievance procedure. One lingering question is...why didn't he take us back out when UPS's management refused to honor their agreement to create the jobs? Could it have been because UPS's management had previously contributed money to his campaign?

Early in his term, one of Hoffa's earliest failures to the UPS members was to appoint Richard Heck to head the Teamsters Small Package Division, and because that Heck was weak, whenever he dealt with UPS's management, which only allowed UPS's management to take advantage of him as they ran all over him like a cheap road. Heck's immediate and constant throwing up of the white flag of surrender to UPS's management, when they began to start subcontracting our feeder work out, left Hoffa with egg on his face, which then in turn left Hoffa with no other choice, but to remove Richard Heck from his position. What has happened to his 'militant' approach that he had preached about on TV and to the press during his campaigning? It wasn't ever seen. UPS's management was later forced to create the new jobs, as they had promised to do, and not because of any effort on Hoffa's part, but it was at the ruling of an independent arbitrator who instructed UPS's management to create the jobs and pay some back wages to the Teamsters who were to fill these jobs, but yet Hoffa immediately stepped in and stood proudly upon his soap box and took the credit for securing our jobs when actually he never really had that much to do with it to begin with.

What about Hoffa's promise to take on Teamster employers like Anheuser Busch to win the members good contracts? Maybe you should ask the 8,000 (+) brewery workers at Anheuser Busch who had to face the relentless contract gutting concession campaigns from their management, about how well Hoffa kept his word, instead of reading the lies that were printed in his tightly controlled propaganda machine, the *Teamster* magazine, which he now uses to deliver his web of deceit and lies to the unsuspecting members.

All this had started back, while Hoffa was running for office the fist time, when he promised those members that he'd visit every plant to meet the 80% of the members who had voted for him, and he made a promise to put them onto the cover of *Teamster* magazine as soon as he took office, as a token of his appreciation for their support. What they got was an issue of *Teamster* magazine with a picture of a teary eyed Hoffa on the cover, along with a contract that gutted their seniority rights, along with other sickening contractual concessions in an industry that is overwhelmingly organized and where new business is thriving in all markets.

What about Hoffa's 1996 convention promise concerning the position of returning favors to his political allies on Capital Hill? This too would prove to be nothing more than a deceit filled lie of monumental proportions.

Remembering back to 1996, when some of Hoffa's closest allies were several of the worst union-hating politicians to have ever walked the face of the earth. Just to mention a few who are now, quite possibly, expecting a little payback for their past efforts of weakening the Teamsters, and thus priming it for his return and the re-infiltration of the old guard. They are as follows, Jon Christensen (R.-Neb), Newt Gingrich (R.-GA), and Peter Hoekstra (R.-Mi).

Hoffa is hard pressed and desperate to get the U.S Government out of the Teamsters Union, although previously he had been crying to the members that the Government needed to get involved with the union, while he was running in 1996, as he was openly embracing and demanding government intervention in a feeble attempt to make his scheme look legit to the members, but secretly behind the members backs he had other plans. Hoffa frantically needs the U.S Government out of the Teamsters union once and for all to achieve his final push to restore the Teamster's union back to the days of old guard domination and control. Hoffa currently stands on his soapbox, and announces to the Rank and File members that the union is now free of corruption, which by saying this, he is delivering to us nothing but another one his mendacities. Hoffa is not interested in cleaning up the union, because by doing so he would remove every facet of support he has due in part from the corrupted old guard locals. The last thing Hoffa wants to do is to have an honest, democratic reformer in control of "one" of his local unions, who could then oppose his trampling of the members rights and voices, because by doing so would be a sure enough self annihilation of any future hope of re-establishing the old guard style of governing.

And besides...rather than removing the elements by ethical means and avenues, he would rather become allies with some of the worst union busting politicians and enlist their aid in removing any government oversight of the Teamsters with the assistance of such politicians like Hoekstra. Hoekstra, who has stated repeatedly that he will try and end the work of the Election Officer by cutting the funding to the office that oversees and ensures that we'll have fair, honest and democratic elections, which this alone should be enough to scare every member in the Teamsters. Hoffa desires to return us back to the days of Fitzsimmons and Presser through the deception to the members that all is well within the union, when in fact it is not, and one way he accomplishes this task is by enlisting the aid of his dictator controlled *Teamster* publication to spread his lies and deceit. One only has to remember that we did not gain the right to vote for our International officers until 1991, when the U.S Government forced the Teamsters to fall under the consent order and allow us the right to elect our leaders, and only then were all the IBT delegates elected in Government supervised elections. 1991 was also the year that our right to vote for IBT officers was written into the IBT constitution, and until then, the right to elect the IBT officers, which before, only fell to an elite old guard few who had control of our local unions. According to Richard A. Ryan, "The Teamsters union has selected Joseph diGenova as it's current representative to the IRB. We need to remember that the IRB is the powerful agency that monitors union corruption, which was created by the U.S Government's consent order. Now after Hoffa's appointment of Joe diGenova to the IRB, Hoffa was quoted as saying, "Joe diGenova has a strong understanding of the Teamsters union and the consent decree." Now remember...that Rep. Hoekstra, being one of the worst union busting politicians on the Hill, and who has voted in support of stripping the funding to OSHA, and various other labor unfriendly bills, then Hoffa goes on to say, and pay close attention to this, "His work with Representative Hoekstra means that the Teamsters union will receive a fair hearing before the IRB." What planet is Hoffa from to make him think of even supporting someone like this, much less appointing them to an office to oversee our union? I mean...here this diGenova guy has worked in conjunction with one of the worst union-hating politicians in existence, and now Hoffa expects us to believe that we'll get a fair hearing before the IRB...yeah right. That's nothing but a load of bull crap! But hold on a minute here...maybe I'm jumping the gun on this. I think... what that appointment actually meant was that Hoffa, and his old guard thugs will get a fair hearing, or a BLIND EYE, before the IRB, because President Bush's administration gets to choose who the third person will be to make up the three member board. But as a consolation to the members...I'm delighted to say that this new IRB member, Mr. DiGenova, should be happy with his new $100,000 a year salary...plus expenses of course. Let's not forget about the extra $35,000 a year Mr. DiGenova will receive in lieu of pension and health benefits. That's a nice cushy job for someone to receive from Hoffa Junior to ensure that everyone in the Teamsters is going to play by the rules...wink, wink.

And while we're on the subject of salaries, benefits and perks lets review Hoffa's progress regarding his 1996 convention promise of reducing the salaries and perks of all IBT officers and employees. We cannot really examine this issue without incorporating his promise of increasing our strike benefits into the equation, so please bear with me.

During the 1991 convention, our strike benefits were raised to $200.00 a week, but they were done so without a funding mechanism. The old guard, before the Carey Administration, had spent millions of members hard earned dues money on fighting court battles to keep them out of prison, and in office, and millions more on high salaries and lavish perks. The old guard officials even went as far as to take $34 million dollars out of our strike fund to finance this little escapade of theirs. Now, Hoffa's 1996 promise to quadruple the Teamsters strike fund and raise our strike benefits without raising our dues...well it will sadly fall well short of its mark, because it was only promised at the time to garner him votes.

In order to fully understand the mechanics involved with the "strike benefits issue," you need to examine one of the many underlying dynamics that has a deciding impact on the creation and maintainability of such a benefit, which is the increase in the IBT officer's, and employees salaries and benefits.

Under the Carey administration, then former Teamster General President Ron Carey had dumped the jets and limousines that had once symbolized the lavish lifestyles of his old guard predecessors, of which the most recent six previous presidents went to jail, a fourth died while under indictment for embezzlement of union funds, and a fifth led to the drain of the Teamsters pension fund. Carey had dumped as well, many double-and-triple dipping Teamster officials who all simultaneously held down two or more full time jobs with the Teamsters union on the local, regional and national level. But this is what Hoffa wants to revert us back to.

In 1996 Hoffa stated during the convention that he planned on cutting the salary of the general president, if he was elected, to $150,000 a year. But sadly...he flat out lied to the members, and once again, he only used this as just another means to get elected with no real intentions on cutting any salaries at the IBT.

Currently, as of October 2001, there are more than 145 IBT staff members drawing multiple salaries, "more than at any time in the history of the IBT, " according to Dan Scott, who was a delegate from local 174 in Seattle, during the 2001 convention in Las Vegas.

One of the first things Hoffa did, when he did take office, was to raise his salary from $150,000 a year to $226,000, a fifty percent increase. Now to fall in line with the increase of his salary, his legions of old guard Hoffanite's, during the 2001 convention, amended Article V, section 1(e) of the IBT constitution, which in part was to raise the daily expense accounts for Hoffa's appointees for meals by 50%, up to a staggering $75 a day, and added an unlimited cost of living adjustment to it as well. $75 a day for meals means that while that IBT representative in conducting union business for the members, they'll get to eat steak and lobster at least twice a day, while some of our own brothers and sisters cannot even afford to take their kids to McDonalds once a week for hamburgers, because of the countless pathetic contracts that have been negotiated by old guard officers like, for example, my own local unions contract with National Linen in Decatur Alabama, even while our own brothers and sisters cannot even afford to buy $75 dollars worth of groceries a week, which all of this comes as a result of previously negotiated weak contracts. But what about Hoffa, and his fat cat, old guard thug's? Well, at least they'll eat well while they're meeting with the bosses. The Hoffa delegates also voted to raise the car allowances by 38%, up to $550 a month, and added an unlimited cost of living raise as well. $550 dollars a month will just about pay the lease payment on a nice, fully decked out Lincoln town car to ride to the lobster house in...it must be nice Mr. Hoffa, since some of our very own brothers and sisters cannot even afford to buy a decent dependable car to drive to work in, all because of your old guards crappy contracts and greed?

I need a drum roll please...will Hoffa live up to his promise of not raising our dues that he made in 1996? He did say that HE wouldn't raise our dues...but he never said anything about our local union's not doing it. At the 2001 IBT convention, Hoffanite delegates voted overwhelmingly for increasing the IBT's share of the initiation fees that are collected from the members on the local level each year, which are roughly $4.7 million dollars. I can honestly say that Hoffa will probably live up to his promise of not raising our dues...but what he'll more than likely do is pass the increase, along with the blame of his actions onto our local union's, and then make it look like they're the bad guys, instead of him, all while he appears to have kept his promise to the membership. Then our local unions will have to pass that extra cost on to the members in the form of an assessment, to make up for the increase that will be sent to the IBT. So in essence Hoffa still gets his $4.5 million (plus) a year in increased initiation revenue, plus the local unions takes the blame and blunt of the members frustration, all the while Hoffa keeps has promise...well sort of. Hoffa thinks he's slick, but he's really only fooling himself.

Another little known victim of the old guard increase of salaries, from over the last three years, was a decrease in funding for organizing. Hoffa had cut funding for organizing by 63%, while the millions had been transferred to pay for the increases in their salaries and perks.

Does it now begin to make sense as to why Hoffa couldn't finance the PPG campaign that our local union had engaged in? It was because he had transferred the millions of dollars that had been earmarked for organizing, and put it into his and his cronies' pockets!

Currently, as of August 2001, there are over 195 teamster officials who are in the $100,000 club, and who all had received well over $29 million dollars of our hard earned dues money last year in just salaries, perks and benefits!

If Hoffa and his old guard cronies had lived up to their 1996 campaign promise to slash IBT salaries, and had cut out the 141 multiple salaries, of which he reestablished after Carey cut back on the numbers of officials drawing multiple salaries which are currently being paid to his appointee's and running mates, there would've been a savings of over $4.3 million per year that could have been used for a strike fund, but lets not forget about recently voted increase in the IBT's share of the initiation fees by Hoffa and his delegates at the 2001 convention, which would add another $4.7 million a year to the total that could've been used to finance, and raise our strike benefits, and with that extra money there would've been almost $18 million dollars in the strike fund just in time that could've been used for leverage in the upcoming UPS and Master Freight contracts which are set to expire in 2002, and 2003 respectively, but this will not be the case.

As Hoffa sat on the sidelines during the 2001 convention, he was likened to a Roman Emperor as he killed any hope of reducing their salaries with a symbolistic thumbs down to his Hoffanite delegates on the floor as all of the proposals was voted down, which wasn't anything but a thumbs down to the members future.

During the 2001 convention the Hoffanite's were in total opposition to decreasing the salaries, and honestly even some of his Hoffanite's even defended them with one of Hoffa's delegates saying that the Hoffa administration was composed of hard working officials who deserved salaried ten times than those that were paid to mine workers. Now talk about a slap in the face to the mine workers! One ardent Hoffanite, defended the increased salaries by saying, "You get what you pay for." Is that right? Because if it is, then what we've been getting out of Hoffa and the old guard leaders from over the past three years, we should've been sending trailer loads of crap up to the marble palace to pay them with, because...that's all we been getting out of the old guard Hoffanite's!

Now that I established a basis for funding, or should I say for a lack of funding for the strike fund, why would Hoffa and the old guard not want an adequate strike fund to begin with? The answer isn't as complex as you might think. It's all a psychological tool.

Ask yourself this question: What is the most dangerous weapon that any union possesses in its arsenal to deal with, and to take on, a company in order to gain, or enforce a contract? Answer: It's a union's ability to strike the employer. Many times just the mere threat of a strike is more than enough to bring the employers to the bargaining tables to negotiate a contract, and affects these hard-ass employers psychological willingness to negotiate with the union for improving wages, benefits and working conditions. It is the strike, and the power of the strike that helps makes a union and its members strong. We already know that there are some local officials out there who are taking kickbacks from certain employers, even in the pristine Hoffa administration. How long do you think that these kickbacks would continue if an old guard official ordered a strike? Not long...right? But is an official stupid enough to sabotage the right to strike language on the surface? Maybe if you're one of the many Hoffa controlled local's you might, but really...how long do you think those members would actually sit back in silence and put up with that until there was an uprising amongst all the rank and file members. Not long. Well...you had better wake up, because it's going on right now under your very noses, and while you watch on. How is this possible you may ask? It's simple.

Take for example that you have members who are living pay check to paycheck just to survive, and they all had debt up to their armpits, and that were living week to week, which that alone would take their whole $300 weekly paycheck just to survive, and to make all of the payments on their house and such, all due in part to a poorly negotiated contract, like some that currently exist in our very own local's. Now if the only way for these members to get a decent contract with one of these employers was to strike that employer, then how many of those same members do you think would go out on strike knowing that all they were going to get was a measly $55 a week in strike benefits? Probably none, because remember...we'd already established that it was taking everything they were making for just this member to survive day to day.

How can these brothers and sisters be expected to survive on just this pathetic amount? They can't, and the old guard knows it.

Thus by keeping the strike fund at this despicable measly amount, they can keep the members working and in check, and thus keep the employers happy without having the fear of a strike looming when it came time for their contract to expire, then the old guard can sit back and try to force a contract down the members throats while keeping the bosses happy. That's how it works. By retaining a poor, and under funded strike fund, this greatly reduces the willingness of most members to strike, just by the member knowing the possibility that they could stand to lose everything they have if the company decided to lock them out in an attempt to bust the union at their site. Although the 1997 UPS strike was different in nature due in part that a rather large amount of the Rank and File members struck the company just out of spite. And along with this weak strike fund in place, it then reduces the chances that any craft within the Teamsters will get a decent contract, and coupled with the recent slowing of the economy in 2001, that then opens the door wide open for Hoffa to negotiate a weak UPS contract and blame it all on the economy, when in fact it was more than likely he'd be retuning the favor to UPS.

The ability to increase our strike fund was there and is there, but Hoffa chooses to line pockets instead of reducing his IBT's salaries, while he continues to blame the past administration for the reasons of a weak strike fund, and while he, and the old guard officials continue to pillage our dues money...while we do without.

Ask yourself one other question concerning funding an adequate strike fund and bargaining for a contract. Do you think that if these same members had a strike fund that almost matched their weekly paychecks, do you think they would be more willing to strike their employers in an attempt to get better wages and benefits? Sure they would, and Hoffa and the old guard know this.

This should infuriate every member within the Teamsters union. The fact that Hoffa and his appointee's gets $75 a day just to eat on, while we only get $55.00 a week to live on if we went on strike to improve ours and our families way of life, and this alone should incite every single Rank and File member into getting rid of these old guard officials once and for all...if only by using the ballot box!

How does Hoffa's 1996 position of supporting and allowing open debate and dissent, along with protecting every member's rights within the union look? Not very good. Lets look at one of the many ways that Hoffa deal's with dissidents.

According to Henry Phillips, "Dissidents who run as reformers are facing enormous pressure to fall in line and quickly tack to the right in order to stay in Hoffa's good graces", or face the wrath of the old guard, and "Given the member's meager legal protections and the enormous power of the office of the general president, meaning Hoffa, Hoffa has many tools for keeping reformers in check." "A good example of dealing with reformers who are encroaching on the thrones of the old guard hierarchy is like what happened in Connecticut's local 1150. It seems that when local 1150 had voted more than 2-1 for Hoffa at first, then later chose to elect a TDU led Reform team to head their local, so what does Hoffa do? He orders that the election be re-run, thus bringing back the old guard tactic of 'vote till you get it right'.

Another example is in old guard held local 396, where a coalition of UPS drivers and Latino sanitation workers teamed up to try and overthrow their local old guard leadership for a third attempt by local reformers. The Hoffa dominated Joint council 42, has ordered another rerun election,". Does this sound fair? Let me finish before you answer. "Guess whose desk that the appeal asking for this election sit's on? If you guessed Hoffa then you're correct.

When Hoffa isn't ordering election re-runs, he is canceling elections altogether, by placing the locals in "emergency trusteeships." This is what happened in local 556, when the members there decided to run a reform slate against the do nothing old guard incumbent officials.

Hoffa's usual answer to the members, who were wanting to exercise democracy in their dictatorship led local unions is like what happened to our brother's and sister's in New Jersey's local 617, when these members submitted a petition to Hoffa asking him to end his two year trusteeship of their local and schedule them a election. Hoffa's answer to those members was that he ignored their petition, and Hoffa has rewarded their democratic efforts by breaking up their local and parceling out it's members to different allied old guard local unions after the reformers had asked for the Government to intervene. Elsewhere, where weak old guard incumbents face opposition, Hoffa uses mergers and local union dissolutions to avoid elections."

What about the members Bill of Rights that Hoffa had preached about so much during the 1996 convention? February 26, 2001, during the convention a Tom Leedham supporter, proposed an amendment to the IBT constitution for a membership bill of rights, and what does Hoffa do? He gave his trademark thumbs down and the proposal was thrown out. But in a pathetic attempt to appear democratic, Hoffa **allowed** a V.P candidate from the Tom Leedham slate, Bob Hasegawa, to read his proposal over one of his Hoffanite delegate's objection.

Among this Bill of Rights proposal was for all Teamster members to get copies of their contracts, as well as the latest financial records, called a LM-2 forms, from their local unions. It also called for the right for the members to elect their job stewards, and for them to be able to attend the meetings of their joint council region or conferences of which their local union is affiliated with. Included in this proposal was a call for the right to vote on dissolving or merging locals.

On June 29, 2001 Hoffa gave his final thumbs down to the Teamster membership, when Hoffa and his Hoffanite delegates voted all of these proposals down. I'm sure that our own local 402 Hoffanite delegate, Matt, was one of the first Hoffanite's to vote these proposals down since he'd been practicing this old guard system within our very own local as I am currently engaged in battling him over these very issues! But if you're still unsure whether Hoffa and his Hoffanite delegates support open debate...then let me throw this one last thing into the pot.

Do you believe that a member's voice should be heard? Do you feel that every delegate who had been democratically elected to represent their local union at the IBT convention should have been allowed the voices of their members to be heard? Unless you're an old guard supporter, and not a real Teamster then you should, but Hoffa and his delegates didn't seem to think so.

During the 2001 convention, as like in the 1996 convention as well, Hoffa's delegates, along with some top aides resorted to several old guard tactic's of using intimidation, threats of violence and the continued disruption of meetings and convention floor speeches while parading around in their little yellow vest, in attempts to squash the voices of the Rank and

File members of the Teamsters union. With hard-line Hoffanite's, like Keegle, who was caught repeatedly cutting off the speakers microphones at the podium during the speeches of their opponents, along with hordes of yellow vested Hoffanite's traveling in roaming packs to block the doorways, hallways and even forced some of Tom Leedham's delegates to run the gauntlet to even get to the convention floor to speak, all of these traitorous actions perpetrated by the yellow vested Hoffanite's were nothing but a disgusting attempt to destroy and strangle the voice and rights of the members...my voice as well as your own. Even at times these very Hoffanite's walked out in the middle of the speeches that were being conducted by General Presidential candidate Tom Leedham and they even walked out on the Election Administrator, Mr. William Wertheimer, during his speech of reprimanding Hoffa and Keegle for using an Ohio Teamster Conference truck at a pro Hoffa rally on that Monday, outside the Bally's hotel which was in violation of the election rules.

The mere fact that these Hoffanistic people didn't even have enough respect to the members, much less to themselves, to act like men and women, should've been of no surprise to anyone. Every one of these Hoffanite's should be ashamed for the way they disgraced the Rank and File members, and if they're not, then they aren't much of an honorable person, and I don't see how they can even look in the faces of their members back home. But, I really can't blame them though for walking out of the convention while Tom Leedham was describing what they had done to the members over the past three years...because If I had done what Hoffa and his old guard cronies had done, I would have had to walk out of there ashamed and embarrassed as well.

Corruption is not a rare visitor to the Hoffa camp. Tom Gilmartin, a candidate for IBT secretary-treasurer on the Tom Leedham Rank and File power slate, has formally asked U.S attorney Mary Jo White in New York to open a criminal investigation of the Teamster scholarship fund set up by no other than Hoffa Jr.

Because of a report in May 2001, by the IRB, found that an owner of a Chicago based company paid $5,100.00 to the James R. Hoffa Memorial Scholarship fund, to be used for golf outings and outlined a scheme that involved several IBT officials linked closely to General President Hoffa. The scheme took hundreds of jobs away from hard working Teamsters and gave them to non-union workers to set up and take down conventions in Las Vegas. In addition the IRB found that the Chicago based company in question would only pay half of the $20 an hour, that the Teamster workers would've received, and without any union benefits to the non-union workers.

Gilmartin wrote U.S attorney White that the company was, "seeking at the time to clinch concessionary labor contract negotiations with Dane Passo, a personal assistant to Hoffa Jr., and then there's William T. Hogan, who is an IBT representative, who had been appointed by Hoffa. Hogan's brother was vice president of the company in question and the CEO of Show Biz USA, a general contractor who was only interested in cheap labor by contracting the Chicago based company. Hogan was Hoffa junior's running mate back in 1996, but withdrew after a government investigation brought internal charges against him citing illegal nepotism in his Chicago local. So what does Hoffa Jr. do with him after finding out about this corruption? The very corruption he pledged to rid the union of during his 1996 convention speech? He hires him as a representative of the IBT. Hoffa should have had him thrown out of the Teamsters for life!

Gilmartin also noted that when the elected principle officer of local 631 wouldn't go along with the plan, Hoffa replaced him with a trustee, who also opposed the deal, and Hoffa ousted him on the recommendation of Passo.

One last bit of 2001 convention news involved a proposal that was turned down by Hoffa and his delegates was one that would prevent Teamster officials from leaving the union and taking the information they learned while in our service to go to work for the employers in labor relations jobs within five years after leaving office. Why wouldn't Hoffa want to support and pass this crucial proposal? One only has to think back to what Hoffa was doing before joining the Teamsters union...do you remember? He was working as a labor attorney and had clients such UPS and Freight! Do you think he'd actually put himself out of a job if he ever gets beat, and be unemployed for five years? Come on now...

There are only two things standing in Hoffa junior's way of lifetime job security...one; a government supervised election, two; TDU...

In order for Hoffa's plans to work he must continue to isolate TDU and local reform leaders, harass reform officials, and block rank and file reform efforts in order to complete his lifetime security project. Hoffa is attempting to use the RULES to attack TDU and his opponents.

But Hoffa is facing a dilemma as well. He has allowed, and is allowing Teamster employers to use their weapons of lean production tactics to undermine working conditions and promote speed up on the job, ridiculous production standards, two tier contracts, part time labor, subcontracting, the rampant use of replacement and temporary workers, and on and on.

Does it begin to make sense to you now, as to why the Hoffa controlled IBT, and our local old guard local unions who are under his rule, and control, have refused to step in and stop UPS's management from raising our stop counts without a time study to justify it? Why has UPS management refused to hire new drivers to replace the ones who have retired, while they still use the PART TIME cover drivers, who are part time employees, to replace them? UPS's management has pushed, and received many of different pay rates for their employees. Why hasn't Hoffa fought UPS for just one flat rate, instead of their two, three, four, five, six and seven different tied wage rates? Why has Hoffa allowed UPS's management to replace what was once Teamster jobs by the hiring temporary non-union replacement workers to replace our union jobs? Why has Hoffa sat back on his dead ass and allowed, until recently, UPS's management to subcontract out our feeder work? Why has Hoffa allowed all of this continue? Why has Matt allowed all of this to continue? Why do we continue to lose our winnable grievances all throughout the grievance process? All one has to do is re-read this little chapter on Hoffa again, and then think back to what you have read so far in the big brown lie.

And if you still don't believe me? Then look at what you have just read about how Hoffa deals with dissident reformers in the union, and then compare that to what happened to me, after I was discharged from UPS back in 1999.

Do you now understand why my discharge was allowed to happen? Do you understand now why Hoffa and Matt never fought to force UPS's management to give me my job back when they possessed the 'militant' power to do so? I was a threat, and I qualified as a dissident reformer if there ever was one, wouldn't you think? It all should now start to all come together, and begin to make a little sense.

The single most dangerous enemy to our very existence, as a union, does not solely lie outside the walls our union...it lies from an enemy that is entrenched within the union itself. Hoffa and the old guard officials are one of the single most dangerous element's that affect's our mere survival.

Chapter 26

Antonio and Fredrick accuse me of shipping a package and not paying for it as retaliation for the complaints to OSHA that I had made earlier. I am running out of patience with these people. I call feeders and tell them that if I see any police cars at the building tonight, that I will not punch in for work."

One evening, after the customer counter had closed I wanted to ship a package to Jamie at our local, who was set to retire the next day, and I wanted to ship her a little going away 'gift', after I figured that we had made amends since after our previous, and many falling out's. I just wanted to send her a little 'joke' box that she, and I had discussed back in January 2000. I was going to send her what was called a 'depression era' shoeshine kit, which textile union members used to send their retiring union officers as a joke back during the 1930's.

I had called the UPS phone center to get a price on the shipping charges for my package that I was going to send to the local. It was going to cost me roughly $4.50 to ship it to her, so I had stopped at a convenience store on the way to work that evening, and purchased a money order for $10.00, and made it out to UPS to cover the shipping charges of the package. I always liked to make sure that I had more than enough money to cover the charges in case they tried to say that I 'stole services' from them.

When I arrived to the building, I already had purchased my box, and I walked into the center and went directly up stairs to the bathroom.

I took some toilet paper and brown shoe polish, and then I wiped the toilet paper onto the show polish. When I was finished it had the desired look I was seeking. I then put it in the box and walked back downstairs, where I had met Joseph who asked me what I was going to do, and after telling him, he thought it was funny and very deserving.

I walked on up to the customer counter and filled out a shipping document, and placed the package on the scale and I bent down to look at the weight. "Less than two pounds," I thought to myself. It weighed a pound lesser than what I had received a quote for over the phone from UPS. Either way...I still had more than enough money to pay for it.

I walked on out into the center and looked for me a supervisor, and I saw that Macy was watching people work on the east belt, and I walked over to where he was, and asked him if I could ship a package out, and he replied to me that it was okay.

"Good," I thought, but not good enough. I wanted at least more than one supervisor as a witness, just in case management would ever say something about it later. I walked around the building for a minute or so, and I found me another part-time supervisor, Stacy, and asked him the very same thing that I had asked Macy earlier. And I received the same answer.

He didn't care what I did, and he told me that it would be all right that I did. But I still wanted one more supervisor. I saw Jack, also a part-time supervisor, who was walking around, and I asked him if he had a minute.

"What do you need James?" Jack asked.

"I need to show you something in the customer counter Jack?" I replied, as we walked toward the back entrance that led into it.

We walked into the little room, and I asked him to look at the weight shown on the scale.

"Two pounds?" He replied curiously, and not realizing what his purpose was as of yet.

"Here's the money order made out to UPS along with the shipping document for this package." I replied, while holding them both up, and waving them in front of him.

"Okay, I see them." He replied.

"That's all I needed Jack, thanks." I replied, as began taping them onto the cash register monitor so the clerk would see them the next morning and then enter them into the computer. I picked the package up and placed it on the belt to go out tonight for tomorrow, because it was important that this gift box arrived at the local the next day.

"Why did you have to go through all that to ship a package for James, heck, drivers do it all the time?" Jack asked, as we walked into the center again.

"I'm not your average driver, Jack." I replied.

Jack picked up on exactly what I was saying, because he knew of all the hell management had put me through. I had to be cautious, and have plenty of 'trusting' witnesses in case anything would come up, and I trusted all three of these guys, because there was no love for UPS in that brood either.

"I've already talked with Macy and Stacy, and they all know that I shipped the package out too, Jack." I replied to him as I stopped as he stopped and turned to face me.

"If anything is ever said about this package being shipped tonight...be sure you don't get amnesia." I replied.

"James you know me better than that. I don't lie for no one." Jack replied. It was getting time for me to start work and we went about our respected duties.

I stopped walking, and pulled out a copy of the shipping document and money order and looked it over again to be safe. I had written the tracking number on the money order as well, and I decided to go ahead and punch them on the time clock to show what time and date they were shipped. I wasn't taking any chances.

I started work, and as I was building my trailers, I thought to myself how silly this whole thing was and how I was acting just to ship a package out. I thought about how paranoid I was acting and then I began to feel foolishly about the whole thing. Maybe I was over reacting and being too paranoid. After all, drivers ship packages out all the time like I had just done, at least several times a week. Maybe I was making something out of nothing.

The next morning when I woke up, after getting off that Friday morning, I called the center and asked for Carrise. Carrise answered the phone, and I asked her if she ran my receipt through, and she said no that she didn't. It seemed that Antonio had told her not to do it, and that he had taken my check and receipt with him. I found this odd, but maybe I just didn't fill something out correctly on the shipping document? Whatever the reason was I had to come into town to pick my check up and run some errands, and I'd talk to him when I got down to the building.

I arrived to the center and walked on inside, and said hello to several people that were working in the building that morning. I walked towards the middle office and stopped to look inside and noticed that Fredrick, the UPS loss prevention supervisor, was talking on the phone, and as he looked at me, I just curled my lip at him. I couldn't stand the mere sight of him, because he made me literally sick. I stomached him long enough to walk into the office to get my check, and as I turned to leave...I caught his reflection in the window looking at me. He was on the talking on the phone, and I just dismissed it as his usual behavior.

I walked on into the west center's office, and saw that Antonio was talking to Gordon in his office. Antonio looked up at me, and I told him that I needed to see him for a minute. I didn't really care to talk to him, but he was the one that had my document, and I wanted to get my receipt for shipping the package. After a few minutes of waiting Antonio came out of Gordon's office and asked me what I needed.

"I need to get the receipt for my package I left for Carrise last night." I replied.

"That was.... your package?" He replied strangely.

"Yeah why?' I asked, while suspecting that something wasn't right with this.

"Sure...follow me James, we couldn't figure out who's it was?" He replied, in a drastic turn of emotion. He seemed as if he was going to bust through the seams with happiness. I just dismissed his behavior as just being flaky.

We walked by the middle office, where Fredrick was at and still on the phone, and Antonio asked me to wait outside as he walked in the office. I noticed that he retrieved my stuff from a file Fredrick had in front of him, as he said something to Fredrick and they both looked at me through the window of the door, and I began to get a very bad feeling about this.

Antonio walked back out, and he began to treat me like I was his long lost brother, and he was asking me about my family and what was going on...the whole bit. He was still acting a little too giddy, and I began suspecting a rat.

I told Antonio that I had to go and that I would just pay for it as I walked out. Antonio told me to have a good day and that he'd see me later. I wanted to see what the problem was that prevented this to be processed like they had always been done, and why this one transaction had been so 'special'.

I walked over to the east side loading dock, and I sat down in between a set of rollers and a ceiling support pole, and I was pretty well hidden from everyone's view by accident. I began to look over the document, and I noticed that what I had done was to have failed to complete the return address section of the shipping document, so I placed it down on the dock and began to fill it out. While doing this I looked up and noticed that

Fredrick and Antonio were walking very fast up towards the customer counter, and I knew then that something was fixing to go down. They entered into the customer counter and looked around, and then turned around, and began walking back towards me, and when they saw me sitting there...Fredrick honestly smiled.

I stood up and I began walking towards the customer counter, and not wanting to get into it with them over this.

"James we need to talk to you okay?" Antonio asked.

"What do you want?" I replied, knowing that if they questioned me about anything without a steward being present that it was not only a contract violation, but an unfair labor practice as well. They had to have a steward there to represent me if this 'discussion' would lead to discipline. I knew this, but I wasn't going to say anything to them about it. I'd just let them hang themselves.

"Did you ship a package out last night?" Antonio asked, with Fredrick standing there trying to look menacing and intimidating with his arms crossed while he bowed out his chest like a rooster or something.

"Yes." I replied, while keeping my answers short, and simple thus reducing any chance of 'tripping up'.

"Was the customer counter open when you shipped it last night?" Antonio asked.

"Depends on ones perspective." I replied, and getting a dumbfounded look from them both.

"What do you mean by that?" Fredrick asked.

I've answered that question I believe." I replied, not falling for the trap. They were going to try and get me to say that it was closed, and drop any further investigating until after I left and fire when I came to work that night, and if I replied yes, then I'd been lying, and then I could have be discharged for dishonesty, but if I replied no, then I could have been discharged for 'stealing services'. So I left them nowhere to go with it.

This response pissed Fredrick off a great deal. I was very capable of going toe to toe with both of them at the same time, and if that's the way they wanted it then so be it. I was beginning to become upset and angry, but I tried to remain calm about it.

"James you realize people has been fired in the past for this very thing." Fredrick popped off in a smart-ass tone.

"No Fredrick...people have been fired for not paying for shipping a package" I replied, as the anger began to swell.

"How could you pay for it if the customer counter was closed James? TELL ME THAT!" Antonio replied, while getting loud. I knew it was only a matter of time before this thing turned real ugly and decided to leave.

"Antonio I paid for it. I weighed it, everything." I replied.

"How do we know that the weight was correct? Maybe you didn't charge enough for it? How are we to know James?" Fredrick replied.

"Where are you going James?" Fredrick asked.

"I'm not on the clock and I don't have to talk to you. I'm going to pay for my package." I replied, and I began walking towards the customer counter door.

"James I'm not going to let you pay for it now until we've done an investigation." Fredrick replied.

I turned and walked back over to them.

"You mean to tell me that you are not going to let me pay for shipping this package?" I asked stepping right in front of them both.

"That's right James." Antonio replied.

"No big deal." I replied, and I turned to walk out leaving them both standing there watching me. They had looks of joy like I had never seen on any set of managers before. It was truly pathetic. They thought they finally had me.

I stopped and turned and hollered back at them. They both stopped and turned around to look at me.

"You better have your ducks in a row on this one boy's." I replied, while standing a short distance from them.

"What do mean by that?" Fredrick replied, as if he was trying to act like a tough guy.

"You need to check with the three supervisors of yours who all told me that I could ship the package last night. Jack witnessed the weight and everything Antonio." I replied smiling.

They just stood there with their mouths dropped open, as all expression had left their pathetic Imbecilic looking faces. They didn't know what to do now, after their glass house had just crumbled on top of them.

I left the building, and drove immediately up to the store on the corner to use the phone. I was unsure of what they'd do. I figured they'd just fire me anyway what did they care?

I called the Birmingham OSHA office, and filed a complaint of 'retaliatory discrimination' against UPS for what I perceived as retaliation for the complaints to OSHA that I had recently filed. The duty officer took the complaint over the phone, and told me that he would issue a notice that I had filed a complaint with his office against my employer. My name would be on this one, because of the type of complaint I had filed, and UPS would know for sure that I had filed one. I then called Matt over at the local and told him what was going on. He started in on "well you've got a receipt right? They don't have anything so don't worry about it."

"That's what you told me the last time remember Matt?" I replied angrily.

"I will not put my family through that again. Do you UNDERSTAND?" I screamed into the phone. Matt could tell that I was through playing games with this.

"I'll call right now and find out what's going on with it." Matt replied, and I hung up the phone. I had to call and tell Lesley, because she had changed jobs last week and lost her insurance. If I were to get fired tonight we'd be without insurance. She became upset and cried after I told her what had just happened.

I drove on home and called Birmingham feeders, and I spoke with my supervisor and explained to him what was going on. The supervisor became enraged. I was shocked to say the least.

"If I come to work and they've got cop cars there I won't even go in, I'll just drive back on home until I can get a lawyer." I said to him.

"If they bring you in the office for anything tonight James, I want you to call me at home, and put me on the speaker phone do you understand me?" He replied.

"They are not going to fire you on this crap." He replied.

I told him that I would call him if anything happened at all.

I arrived for work that night, and I didn't see any police cars there like that were there back in August of 1999. I walked on into the shop, and asked the mechanics if they had heard anything that might be going to go down tonight, and they both replied no that they haven't.

"Have you seen any big wheels up here, or anyone from loss prevention?" I asked.

"Nope, no one James." They replied.

I eased on into the office and punched in on my computer. I didn't notice anything out of the ordinary. I walked on out from the middle office back into the center, and I looked around, and didn't notice anyone there either. I met up with all three of the part time supervisors, and asked if anyone had talked to them about shipping the package, and they replied that Gordon had talked to them, and they all told him that they said it was okay for me to ship it. No wonder I didn't see them. They were too ashamed that their little scheme fell short of its mark.

The following Monday, I would catch Gordon in the building, and I asked him again to settle this matter once and for all. He told me to just pay in cash whenever I had a chance to, but I refused to do this, and I told him that UPS could just keep the money that was left over from the difference.

Several days later Gordon called me into the office, and that he had my change. Gordon had laid the change out on the copy machine, and he had made a copy of the full amount that he was giving back to me. Management wanted me to sign a paper, which had the copied money on it, showing that they had given me my change back, and I signed it while, I was thinking how funny this all was.

Matt had stated to Josey, that he was considering letting me be steward of just feeders and no one else. I wanted to be steward again, but not at the expense of representing just one classification, and not being able to serve everyone as a whole.

Management doesn't want me to have any say about the part timers on both the reload and preload, because that's where most of the problems were that currently existed in our building, and Matt figured that this move would settle and pacify both sides of the issue. The fact of the matter is our side is the only side that counts on this subject. I will have to decline the offer, if he actually makes it, concerning limiting my power as a steward, because...I'm not for sale.

DATE GRIEVANCE FILED: 7-18-01

EXPLAIN GRIEVANCE: *The monthly CHSP meeting was scheduled today. When I arrived at 8:00 a.m. I waited until 8:13 a.m when Gordon came up and told me it was cancelled. I find this extremely inconsiderate and unprofessional.*

REMEDY SOUGHT: *one hours pay @ 1 ½ rate.*

Gordon and I had had words about this little stunt that they had pulled concerning me, and the CHSP meeting. I wasn't going to worry too much about it, but someone was going to pay me for showing up. I had gone ahead and punched in on the clock just right before the meeting, and punched out before I left, and I then faxed my timecard down to feeders in Birmingham. I was being sure to document the time that I was there to correspond with what I was saying I was, because I knew how Hembry operated in the office during the local, and he might throw out the grievance for a lack of documentation.

I continued to watch the CHSP board, that was just outside the west center office, and I was waiting for some sort of notice announcing a new time and date for the next meeting to be posted on it. I checked it every morning before leaving the building, and every evening when I arrived back to the center, but nothing yet.

One evening I came into work and Gary, a mechanic, stopped me as I walked into the building.

"James someone's here to see you." He replied, while looking back toward the offices as he wiped off one of his tools.

"Who is it? Do you know?" I asked.

"No I don't, but I know that it's some big wheel from Birmingham." He answered.

I didn't know whom it could be, and I walked back outside, and peered around the corner to look at the back of the building.

"No police." I thought to myself, and I walked on around towards the offices. I went on inside the middle office and punched in for work, and as I walked back outside into the building, this individual who was looking for me walked up. I knew who it was. It was Kendall Borton, the Alabama District safety manager.

"James Earls?" He asked, while not knowing for sure of who I was.

"Yes sir," I replied.

"I need to follow up with you about a complaint you filed against us with OSHA." He replied, while crossing his arms behind his back. I had forgotten all about calling OSHA that day when Antonio and Fredrick had tried to fire me for shipping the package.

We proceeded to discuss the matter and I outlined for him what had happened that warranted this type of complaint. He didn't really seem that enthused to be here discussing this matter with me, but so what.

Finally towards the end of our discussion, he replied, "I have never seen a complaint from OSHA with a name on it. Most of the time it's anonymous."

"They have to disclose the name of the person filing it on this type of discrimination complaint." I replied.

"I prefer y'all to know that it was me anyway," I replied, while smiling. He didn't seem to share in my sense of humor.

By this time Abel had arrived to work, and I asked him to join in the conversation with us. Abel began to tell Kendall about the constant egress problems they were having on the reload, and Kendall said that he was interested in fixing the problem. It was such a serious problem that one of the part time supervisors had been coming to Abel and me to fix for him, because every time he went to management they'd just brush him off.

The problem was that management wasn't giving him enough people to keep the work caught up during the sort due to "LEAN PRODUCTION TACTICS", which caused everyone else to have to speed up. The supervisor said, that he had been trying over and over to fix the problem, but he never got any results, so that's when he decided to come to us.

Kendall assured us that the problem would be fixed, and he went on his way. Abel and I had heard all of this before. "Yeah right," We thought.

A few days later, and management had still not posted a new date for the safety meeting, and I was looking forward to bringing up the issue of egress, so I could demand an answer as to why nothing had been done about it since the last meeting of the CHSP committee, when I had brought it up then.

I came into the building earlier than normal the next evening, and noticed that nothing had been done to correct the problem of egress like Kendall had said that he would do. It was the biggest mess I had ever seen.

Packages were literally falling off of the slides that connect to the rear of the trailers. Packages were piled up on both sides of the trailer and were preventing the Teamsters, who were working in the trailers, to escape in case of a fire. If that would've happened they would have probably been killed before we could get them out of the trailers. I knew just what to do.

The next morning I called, and filed another complaint with OSHA for Huntsville's egress violations. And after day or two, after I had made the call, OSHA came in and conducted another surprise inspection, and once again, management was caught with their pants down.

The management in Huntsville knew that I had called OSHA and most of them wouldn't even look at me. They hated me more than ever. But they were going to fix the problem in Huntsville or I'd have OSHA in there every week.

The problem of egress managed to be straightened out for a day or two, and then it was right back to square one. They were more concerned with keeping the sort on schedule, and making sure that it went down on time, rather than providing us a safe place to work. If they had cut the belts off to clean up the egress problems during the course of the sort it would have put them slowly behind each time it was done, but once again management had put the almighty dollar before workplace safety.

I came back into work that evening and I looked around the building and there it was. The problem was there in the Montgomery trailer. I walked on around, and under the slides, and looked inside. Inside the trailer were Walt, and another supervisor working inside with a new guy. They both looked up and saw that I was standing there, and they knew they were fixing to have hell to pay, because they climbed out and cut the belt off to clean up their mess, but it was a little too late for that now.

I walked back around to the offices, and I looked through the file of a package car steward and found several grievance forms. I walked back around to the east office and sat down, and began filling them out, only this time I'd include a personal letter to Kendall, the UPS safety man for Alabama, telling him that I would be following up with another OSHA complaint once again. I explained to him that I was very concerned that if something wasn't done about the egress problem soon that someone could get killed in an event of a fire, and as well, that I disappointed in his lack of interest, as I perceived it, in correcting the egress problem, and I was sure to throw in there as good measure, what I thought about the CHSP team in Huntsville.

I had earlier reported to the safety committee in Huntsville that there was a problem with egress on the reload shift. They sure talked a good game about how they were going to correct the problem, and follow up with everyone. What a joke. Nothing was ever done by any of them. But I had managed to correct the dangerous problem of egress with just two little phone calls to OSHA, and one letter and grievance to Kendall. That's were the power is to correct the problems like we face at UPS. It's in exercising your federal rights under the OSHA Act, and not in some little pathetic little Mickey Mouse committee like what was in Huntsville.

The following Monday night I was pulled off to the side by Walt, who was now the reload manager, to talk off the record, as Abel stood there watching me, as I walked off to the side with Walt so no one could hear our conversation.

He began the conversation off by stating that he wasn't trying to discourage me from not filing my grievance about egress.

"That's good," I thought, because this conversation could turn into an unfair labor practice charge if he wasn't careful. Walt proceeded to tell me that he was really trying, and that he had made progress since taking over the reload, and on, and on. I stood there letting him say his peace, and when he finished, I stood there thinking about what I was going to say.

"Walt, the problem I had with the egress thing the other night was that you did not turn off the belts to clean up your mess...now did you?" I asked.

Walt never said anything.

"It's always been that way with this management team, and it's that way now. All y'all care about is getting the sort down on time, regardless of what is happening to affect safety." I said.

"We're trying James, and the problem won't happen ever again. I promise," he replied, and I walked off just leaving him standing there.

It was the same old story. I mean, they continue to ask us to turn the other cheek and over look safety issues, and then they make promise after promise to us to fix the problem, but nothing ever comes of it.

It's just like the old saying goes, "Fool me once shame on you, fool me twice...shame on me." I would fix the egress problem in Huntsville one way or another.

Chapter 27

"We all met with other influential members from each job site and tried to form a slate to defeat Matt and the other old guards who have seized control of our local union. Little did we know that we were being set up, and that we would be betrayed once again, for political reasons, by two of the very people that we had trusted and had formed an alliance with."

I was looking forward to bringing this latest turn of events up during the next safety committee meeting. I was still looking and waiting for the date of the next meeting to be posted on the board, but still...nothing yet.

In the meantime, Abel had been working on an idea that had regarding the upcoming local union election, which was only a few months off. We discussed it several times on our way up to Whites Creek, and with several of the other trustworthy drivers that we ran with, and we all agreed that it was a good idea. We were planning to hold a meeting, so anyone interested in running against Matt in the fall of 2001 could meet, and sit down to discuss the best course of action. We all would have the same goal, which was to get rid of Matt and the old guard.

We wanted to put the best man we had to run against Matt and concentrate only on getting him elected along with his slate. The date of the meeting would be set for the last week in August 2001.

During the next couple of weeks Abel spent a lot of time trying to secure a date for the meeting, and word had leaked out about the meeting, and then several "questionable" drivers began asking us questions about it, and what it was for, but we all knew that they were asking on behalf of Matt. It wasn't as if it was top secret or anything, but we weren't expecting this sort of questioning just yet. So all we did was pump them up with a bunch of crap so they'd then run back and report to Matt about what we were saying. We always told them something different each time, and sure enough it would get back around to us by other drivers a day or two later.

The Tuesday after talking to Walt about the grievance, I finished my run from the Whites Creek hub, and walked into the center to do my check out to go home. I looked on the safety board as I walked by and stopped after realizing what I had seen...and I saw it was written in black and white.

They had had their safety meeting without telling me.

I waited for five days before filing the grievance. I wanted them to think I had given up about being permitted to attend and I wanted to surprise them at the last minute.

DATE GRIEVANCE FILED: 8-7-01
EXPLAIN GRIEVANCE: *The management refuses to allow me to at-*

tend the CHSP meetings. Management failed to mark a new date on the minutes of the old meeting on 7-31.

REMEDY SOUGHT: *Pay for all time in meeting @ 1 ½ times hourly rate.*

It was obvious now what management was doing. They were openly discriminating against me, and they did not want me there, but I now become more determined than ever, to force management into allowing me to attend these meetings...one way or the other.

I received a call from a representative with OSHA, who wanted to meet with me to discuss the complaint I had filed against the UPS management. I figured it was about the retaliatory discrimination complaint that I had called in against Antonio and Fredrick about shipping the box.

I drove on out to Madison Alabama to a Day's Inn hotel where he was staying. I met with him and we both sat down, and I discussed what was going on. I proceeded to tell him about shipping the package and what Antonio and Fredrick had tried to do, and I told him as well about the safety committee, and how they wouldn't let me attend. He took down my statements, and I signed the affidavits.

"I'll send UPS a nice letter about letting you attend these meetings if they're allowing everyone else to do the same Mr. Earls." He said, pausing for a minute. "I'll get you in." He finished.

I was very satisfied with the results of the meeting with OSHA. I had tried to work out this matter with UPS before resorting to intervention by the Federal Government, but they refused to straighten this problem out, and do the right thing. So then the U.S Government would force management to let me attend the CHSP meetings whether they wanted me in there or not.

I started to leave the hotel and thanked him for his time, only he wasn't finished. He was interested in discussing an incident that had happened at one of our sister centers several months ago.

The little Colonel had had enough with people getting injured, so he stood up during one of his morning PCM's with his drivers and stated to them, "The next one who gets injured he'd fire them." Which, this was illegal, and was nothing more than an unlawful tactic used to discourage people from reporting injuries.

Everyone over there filed a group grievance against the Colonel for saying this, and then when I found out about what he had told them, I called in a complaint to OSHA about it. Management had been, and still does, disciplining people for getting injured. They always had. They say that they failed to work safe, or not as directed and so on. This time it had finally caught up with them, and with none other than the little Colonel.

It seemed that someone up high at OSHA had taken an interest in the matter of this practice by UPS management.

I asked him what could come of it if anything happens. His reply was maybe a class action lawsuit against UPS for this practice. The remedies ranged anywhere from a Federal Judge ordering the removal of all related discipline from "ALL" employees records to UPS being forced to send a letter of apology to all of its employees. He wouldn't go any further with anymore information. The case was still open, although management thinks it's closed.

Several days after the initial complaint, the Colonel stood back up during a PCM, and in front of everyone, and craw fished, and even tried to intimidate several drivers into saying that it was all just big a misunderstanding, which was typical of management anytime the Federal Government has busted them on something.

On August 14, 2001 I arrived back to the building at around 3:00 a.m and waited for a member of management to show up to let me in. Finally, Chasity came in and unlocked the door for me. Before I punched out, I asked her if the safety meeting was today, to which she replied that it was. I told her that I'd see her there and I went on home.

I managed to get a few hours of sleep and awoke just in time to make the drive back to the building to attend the meeting. I walked on into the building and punched in, and then after a minute or so, Gordon came walking up to me while I was talking to Georgianna and Candy.

"James do you have some reason to be here?" He asked, while acting very cocky.

"Yeah, I'm here to attend the safety meeting Gordon." I replied calmly. I knew what was coming next.

"No, you're not welcome, and are not invited to the meeting, and you need to leave the property immediately." He popped off.

"Okay Gordon, thank you." I replied, while walking off. I think this shocked him more than anything, because here I was just walking away and had elected not to fight it out with him about the CHSP.

I walked on over to the job stewards folder, and removed two more grievance forms from it, and walked back over to the hood of a package car, and used it as a desk to write on. As I stood filling the grievance papers out, people filed by me, looking over my shoulder, and asking me what I was filing on.

"I'm being discriminated against." I replied, while sighing.

After a minute or so, I walked around to the clock to punch the grievances on, and Antonio walked by me smiling, so I smiled back, and winked at him. He then quit smiling, and walked on off.

There wasn't a steward there yet, and I saw Tracy, a west center supervisor, come walking by, and he replied, "Are you going to the meeting this morning James?"

"No, Tracy they won't let me." I replied.

"Who won't let you?" He asked concerned.

"Gordon told me I couldn't attend it." I replied.

"I can't believe it" He replied, as shook his head in disbelief.

By now Gordon had come walking up to us, and he began to stand there with his arms folded.

"Tracy, I'm coming to you to invoke the company's in house procedure regarding reporting discrimination." I replied, as Gordon's mouth dropped open.

"What's going on James?" Tracy replied.

I began to explain to him how management wouldn't allow me to attend the meetings, and then how they had allowed me to attend in the past, and then changed their minds. Management had changed their position from "anyone can attend", to that of, 'you have to be a member' in order to attend position. I explained to him about filing the complaints to OSHA, and the numerous grievances concerning safety, and how they were now discriminating against me by not allowing me to attend these meetings.

"You need to tell a manager, and not him." Gordon fired off at me.

"Tracy, the complaints against Gordon here, and I felt that I couldn't come to him with the problem...you know, a conflict of interest kind of thing." I replied, while not making any eye contact with Gordon.

"Well James, you need to tell Antonio then." Gordon said again while Antonio stood there watching the whole thing unfold.

"Well Antonio.... He's mixed up in it too Tracy." I replied, and I could tell that Gordon was about to explode.

By now Fredrick was coming down the stairs, and Gordon called Fredrick over, and told him what was going on, and that he was going to be the one that probably would be involved in the investigation concerning my new allegations.

"James I'll get on them right away, and I'll do the necessary things to get the ball rolling." Tracy replied. I knew that Tracy was a decent manager, although some people didn't like Tracy while he had been a center manager years ago, but I liked him, and I knew that he was somewhat ethical, and I knew that he'd do the proper thing, and not employ the 'buddy system" in handling my complaint.

I walked on out side, and saw that Joseph was sitting at the back of the building. I walked over to his truck, and told him what had just happened.

"Are they that damn stupid? Why don't they just let you go to the meetings like they did for everyone else?" Joseph replied, while taking a draw off his cigarette. I handed the grievances to Joseph, and he looked them over.

"Be sure to give them to Gordon." I replied, and went home.

DATE GRIEVANCE FILED: 8-14-01

EXPLAIN GRIEVANCE: *I am being discriminated against for filing grievances and complaints to OSHA. Management is still refusing to allow me the right to attend these safety meetings as any other employee can.*

REMEDY SOUGHT: *I will be filing a complaint to OSHA and an unfair labor practice charge against management.*

I made the drive home and called Matt at the union hall, and told him what was going on, and he sat there on the phone listening to everything I had to say. He wanted me to drive to Atlanta, Georgia next week to be called as a witness for my grievances that were on the docket to be heard, but I told him to just defer them, and that I wanted to wait and see what the NLRB had to say about what management was doing to me, and there was no way that management wasn't going to be able to reverse themselves now. I went ahead and called Donny, with OSHA, and discussed with him what was going on. He had told me that Kendall was supposed to have talked to me about the CHSP, and see if we could settle the issue regarding whether I could or couldn't attend the CHSP meetings.

"Donny, he hasn't talked to me about it yet." I replied.

"Well, I spoke to him several days ago, and he said that he would be getting in contact with you Mr. Earls" He replied.

"If they're not allowing anybody into these meetings, but the safety committee 'members' then there's nothing I can do. They can do that. But on the other hand though...if they are allowing others who are not members to attend, then we have a problem with that practice." He replied.

Nonetheless, I had achieved what I wanted. Management was arrogantly using this revelation by OSHA to prevent me from attending the CHSP meetings. That was fine. Management had now concreted my position that I had been trying to establish all along, which was that they had hand selected several people whom they wanted to represent us, and these people were not chosen by us, the employees, along with management not allowing 'outside' people to participate in the meeting's only established that it was in fact, an employer-dominated group. I would just let the NLRB take it from here. Management may have finally cut their own throats on this one. Management had fallen victims to their own arrogance. I had manipulated them into finally admitting that this practice was going on.

August 15, 2001 as I walked into the building that morning, after completing my run to Whites Creek, I found Abel standing with Josey, Ronnie, Brian and several other drivers in front of the stairs. They were discussing a new policy Gordon was considering implementing building wide.

Abel motioned for me to come over to where they were. "James have you heard this?" He asked, while laughing and shaking his head.

I walked on over to where they were, and asked, "What is it now?"

"All the feeder drivers cannot come to work ten minutes before their scheduled start time and they have to leave right after punching out." Josey replied.

"Who told you this crap?" I asked.

"Gordon did."

I noticed that we had a rat standing amongst us, and I knew that this person would run back to Gordon the minute he showed up for work and spill his guts. I wanted to get my message back to Gordon and I knew now that I had a messenger.

"Fine. If that's how he wants it to be then that's the way it'll be." I said loudly, trying to draw the attention of several part time managers standing around. After I noticed I had their attention and I began to put on my show.

"It may happen, but I'll guarantee you this...that it will be everybody, drivers, butt kissers and all. These butt kissing drivers will stop coming in a half hour early everyday just to smooze up to Gordon and going through their loads off the clock.

"That goes for everyone." I replied in a rather loud tone. The part time supervisors had come a little closer to our little group discussion to hear all the facts, but that wasn't necessary, because the rat had taken the cheese.

The buzzer sounded for the pre-loaders to start work and everyone dispersed and went to work.

Abel just looked at me and smiled knowing that the rat had taken the bait. I walked on upstairs to the locker room to wash up and came back down the stairs and noticed that Abel and Josey were in the west center office, and as I walked on in, I noticed that Josey was standing in front of the vacation schedules marking something out on it.

I walked in and Abel was saying to Josey as I grabbed a chair to sit in, "Someone may steal your identity Josey."

"No they won't either." Josey replied, while marking out his social security number on it.

Abel was just aggravating Josey trying to get him stirred up a little bit.

"I called over to the union hall yesterday to talk to Matt about sending that letter over here, to UPS in Huntsville, and making you feeder steward." Josey said.

Abel looked at me, and I replied, "I'll believe it when I see it."

"No...seriously, I got on Matt's butt and told him we needed a letter sent to UPS. He's going to make you, and Donnie, both full time stewards." Josey replied.

I still didn't believe that Matt was going to do this. We'd been without a steward now for about three months, and after all the hell that we rose trying to get him to appoint me had done very little good. Management still didn't want me in there and neither did Matt.

"I told Gordon too." Josey replied, while beginning to smile.

"What do you mean you told Gordon?" Abel asked, while sitting up in his chair.

"I walked into Gordon's office yesterday, and asked him if he'd heard the news?" Josey replied.

"Gordon then asked me what news?" I then told him, " James Earls is fixing to be feeder steward over here, and that Matt is sending a letter to you." Josey said.

"What did he say then?" Abel asked.

"He didn't say anything for a minute or so." Josey replied.

"Well what did he do?" I asked.

"He stood there with his mouth open like this." Josey replied standing with a dumb look on his face with his mouth wide open. We both started laughing.

"Then he said, what did you say...what did you say?" Josey replied.

"Yeah all the color left his face. He looked like he had heard the worst news of his life." Josey replied.

Abel couldn't stop laughing.

"Yeah, he looked like he was really worried about it." Josey replied.

"Well, I'll believe it when I see the letter." I replied, still being doubtful.

DATE GRIEVANCE FILED: 8-15-01

EXPLAIN GRIEVANCE: *I Want to see the agreement between UPS and the IBT, and Teamsters Local 402 regarding the formation of the CHSP committees. I want to see the agreement authorizing the non-observance of seniority, bypassing the grievance machinery language and discrimination of Teamster members.*

REMEDY SOUGHT: *disband safety committee.*

DATE GRIEVANCE FILED: 8-15-01

EXPLAIN GRIEVANCE: *I was told by Gordon, west center manager,* that I was not welcome and not invited to the committee meeting. This is after I had been invited and told I could attend the meeting by Antonio in the presence of Josey and Abel. I was humiliated and embarrassed by Gordon in the presence of a co-worker and another member of management. I was treated without dignity.

REMEDY SOUGHT: An apology to myself and as well to the hourly employee and the member of management that was witness to this humiliating act.

I came into work the night of August 15, 2001 and handed the grievances to the part time steward on the reload, named Mark, and told him to give them directly to Gordon the next day, and to no one else...period. Everything was being set for the next day.

Abel and I made the our runs to Whites Creek, and on the way back we discussed what was going on and how childish management was acting about the issue of the CHSP committee, and how Gordon had been treating me about attending the meetings. We wrote it off as typical, and gave it no more thought.

We both arrived back into Huntsville on time, around 4:15 a.m, and pulled onto the yard, and we both began breaking our equipment down. Josey pulled in right behind us, and pulled his feeder right up along side mine.

I started to climb back into mine, after unhooking the rear trailer, and saw that Josey was standing over beside Abel's door talking to him, and Abel had a strange look on his face. I wasn't sure as to what was going on, then Abel motioned for me to come over, and as I walked on over to where they were, I was thinking it had something to do with the steward letter that was being sent over, but it would be something totally different.

"James when y'all get done I need to talk to you and Abel in the office." Josey replied.

"What is it?" I asked, while looking at Abel for some sort of clue. Abel looked me and then looked back to Josey. I began to get a funny feeling that something was going on.

"I'll tell you inside." He replied, while acting kind of strange.

"Josey you're making me nervous, what is it? Are they going to fire us or me?" I asked impatiently.

"No...it isn't that." He replied, while shaking his head as he sort of walked off and then stopped.

"Josey I can't handle this kind of stress this early in the morning." I replied, while becoming a little perturbed in the fact that Josey was acting like something important had happened that would be detrimental to my job.

I went ahead and climbed back into my tractor, and put my trailer on the door, and then I quickly unhooked from it, and pulled around and parked my tractor on the other side of the building. Josey was standing around there in the shop area, waiting for us both to get out. I climbed down, and Abel joined me for the walk back into the building. I continued to quiz Josey about what it was that was so important, and he still wouldn't answer me. I had punched on out while in the parking lot and dropped off my paper work and plugged my computer into the phone line so it could down load my time card. I walked on upstairs with Abel to wash up and use the bathroom. Josey motioned to us to follow him outside and we walked on out of the locker room and into the office that was located just outside the locker room. We walked on in and all three of us took a seat.

I sat there waiting anxiously for Josey to tell 'us' what it was that he needed to tell me so bad.

"James I had a talk with Gordon yesterday." He replied, while letting out a sigh.

"Yeah, and?" I replied.

"He asked me about that package you shipped over to the local to Jamie a few weeks ago and asked me if I knew anything about it." He replied.

I sat there looking at him not saying a word.

"I told him no...that I didn't, and he didn't believe and so on." Josey replied, as Abel was biting on his fingernail and listening to what was being said.

"He told me, that if James wants to 'gouge me' that I'll gouge him back." Josey said.

My blood pressure was rising fast, as I could tell from my face getting hot, but I sat there not saying anything...yet. Gordon was making reference to retaliating against me with some sort of reprisal for filing the grievances, and the internal UPS discrimination complaint against him. THIS IS ILLEGAL and is against Federal Law.

"Gordon then told me that he still had the package that you shipped over to the local that had been addressed to Jamie. He then proceeded to tell me that if he needed to that he could raise the issues of the package itself." Josey replied.

"What do you mean about the package?" I asked angrily.

"He raised the question of where did you get the box to ship it in, and how it looked exactly like the one's sold by UPS over the customer counter. He then raised the question of the shipping peanuts in the box and where did you get them? Where did you get the toilet paper that you used? Where did you get the brown shoe polish? Where did you get the DR bag, a plastic bag used to put packages in by drivers when delivering to protect the package from rain? He then said, 'we don't sell those'." Josey replied.

Abel had stood up, and had walked to the other side of me, and then leaned up against the counter with the coffee maker on it, and by now my blood was boiling, and it was becoming harder to contain myself.

"Look Josey...you tell Gordon that if he wants to go down this road with me he need's to think this through. First of all, this matter of shipping the package has been settled. You tell him since he's not man enough to face me himself, that I have three of his supervisors on tape telling me that I could ship it. Tell him as well that I have him on tape telling me that this matter was over and that it was just a big misunderstanding. Last thing you tell that piece of crap that my mother in law works for a place that handles shipping UPS and Federal Express packages. They are a Pack and Ship provider and sell peanuts and all sizes of boxes like I used in my package. I asked his supervisor if I could have a 'D.R' bag, and how he said it was fine that I could have it. You tell him that." I replied very angrily.

"James if they had anything at all or they would have fired you the night it happened. They don't have crap." Abel replied.

"Abel's right James they don't have anything." Josey said, trying to back up Abel's claims.

"James if they're looking at using stealing a piece of toilet paper against you, and are looking for a way to fire you for something that stupid, you know then that they're watching every little move you make." Abel replied.

"I know that they don't have anything." I replied, but I knew that Gordon had been in loss prevention for a few years before getting promoted to being a center manager, and this concerned me.

He had the knowledge and expertise in 'this area', and he was just trying to intimidate, and strong-arm me like a common criminal into withdrawing the grievances and complaints against him. He had a reputation for bull crapping, and bluffing people with these sorts of scare tactics, but I wasn't scared of him. Josey and Abel suggested that I call Gordon's boss, Stanson, the Mountain Division package car manager, and explain to him what Gordon had said, and how he was threatening me.

"Oh something else too, James. Matt and Jamie had helped them with their little investigation, it seems that Matt made the call to UPS that morning and then he turned the package over to UPS." Josey replied.

"What?" I replied, while sitting up now.

"Yeah that's what he said." Josey replied.

"Well old boy it looked like your local union leader tried to get you fired." Abel replied, while shaking his head.

This wasn't really any surprise. I felt like a chump though after having called Matt the morning this had all went down, and he acted like he knew nothing about it, but he had been the one to call UPS in the first place. I decided that I'd just sit on this for now, and when I get Matt over here in person, face-to-face, I corner him up, and 'discuss' this matter with him.

I called down to the Birmingham, Alabama feeder office, and asked someone to give me the number to Stanson's office in Birmingham.

I made the drive on home and managed to lie down for a while. When I woke up, I went ahead and called the number that I had for Stanson, and was told that he was at the Florence Alabama center, so I asked for the number to there, and then I called it. Stanson was on the phone at the time, and the center manager in Florence, Pablo, took my name and number down, and said that he'd give my message to Stanson. I lay back down on the couch, and had dozed off when the phone rang. It was Stanson.

I explained to Stanson what was going on, and what was told to me by Josey concerning the conversation between him and Gordon. I told Stanson about how I had filed the OSHA complaints, and the grievances about the CHSP committee, for then not allowing me to attend the meetings. I also told him, as well, about invoking the internal, 'in house' procedure for reporting discrimination in the work place. Stanson agreed with me that an employee should, and WOULD, have the right to file grievances, and complaints without any fear of retribution from the company. I explained to him about the tape recordings that I had of Gordon saying this was over, and of the three supervisors giving me permission to ship the package.

"Stanson this may very well turn into a 'labor issue', but keep in mind that I was a customer while I shipped the package, and with what he's trying to pull on me...this is nothing but damage to my character and slander against me. I will not only sue him and UPS for this, but everyone else who is involved with this incident all the way up the ladder, including you." I said.

Stanson wasn't saying much at all. I finished with what I had to say, and told him that I'd give him a chance to get this matter resolved, or then I'd be forced to get the Federal Government and my attorneys involved if Gordon's course wasn't stopped.

"I'll call him right now when we hang up James and find out what the problem is, and why he's threatening you." Stanson replied. We hung up. We'll see where this goes tonight when I report to work. I figure Gordon will be there tonight either wanting to meet with me and settle this or the company will side with him and go ahead and discharge me. Time would only tell.

I arrived to work that night and nothing was happening out of the ordinary, so I walked on into the building and punched in for work. I was still early and then I flagged down one of the part time supervisors.

"What's going on tonight James?" He asked while shaking my hand.

"Same 'old same 'old." I replied, while looking around.

"Who's here tonight?" I asked.

"No one that I know of James just Walt." He replied.

"You haven't seen Gordon or anyone from Birmingham around have you?" I asked.

"No I haven't." He replied.

We finished our conversation, and he walked on off. I thought this was sort of odd especially after the talk I had with Stanson earlier this morning. I figured someone would have been up here if not, or at least on the phone, wanting to talk to me about the matter. UPS' open door policy, and all the hotlines to call, and such, that they had posted to report this sort of activity was plastered all over the place. I mean...you couldn't take a bowel movement without coming across one of these posters hanging up in the John.

I went ahead and started work, and on the way back from Whites Creek, Abel and I discussed this latest problem with Gordon over the C.B. Abel seemed to feel that they weren't going to do anything at all about it simply, because it was I who was making the complaint. Abel would be surprised if anyone at all from management would even talk to me about it. I felt the same way, but I tried to remain optimistic that someone from UPS would call me to ask me about what was going on.

The following Monday morning after I walked out to the mailbox to check my mail, I thumbed through the usual junk mail, but there, close to the bottom of my stack, was a letter from the NLRB. I opened it, and began to read it as I walked back to my house. It was the charge notification form and a notice for a hearing. This was rather fast I remembered thinking to myself. I stopped and looked at the back cover page. It was addressed to the center as well. That means that Gordon should get his copy today as well. I had addressed them both to Hembry on the complaint form, but I knew that he would still see them regardless, and hopefully it would get him to thinking that I wasn't going to play games with his threats against my job.

I spoke to Abel that evening, and he figured management wouldn't do anything in regard to investigating my claim of discrimination, and threats, out of fear of saying something to me that might tighten the noose that was already around their necks.

I came in a day or two later, and saw that Tracy was working in the center late that night. I asked several of the drivers who were standing around why he was here, and they said that he had conducted a ride with one of them today. I walked on up to Tracy and asked him about the complaint that I had asked him to initiate several weeks ago.

"James hasn't feeders got with you yet?" He asked me puzzled.

"No Tracy I haven't spoken to anyone about it." I replied.

"William is supposed to be coming up here to talk to about it, this coming up Monday night." Tracy replied.

"Well that's the first I heard of it Tracy." I replied.

"Well that's all I know about it for now James." He replied, and I thanked him and walked on over to punch in for work.

I really didn't believe that anyone would be coming up here to talk to me about this latest incident. It really wouldn't have been a smart thing for them to do especially with two unfair labor practice charges, and a retaliatory discrimination complaint filed with OSHA against them, but I would think that if it were going to be done, that their labor manager, Hembry, would be the one to question 'my side' of the story.

Abel was still busy trying to coordinate a time and location for our upcoming meeting, and we had settled on a date to have our meeting with all the Teamster members who were considering running against Matt. We were going to try and select one candidate and build a slate around him, and then we'd have a very good chance of beating Matt and his old guard goons with a unified slate, rather than three or more people running for his job, and splitting the votes between them. The meeting was set for the following Sunday.

I decided to call Matt that Thursday, and check into why he hadn't sent the letter over to Huntsville announcing my appointment back as a steward. I just asked him about it point blank. His response was that he had the letter signed and ready to be mailed but he was waiting. He was waiting to see the outcome of these charges and grievances that I had recently filed against management.

"I don't want what happened to you the last time when you were a steward to happen this time." Matt replied.

We had been trying to get him to send the letter over well before I had filed the grievances and labor board charges. This was a just lame excuse of not wanting to appoint me at the very least, but I chose not to argue with him on his illogical thinking. Whether I'm a steward, or not, should not have had any bearing on my grievances, because I had management dead in the water on this one. I seemed to think that management was still exerting some sort of 'influence' over the governing of our local union, in regards to whom Matt appointed to represent the members. Matt tried to fish me for information about what was going on with OSHA and the NLRB, and I simply told him that if they wanted him to know they'll call him, and I left it at that. I knew that he'd run right back to Hembry and spill his guts about what I said, so I couldn't chance trusting him, because that's why I had got the Federal Government involved in all this in the first place.

We attended our meeting the following Sunday afternoon at an IHOP restaurant in Decatur Alabama, and in attendance were all of the influential people from all of the UPS centers in North Alabama along with a Consolidated Freight driver.

We all sat around for almost six hours debating the issues and finally a slate was chosen that everyone was happy with. It was looking as if we were going to have a good chance of beating Matt in 2001, but I was still feeling uneasy about a few of the candidates, namely Ted and Charley, who were chosen to run on our slate, after remembering back to Ted's and Charlie's position concerning the CHSP back during the special meeting in July 2000, and when I later brought up claims of member rights being violated by not only the company, but the local union as well. I felt better though with Abel running on the slate with everyone, but I still didn't like the fact that Ted, Jim and Charley, who both were a current local 402 old guard trustees, were running on our reform slate. Hell they were the one's who failed to do anything about Matt, and here they were wanting to help us get Matt out of office? Something wasn't right with this whole picture.

Ted, the Florence steward was picked by most of everyone to be the one to run against Matt, at my disapproval, followed by Jacob for President, Abel as Vice president, Charley as a trustee, and Jim and another person where chosen to round out our slate. It looked like we had all four UPS centers, CF Freight, Yellow Freight and part of Wise Aluminum and Construction covered which would leave Matt very little to expect in regard to support.

One of the executive board member, named Charley, who had attended the meeting with Ted, sat around and talked about how sorry and crooked Matt was, and how he had run the local's finances into the ground and so on. They both swore that they'd never run with that "crooked son-of–a-you know what," and said they would never support him... ever, while swearing this to us.

The only problem now was getting people off of their butts and vote. We all knew that we were going to have a long fight ahead of us in the upcoming weeks, and that Matt wasn't going to give up his stranglehold on the local union without a fight, but we were prepared for that if, and when the time comes. The future and very survival of our local union was at hand, because Matt had stated during his acceptance speech for another term in office, he stated that the IBT was considering dissolving these smaller locals, like ours, and merging them into larger ones, and this concerned me tremendously. Sounds a little like what Hoffa was doing elsewhere...huh?

OSHA is scheduled to meet with several of the Hartselle UPS employees who had overheard the little Colonel threaten to discipline people for reporting injuries, for the week of Labor Day 2001. The Federal Government may finally have what they need to put an end to this practice that is being committed by UPS's management once and for all.

As far as the formation of our 'unified' slate goes in an attempt to try, and oust Matt...Ted later called Abel the night before the election nomination meeting was to take place, and Ted told him that he had changed his mind, and that he, Jim and Charley were going to run on a slate with Matt, along with the other "old Guard" officers to form their own slate. Matt had agreed to let Ted run as president on his slate while pushing poor old Dwayne down to vice president. This was probably done only to please Ted and to pull what very little votes he'd get out of UPS in Florence. I felt strongly that this was their plan all along, which was to sabotage our campaign. They had intentionally misled, and betrayed us, and every member in this local union as far as that goes to help Matt win another three years for his retirement.

I'm going to go out on a limb and make a prediction that Ted will probably be the one who will replace Matt as soon as he retires, which will probably come in little over a year, as Secretary Treasurer of local 402, which had probably been his plan all along. I had discussed this very matter with Ted earlier in the year, about how Matt probably would do the same thing, only by using Dwayne instead, and Ted expressed zealously how he was so against the practice, but evidently it seems that he might have sold his soul to the devil, in order to get control and keep the old guard power structure in our local union. I just hope it was worth the price he paid for our betrayal, and thus becoming branded for life as an old guard betrayer who can never be trusted again, all for his personal political gain.

I decided to go ahead and make a run against Matt in this election as I attended the nomination meeting on September 8, 2001. Matt allowed me to be nominated for secretary-treasurer while I read the letter that he sent to me last year where he found me eligible to run in the election and without any objection from the floor and the membership. But Matt wasn't about to make a scene during the nomination meeting, and he cowardly waited until after the nomination meeting was closed to make his underhanded move to disqualify me, which was a typical old guard tactic. A few minutes after the meeting was officially closed Matt asked me to accompany him into his office where he told me in front of plenty of witnesses that he just got off the phone with the IBT and he told me that Hoffa Jr. was going to rule me ineligible. Needless to say crap hit the fan when he told me this. Jamie was there and decided to jump in with Matt and try to double team me by telling me that she was going to bring internal charges against me for sending her the "retirement package" from several weeks ago. I simply laughed at her and replied, "I see that you still don't know shit from shoe polish Jamie." I thought she was going to have a stroke right there on the spot. I decided to go ahead and leave before things got even more out of control, and as I walked out of the union hall I asked that Ted, who had been appointed as local 402's new president, to come outside for minute so I could talk to him in private. I walked over to Abel's Jeep and opened the door to retrieve the file that I had brought along with me to the nomination meeting. Inside the file were copies of every bit of correspondence that Matt had sent me, along with his testimony (transcripts) to the Election Administrator stating what he had told them about his "commitment" that the local union would pay my dues for me. I tried to explain to Ted what was going on and I even showed him my evidence regarding Matt's testimony and how he had abused the power of his office. Needless to say...it fell upon deaf ears. Matt never sent me anything, that I was aware of, citing the fact that I was disqualified from running against him as he had Ted call me to find out if I was going to get the Department of Labor involved with my rights violation. I knew that Ted was calling for Matt, but I really didn't care so I told him what I was going to do. I told Ted that I was going to appeal the decision to Hoffa, as provided for in our bylaws, but there is a problem with this. How could I appeal the decision to Hoffa if there hasn't been a protest by a member of the local union? Why did Hoffa jr. step in right away when the truth of the matter is that he shouldn't know really anything it unless...it was part of their master plan all along? Hoffa would drag the matter out for several weeks before he sent a formal reply to me stating that he was going to uphold the decision of the executive board and rule me ineligible to run in the local 402 election. Matt would later winding up winning the election, along with his entire slate of old guard members due in part, because less than 300, out of 650, members voted in the election.

After the recent tragedy that occurred on September 11, 2001, many of UPS's Teamsters wanted to show their support and love of patriotism by displaying red, white and blue ribbons on their uniforms and flying displays, and in some cases actual flags from their UPS vehicles. UPS management's response was slow to come, but it still came as everyone had expected.

While I was traveling back to the Huntsville center, after leaving the Whites Creek hub, I was listening to a syndicated talk show host, Mike Gallagher, in which he was discussing the topic of "Employer retribution" for displaying and showing patriotism in the work place. In one segment of the show he received an E-Mail from a UPS driver who said that his management team forced him to remove the flag he was flying from his mirror post. I can understand management's position if it involved a 'safety' related issue, but not all of the cases were involving the issue of 'safety'. Shortly into the discussion of this topic Mike Gallagher received a call from a spokesperson from UPS's corporate office that spoke on the phone to Mike and explained UPS's position on the topic. The spokesperson made it clear that UPS was patriotic and stated that the company would NEVER stand in the way of an employee displaying their patriotism...unless it involved safety. It was clearly evident that UPS management was facing a public relations backlash of biblical proportion on this issue if they didn't lax their stance, and to my surprise they allowed people to wear what they wanted to. This position lasted for a few weeks, and with the mentality of management being what it is they decided to manufacture lapel pins and window decals to 'satisfy' their employee's desire to be patriotic. I was actually looking forward to receiving one of these pins to wear on my uniform, but when I saw what it looked like I immediately refused to wear one. UPS's answer was to incorporate their corporate flag into the pin as sort of an advertisement ploy. I found the pin to be repulsive and very, very tacky for them to try and take advantage of a stressful and trying time for a Nation in order to make a "company statement". In my opinion their flag had no business being along side the American flag in what I felt was instead of a display of patriotism, it was more of a display of commercialism. The window decals they placed in the windshield left a lot to be desired of as well. I was expecting something more than the pathetic two inch by two-inch transparent sticker that they were placing in the bottom right corner of the windshield. When I reported to work that evening, the mechanic at the building asked me how I liked the new stickers. At first I couldn't find it, and after about ten seconds of searching for it the mechanic finally pointed it out. When I finally found it I shook my head in disbelief. In order to see it, you'd have to be right up on it and standing in the light just right, because that the backing was transparent it blended into the colors of the truck and 'disappeared'. There would be very little chance of any passing motorist ever seeing it unless they were riding on the hood of the truck as it went down the road. But...they satisfied the 'publics' demands, while maintaining theirs.

Several drivers were wanting UPS to put up a flag pole out in front of the building to fly the American flag from, which UPS in Huntsville doesn't have a flag pole. The drivers went to Gordon and asked him about the idea and he said he'd get back to them with the answer to their request after he called the Birmingham district office to discuss it with the 'appropriate' people. The next morning the answer was more in line with UPS's manager's mentality. The answer was no...unless WE paid for it and then they'd ALLOW us to fly our American flag from it, and I'm sure they'd want to fly their corporate flag from our pole as well. The response amongst the drivers from this answer was one of utter disgust, but everyone felt the same in finding their answer to be just the type of response that would come from a multi-billion dollar company. Several people vainly attempted to spearhead a campaign to raise the money from every employee, which would have cost everyone about $5.00 a piece, but when everyone found out what management was wanting to do they refused to contribute to something that they felt was UPS' civic duty to do. That's when Matt stepped in and he made a few phone calls and found us a pole, and a contractor who offered their services for free, and we already had a commitment from a local flag company who told their delivery driver that they'd give him any size flag he wanted for no cost because they liked him. UPS answer to this was, "they didn't want anything that looked "junky" out in front of the building." After Gordon realized the amount of hatred that was stirred up by this un-American move, he offered to split the cost of having a flagpole put up with the drivers. Our answer to that was...NO! After that last episode the flag issue died away and nothing was said anymore about it especially after we had a flagpole, and the labor along with a large flag in our hands at no cost to anyone.

There was one other disturbing incident, which happened at UPS as I was working on an ending to my book, and I felt very compelled to include it in the ending. The incident happened at the Whites Creek hub on October 22, 2001, which can sum up the UPS's managers thoughts and feelings concerning us. Upon pulling up to the phones at the gate of the hub, I noticed that there were a couple of police cars, a fire truck, and an ambulance parked at a loading door on the front of the hub. After asking several different witnesses what had happened, they all concurred that there was a 40, some odd, year old part timer, a Teamster, who was loading an outbound trailer when someone noticed that he had collapsed inside the trailer. Another part timer, who was working just outside and above the trailer picking off the packages that were to go into the trailer, tried to come down to check on him after he noticed that his friend could've been hurt, but he was told to stay up there and not to stop working. Several member's of management had the part timer carried out of the trailer and stretched him out onto the floor of the hub, right behind his trailer. By now packages had began to build up on the slide and they started falling off of the slide that fed into his trailer, and began to cause the sort flow to pile up. Management then puts two part timers into this mans trailer to get caught his flow caught back up and the sort kept on rocking along. Management never cut the belt off one time during extracting this man from the trailer. I'm sure that UPS' management is very happy that they never allowed the belt to be cut off one time while all of this was happening, and how they didn't allow the mere death of this man, a brother Teamster, to stand in the way of getting that trailer loaded so it can be pulled off of the door on time. That's right...that man died while loading the trailer, and they never missed a lick. This should sicken anyone who has a heart. This is how they view us, a soulless machine...an instrument to achieve their demands, and not as a human being. Here this man was trying to provide a living for his wife and kids and UPS's management disgraces this man by not having the human decency to cut the belt off for one second...this says it all for me about them.

The "wearing of the flag" issue hadn't died, even after several weeks with management turning a blind eye and biting their tongue, but management was just buying their time with the employees wearing signs of patriotism that was in total contradiction of their established uniform policies. It was honestly killing management to see the drivers walking around while wearing ribbons, and pins and they were just waiting for the right moment. They were waiting for the 'hysteria' to die down and then they'd make their move to bring the drivers back under their guidelines with little fear from a public backlash. That move would come in Canton Ohio in the first week of December 2001.

A twenty-eight year employee, who was a package car driver was fired Thursday morning for wearing a ribbon on his uniform. The driver happened to be a union steward as well, which the labor agreement afforded him the "right" to wear a union steward pin to identify him as being a union steward to all the employees and management. The Teamster pin the driver was wearing that day came with a red, white and blue ribbon attached to it, and when a supervisor told him to take the ribbon off...he refused and he was fired on the spot. UPS management didn't figure on the unions answer to their disgusting unpatriotic move, because they weren't dealing with a weak, southern local who is in bed with them. Teamsters local 92's business agent, called a special meeting with the employees of the center and he conducted a vote requesting that the affected members of the local union give him the authority to call a strike against the center that fired their union steward. Their answer came with support of their steward in the form of a vote of 137 – 12 in favor of striking UPS over this mans discharge if the matter was not settled. That's when it hit the media and it was shown across the nation on the world news what they had done, then coupled with the vote to strike UPS management made the right move. They immediately put the man back to work, but not without having the last word, which according to a UPS corporate spokesperson, "We make no apologies for a stringent uniform regulation."

This is what a union is about and I'm thankful that for two things in that particular incident. One being that the driver was a true American and a strong steward who believed in and stood up for what he thought was right, and I'm proud to be associated with him as a union brother. The second thing I'm thankful for is that the driver's local union officer wasn't like ours, in which if he had Matt to deal with he would've probably been out of work for several months before he got his job back. I'm thankful for the strong leadership that local 92 exhibited. The one thing that UPS management fears the most out of the employees in the union is solidarity.

I met with a representative of the Department of Labor on December 13, 2001, and I filed an election protest to try and have the local union election overturned, and a new one ordered. I will once again try and argue my case so I can be ruled eligible to run in this election while trying to have Matt, and his old guard regime disqualified for corruption. I met with the agent for about two hours at the Books A Million in Huntsville. I discussed with him everything that had gone on since our last discussion and he was very interested in how I was presenting my case to him after I had obtained some new evidence since the last time we met. There were a few things that I was short of, as far as documentation, and I told him that I would send them to him as soon as I got home that evening. One of the things he wanted was a copy of the letter that Hoffa Jr. sent me where he found me ineligible to run in the election. I went on home and was going to wait until the weekend and look for the letter when I would have more time on my hands to spend on the search. I found the letter, and I sat down and began to read it aloud. This was the first time that I actually read the entire letter since receiving it from Hoffa. As I read into it, I began to slow down and then I stopped. I remember saying to myself, "Oh crap!" as I ran back to my bedroom with Hoffa's letter flying out of my hand and onto the floor. I knelt down onto the bedroom closet floor and dialed the combination to my safe as I opened it as fast as I could. I reached inside and began looking for the transcripts from the testimony that Matt had given to the Election Administrator back in January of 2001. After a minute of frantic searching I found what I was looking for. I stood back up as my heart was racing as I began walking back through the hall picking up Hoffa's letter that he sent to me. I walked back to the living room and I sat down in the chair and took a deep breath as I began to study his testimony.

Matt's testimony that he had given to the Election Administrator (case: *Earls*, 2001 EAD 98) on January 24, 2001 read:

"Mr. Earls stated that he asked Matt if he should take an honorable withdrawal (which, in these circumstances, would have cut off Mr. Earls' eligibility during the 24-month continuous period). Matt told Mr. Earls that he need not do this as he expected that Mr. Earls would be back to work the following week. According to Mr. Earls, Matt also stated that during the illegal discharge, Matt would make sure that Mr. Earls' dues were paid even if Matt had to pay them himself. **Matt didn't remember using these exact words, but did remember telling Mr. Earls not to worry about paying his dues, that the union would take care of them."**

ELECTION ADMINISTRATOR

Matt's testimony to the IBT, which is stated in the letter from Hoffa to me, dated October 4, 2001, which reads:

*"According to the Election Administrators decision, Brother Matt acknowledged that he advised Brother Earls that he did not have to pay dues while his discharge was pending, however, **denied stating that the local union would pay the dues on his behalf.**"*

Hoffa Jr., October 4, 2001

"I've got his ass now!" I screamed out loud as I stood to my feet. What I had just accidentally discovered was that Matt had intentionally given false testimony to the office of the General President, which could result in his expulsion from the Teamsters union for life, and with him losing his pension, for bringing reproach upon the local union. I walked back to my room with the biggest smile on my face as I was feeling as if the weight of the world had just been lifted off of my shoulders. I stopped for a moment and thought about how I was going to handle this new situation, and I decided that I would wait until after Ted is sworn into office as the president of local 402, and then I would make my move during the next general membership meeting, and expose to the members what had been going on between the old guard and myself over the last two years and how Matt has lied to the IBT in his statement concerning my dues case. I think I will give the entire executive board one last chance to act, on my terms, and remove Matt from office, and try him in accordance to the Bylaws and IBT Constitution, and if they choose not to...then I will be taking them all down with him once and for all now that I have hard concrete proof. As far as Hoffa junior goes, I will be sending him a certified letter as soon as possible, along with copies of both sets of Matt's testimony, demanding him to bring charges against Matt for providing false testimony to the office of the General President, and if Hoffa refuses to act on this...then I will immediately file charges against him with the IRB and then I'll get the Federal Government involved and attempt to take him down as well. I wonder if Matt will finally roll over on Hoffa and tell the Federal Government just actually what went on and how much Hoffa was involved. When a man is facing losing his pension for something like this, it seems to bring out a cooperative spirit in a person, which in turn causes them to 'spill their gut's' about everything they know. In the meantime I will be writing to my Congressman, and both of my U.S Senators as well as the news media outlining what has happened over the last two years describing the history of my battle with Hoffa and the old guard, and solicit help from them as well. It finally looks like justice will actually be served.

As for me, and my charges against the UPS managers... my depositions are scheduled to go before a Board Agent from the NLRB in Birmingham Alabama in early 2002. I'm hoping that I have enough against management to finally get them off of me and to put an end to my personal daily Hell.

In regard to my final personal injury tally to this story which includes, along the lines of other additional work related injuries; Two peptic ulcers, problems sleeping which required a sleep study to be performed, two more pulled groin muscles, one more strained neck muscle, one more torn forearm muscle, and a broken right hand, and this is in addition to all of the other injuries that I had sustained from over the years. I had asked my local management for more detailed information concerning UPS's loss workdays due to injuries to update my numbers for this story, and as always, I was told that it was confidential information and I was refused access to their records.

As far as the current state of the Huntsville center...its nothing like it was back when I was chief steward right before my discharge. Matt has allowed the Huntsville management to eliminate several Teamster jobs only to be replaced with workers from a non-union temporary agency doing our bargaining unit work. We still have several of our feeder drivers on lay off while management continues to run other drivers through our center to pick up our work, which in turns guarantees that their drivers will not be laid off in their home centers. Huntsville's management personnel continue to work everyday on the preload and reload while some stewards just sit back, and often times work right along with them. And if someone were to call a parking lot meeting now...you'd be lucky if you'd get a dozen people to even show up much less the numbers that we had who walked with us back in August 1999. Solidarity in Huntsville is dead, with Matt and UPS killing it, because there is no real leadership in Huntsville other than who UPS wants the union to appoint to represent us. Although Huntsville is still a thorn in the side of management due in part to a handful of members like myself, Abel, Ronnie, Petey and 'Burr, but it's nothing like it was. I guess that the members in Huntsville are happy with the current state our center is in and the rampant abuse against their fellow workers by the management, because nothing is ever said.

There is no actual ending to this story, because our experiences are day to day, and never cease, and I could never really stop writing about what goes on here as a UPS Teamster. All we can do is stand strong as one, and continue to battle the ruthless and oppressive style of management that UPS is accustomed to enforcing on us, and as well, battle the poor representation of our corrupted union officers, and their continuing trampling of our union rights, but there is very little I can do without being a steward. So now I am preparing to finish the battle that the old guard had started two years ago, in the upcoming weeks with "the enemy within the union."

In Closing

Many people have often asked me the same question. Why did I continue to stay and work for this company if indeed my working conditions were truly this horrible?

I've often asked myself the same question numerous times over the course of my career, especially during the last few years, but the answer, in my case, isn't as complex in the number of reasons as one might expect.

I wanted to provide a comfortable living for my family and to try and give them some of the finer things that life had to offer. I figured that I'd endure what I had to in order to provide a good living for them. Was it about the money? Where else could I go, and make what I made with just a high school education? Was it about the years of my life invested here? I have eleven years of my life, eleven hard years, invested toward a retirement to which, one day hopefully if I do make it to retirement, that I may not have to work ever again, and finally I will be able to spend quality, stress free time with my family and loved ones.

Others ask me why didn't I just give up and simply walk away from it all? How easy is it for one who has a mortgage, and is in debt up to their neck to just simply walk away? What actually stands in the way of us all, from leaving the UPS life, and moving on? Is it fear, pride, stubbornness or just plain ignorance and greed that prevents our exits?

Managers at UPS are very smart when it comes to this age-old question of labor relations and economic psychology. Top level management knows that many of its employees are living paycheck to paycheck, and that they cannot afford to leave, or by doing so they then risk losing everything they have. So in one sense...it's sort of like corporate slavery. Management feels that they can treat you anyway they want to simply because they pay you well, and this alone makes them feel as if they own you. At the time, I too had fallen into their trap as well.

I wasn't about to cave in and just simply walk away. I wasn't about to simply give up and quit like management, and the old guard officials had desperately hoped that I would've done. I was not about to let these people win. But in the end, what did I win? What do I have to show for it? I had lost my house, cars, I had to file bankruptcy, I had to resort to selling every valuable I owned just to try and survive, but I almost lost the most important possession of all...I had almost lost my family.

I had managed to win the war...and I had won the right to walk back into the lair of my perceived enemy, long after most everyone had given up and hoped that I was finally gone.

I simply could not, and would not let UPS's management, and the corrupted Teamster old guard officials, who all held the power to end this tragedy, to beat me. I was much stronger than that, but in reality, I had nothing else to lose, because I had lost it all.

Walking back into the building that day was not only done for myself, but I had done it as well for everyone who had not had the strength to ride out the storm, and had given up and quit.

Many people have asked me if I was I ever fearful for what management could, and would, do to me for partaking in my endeavor to protect and preserve the member's rights, while even at times, putting my own job on the line for individuals, even some of whom wasn't deserving of the type of effort that I would give at representing them? No...I wasn't.

My biggest fear, as a steward, was in failing to do everything in my power to truly, and whole-heartedly represent that particular member in the office without bias or prejudice. To simply put it... I was scared of failing the member.

As a steward of the Teamsters Union, I was charged with the responsibility of fighting for every member's rights, and that is something that I still take very seriously, even to this day. And I strongly feel that I have done what I was sworn to do, which was to serve and protect the members the best that I could from managerial and old guard oppression, and to battle for workplace, safety and even...union rights. I gave all I could give. I had sacrificed my job and my family structure for another member.

My story isn't unique in its nature, but in fact...it's quite typical within this company.

This book wasn't written out of anger by some disgruntled employee, or by a disgruntled union member, bent on trying to bring down the company they work for, and the union they believe in. This book was written out of concern for the future of our union, and to educate others outside the realm of organized labor of actually what goes on behind the iron brown curtain in regards to the dark art of industrial labor relations. I had become disgusted with the daily deceit of UPS's management to my customers, to the public and to the unknowing family members of those managers who had a hand in the enforcement of UPS's labor policy, and to the individuals who instruct, direct and order this campaign of corporate terrorism against us, its employees, through their labor relations policy, and I felt that this needed to be finally made known to the world of their actions, and the consequences that affects peoples lives from their such said actions.

For a Fortune 500 company, like UPS, to be awarded the honor of being recognized as Forbes Magazine "Company of the Year 2000" is the ultimate blatant display of hypocrisy and is nothing more than a slap in the face to every working man and woman in America. What is the management at UPS most admired for other than making money? I doubt that their brutally abusive labor relations' policy came into play when the magazine was weighing its decision to award them with this prestigious honor.

If the world just knew of the pain and heartaches that are being felt everyday by thousands of UPS employees, then, and only then would it be a different story. For UPS's top managers to stand up before the world and accept this honor, while knowing how, and why they treat us the way that they do, is like a child abusing parent standing up in front of the world, and accepting a "parent of the year" award while knowing that they have their dirty little secret locked away in a closet back home. It just doesn't make sense.

When UPS's management used to subject us to letter writing campaigns on work time, asking us to solicit our U.S Congressmen and Senator's and for us to complain to them about some certain bill that was going to be voted on that would've harmed "UPS's ability to compete on an even playing field", without actually telling us the whole truth of how it would negatively affect us, and harm us as Teamsters, as families, and as consumers...this act alone should say enough about their integrity.

I had learned long ago that integrity, responsibility and honor are for sale at UPS as long as it'll generate a profit.

The impact that this company's labor relation policy has on society not only affects the employee(s), but our families as well. UPS' management style slowly eats us away, and consumes us like a cancer, only until later, after realizing that its too late, and that the damage has been done, and like in most cases...too many years have passed to try and recapture, and reverse what was lost in the youth of their lives.

No greater example of a real life impact from their labor relations policy can be made any better than when I was illegally discharged, and hung out for ten months by a sect of managers and old guard officers who were trying to teach me, and everyone else a lesson, and the effects it had on my life, and that of my family's lives as well. The intentional man made hell that management, and the old guard had created for me to survive in not only affected me, but it also has had a detrimental impact on my family as well. The emotional, and mental stress alone, then coupled with the heartfelt pain from losing our home, and possessions, and almost our marriage from this unnecessary ordeal has taken a toll on all of us. Not to mention the most important one of us all...our little, innocent two-year-old daughter.

How does someone explain to a crying little girl why were having to leave our home never to return to it? Why were never going back to play on her swing set ever again? Or why don't we have our things anymore? But the most important question of all...why mommy and daddy are not living together anymore?

Maybe UPS's top managers should answer that to her.

This company's management attempted to ruin me not only financially, but also mentally, and emotionally as well. Will I ever be the same as before I ever went to work at UPS? I doubt it. I can only hope.

UPS's management, and the old guard union officials had failed to accomplish what they sat out to do when they fired me. I managed to overcome the odds, and beat this multi-billion dollar company, and thwart the crooked tactics of the old guard, and I'm now able to proudly walk back through the doors everyday with a hard earned grin on my face, while knowing in my heart the truth, and this is indeed a very bitter pill for them all to swallow...even to this very day.

My blame does not lie with the entity itself known as United Parcel Service. For if I blamed UPS, the entity itself, for the atrocities carried out against its employees on a daily basis by its managers, then I would be blaming myself as well, which is simply not the case.

For I am just as much UPS, and even more so, than the very management who runs the company. We, the Teamsters, are the ones that perform the labor that keeps the company going, not them.

This was no greater demonstrated than during the strike of 1997, which if the management of UPS was the company, as they so arrogantly claim, then they wouldn't have lost six hundred plus million dollars, and there wouldn't have been a need for us to return. We, and we alone, the Teamsters, rebuilt UPS into what it is today and management knows it. Without the Teamster laborer's there is no UPS.

To all of the fair and "good" managers, and supervisors, I want to say thank you, and I appreciate everything that you do, and have done in the past when you stood up against the deliverers of injustice and defended us thank you. I want you to know that this book does not reflect upon you, but out of fear of some sort of reprisal against you from corporate UPS I will not name who you all are, but you know in your heart who you are, and we thank you for that. I want to make this a better and safer place for you as well. Thank you for all the honest, and true union leaders that we have who stand up and battle for what's right. God bless you all, we need you all very much.

UPS cannot survive without the Teamsters, and in turn, nor can the Teamsters survive without UPS. It's a co-existence that must be preserved. For the level of professionalism that is demonstrated, and carried out by all its employees on a daily basis, along with the level of pride taken in saying that we are a UPS'er...can only be found within the ranks of being a Teamster.

Those of us, including myself, employed at UPS are not looking for pity. None of us at UPS are. We just want an understanding that the money we make often comes with a price. A very high price at times, and I challenge you to 'encourage' UPS's management to change its brutally abusive style of management for our sake, and quite possibly for one of your very own family member's sake. Share these confessions with others, because it's important that everyone finally learns about what actually goes on here at UPS and in the Teamsters.

It's very easy for management to abuse its employees when in reality they only view them as a number. When you abuse something that hasn't a face, or soul then the task becomes evermore so easier to perpetrate.

In my opinion, the Teamsters union, and as well...every other union in America needs more stewards like myself. Stewards who are willing to stand up and make the sacrifices needed to protect and preserve our union as the institution that it is, one to fight for and protect workplace rights, and if stewards like me didn't exist...then UPS, and other corporations would be unbound to create a more definitive- hell on earth for ALL workers.

I am but a small figure in this battle being waged, fighting in the trenches, and facing insurmountable odds on the battlefield known as corporate America. For there are many people like myself, even non-stewards, who have chosen to take up the flag of reform and charge headlong into the thick of the battle. I am very thankful for them, because they all try to make this company a better place to work, and make this union stronger, and they need to be commended for their courage and determination.

This book was not written about UPS the corporation as some might think it was. I had written it, hoping, to generate a spark of interest in the reform movement within the Teamsters union, and I wanted the Teamster members, and UPS's employees to actually see the effects of UPS's managements, and the old guard union officers, labor relation's policy has on our health, and on society as a whole.

I wanted to show in the end, the whole picture of the labor movement in the Teamsters, and at UPS, and unless things change soon...we will continue in a death spiral with leaders like Hoffa and Matt at the helm, with the possibility that many locals will fold, or be dissolved and merged into larger old guard controlled regimes if members don't start voting these bums out of office. Every member of the Teamsters, whether they like it or not, are bound by an oath, which is found in their local union bylaws, to protect and defend this union, and to preserve it as an institution. We all have the duty and obligation to root out these old guard officials who are serving us only for their selfish reasons, and who are trying to damage and severely cripple our union, by denying us our rights, and by ransacking the union treasury. It is our DUTY to rid our union of these cancerous vermin once and for all by exercising our rights by voting these traitors to labor out of office.

I literally stood on the brink of sanity, and peered over the edge into the black, bottomless abyss known as insanity. I teetered on its edge, like a tightrope walker, hoping not to stumble and fall into the dark void.

I managed to overcome the destructive temptations from the demon's of alcoholism that were wanting me to search for my faith, and for the answers to my problems at the bottom of a bottle, and to simply just drink the problem away. I managed to have fought many demons during my time of despair, all of which who wanted the very same thing...my hope, my will, my faith and my family. I continue to work hard everyday at trying to bury the overwhelming amount of guilt I feel for denying my family the sanctity of being just that. A family.

I was carted to the edge by certain members of the management of this fine company, and by several of the old guard union officers, and abandoned. I had almost lost everything...my identity, my dignity, will and faith in the system, but the one thing that I managed to hold onto was my faith in God. I personally feel that now I am a stronger person than ever before, and I want to thank the UPS managers and the old guard Teamsters for that.

Working for the management of this great company indeed makes you hard hearted, because it carries over with you in whatever you do and whomever you meet. It's a curse. It makes you a victim and also...it makes you a survivor. We managed to weather one of life's trials and we managed to come out on top. There are victims on both sides of the battle. I have seen in the eyes of many management people, the shame, sorrow and regret for their actions, but they knew in their heart that what they were doing was wrong, but they chose to abandon any responsibility of their actions by blaming their superiors. This was their rationalization for there deeds. But those of you need to understand that it is you, and you alone who are responsible for what you have done to us over the years, and that you have a greater obligation than the one to the company you have a moral obligation to us to treat us as human beings instead of like soulless machines. I hope this book improves your working conditions, as well as relieves the ramifications of having to carry out this labor policy.

There were very few happy times while I have been working for UPS, but those good times that I did have were always centered around the time that I spent with my union brothers and sisters, and rarely ever involved management.

Many fail to realize that I am a product, a creation of my work environment, and that it was UPS's management style that had created the monster that they have desperately tried so many times to destroy, because I was not like this before I started working for UPS. Now that they have produced me from years of abuse through their labor relation's policy, they are unable to deal with what they've created.

The one bit of good that has come out of all of this was the fact that I was finally able to establish the type of 'fatherly' relationship with my daughter that I had prayed and longed for. I was also able to renew my marriage to my wife and re-establish a loving relationship, something that I have not had prior to the discharge. I've often prayed to God asking him to give me this special gift, and I was very blessed to have received it from him, although by a different means than I had expected. God does truly work in mysterious ways.

Truthfully, this book was written about the selfish union member who elects not to get involved, which the end result from their actions, along with their lack of caring is that they are the ones responsible who for our working conditions, and our treatment. They are the ones who are responsible for the labor relations policy that we are forced to work under, and as well for our weak, corrupted union for their unwillingness to simply vote for those of us who are willing to make a stand against employers who abuse their workers, and against corrupted old guard local leaders who do nothin for us.

Many will hear of this book, and they will refuse to read it. Many will even read it, and dismiss me as just being eccentric, and a lunatic who is delusional. Many of the employees, and members are still being deceived daily by UPS's managers, and by old guard officials, and they honestly think that what's currently happening to me, and has happened to me, cannot happen to them and their family. They actually think that they are above the rules, and are untouchable, and are in good with "Uncle Buster", and the union.

They continue to think that the labor relation's policy of UPS's management doesn't affect them at all after I have shown them the effects. The truth is that they're still a number in the eyes of UPS's management, and just a mere stepping-stone for an old guard officer to get what they want, and if they think that what has happened to me and my family cannot happen to them, as they foolishly continue to believe that this labor relations policy doesn't affect them and their families health... then they are only fooling themselves, and they are truly living...the Big Brown Lie.

Appendix A
MOTIVES BEHIND THE STRIKE

Why does UPS's management want control of our pension plan? Why the shift to more part time workers? Why the shift to replacing union jobs with temporary agency workers?

Why control the pension fund?

How big of a role did the issue of "pension control' play in the underlying motives to the strike? It played a very huge role, which could have led to the slow death of the Teamsters union, as we know it. Why was UPS's management so adamant about withdrawing from the jointly controlled plans, which was established in 1955, and which is one of the largest Taft Hartley funds in the United States? Their motive could have been spawned from one little word...greed.

The pension plan, which is made of 31 separate plans consisting of about 400 different employer contributors, holds assets that exceed $18 billion dollars, and has over 450,000 participants, and just during the year 1997, they paid out over $1.6 billion in benefits to over 185,000 retirees and beneficiaries. The two best known of these plans is Central States and the Western Conference plans. UPS reports twenty percent of the total pension dollars reported to the fund each month. For UPS to contribute a whopping twenty percent out of 400 employers in a staggering amount of cash being pumped into the plan, and it sets up the basis for their possible argument to pull out.

UPS's management was claiming that if they weren't required to pull the weight of the other "less prosperous' companies that their contribution would by a higher pension benefit than the members now get in the trust. This may be true but their claims to being able to raise the benefits by 50% are highly doubtful.

This motive sounds good on the surface but we need to dig a little deeper to ascertain the real benefits of who would receive the bulk of the benefits from this move. UPS recognizes that if they had total control of the plan they then could establish and make changes in the funding formula. Their immediate reward from them being able to administer their own plan would mean that they could possibly get by with a much smaller contribution to maintain the funds current levels of payments to participants. But the real gain could come down the road when management decides that the funds needs to shift form a defined benefit to a defined benefit contribution basis, which then opens the door to them raising the eligibility standards, for example...like increasing the number of hours per year that will be required before an employee is even able to participate. But enter the greed factor. Typically in single employer plans, the management has a greater control over how the plans money will be invested. This opens the door to allow them to be able to invest our pension money into their company stocks, which if this happened they would reap double rewards. Ask yourself a question. Say, for example, it takes $100 a week to fund our pension plan, but if UPS's management had control of it and could fund the SAME benefit for $75 a week...then who gets the $25 that is left over from the difference? Do you honestly think we would get that $25? I doubt it. It's just another source of revenue for them...that's all it is.

If the Teamsters union had allowed UPS's management to abandon the multi-employer plan, we could possibly see other companies try and follow. That could have seriously weakened the pension plan as a whole- and perhaps even sent them into a death spiral. This move would've have drained the union of one of its most powerful organizing weapons...the pension plan.

Do not believe what UPS management tells you about how they can better administer the plan than the way it's set up now. Your future depends on it.

Why the shift to part time, and temporary agency workers:

United Parcel Service delivers more than 80% of the nations packages had began years ago shifting its workforce to a more defined part time status, thus creating a "throw away" job perception amongst its employees. Of the new jobs created at UPS, a whopping 83% of them are part time. With a national average of 18% of the work force being part time...at UPS the story is much different. Of the 46,300 new jobs added at UPS since 1993-1997, 83% of them, or 38,500 are lower wage part time jobs. UPS's management has shifted to over a 60% makeup of its work force being part time jobs, which is up 18 percentage points in the last ten years. This shift has come at a time when other U.S companies have become less reliant on a part time, high turnover jobs strategy. Since 1993, UPS has accelerated its creation of part time jobs at the expense of full time job opportunities. Across the Nation, the amount of UPS jobs that are only part time has grown considerably from 42% in 1986 to over a staggering 60% as of just 1997!

The fact of the matter is that the thousands of part time employees are really just "part time" in the name only. Many of the 1000's of UPS part timers are classified only as part time and are subsequently paid the lower wager and benefits that are associated with the title, but yet they continue to work over 35 hours a week. This shift coupled with a starting wage of $8.00 an hour, which hasn't changed since 1982, has radically altered the work experience and damaged morale at UPS, which has created an annual turnover rate of 400% amongst part time employees at UPS. For example, in 1996 UPS recruited and trained 182,000 people for part time jobs, which only 40,000 of whom were still with the company at years end with only a vast majority of those left only stay about a year and then quit.

In an attempt to answer the nagging question that plagues UPS, the Teamsters commissioned a study by Cornell University's school of Industrial and Labor Relations. The Cornell researchers found that the elimination of any chance at a full time job opportunity was a major contributor in the high turnover rate, with three out of four part timers citing this very reason when they quit the company.

The practices of UPS' claims that this is necessary in order to create "flexibility to meet the competition" is not very accurate, but it has everything to do with nickel and diming the workers.

Many major hubs, like a major sorting hub in Chicago, employees only part timers, although they run around the clock. The Chicago hub employs 6,000 people with less than 300 of them being full time. In Chicago overall, the percentage of part timers at UPS has risen to a sickening

70%, which is 10% above the UPS average and up 15 percentage points since 1993. In other major hubs across the nation part time positions at UPS's workforce have risen to a whopping; New York (61% of the workforce is part time), Newark/Northern New Jersey area (72% are part time), Boston (67% are part time), Dallas (68% are part time), Los Angeles (72%), San Francisco (76%), Louisville- a disturbing 90% of its work force is part time! The affect on society as a whole has two sides. First...lets examine the economic backlash that affected the above-mentioned eight cities. In a combined loss of at least 11,648 full time jobs in just the last 10 years, as of 1997, has lost a total of $153.9 million in worker income and business sales each year and another $83.4 in annual tax revenues. Without a doubt this cause severe economic damage to these cities where its major operations are based. Second...are the affects on the employee. Many part timers are having to work several jobs just to try and survive with wages at a stagnated $9.00 an hour after two years service, if they make it to then, leaves them with a mind blowing $27 a night, before taxes, to live on while UPS's after tax profits of $1.15 billion during 1996 (on $22 billion in revenue) and $4 billion over the prior four years.

One final thing that UPS must be refusing to see is that as turnover rises...productivity falls. Since 1993, in several central-sorting facilities the number of pieces per worker per hour has declined from 139 to 95, a drop of nearly 32%. UPS's claims to building communities remain in question as a result of such antics as the "part time" problem which is still being rampantly applied across the nation only UPS's management has shifted to a newer and stealthier accomplish to this problem which is the shift to temporary workers.

According to prominent researchers, countless features of the workplace society have been changed with one of the more significant changes have been the increase and deployment of a more 'flexible workforce'. In most cases many of the 'flexible' workers are combining together various jobs just in an attempt to make a living wage. This task has become evermore so difficult to do since the slow conversion of the U.S manufacturing economy to a service economy, which has been associated with a substantial increase in the 'short term contracts' between the labor relationships of both parties such as with the rise of "temporary workers" in the workplace.

There are several major reasons corporations incorporate the use of "temporary" workers into the labor relations, and human resources policy which include; they earn much less than the workers they replace, provide companies with flexibility, they receive and require very little investment, and THEY MAY USED TO BUST UNIONS or avoid unionization altogether in various labor relationship scenarios.

Of all of the jobs that were created in the 1980's almost a staggering 50% of them were part time and temporary jobs with many of the new jobs being created in the "SERVICE" industry. The number of contingent workers in the United States has been estimated to range from 29.9 million to 36.6 million, or 25% to 30% of the workforce, and since 1982, temporary employment has grown10 times faster than overall employment of the American workforce, which the majority of those employed are minority.

Some of the social ramifications from corporations, like UPS, who are shifting to temporary workers, include the erosion of adequate health and pension plans. According to leading researchers there was four basic changes in traditional employment that is associated with temporary workers. The first was a change in how long and when people work. A second change concerned that the workers can now be hired on a 'temporary basis' with no promise of future employment. Third, temporary workers may be part of a "fashion" trend in which the site or location is becoming more fluid. Fourth, concern for the *social* contract, which refers to federal laws that guarantee certain protections (workers compensation, overtime compensation for nonexempt employees, unemployment, equal opportunity, and OSHA regulations, as well as the absence of formal labor control with unions, which is clearly prevalent in the Huntsville center.

In regards to production quotas staying the same when temporary workers replace union jobs is nothing but a farce and they are only used to benefit the company who uses them, because often times they are held to a substandard level in terms to wages and benefits. It is quite possible that the companies who use the "temps" can achieve the same amount of production out of a ratio of 2:1 ("temps" to union workers) while still maintaining acceptable levels of production at a cheaper overall cost. The assumption that the use of temporary workers is only a means of being a cost saving tool has begun to receive some firsthand attention. Many of the employers have used these throw away jobs to reduce the cost of wages and benefits in order to substantiate their claims of only doing so to remain competitive and retain some sort of flexibility to the competitive markets and demands. But sadly the truth of the matter is that the implementation of such human resources has been at the least "a mixed blessing" as wages and productivity have followed one another in a drastic and overwhelming down turn.

Employers, like UPS, which hire these secondary part-timers, gain without any question lower wage and benefit cost, which include a higher turnover rate, lower productivity, and much lower retention rate. Strangely enough it has been found that for these types of workers to be cost effective they must remain on the job for a reasonable amount of time, which is rarely the case in which the UPS center in Huntsville hires its temporary employees who are college kids and they know that chances are they will not remain with the company after graduation.

The perception of these workers, by the companies who use them, are even lower than that of most others who work full time and are permanently retained by their employers and maintain a level of morale which is much lower than the standard employee. They view these temporary workers as a article of trade rather than as an investment and treat them as such by refusing to invest in their known methods of increasing productivity and subsequently refuse to hold them to the same standard as the union employees, which has a dramatic and costly effect on production and morale. These workers are viewed, by UPS managers, as replaceable and disposable workers at best along with their throw away jobs, and they feel that if the 'Temps" don't like the way they are treated that they can leave without fear of being held accountable to an agreement like the one that exist between the Teamsters union and UPS.

With the fact that these new workers have emerged on the scene, and how they are viewed and regarded by the employers as being 'separate' from bargaining unit employees and are not covered under any formal labor agreement, this prevents the union from organizing these "temporary" employees, which they could be used to scab and replace the union worker in the event of a labor dispute arising.

The cost of these non-union workers to unions is enormous and the use of these 'temps' affects them not only financially, but it also attacks the very psychological structures of solidarity among the rank and file members. In order to understand the psychological ramifications from this practice in which its attributed by a decline in the support of the union by the rank and file members is due from the result from when the members see what was once a union job being replaced by a non-union worker as the union sits idly by and allows it to happen. When a union loses any union paying jobs to these replacement workers, which is currently going on at UPS, it has a ripple effect, which affects all of the core areas of the union itself. First, it affects the union financially. With the loss and replacement of a union worker, but not the loss of a union job, there is a decrease in overall dues revenue. Accompanied with the loss of dues revenue is a loss of pension contributions into a centralized health and pension plan. At first this may not seem like much, but when you compound the numbers nationwide the cost are astronomical.

Since Hoffa has taken over the Teamsters union there has been a reported decline of union membership of roughly 11,000 members. How many of the 11,000 members jobs were lost to temporary workers? For example say that you have 1000 full time UPS drivers retiring. Who's going to replace them? The part timers are going to replace them by being promoted to full time, but in the process the part timers jobs are 'eliminated' and replaced by temporary workers. In our Huntsville building we lost about five part time union jobs (revenue auditors and scanner positions) to temporary employees. Now if 1000 of these part timers jobs are 'converted' over to temporary non-bargaining unit positions and lost then the union has lost the dues revenue, and pension contributions, which weaken the overall pension plan and could quite possible have an impact on the plan governors willingness to increase future benefits, from 1000 new part time members that would've been hired to replace those that were promoted to full time to replace the ones who retired. If those 1000 members each paid $27 a month in dues, which would come to $27,000 in lost dues revenue each month and $324,000 a year not counting the loss in health and pension contributions to a centralized plan like Central States.

One of the single most dangerous threats to the Teamsters union in the future is the intension of slowly and cleverly destroying our union jobs by replacing them with these temporary workers by UPS' management. UPS's top brass probably figures that they'll slowly bust the union at UPS from within by casually replacing union workers with non-union workers all while our locals sit back and allow it to happen. It is a problem that must be addressed and it is without a doubt a new and subversive attempt to undermine and bust the union. It is a new cancer on the body of organized labor.

STATEMENT OF RIGHTS

DISCLAIMER

For information on discounts or bulk purchases,
write: RLM Publishing Co.
PO Box 265 • Hazel Green, AL 35750~0265
Visit our homepage at http://www.thebigbrownlie.com